SPEAKER NANCY PELOSI
AND THE
NEW AMERICAN POLITICS

SPEAKER NANCY PELOSI

and the New American Politics

RONALD M. PETERS, JR.
CINDY SIMON ROSENTHAL

OXFORD
UNIVERSITY PRESS

2010

OXFORD
UNIVERSITY PRESS

Oxford University Press, Inc., publishes works that further
Oxford University's objective of excellence
in research, scholarship, and education.

Oxford   New York
Auckland   Cape Town   Dar es Salaam   Hong Kong   Karachi
Kuala Lumpur   Madrid   Melbourne   Mexico City   Nairobi
New Delhi   Shanghai   Taipei   Toronto

With offices in
Argentina   Austria   Brazil   Chile   Czech Republic   France   Greece
Guatemala   Hungary   Italy   Japan   Poland   Portugal   Singapore
South Korea   Switzerland   Thailand   Turkey   Ukraine   Vietnam

Published by Oxford University Press, Inc.
198 Madison Avenue, New York, New York 10016

www.oup.com

Oxford is a registered trademark of Oxford University Press.

Library of Congress Cataloging-in-Publication Data
Peters, Ronald M.
Speaker Nancy Pelosi and the new American politics / Ronald M. Peters, Jr.
and Cindy Simon Rosenthal.
    p.   cm.
Includes bibliographical references and index.
ISBN: 978-0-19-538373-7
1. Pelosi, Nancy, 1940–   2. United States. Congress. House—Speakers—Biography.
3. Women legislators—United States—Biography.   4. Legislators—United States—Biography.
5. United States. Congress. House—Biography.   6. United States—Politics and government—1989–
I. Rosenthal, Cindy Simon, 1950–   II. Title.
E840.8.P37P48 2010
328.73092—dc22   2009027936

9 8 7 6 5 4 3 2

Printed in the United States of America
on acid-free paper

PREFACE AND ACKNOWLEDGMENTS

Nancy Pelosi's election in January 2007 as the first woman Speaker of the House of Representatives was a milestone in U.S. history. In addition to its obvious historical importance, it also raised new questions for scholars to address. On the one hand, those questions focused on the return of the Democrats to power after 12 years in the minority. Would the Democrats proceed as had the Republican majority they replaced? Or would they return to the familiar patterns of a previous incarnation? On the other hand, would the fact of Pelosi being a woman make any difference in her conduct of the speakership or the reaction of the political system to her? Scholars have developed sophisticated theories of congressional leadership, but none of them account gender, a significant variable. Should they?

As the 2006 election and Pelosi's elevation to the speakership unfolded, the authors of this book, situated just across the hall from each other, began a dialogue that has resulted in this book. Peters has spent the last 30 years studying the speakership and the Speakers of the modern era. He has had the privilege of interviewing every Speaker from John McCormack forward, and has written one book and edited another on the speakership. Rosenthal is a student of women's political leadership (and, as mayor of Norman, Oklahoma, a practitioner herself). She has written a definitive study of women in leadership roles in American state legislatures and has edited a book on the impact of women on the U.S. Congress. Our collaboration on this book appears (to us at least) inevitable.

Our most immediate aim in this book is to analyze and assess Nancy Pelosi's service as Speaker. We tell her story as we have come to understand it: not simply as an exercise in narrative history but as offering a window on the American political system today. As our conversations about Pelosi began in earnest in December 2006, Pelosi was drenched in the deluge of publicity that attended the Democratic takeover of the House and her enhanced stature as the first woman ever to be in line to become Speaker. We were reminded, of course, of the attention Speaker Newt Gingrich had gathered after the 1994 election, when he was hailed as a sort of messiah who had led his party into power after 40 years in the wilderness. The election of the

Democratic majority in 2006 had perhaps less historical significance than the Republican revolution of 1994, but the fact that it was a woman who had led the Democrats stimulated public interest.

We also recalled that Speaker Gingrich's tenure had been brief and had fallen well short of the expectations that surrounded his electoral triumph. In fact, since the late 1980s, the House had experienced a series of speakerships that did not end well. Jim Wright had been forced to resign in 1989 under a cloud of ethics charges. Tom Foley had lost his seat in the 1994 upheaval that ejected the Democrats from power. Gingrich was pushed out by the Republicans when they lost seats in the 1998 election. And Dennis Hastert, while surviving to become the longest serving Republican Speaker, had presided over his party's reversal in 2006.

These considerations led us to reflect on the condition of the speakership during the current politically charged era in American politics. What changes have occurred in the American political system that put House Speakers so consistently at risk? What is known about the experience of these previous Speakers that might inform our understanding of the challenges Pelosi faced? What skills do Speakers need to succeed in this environment? How would Speaker Pelosi respond to challenges that had brought her predecessors low?

We concluded that our study of Speaker Pelosi also needed to describe how American politics has changed over the past 30 years. The fact that a woman could be elected Speaker was itself an indication of one important change, the greater diversity in representation. But other changes seemed equally important. We have arrayed them under the rubric of the "New American Politics," in which we include, along with diversity, partisanship, organization, technology, and fund-raising. As we thought through the implications of these changes, which we describe in more detail in chapter 1, and learned more about the evolution of Nancy Pelosi's political career, we realized that in many respects her career paralleled and reflected the changes that have occurred. The story we needed to tell would describe and explain how Pelosi's rise to power and her exercise of it has intertwined with the rendition of the American political system in which history has called on her to serve.

This book is the result of these deliberations. We hope it will provide the reader with information and insight about Pelosi herself, but also an enhanced understanding of American politics today and the ways and means of the contemporary House of Representatives. By bringing together theoretical constructs from congressional leadership theory and gender theory, we hope to offer a unique perspective on these broad topics that will be of interest to scholars, students, and lay readers alike.

We owe many debts to those who have helped us in writing this book. These include a team of able research assistants: Deidre Neal, Simon Haeder, Jessica Winski, Stephanie Holliman, Barri Bulla, and Caitlin O'Grady. Laurie McReynolds assisted with document production. Steve Gillon provided an introduction to Oxford University Press. Research information and advice were provided by J. R. Reskovac, Don Wolfensberger, and Valerie Heitshusen. In addition to cited sources, we have drawn on several dozen confidential interviews with members and former members of Congress, present and former congressional staff, and other observers. While we do not list them due to the confidentiality they were assured, we thank each of them for sharing their time and insight with us. We were assisted in arranging some of these interviews by Congressman Dan Boren, his communications director Cole Perryman, Clyde Henderson, and Jonathan Rucks. Joel Jankowsky, a generous supporter of the Carl Albert Congressional Research and Studies Center at the University of Oklahoma, also facilitated several interviews. We would like to thank Speaker Pelosi who granted us an interview and was generous in sharing the time of her staff. We want to especially thank her communications director, Brendan Daley, for his assistance and insight. At Oxford University Press, we thank our editor, Dave McBride; editorial assistant, Alexandra Dauler; senior production editor, Jessica Ryan; and copy editor, Martha Ramsey. Alexa Selph provided careful indexing of the manuscript.

We benefited greatly from the advice of readers of the first draft of the manuscript. We want to thank Randy Strahan of Emory University, Michele Swers of Georgetown University, Dave McBride and anonymous readers for Oxford University Press, and Barri Bulla and Caitlin O'Grady of the Carl Albert Center. As usual, any errors of fact or interpretation are strictly our own.

To our families is owed immense gratitude for their patience and support. To Glenda Peters, we credit the initial inspiration for this partnership. To Jim Rosenthal, thanks for steady encouragement both on and off the golf course.

CONTENTS

SPEAKER NANCY PELOSI
AND THE
NEW AMERICAN POLITICS

Chapter 1

Madam Speaker

I'll tell you what I think. I think that someday a man will be elected who'll bring the speakership into real respectability again. He'll be the real leader of the House. He'll be master around here, and everyone will know it.

—Sam Rayburn (1923)

The day will come when men will recognize woman as his peer, not only at the fireside, but in councils of the nation.

—Susan B. Anthony (1899)

On January 4, 2007, Nancy D'Alesandro Pelosi, a Democrat from San Francisco, was sworn in as the fifty-second Speaker of the U.S. House of Representatives, the first woman to serve in that high office. Accepting the gavel from Republican Leader John Boehner, Pelosi wielded it like a hammer, and then gathered around her the children and grandchildren attending the ceremony to join in the celebration.[1] The dual themes of political power and motherhood framed succinctly the image she aimed to project. Her formal election as Speaker culminated four days of celebration and ceremony during which she claimed the historic moment as an occasion to define herself and the Democratic Party she would now lead.

The opportunities were evident. In November 2006, Pelosi had led the House Democrats to their first majority in 12 years. Congressional Republicans were in disarray. Republican president George W. Bush had reached new lows in job approval ratings. In Congress and around the country, Democrats basked in the glow of their return to power. As the first woman to serve as Speaker, Pelosi became the focal point of public attention in the United States and around the world. She had been a notable but not widely known leader of the minority party in the House of Representatives; she was now one of the most powerful political figures in American politics, certainly the most powerful woman.

In framing her inauguration, Pelosi stressed her eastern roots as the daughter of longtime Baltimore mayor Thomas D'Alesandro and her Roman Catholic upbringing and education. Even though Tony Bennett regaled celebrants at one dinner with his classic rendition of "I Left My Heart in San Francisco," much of the celebration's emphasis was on her Maryland background, and not on her rise to power in California. The "eastern" focus was all the more interesting in its contrast to the very "western" themes around which her political career had been built. Pelosi had always stressed the "entrepreneurial spirit" of the West in explaining her approach to politics and party leadership. She had always run as the western insurgent against more established eastern politicians. Now, having risen to the pinnacle of power, she sought to present herself as both the political daughter of the East and the housewife turned politician from the West.[2] This positioning aimed to take the edge off of her image as a "San Francisco liberal," a recurrent claim of her political opponents.

In this book we seek to understand Nancy Pelosi, not just as a Speaker of the House, or even as its first female Speaker, but also as a reflection of a new era in American politics. In her career, one can see how the House of Representatives and the American political system more generally have changed in the last thirty years. We will describe and explain both the forces that shaped Pelosi's speakership and her approach to harnessing them in order to fully lay hold of the office's potential. Our account traces her rise to the speakership (chapter 2), her use of institutional power (chapter 3), her approach to politics and image-making and her communications strategy (chapter 4), the challenges that faced a unified Democratic government (chapter 5), and the gender dimensions of her leadership (chapter 6). We conclude (chapter 7) with an analysis and assessment of her approach to the speakership in the context of the institutional life of the House of Representatives and the current state of play in the American political system.

In this chapter, we map the terrain and introduce the themes that guide our narrative. Pelosi's story opens a window on social, political, and institutional forces that have framed her career, shaped her leadership, and transformed the context within which the speakership has evolved. We label these trends the "New American Politics." Since Pelosi is the first woman to serve as Speaker, we specifically explore the gender dimensions of this new incarnation of the political system. Finally, we turn to the implications of these trends for the speakership itself.

THE NEW AMERICAN POLITICS

Historical Backdrop

After President Lyndon Johnson trounced Barry Goldwater in the 1964 presidential election, a period of Democratic liberalism took shape in Johnson's Great Society legislative program. But the political geography was shifting. The enactment of the Civil Rights Act of 1964, as Johnson predicted, led to the realignment of the "Solid South" from Democratic to Republican control. Led by Ronald Reagan, a reconstituted Republican Party emerged from the ashes of Goldwater's candidacy. The GOP would no longer be the bastion of blue-stocking Yankees from the East or small-town bankers and merchants from the Midwest; it would come to be dominated by antigovernment ideologues from the West and social and religious conservatives from the South. In gendered terms, the Republican Party would evolve into the "daddy" party representing muscular foreign policy and stern traditional authority, while the Democrats would become caricatured as the "mommy" party, soft on military matters and permissive in the realm of national security and on some aspects of family values.[3] The excesses of the Great Society and the tragedy of the Vietnam War fed these stereotypes and opened political space for Republican presidents Richard Nixon and Gerald Ford. And in 1980, Ronald Reagan's sweeping victory over Jimmy Carter carried the Senate into Republican hands for the first time in almost thirty years. Republicans were on a roll.

The only elected branch of the federal government that resisted this Republican trend was the House of Representatives. Led by the iconic Speaker Thomas "Tip" O'Neill (D-MA, 1977–1987), the House remained under Democratic control until 1994, even as its membership became more polarized along partisan lines. Gradually, conservative southern Democrats were replaced by even more conservative Republicans, while in the North and the West, moderate Republicans gave way to more liberal Democrats. The House congressional parties became more ideologically homogenous, the Democrats more liberal, the Republicans more conservative. The center shrank.

The Republican failure to capture the House in the 1980s was not for lack of effort. Beginning in the late 1970s, House Republicans assumed a more confrontational style in challenging the majority Democrats. Led by firebrand Newt Gingrich of Georgia and his Conservative Opportunity Society rebels, House Republicans sought to put the Democratic majority on the defensive. By 1987, relationships between House Democrats and Republicans had become rancorous and polarized. Party leaders developed strategies that aimed at fostering unity within their caucuses.[4]

Political scientists have stressed party polarization in explaining the changes in the American political system that began in the 1980s. However, polarization is not the only significant change that occurred. Nancy Pelosi was first elected to Congress in 1987 and became Speaker in 2007. During those two decades, American society and politics underwent a number of dramatic changes. Consider, for example, the transformation of information technology. In 1987, a simpler media environment prevailed. Personal computers were only beginning to take hold, and the internet had yet to come "online." E-mail was nascent and the blogosphere unimagined. Cellphones were executive luxuries. Most Americans got their news from the three broadcast networks' evening news programs, presided over by telegenic white men possessed of fatherly seriousness and authority. The fledgling cable news network CNN had yet to establish itself with its coverage of the first Persian Gulf War (1990). Fox News did not exist. The twenty-four-hour news cycle had yet to develop. Americans still read newspapers they held in their hands. Politics in 1987 was played according to the rules put in place in the 1970s. Money flowed through PACs to political campaigns. Grassroots organization meant developing voter lists, which were beginning to be computerized. Campaigns and congresspersons reached voters and constituents through direct mail. Baby boomers were on the leading edge of their political power. As Bill Clinton, the first baby boomer president, has noted, the political alignments of the 1990s were basically defined by where one stood during the 1960s.[5] During a period of relative prosperity, cultural issues came to dominate political discourse. The "Reagan Revolution" had put liberal Democrats on the defensive on the matters of war and peace, the role of government in society, and social issues such as abortion.

Consider, too, the transformation of women's roles in the workforce and politics during the 1980s and beyond. On June 30, 1982, the deadline for ratifying the Equal Rights Amendment to the U.S. Constitution came and went, just three states short of the needed 38 required. In its wake, the activists who had pursued the amendment turned to the electoral process and achieved steady, if incremental, increases in the number of women representatives. The term "gender gap" was coined by leaders of the National Organization for Women to keep attention focused on women voters and their importance.[6] Feminists used the evidence of a "gender gap" to pressure Walter Mondale to choose Geraldine Ferraro as his running mate in 1984. The 1992 elections gave rise to the moniker "Year of the Woman" after law professor Anita Hill galvanized the country with her 1991 testimony before the Senate Judiciary Committee hearings on the appointment of Supreme Court Justice Clarence Thomas in which she described sexual harassment she said she had experienced while working for him. Talk of women in politics that year was dominated by the question whether or not Hillary Clinton would "stand by her man" and live up to expectations to bake cookies and serve tea in the White House as first lady.[7] As election experts contemplated how carpool moms, soccer moms, national security moms, and most recently hockey moms would vote, the numbers of Democratic women were slowly but steadily increasing in state legislatures, within the U.S. House, and as a political bloc to be reckoned with in the House Democratic Caucus.

Thus, the two decades of Nancy Pelosi's House career preceding her election as Speaker witnessed dramatic changes. Partisan polarization, to be sure, remains a defining feature of the political landscape. But partisanship now plays itself out in a transformed social and political environment. Information and communications technology has changed the way Americans live and interact. While the face of the traditional news media has been transformed—Katie Couric, Diane Sawyer, and Gwen Ifill head a list of prominent female journalists who now visit our living rooms to report the news—many Americans obtain their information from the internet. In a survey the Pew Research Center for the People and the Press released in August 2008, respondents reported on the sources of information they frequently accessed ("got news there yesterday") as follows: local television news 52%, cable television 39%, internet 37%, radio 35%, newspapers 35%, and nightly network news 29%.[8] Pew also notes two clear patterns emerging that differentiate younger and older citizens. Older Americans are much more likely to get their information from traditional television and newspaper sources; younger Americans rely on the internet and social networking sites. An emerging group—"integrators"—draw on multiple sources of news.

This rise in integrators is no doubt connected to the transformation of telecommunications. Cellphones are now ubiquitous. The BlackBerry generation has, to some extent, been set free of institutional filters to the world such as the traditional media had provided. The development of the internet, the blogosphere, social networking websites such as MySpace and Facebook, and information search engines have decentralized information dissemination and collection while eliminating the quality-control filters that the old institutional gatekeepers tried to provide. The audience for broadcast news has shriveled, and cable networks seek audience share by infusing news programming with entertainment values involving a minimum of social and political nuance. Talk radio fans the passions of its fervid audience; misogynist and racist rants are not off limits. This balkanization of information dissemination and opinion formation has led to a self-reinforcement of attitudes that has exacerbated the underlying partisan trend.

While the political landscape has developed a familiar red state/blue state divide, the international map has undergone its most radical redrawing since the ending of the colonial era during the two decades after World

War II. The breakup of the Soviet Union has altered the context of American foreign policy and brought forth new challenges, such as the civil wars in the Balkans and the eruption of Islamic fundamentalism and geopolitical terrorism. China has emerged as the major strategic competitor to the United States. At the same time, the American economy seems even more fragile now than it did two decades ago.

The American political system and its government face enormous challenges today: a mountain of public and private debt, huge unfunded liabilities in social insurance programs, crumbling infrastructure, a dysfunctional health-care system, the threat of global climate change, and regular doses of corporate malfeasance causing economic losses in the billions. Estimates of the financial policy deficit (the amount of money required to pay all of the government's future obligations under current policy) exceed $50 trillion over the next generation. And in 2008, things got considerably worse, with the onset of the greatest financial crisis since the Great Depression.

This transformation in the terrain of American politics has produced a new political and policy dynamic. Ronald Reagan anchored the Republican Party in a triumvirate of policy positions: strong national defense, tax cuts, and conservative social values. These positions united the national security, economic, and cultural conservatives. Republicans were free traders as well. The Democrats were, as usual, divided. Liberals on the party's traditional ideological left have adhered to New Deal and Great Society application of government power to address social and economic problems. They have been suspicious of globalization and free trade. Centrist and conservative Democrats have concluded that the party can win elections only by moderating its positions. These "Third Way" Democrats have sought to "reinvent government," favored reliance on private sector solutions where possible (privatization), and supported former heresies such as welfare reform and free trade.

These policy cleavages have run side by side with considerations of political expedience. Republicans have settled on a strategy of uniting their party's base voters around the three pillars of Reaganism. This approach produced huge federal deficits under presidents Reagan and George W. Bush. The Democrats were internally divided over political strategy as they were on public policy. Moderate Democrats concluded that the party needed to reposition itself to recapture the center ground of American politics, in effect asking liberals to sacrifice their policy preferences in order to gain political control. Liberal Democrats took their playbook from the Republicans, arguing that what was needed was more effective political organization; they derided the centrists' approach as "Republican Lite." As we shall see, this strategic controversy had powerful implications for the Democrats' choice of legislative leaders.

Elements of the New American Politics

The changes we have described have contributed to the emergence of what we call the "New American Politics," a phenomenon we think rests on five interrelated elements: partisanship, money, organization, technology, and representation. The partisan divisions in the government, reflecting those in the country at large, are evident in the results of the recent presidential and congressional elections. We will have more to say about the partisanship in Congress in this book. Here, we wish to stress that both the major parties have focused on cultivating and motivating their base—that is, their most loyal—voters. While both political parties have been complicit in this race to the base, scholars have credited the Republican Party with the first and, over time, most effective deployment of this strategy.[9] It was the essence of Bush political advisor Karl Rove's approach to winning the presidential elections of 2000 and 2004 and the key to the Republican capture of Congress in the low-turnout election of 1994.

This base-voter strategy has fundamentally altered American politics. Historically, the two major parties sought to win elections by capturing the center of the electorate, where the majority of voters are presumed to reside.[10] The fight to win over the median voter had the effect of moderating the nation's politics. Presidential candidates ran to the base in the primary election and then scrambled to the center in the general election. Rove concluded that this approach was not necessary if your side could turn out more base voters than the other side. Kindred to the base voter strategy is the "culture wars" approach. Scholars have questioned the existence of a "culture war" in the United States, citing data suggesting that most voters are middle-of-the-road when it comes to public policy.[11] These scholars assume that a culture war would center on policy issues, about which Americans disagree, and argue that those disagreements are less substantial than the culture wars approach suggests.[12]

But the culture war may be less about policy than about people. The oldest divisions in political life are between *us* and *them*, whether these be southerners and northerners, Catholics and Protestants, blacks and whites, Yankee fans and Red Sox fans, immigrants and natives, Republicans and Democrats. Each party aspires to be the party of *us* and to make the opponents the party of *them*. Then, the strategy is to turn out more of *us* to vote than the opposition can of *them*. As Rick Perlstein has recently argued, this kind of cultural alienation, which goes deeper than values, has been a staple of Republican politics since it was debuted by Richard Nixon.[13] We see it manifested when Gingrich calls Democrats the "enemies of normal people," Sarah Palin evokes "hockey moms" against the Washington establishment, and conservative commentators characterize the Republican Party as comprising "typical Americans" and the Democratic Party otherwise.[14]

One particular fault line in this culture war runs through the playground, dividing stay-at-home mothers and working mothers in heated debates about women's choices for their families and careers. When the General Social Survey of 1986 asked "Do you agree or disagree: Women should take care of running their homes and leave running the country up to men?" more than 39% of housewives concurred, in contrast with 14% of working women. The divide between housewives and working women narrowed to its lowest level (15%) in 1993 and then rose again through 1998, when the question was last asked. By 1998, the divide had grown to 24%, with almost one in three housewives (31%) embracing the "run the home" view, compared with only one in ten (8%) women in the workforce.[15] There is, of course, a partisan twist on these numbers: in most of the survey years, more women claimed a preference for the Democratic Party; and among working women, Democrat outnumbered Republican working women by almost two to one.

For the past fifty years, starting with Nixon, the Republican Party has sought to identify itself with a core of white, conservative, religiously oriented (at first mostly Protestant, then increasingly Catholic), middle-class voters. The Republicans have portrayed the Democrats as the party of minorities, intellectuals, media, and entertainment elites—in short, an odd combination of people too poor and alien to be one of "us" with the "effete corps of impudent snobs" who look down their noses at regular, hardworking Americans.[16] Democratic presidential candidates have been portrayed as arugula-loving and somehow foreign. This portrayal has also had gendered dimensions—"traditional" families of happy stay-at-home moms and angry white working men are allegedly under siege from prochoice feminists, homosexuals, and illegal immigrants who threaten the essential fabric of society and traditional family values. If one city more than any other represents this caricature of the Democratic Party it is San Francisco, California. Democrats have sometimes responded with exaggerated representations of Republican constituencies, describing them as parochial, prejudiced, gun-toting rednecks. The cultural divide runs in both directions.

This cultivation of cultural and gendered partisan divisions is reflected in two other aspects of the New American Politics: money and organization. The 1974 Campaign Finance Reform Act set up the political action committee (PAC) system, which was designed to put constraints on the flow of money into politics. In order to enhance the role of the political parties in the process, the law allowed unlimited contributions (sometimes called "soft" money) to political parties. This arrangement put a premium on organized fund-raising through PACs to fuel individual campaigns; but it also opened the spigot for big-money givers to write large checks to the political parties. This largess is ostensibly for "party building" activities such as get-out-the-vote drives, but in practice has also been used for sham "issue" advertising plainly directed at individual races. The premium now is on party operatives and supporters who could reach out to large numbers of "limit" donors, that is, those who could afford to give the maximum contribution the law allows. Lobbyists with access to PAC funds have become more influential. Forced to devote considerable time to fund-raising, members of Congress have come to rely on those who could most easily help them.

The 1974 law did democratize political fund-raising to some degree. The days of Nixon's Committee to Reelect the President stuffing its safe with hundreds of thousands of dollars in cold cash were over. But the continuous need to raise money created a dependency on those best able to raise it. For women candidates who were struggling to compete on the national scene, EMILY's List began to level the playing field. First created in 1985, this grass-roots organization perfected the bundling of donations to benefit prochoice women running for Congress or state legislatures. Claiming more than 100,000 members, EMILY's List received and disbursed some $35 million in the 2008 election cycle.[17]

The new fund-raising regime created a role for those who were well con-nected, could hold fund-raisers, and could close the deal. This required not only personal connections but also organizational skill, the third element of the new politics. Here once again the Republicans were well out in front of the Democrats. Historically, the Democrats relied on labor unions to turn out the vote in states they needed to win, but over the past generation, the unions have atrophied, their membership in decline. Shrinking trade union-ism was caused primarily by an underlying transition from an industrial to a service economy, but it was assisted by Republican efforts to undermine union power itself. Even as the Democrats' organizational infrastructure was breaking down, the Republicans' was developing. Republican operatives such as Richard Viguerie and Karl Rove were experts in direct-mail fund-raising with its typical stress on negative politics. Relying on microtargeting as well as church- and neighborhood-based networks, the GOP brought political orga-nizing to new levels. They drew districts favorable to their candidates, identi-fied their contributors, and turned out their voters. Both parties drew on new redistricting computer software to secure safe seats for their incumbents.[18]

The Democrats lagged in organizational capacity from the outset. The California Democratic Party, for example, did not have computerized voter lists until the early 1980s, when its young state chair, Nancy Pelosi, imple-mented a new system. Not until after the shock of the 2000 election did the Democratic National Committee (DNC) seek to upgrade its capacity to identify and target voters. In the 1994, 2000, and 2004 elections, turnout was key and turnout strategies carried the day. One reason the Republicans prevailed was that they had the organizational advantage. In response to it the DNC, under the leadership of Terry McAuliffe, sought parity through an intensive effort to develop computerized donor lists, marketing databases, voter registration, and other data. The result was a massive voter database that rivaled that of the Republicans.[19]

Political parties identifying and communicating with voters by means of databases and microtargeting is one dimension of the new political technology. Another is voters gathering information and communicating with one another. At the time of the founding of the United States, James Madison posited that the size and diversity of the country would inhibit the development of majority factions. He regarded factions as a necessary byproduct of republican government but feared that majorities would use the democratic process to tyrannize minorities. In *Federalist No. 10* he argued that in a large country like the United States, majority factions were less likely to emerge and, if they did, less able to communicate and coordinate their activities. He offered his theory of the "extended sphere" to explain how the size and diversity of the country would impede majority tyranny. Of course, the size of the country, by impeding communication and coordination, makes it difficult to organize for political action of any type. America's political parties developed in response to the need to coordinate political action. Technology now abets the work of both political parties and interest groups. In the twentieth century, radio and television supplanted newspapers as the primary avenues of political communication, through which citizens shared common sources of information. Toward the end of the twentieth century, economic trends, an altered regulatory structure, and the technological development of cable television led to a fragmentation of the media market. In the twenty-first century, the development of the internet has dramatically accentuated this trend. The result is a fragmentation of society and culture in which the cleavages produced by residential housing patterns have been reinforced by group polarization and what scholar Cass Sunstein calls "enclave deliberations."[20] Essentially, citizens tend to gather information from sympathetic sources and converse with like-minded persons.

Even as the internet breeds further political division and partisan polarization, however, it creates opportunities for coordinated political action. Independent organizations such as MoveOn.org and Tea Party Patriots would have had little prospect without it. Influential blogs like the Daily Kos manifest the role of the internet.[21] Conservative pundits like Michelle Malkin and Glenn Beck extend their reach through the internet. The internet effectively shrinks James Madison's extended sphere (narrowing political space) while at the same time it empowers the organization of an even larger number of groups (proliferating factions within it).

The technology that enables MoveOn to raise money, and left-wing organizations like the Daily Kos and right-wing organizations like Focus on the

Family and Americans for Tax Reform to reach millions of voters is also available to the parties themselves, both boosting and weakening them. The internet has strengthened parties by creating new pathways for raising money, coordinating and disseminating their messages, and running campaigns. This development has also, however, accentuated conflict within the parties. The congressional parties are now tugged in one direction by their activist bases in the ideological blogosphere and in another direction by the more moderate members on whose election a congressional majority usually rests. This tension has been more evident within the Democratic Party because it is more ideologically diverse.[22]

These technological and organizational features of the New American Politics have contributed to the development of the "permanent campaign."[23] The two political parties, their candidates, incumbent members of Congress, and party leaders now incessantly compete over money and message. The permanent campaign infuses politicking into every aspect of policy-making as well. Party leaders, including the Speaker of the House, are responsible for fund-raising and are also expected to control the policy-making agenda for political advantage. With an attentive eye toward campaign advantage, the leaders forego the middle ground on which political compromise might be forged. We believe that the permanent campaign is an important dimension of the New American Politics but not its primary cause, which we situate in underlying cleavages in the electorate.

Finally, the New American Politics has put a different face on political representation. While the U.S. population remains majority white and non Hispanic, minority populations overall are growing much faster than the white population, and America faces dramatic changes in its ethnic, linguistic, and racial composition in the future. According to the census, 88% of the U.S. population was white and non-Hispanic in 1970; that figure dropped to 76% in 1990 and 69% in 2000. According to 2008 census projections, only 60% of the population is estimated to be white and non-Hispanic by the year 2010 and only 46% by 2050.[24] As the country has become increasing diverse over the past 40 years, so have elected representatives. Figure 1.1 charts the incremental transformation of the representation of women, African Americans, and Hispanics in Congress and in state legislatures.

The emergence of women as political leaders is a central concern of this book. In the long view of American history, women constitute a small sliver of the individuals who have served in the U.S. Congress—only 2% of the total since 1789. But significantly, the 88 women who served in the 110th Congress made up over one-third (36%) of that sliver. The story of the last 20 years for women in politics has been steadily incremental increases, first in state legislatures and more recently in Congress. Similarly, more than a third (41 of the 119) African-American members who have served in Congress

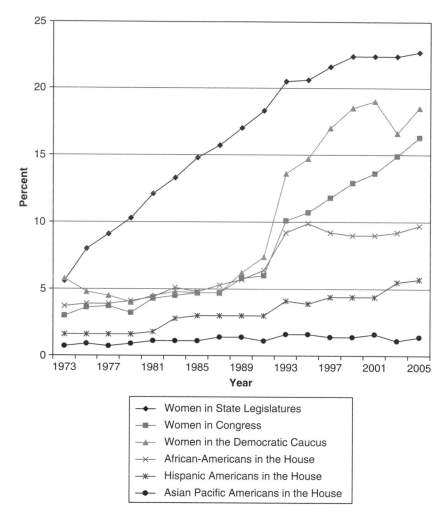

Figure 1.1   Diversity of Representation in Government

Sources: Center for American Woman and Politics, www.cawp.rutgers.edu; Joint Center for
Political and Economic Studies, www.jointcenter.org; U.S. House, Black Americans in Congress,
"Historical Data," http://baic.house.gov/historical-data/representatives-senators-by-congress
.html?congress=110; U.S. House, Women in Congress, "Historical Data," http://women
incongress.house.gov/; Library of Congress, "Hispanic Americans in Congress, 1822–1995,"
www.loc.gov/rr/hispanic/congress/chron.html#1993.

since 1868 are current members. In actual numbers, women representatives
outnumber racial and ethnic minorities, and the trend lines for women in
figure 1.1 show larger percentage increases in recent years. Together, women
and minorities contribute to congressional diversity. This diversity is most

evident in the Democratic Caucus: Democratic congresswomen outnumber their GOP counterparts by more than two to one, and all of the African-American representatives are Democrats. A significant percentage of Asian and Hispanic members of Congress are also Democrats. This partisan twist on the changing demography of representation has implications for policy, politics, and political participation in the twenty-first century.

Gender is, of course, an important aspect of this diversity and is central to our narrative about Speaker Pelosi. We turn now to a more detailed discussion of how gender and the New American Politics interface with each other, shaping trends and opportunities. We focus on gender not only because of our interest in Speaker Pelosi but also because each element of the New American Politics has a gendered dimension that we believe warrants investigation.

THE NEW AMERICAN POLITICS AND GENDER

In 2008, the presidential campaign produced a new political drama in which gender played a central role. The stage of presidential politics featured a cast of women players never before seen: a woman U.S. senator was considered the front-runner for much of the Democratic primary campaign, only to be edged out in the final tally of delegates; a woman governor winked her way into the hearts of GOP partisans as the darling vice presidential candidate of the Republican ticket; and a woman Speaker presided over the national convention for the Democrats. On the basis of data about new registered voters and historical patterns, women were estimated to outnumber male voters in the 2008 by more than 9 million.[25] The women in the spotlight of the 2008 presidential election marked a high point for women in the era of the New American Politics.

The two parties took different and defining paths on women's issues in the 1970s and 1980s, contributing a key dynamic to today's partisanship. Before then, women's issues and women's place in politics were not priorities for either party. After women won the right to vote, both parties created auxiliaries for women, which often had the effect of marginalizing their participation in party politics.[26] Throughout the first half of the twentieth century, neither party adopted gender equity issues with much enthusiasm; women were generally relegated to second-class status. When the Equal Rights Amendment was first introduced into Congress in 1923, bipartisan opposition arose from organized labor and Progressive organizations. Between 1925 and 1970, women were unable to transform the vote into policy benefits; then the emergence of independent women's organizations like the National Organization for Women brought increasing clout for women in the political arena.[27]

The emergence of the modern feminist movement in the 1960s coincided with a number of other trends: more women entered the workforce, birth rates were declining, and divorce was on the rise. Betty Friedan's *Feminine Mystique* spurred a generation of middle-class, educated women to aspire to something beyond traditional domestic roles and to demand better job opportunities, equal pay, and greater personal liberty.[28] Both parties responded and adopted extensive women's rights planks in their party platforms while avoiding the abortion issue. Both parties increased the number of women delegates to party conventions, though the Democrats went the furthest and mandated equal representation for women among the national convention delegates in 1972.

The political focal point of the modern women's movement was the Equal Rights Amendment, which Congress sent to the states for ratification in 1972 on a bipartisan vote. That bipartisanship, however, soon dissipated. The feminist movement inspired an antifeminist backlash led by Phyllis Schlafly of Eagle Forum and Beverly LaHaye of Concerned Women of America, who became a force to transform the Republican Party. That party, beginning with Ronald Reagan, increasingly aligned itself with antifeminist organizations and courted Democrats disaffected by their party's stand on abortion. On many other gender-related issues, the parties did not take different issue stances, but the abortion conflict became the realigning topic for the electorate.[29] While both parties continued to send roughly equivalent numbers of women to Congress through 1990, the "Year of the Woman" election in 1992 dramatically altered that trend, and today Democratic women outnumber Republican women two to one.

The growing role of money in campaigns vaulted a number of women to the political forefront. Not only did the potent grassroots fund-raising of EMILY's List and other women's PACs create conditions of success for women candidates but also women who had previously labored in obscurity in party organizations rode to greater political recognition on the strength of their fund-raising skills. Nonetheless, conventional wisdom held that women candidates had less success than their male counterparts in the money game. Dispelling this myth, Barbara Burrell analyzed campaign giving from 1972 to 1992 and found parity in fund-raising on a variety of measures. Burrell concluded that conventional wisdom persists in part because women generally earn less than men and hold a smaller share of top positions in the private sector.[30]

Conventional wisdom dies slowly; but recognition of women's talents in fund-raising has grown apace. Among the best is Nancy Pelosi, but she is not alone. Among Democrats, Roz Wyman of California and the late Pamela Harriman were leading fund-raisers for many years. Chicago's Penny Pritzker chaired Barack Obama's campaign fund-raising committee in 2008. On the

Republican side, Doro Bush played a major role in raising money for her brother's presidential campaigns. According to a *USA Today* report, "women account for 59 out of more than 500 top fundraisers in Republican John McCain's campaign. Democrat Barack Obama has 148 female fundraisers out of more than 500."[31] In Congress, women also have come to play a more central role as party fund-raisers. In 2001, U.S. Senator Patty Murray (D-WA) became the first woman to serve as chair of the Democratic Senatorial Campaign Committee, and Representative Nita Lowey (D-NY) became the first woman to chair the Democratic Congressional Campaign Committee (DCCC). If money is the currency of the New American Politics, then women are beginning to move to the fore in securing the power it purchases.

The gender lens also suggests a different understanding of the organizational skills required in the new politics. The parallels between household organization and political life have deep roots in American history. Historian Glenna Matthews traces how an ideology of domestic feminism flourished in the nineteenth and early twentieth centuries and linked the womanly arts to public housekeeping.[32] As leader of the settlement house movement, Jane Addams in 1910 urged city governments to use the talents of women who were "accustomed to detail and variety of work, to a sense of obligation for the health and welfare of young children, and to a responsibility for the cleanliness and comfort of other people."[33] At midcentury, women sustained the war effort at home and in the factory, transforming forever the role of women in the paid workforce, and double-duty obligations (and expectations) were imposed on women. The organizational demands of the New American Politics seem well suited to the skills many women perfect as they balance paid work, family, second-shift housework, and community service in their busy lives. Pelosi has given voice to the linkage between household management and political organization. She often attributes her political organizing skills to her mother's example and to her own experience keeping track of the many functions of a busy household of five children. Other women in politics for whom life is continuous multitasking and balancing of public and personal obligations also see the linkage.[34] The modern household also demands the blending of the "high-tech and high-touch" characteristics required in modern organizations.[35]

Finally, we consider the gendered implications of technology in the New American Politics. Technology, like science and math, has long been identified as an arena where men dominate.[36] That may be changing in the new media of the blogosphere and social networking. Nielsen Online reports that women between the ages of 25 and 54 are nearly twice as likely to use online services like e-mail, online forums, and social networking websites to seek information and build relationships.[37] BlogsbyMoms lists 13,040 blogs that appeal principally to women, on topics ranging from politics to parenting, with lots of issues in between. Momsrising.org advocates for paternity and maternity leave, child-care and health-care issues, flexible work accommodations, and a host of local, state, and national initiatives. In the information-rich world of blogging and social networking, analysts are taking note of some interesting gender differences. In 2005, the Pew Internet and American Life Project reported that women were catching up with men in all areas of internet use.[38] Just three years later, Rapleaf, an online search and social networking company that tracks consumer demographics and social media, reported a study of more than 13.2 million people showing women as dominant users of social media and on some social networking sites constituting two-thirds of the users:

> Traditionally, men are the early adopters of new technologies. But when it comes to social media, women are at the forefront.... While the trends indicate both sexes are using social media in huge numbers, our findings show that women far outpace the men. As a result, with the next wave of innovation likely to target women more than men, this gender gap on social networks (and increasingly in all of social media) will only widen.[39]

The Rapleaf study also suggested important stylistic differences in the way men and women use the internet. Men are engaged in competitive games, fantasy role playing, and transactional connections, while women are into social networking, information sharing, and building relationships. Given the fact that women outnumber men as U.S. voters by almost 9 million, the role of new media is likely to have important implications for their ongoing political role.[40]

Thus, we see that each element of the New American Politics is affected by gender and contributes to an understanding of the environment in which Nancy Pelosi rose to become the first woman Speaker of the House. In a broader sense, we suggest that the New American Politics is the product of a variety of trends in the American culture, demographics, economy, and structure of politics and the technologies that shape them all. It is certainly more partisan, considerably more fluid, and arguably more challenging than American politics has been at any time in history. It sets the context of American political institutions and the officials who lead them, including, of course, the office of the Speaker of the House.

THE SPEAKERSHIP TODAY

The office is a complex one, a hybrid of constitutional, institutional, and partisan obligations.[41] The Speaker is one of the only four officers specified in the Constitution (the others are the president, vice president, and chief justice of the Supreme Court). The office stands second in the line of succession to the presidency. The Speaker has an obligation to sustain the constitutional prerogatives of the House of Representatives in the constitutional system of separated powers. Institutionally, the Speaker serves as the presiding officer. As such, she has an obligation to enforce the rules of the House impartially and to offer fair treatment under those rules to all members. Enforcement of the rules and normal adherence to "regular order" (the process of developing legislation in committee) are related to the Speaker's broader obligation to ensure deliberative government in the House. The rights of the minority party under the rules must be respected as well. This responsibility occasions regular tension with the Speaker's third role as leader of the majority party in the House. In that capacity, she must seek to hold and enhance her party's majority, develop cohesion in her caucus, and pass her party's legislative program.

Scholars debate the extent to which legislative party leaders are hostage to the preferences of members. Political scientist Barbara Sinclair has characterized party leaders, including the Speaker, as agents acting at the behest of their principals, the members who elect them. Other scholars have argued that Speakers are capable of acting autonomously of (and in some cases contrary to) member preferences, depending on the context in which they govern. Surely, there is truth on both sides of this argument. No Speaker will last long by ignoring the preferences of her members; but a Speaker can and should act according to her best judgment about party and public interest. In assessing any Speaker, the question to ask is whether the Speaker commands sufficient support within her party caucus to enable her to challenge it on those occasions when the public interest requires it.[42]

Concurrent with the rise of the New American Politics, the office of Speaker has undergone significant changes since the reform movement of the early 1970s.[43] During the 60 years between the revolt against Speaker Joseph G. ("Uncle Joe") Cannon (R-IL, 1903–1911) in 1910 and the passage of the Legislative Reform Act of 1970, the House developed into a "feudal" institution in which power was largely centered in the committee system and the powerful chairs who ran its fiefdoms. A liberal tide that swept through Congress in the 1960s produced pressure for institutional reform. These reforms aimed at diminishing the power of the committee chairs by both decentralizing power to the subcommittee level and enhancing the power of the Speaker. The "Subcommittee Bill of Rights" ensured that committee chairs could no longer dominate the legislative process. The Speaker was given more control over bill referral, effective control of the Rules Committee, and for the Democrats, a stronger hand in making committee assignments. In the wake of these institutional reforms, in 1975 the House Democrats replaced three senior committee chairs, a harbinger of what was to come. Power gravitated away from the committee chairs down to the subcommittees and up to the leadership. While Carl Albert (D-OK, 1971–1976) and Tip O'Neill had more institutional power as Speakers than John McCormack (D-MA, 1962–1970) and Sam Rayburn (D-TX 1942– 1946; 1949–1952; 1955–1961) had before them, they availed themselves of it infrequently. The Democratic Caucus remained divided between southern conservatives and northern liberals, and it ill behooved the Speaker to get caught between them.

Reforms transformed the Speaker's power in controlling the process by which legislation is brought to the House floor. The House Rules Committee acts as the gatekeeper to the floor, establishing the time limits for floor debate and the number and nature of amendments that can be considered on each bill. The House stripped the Speaker of control over the Rules Committee in 1910, but this power was restored in 1975 by granting the Speaker the power to appoint its Democratic members. Traditionally, the House had considered legislation under open rules, allowing substantively relevant (germane) floor amendments to committee bills.[44] Since bipartisan accommodation within the committees was more likely to produce committee consensus, the minority had less need to offer floor amendments. There was a strong institutional norm that committee bills would be backed on the floor. And there were few recorded votes, with most amendments considered in the Committee of the Whole House by unrecorded teller votes.[45]

In the 1970s all three factors changed. First, the transition of the South to the Republican Party diminished the conservative coalition and increased partisan tensions in the committees. Republicans were no longer satisfied with the committee product and wanted to offer floor amendments. Second, the House implemented an electronic voting system that made it practical to conduct recorded votes on any question. The rules required a recorded vote at the request of 20% of the members present and voting, a threshold that both parties routinely met. Third, the Republican minority began to offer amendments that often had little prospect of passing but were designed to put Democrats representing more conservative districts on the spot. Interest groups began compiling voting indexes, which provided a vehicle to realize the Republican goal of defining Democrats negatively on the ratings. These developments played into the widening partisan divide.

In response, the majority Democrats moved from the traditional practice of open rules to a hybrid system in which they often limited the number and nature of the amendments the Republicans could offer. Through the 1980s and early 1990s, House Republicans assailed the Democratic majority for its overbearing tactics and unfair floor practices. In the 103rd Congress, the Republicans made alleged abuse of power by the Democratic leadership a major focus of their successful 1994 campaign. Once in the majority, the Republicans ended up being every bit as controlling as the Democrats about whom they had previously complained. The Republicans knew that the Democrats would offer floor amendments that would substantively alter Republican bills or else force Republicans in marginal districts to cast tough votes. The Republican leaders were every bit as anxious as their Democratic predecessors had been to protect their members. And the minority Democrats complained just as loudly as the Republicans had.[46]

The trend toward use of special rules to control the floor agenda was but one of the strategies employed by Speakers in the postreform House. The leadership also used the Suspension Calendar to deny minority amendments.[47] On some occasions, the minority was even denied an opportunity to send legislation back to committee via a motion to recommit (MTR).[48] The Speaker was also given greater latitude in referring bills to committee, including the power to refer complex legislation to more than one committee. Within the Democratic Caucus, the Speaker was given greater influence over committee assignments through control over the Democratic Steering and Policy Committee (SPC), which made the appointments. Still, Democratic Speakers adhered consistently to seniority in nominating committee chairs, and the selection of subcommittee chairs was made by and within each committee.[49] These concessions to the autonomy of the committee process set constraints on the power of Democratic Speakers due to the influence of senior committee chairs.

Democratic Speakers O'Neill, Jim Wright (D-TX, 1987–1989) and Tom Foley (D-WA, 1989–1994) developed new strategies and techniques to build winning floor coalitions.[50] These strategies included a larger whip organization (whose task was to count votes and rally support), the use of task forces to build support for important bills, referring all or parts of bills to more than one committee to build coalitions across committee jurisdictions, and the use of special rules to orchestrate policy choices on the House floor. These strategies stressed intraparty communication aimed at unifying the often fractious Democratic Caucus. While retaining a good deal of autonomy in managing their fiefdoms, the committee chairs cooperated with the leadership more often than not. These strategies created substantial pressure for conformity within the caucus. The members most resistant to this pressure were the southerners representing more conservative districts. These "Blue Dog" Democrats sought to moderate party policy, especially on fiscal issues, but their arguments were usually unavailing against their more liberal colleagues.[51] Reconciling the divergent policy preferences and political interests of the liberal and conservative wings of the caucus was the central challenge of these Speakers.

By the election of 1994, when the Democrats lost their congressional majority, the speakership had become much more powerful than at any time since the beginning of the twentieth century. Under Newt Gingrich (R-GA, 1995–1998) and Dennis Hastert (R-IL, 1999–2006), the Republicans took the stronger speakership and upped the ante. They effectively stripped committee chairs of their autonomy. The leadership controlled all committee assignments and nominated the chairs. Aspirants to become chairs were expected to raise substantial amounts of money for the National Republican Congressional Committee. Under Speaker Gingrich, the Republican majority sometimes bypassed committees altogether, developing legislation through ad hoc task forces or writing bills in the Rules Committee. Speaker Hastert enunciated a "majority of the majority" principle that in effect discounted the role of the minority party in the legislative process, seeking floor majorities within Republican ranks while ignoring the Democrats.[52] Standing behind Gingrich and Hastert, Republican whip and then majority leader Tom DeLay enforced party discipline. Eager to hang on to power, the Republicans, working with President George W. Bush, abandoned the fiscal discipline they had demonstrated in negotiating a balanced budget agreement with President Clinton in 1997. The skyrocketing increase in the number of congressional earmarks and in the number of registered lobbyists directly linked. Earmarks were commonly used to whip votes on other issues. Democrats, to recall the words of Speaker Tom Reed (R-ME, 1889–1891; 1895–1899), were there to make a quorum and draw pay.[53]

The increased partisanship that had emerged under Democrats Jim Wright and Tom Foley was taken to new heights under Gingrich and Hastert. Partisan bickering, a decline in civility, and all-out political warfare became common features of House proceedings.[54] Scholars and other observers came to wonder if Congress had the capacity to address the most important issues on the national agenda. Each party was pulled to its ideological extreme by districting plans that created safe seats for most members. A safe-seat Republican or Democrat had to worry more about an intraparty challenge in the primary from the Republican right or the Democratic left than a general election opponent.[55] Even as the Republicans used their institutional power to protect their majority, the Democrats drew on tactics developed by the previous Republican minority. To complete the role reversal, the Republicans extended the legislative tactics the Democratic majority had used in defending its position.

This institutional partisanship, directly reflecting the underlying cleavages of the New American Politics, has had obviously deleterious effects on the House as an institution. In their 2006 study, political scientists Tom Mann and Norm Ornstein lamented the decline in civility, the erosion in institutional norms, and the inability of Congress to address the most important concerns facing the nation.[56] The House had in recent years failed to perform even its most basic oversight responsibilities. It met in short sessions each week, while its members spent more time campaigning and fund-raising at home than they did governing on Capitol Hill. The GOP majority was the main target of Mann's and Ornstein's criticism, but the underlying institutional trends had affected both congressional parties. Mann and Ornstein left open the question of whether a new Democratic majority might proceed differently.

ENTER NANCY PELOSI

By 2007, when Nancy Pelosi became Speaker, the Republicans had thus brought the office to a level of power not seen since the heyday of Uncle Joe Cannon a century before. The Republicans had mastered the New American Politics and translated that mastery into legislative power. However, they overreached, in both politics and policy. Burdened with an unpopular war, an unpopular president, and a tarnished brand name, the Republicans lost their grip on power in 2006. As the Democrats resumed control of the House for the first time since 1994, they had to decide just how strong a speakership they wanted to establish. They had been led back into power by their new Speaker, and it would be she, more than anyone else, who would craft the new Democratic rendition of the office.

Consider Nancy Pelosi's situation as newly elected Speaker in relation to those of her predecessors in the postreform House, as shown in table 1.1.

Besides the most obvious difference of sex, the biographical, career, and institutional dimensions shown in the table suggest that Pelosi is situated similarly to her recent peers in many ways.[57] Like them, she served in the House for a considerable length of time before becoming Speaker. She was elected to prior party leadership offices, as most of them were. She was relatively high in party seniority, as they were. She was, at first election to the House, the oldest among these Speakers, and she was also the oldest to become Speaker, a fact not unrelated to her sex and about which we will have more to say in chapter 6. Table 1.1 reveals, however, that in key institutional respects Pelosi's situation was more similar to Republican speakers Gingrich and Hastert than to Democratic speakers Albert, O'Neill, Wright, and Foley. The four other Democratic Speakers enjoyed average margins of around 70 seats in their first Congresses. Pelosi and the two Republican Speakers averaged just a 20-seat margin on entering office. Average party unity was higher for the three most recent Speakers than their predecessors, reflecting their narrower margins. Ideological polarization in the House was also much higher. Thus, Pelosi had to govern in a polarized environment with a narrow majority, just as her Republican predecessors had.[58]

None of these statistics captures the most obvious difference, Pelosi's status as the first woman to become Speaker. To understand the context for her,

Table 1.1 Profiles of Recent Speakers

Speaker	Age at first election to House	Age at becoming Speaker	Seniority first Congress as Speaker	Prior elected leadership offices	Margin of first majority as Speaker	Party unity first Congress* as Speaker	Polarization first Congress* as Speaker
Albert	38	62	24	Whip, leader	75	.709	.56
O'Neill	40	64	24	Whip, leader	149	.725	.55
Wright	32	64	11	Leader	81	.880	.66
Foley	35	59	18	Caucus chair, whip, leader	85	.861	.66
Gingrich	35	51	19	Whip	26	.918	.79
Hastert	45	57	49	–	11	.893	.83
Pelosi	47	66	33	Whip	28	.984	.96

Source: Data from Biographical Directory of the United States Congress 1774 to the present, http://bioguide.congress.gov/biosearch/biosearch.asp, accessed March 31, 2009; Jackie Koszczuk and Martha Angle, editors, CQ's Politics in America 2008: The 110th Congress, Washington D.C.: CQ Press, 2007, and previous editions of CQ's Politics in America for 1986, 1988, 1990, 1992, 1996, and 2000. The calculation of polarization scores is based on the measure developed by Keith T. Poole and Howard Rosenthal, DW NOMINATE data set, http://voteview.ucsd.edu/Polarized_America.htm. The party unity scores are taken from Keith T. Poole and Howard Rosenthal, "Party Unity Scores by Chamber for All Two-Party Systems," http://pooleandrosenthal.com/party_unity.htm, accessed October 2, 2009.

*The party polarization score is the absolute value of the difference of Republican and Democratic means on the DW NOMINATE first dimension (for further explanation, see note 58). A party unity vote is one that pits a majority of one party against a majority of the opposite party and the score represents the proportion of members voting with a majority of their party on party unity votes during that particular congress.

attitudes about women in politics must be understood. None of her male predecessors had to contend with fundamental doubts about whether they belonged in politics or were suited to the task of political leadership, doubts arising specifically from her gender. To be sure, public attitudes have been transformed over the period of Pelosi's own adult life, but doubts remain among significant portions of the population. For more than 30 years, the General Social Survey has been asking: "Tell me if you agree or disagree with this statement: Most men are better suited emotionally for politics than are most women."[59]

Figure 1.2 demonstrates that a substantial segment of the populace doubts women's qualifications for political office. Even in 2006, 24.6% of men agreed that men were better suited for politics than women. Among women, 18.9% of those working outside of the home and 27.2% of housewives also agreed that men are better suited for politics. At the same time, 15% of Democratic women agreed with that statement, compared to 34% of Republican women. While the general trend has been one of declining resistance over the past three decades, the figure also reveals more volatility in opinions held by house-wives compared with men and women in the paid workforce. It is interesting to note the increasing doubts of housewives following major milestones for women in politics, such as Geraldine Ferraro's unsuccessful vice presidential candidacy and the so-called Year of the Woman in 1992. With the Republican

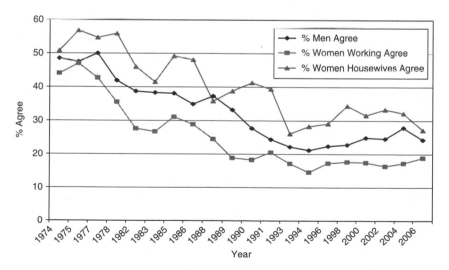

Figure 1.2   Percent of People Who Agree Men Are Better Suited for Politics Than Women

Source: Calculated by the authors from the General Social Survey, www.norc.org/GSS+Website.

dominance and the emergence of cultural conservatives as a force in the mid-1990s, acceptance of women in politics has changed very little over the past decade. Pelosi, who often defines herself as a mother, grandmother, and wife, has had her personal ambitions shaped by such attitudes, while at the same time she has had to confront an electorate that includes a significant portion of voters who think a Y chromosome would qualify her better for politics. Carl Albert has acknowledged that "from early on, everything I did was calculated to being elected to Congress," and Tip O'Neill has confessed to his ambition to secure the speakership from the first day of his House service, but Nancy Pelosi's ambition could hardly have been as bold or unconstrained.[60] How she is judged as Speaker and how she shapes the speakership will never be wholly separable from her gender and the historic spotlight that shines on her as a woman. Hers is very much a story about the transformation of women in politics, yet because of her success, her unique narrative raises new questions about opportunities for women in politics, especially those who aspire to lead.

What kind of leader would Pelosi be and what style of leadership might she (or another woman) pursue? The available research on women in political leadership offers a few clues. Because women often follow a different and more circuitous path to political leadership, their formative experiences may involve different skills and leadership opportunities. Socialized as caregivers and nurturers, women have been portrayed in the leadership literature as differing from their male colleagues in several areas; for example, attending more closely to relationships, emphasizing consensus building, being good listeners, and being focused on integrative skills that bring people together.[61] Research suggests that power motivates men and women differently and women are much more likely to share power and use it to promote change, whereas men use power to reward, punish, or have influence over others.[62]

Women's voice is said to be distinctive. They articulate and act on goals that are rooted in the preservation of relationships, personal commitments, and an orientation that focuses on others rather than self.[63] There is an abundance of evidence that women lawmakers are more likely than their male colleagues to advocate for policies that affect social well-being and families, speak for underrepresented groups, introduce more feminist and social welfare legislation, invest scarce legislative time in women's issues, emphasize constituency service, and facilitate rather than dominate in committee communications.[64]

While these differences have been well documented, James MacGregor Burns describes the archetypal style of legislative leadership as transactional—competitive bargaining and win-lose-or-compromise strategies. Indeed, he calls legislatures and legislative committees "the classic seat of transactional leadership," which is characterized by calculating interests, logrolling, competing, and maneuvering for strategic advantage.[65] As one former Speaker of the Oregon House of Representatives noted: "Traditionally, legislatures have fostered the spontaneous generation of conflict and competition. Members are taught to look out for themselves. Protocol and titles are considered of central importance. The victor in any given struggle is often the one who pushes the hardest and the longest."[66] There is some evidence that in more professionalized legislatures—certainly Congress fits that description—institutional imperatives and norms may push all leaders toward the transactional style, irrespective of personal preferences.[67] In addition, the hyperpartisanship of the New American Politics has pushed contemporary congressional leaders toward a "take-no-prisoners" posture that may work against the possibilities of—to use Carol Gilligan's famous term—a "different voice."

This is a central puzzle to solve as we seek to understand Nancy Pelosi as the first woman Speaker of the House. The epigraphs to this chapter convey the core issue we address. Sam Rayburn looked forward to a Speaker who would be in charge of the House.[68] He became its longest-serving Speaker, legendary in spite of very real limitations on his power due to the dominance of the committee system. He certainly did not contemplate that the Speaker of his dreams might be a woman and not a man. Susan B. Anthony envisioned the day when women would stand equal to men in the councils of government.[69] In Nancy Pelosi, these two predictions come together in a political context that neither Rayburn nor Anthony could have anticipated in their lifetimes. Is Pelosi's approach as Speaker well suited to the contemporary Congress and the New American Politics in which she leads? Will history portray her as leaving a new imprint on the speakership? Does her gender make a difference? We address these questions as we explore her rise to power, her management of the legislative process, her electoral and communications strategies, her ambition and voice, and her leadership.

Chapter 2

Getting There

This is an historic moment—for the Congress, and for the women of this country. It is a moment for which we have waited over two hundred years. Never losing faith, we waited through the many years of struggle to achieve our rights.

—Speaker Nancy Pelosi (January 4, 2007)

Nancy Pelosi's election as Speaker of the United States House of Representatives was indeed a historical moment.[1] How did she get there? The answer to this question is the remarkable personal story of a housewife and mother who, as she has put it, made it from the kitchen to the House. But it is also a narrative about the changing face of American politics and the changing character of the House of Representatives. Considering Pelosi's rise in California politics, the way she built her career in the House of Representatives, and her rise to the speakership enables us not only to understand her career in the context of the political forces that shaped it but also to better understand those forces through the prism of her career.

What we learn by studying her path to power are the lessons and assets that define success in the New American Politics. Pelosi's career illustrates how partisan polarization, identity politics, representation, and diversity shape opportunities particularly in the Democratic Party. In addition, her story reveals how coalition building, fund-raising, new technologies, and strategic choices create the building blocks of a national leadership career in the contemporary Congress. In addition to the political and institutional lessons learned, there is also the personal—Pelosi's inclination to start early, to out-organize and work harder and more persistently than others, and to deny others the opportunity to define her persona and career. Pelosi's rise to the speakership provides at least one—albeit perhaps not the only—recipe for political success in the New American Politics.

CALIFORNIA

Getting Started

In 1976, the Democratic Party stood on the verge of winning the presidency after eight years of Republican administrations under Richard Nixon and Gerald Ford.[2] The Democrats had made substantial gains in the 1974 congressional elections and liked their odds of ousting the unelected Ford. California in this, as in many other ways, was a leading indicator. In 1974, Jerry Brown had reclaimed the governorship Ronald Reagan had wrested from his father, Pat Brown, in 1966. The ascetic Jerry Brown was an icon of the left wing of the Democratic Party. Refusing to live in the posh new governor's mansion that Reagan had built, Brown chose instead to live in a small apartment. Rejecting the governor's limousine, he drove himself to work in a compact car. The man who became known as Governor Moonbeam symbolized California "New Age" thinking arising from the counterculture of the 1960s. He brought together the political instincts of his powerful father and the sensibilities of the seminarian he had once been.

Liberal Democrats like Jerry Brown were caught by surprise when the most conservative among their presidential candidates, former Georgia governor Jimmy Carter, emerged from the pack to become the front-runner for the party's nomination. While it was not apparent at the time, Carter's candidacy was an early indication that the country was beginning to move to the right. While presenting himself as the son of the "New South," Carter was in fact the most conservative Democratic nominee since Grover Cleveland. His election and subsequent administration would reveal a clear split among Democrats between northern and western liberals and southern and border state conservatives.

Although he had been in office less than two years, Brown contemplated a late entry to the race, hoping to pick up the ABC (Anybody But Carter) banner. Though the June California primary would presumably be his for the taking, he could hardly afford to wait until summer to win some delegates. But where else could he run and win? At a Democratic fund-raiser, Brown was introduced by Leo McCarthy, the Speaker of the California House, to a young housewife, Nancy Pelosi, who had been active in raising money for California Democrats since moving to San Francisco in 1969. Pelosi and Brown had much in common. Pelosi was the daughter of former Maryland congressman and Baltimore mayor Thomas D'Alesandro. She had been raised in a political environment from birth. Having helped in the family business as a young girl, she had well-developed organizational instincts. A staunch liberal, she was attracted to grand political visions. When she later talked about saving the planet, one could recall that the environmentalist Brown had often spoken about the survival of the planet in the 1970s.[3]

Pelosi suggested to Brown that he could win in Maryland and offered to enlist the support of her family and its political connections in Baltimore. She went to Maryland with him, introduced him to her brother and other members of the D'Alesandro political circle, and raised money for the Brown campaign. Pelosi proved correct, and with her help Brown carried both Maryland and California. But Brown had started too late to deny Carter the nomination—a lesson Pelosi would witness more than once in her political career.

A basic rule of politics, especially in Baltimore and San Francisco, is that one rewards one's friends. Brown thanked Pelosi for her support by endorsing her as the Northern California chair of the state Democratic Party, a position in which she served until 1980. In 1981, she was elected state party chair and delegate to the DNC.

With her emergence into active participation in party politics, Pelosi's challenge was to build and maintain her party in the face of the Reagan Revolution. She sought to modernize the party's technical organization and to rebuild the urban-rural coalition on which the party had always relied. She had extensive personal experience as a fund-raiser, but now she had to develop a party infrastructure. It was necessary to develop voter registration lists and a polling capability.[4] In implementing these organizational reforms, Pelosi drew both on the Baltimore tradition of urban machine politics and on newly developing technology. The personal computer would revolutionize campaign organization, and nearby Silicon Valley was the heart of the computer revolution. Computerized donor lists and telephone banks would be developed and would supplement the traditional fund-raising receptions and dinners. Pelosi also sought to reconstruct the Democratic coalition. Reagan had appealed to conservative Democrats, many in the eastern part of the state. Pelosi was determined to reconcile farmland conservatives and seacoast liberals. Her earliest political work reflected the elements on which her political career would be built and sustained: coalition building, money, and organization.

The National Party Stage

Pelosi developed a reputation within the San Francisco, California, and national Democratic Party establishments, but aside from the Brown campaign, California remained her field of operations. That changed in 1983 when she led the effort to bring the 1984 Democratic National Convention

to San Francisco and the following year when she chaired the host committee for that event. Many feared that by picking San Francisco the party would
only reinforce its liberal image at a time when the electorate seemed to be
turning more conservative. Pelosi argued that ideology was less important
than organizational capacity. In the end, San Francisco won out because of
its amenities and the hard work of the host committee to meet the needs
of the delegates. The reservations about it proved well founded, however, as
the Republicans, meeting that year in Dallas, lampooned the "San Francisco"
Democrats as the party of tax increases and soft foreign policy. Reagan went
on to a landslide reelection victory.

Two memorable speeches marked the San Francisco convention.
Minnesota senator Walter Mondale in his acceptance speech promised to
raise taxes, and New York governor Mario Cuomo made a biting attack on
Reagan and a soaring defense of the policies of the Democratic Party. At this
convention, Pelosi forged relationships with Cuomo and other Democratic
Party leaders that would prove valuable as her career developed. She understood the value of interpersonal relations and reciprocal favors in building a
political network and career.

The 1984 election was a disaster for the Democrats that led them to
both introspection and internal strife. In the House, much of the discontent
was directed at Speaker Tip O'Neill, an early and strong supporter of the
Mondale-Ferraro ticket. Republicans had sought for years to gain political
advantage by associating O'Neill with the excesses of New Deal and Great
Society liberalism. O'Neill was said to be like the federal budget: "fat, bloated,
and out of control."[5] Republican efforts to run against O'Neill were, however,
unsuccessful, as the Democrats retained control of the House. Still, there was
increasing disgruntlement among moderate and conservative Democrats
who concluded from the election results that the party had moved too far
to the left. From this concern emerged the Democratic Leadership Council
(DLC), a national organization of party moderates, and in the House, the
Mainstream Forum, led by Oklahoma Congressman Dave McCurdy.

The tensions within the national party were revealed in late 1984 and
early 1985 as the DNC moved to select a new national chair. The contest
reflected the disarray into which the party had fallen. The Democratic governors sought a candidate of national stature who would be perceived as
independent of Washington and its organized interest matrix. They eventually settled on former North Carolina governor Terry Sanford. The other
announced candidates were party activists of one description or another,
none of whom had held national appointed or elective office. Among them
was Paul Kirk, a Massachusetts lawyer and former aide to Senator Edward
Kennedy. Kirk was the candidate of the East Coast party establishment, the
Kennedy liberal wing, and the labor unions. Pelosi, riding the increased

visibility she had attained at the San Francisco convention and drawing on her decade of service to the party, launched an insurgent candidacy and cast herself on the national stage for the first time in seeking election to the DNC post. As with all of her undertakings, her campaign was well organized and well funded. She spent $100,000, hiring a public relations firm to promote her candidacy.[6]

Her campaign presaged positions she would later take as a member of Congress and its Speaker. Kirk, she claimed, was a front man for Kennedy. The reason the Democrats had lost in 1984 was not because the party was too liberal but because it was too set in its ways and beholden to its entrenched interests. Unlike those Democrats who associated with the DLC or the Mainstream Forum, Pelosi did not argue for a more centrist Democratic party but for a more effective one. The party had to get back in touch with average voters, and to do so it needed a leader who was not a part of the Washington establishment. Pelosi offered to bring a "western" perspective to the Democratic Party. She was the "outsider" running against the "Washington Establishment."[7] Interestingly, her most prominent supporter was Governor Cuomo.

Pelosi's candidacy was complicated because the incumbent, Charles T. Manatt, was a Los Angeles attorney. This made it more difficult to argue for a California successor, especially one who, like Pelosi, was a Manatt ally. Manatt was also at the time involved in a fight over delegate selection rules, and Pelosi had been in charge of enforcing the rules in San Francisco. And she encountered additional obstacles. To some labor leaders, she appeared insubstantial—an "airhead," according to a statement attributed to an unnamed labor leader.[8] To other DNC members, she was simply too liberal, representing a city that was well known for its left-leaning politics and substantial gay community. And, it was said, Pelosi suffered from a reaction against the vice presidential candidacy of Ferraro, who some believed had been a drag on the Mondale ticket. This was not the time for another liberal female leader of limited national experience.

Before the balloting, Pelosi determined that she could not win and withdrew from the contest. Sanford never generated sufficient support, and Kirk was elected. This defeat, the only one Pelosi ever experienced, offered lessons to and about her. She had traveled a considerable distance from her origins as homemaker and fund-raiser in 1976. In seeking the position of national chair, she had encountered four points of resistance: she was an outsider, more liberal, reflective of the state party as opposed to the Washington establishment, and a woman. There had been too many hurdles to leap. As we discuss further in chapter 6, she learned from this experience that the path ahead for a liberal woman from San Francisco would necessarily face the ideological cleavages within the Democratic Party and the biases of some of its important members. And she learned two practical strategic lessons: first, do not let your opponents define you; second, start early.

Pelosi's defeat in the DNC chair race did not lead to her retirement from politics. Instead, she carried her primary political asset, her ability to raise funds for the party, to a new venue. In 1986, Senator George Mitchell asked her to serve as finance chair for the Democratic Senate Campaign Committee, which he led. The importance of the 1986 election to Senate Democrats can hardly be overstated. The Republicans had won control of the Senate in 1980 for the first time since 1955. The twelve Republican senators who had been swept into office on Reagan's coattails in 1980 were up for reelection, presenting Democrats with a chance to retake the Senate. Mitchell's future in the Senate depended considerably on the results. That he recruited Pelosi to head his committee's fund-raising indicates the reputation she had established nationally. Her service as finance chair led to tangible results. The Democrats did retake the Senate, and Pelosi's fund-raising network was extended nationally. Her political career had proceeded stepwise, as each opportunity she seized led to new ones. As she completed her work on behalf of the Senate Democrats, she did not know that her most important opportunity yet would soon emerge.

Running for Congress

She had often been encouraged to seek political office but had always resisted. She understood from her childhood how unrelenting is the life of an elected politician, and she saw her role more as a party fund-raiser and organizer than as an elected official. Then, in 1987, fate intervened. Congresswoman Sala Burton, who had succeeded her late husband Phil Burton as California's Fifth District representative, succumbed to cancer. Before she died, she endorsed Pelosi as her successor. The special election to replace Sala Burton was set for April 7, 1987, and Pelosi was among four Democratic and one Republican candidates to seek the office. The rules in place for special House elections in California gave definition to this one. In an initial open election, all candidates from all parties competed. If any candidate won at least 50% of the votes plus one, he or she would be declared the winner. If no candidate attained that threshold, a runoff would be held. However, the runoff would be held between the Democrat receiving the most votes and the Republican receiving the most votes, not the two highest vote getters. Given the substantial Democratic voting edge in the district, the competition to become the leading Democrat would likely determine the outcome of the race.

The Burton machine had dominated the district and much of San Francisco politics for two decades, and as Sala Burton's anointed successor, an easy victory for Pelosi might have been assumed. The reality was more complex. Underlying it were the political cleavages that defined Democratic politics in San Francisco—involving the various ethnic groups, organized labor, the increasingly influential gay community, environmentalists, and of course business interests. The backbone of the Burton machine was a coalition of liberals, labor, minorities, and environmentalists. Now that both Phil and Sala Burton had passed from the scene, that coalition was fragile. In the first place, the Burton machine without Phil Burton had lost much of its potency. San Francisco politics had become increasingly eclectic, as the city's cultural mix became ever more differentiated. High housing costs pushed many blue collar workers out of the city. Immigration brought many more Asians into it. San Francisco continued to be a magnet for gays, whose numbers had increased substantially.[9] Second, Pelosi could not count on all of Burton's supporters, especially among organized labor and blue-collar voters.

She faced other challenges as well. For a time, it appeared that San Francisco mayor Dianne Feinstein would enter the race, and she would have been in an advantaged position as the incumbent mayor. When Feinstein announced on February 13, 1987, that she would not run, Pelosi declared her candidacy the same day.[10] Pelosi had some liabilities. She had never held public office and had no constituency in San Francisco. She had never been the favorite of organized labor, as evidenced by its opposition to her candidacy for her party's national chairship. Her most formidable Democratic opponent was Harry Britt, a member of the San Francisco Board of Supervisors, a leader in the gay community, and the first serious gay candidate from San Francisco to seek election to Congress. For many gays, their time had come.

Pelosi was not without assets. Money would not be a problem because of her extensive fund-raising network. She understood urban politics and its basic organizing principles. She also had substantial name recognition due to her role as state party chair and her work on the 1984 Democratic convention. Perhaps most important, the role she had played in California politics had called on her to build bridges between competing factions, bring the party together, and straddle whatever political divisions she encountered. For example, Leo McCarthy, who had led her to Jerry Brown and her appointment as state party chair, would serve as an important advisor to her campaign for the seat once held by his old rival, Phil Burton. In her approach to politics, she was unflinchingly liberal, yet she built relationships with both liberals and moderates. She was a more establishment figure than Britt, yet she ran as an outsider. She embraced the gay community yet appealed to those who rejected it. Unable to rely on the Burton coalition, she sought to build one of her own. As always, organization was at the heart of her effort.

The special election became an exercise in political definition. Britt was banking on the breakup of the Burton coalition. His strategy was to portray Pelosi as a rich and privileged socialite, a "party girl" who would not be an effective voice for the working class. He hoped to galvanize a substantial majority among the gay community, gain a sufficient number of working-class votes, and ride to a plurality in the first election that would carry him into a runoff with the Republican candidate.[11] As a member of the Board of Supervisors, he had the credibility that attached to service in elective office; Pelosi did not.

Recognizing that she could not simply ride the Burton coalition to victory, and with labor suspicious and most gays supporting Britt, Pelosi sought to drive Britt back on his base, split it, and bring new voters into play. She would do as she had always done: organize her way forward. Her campaign theme was "A voice that will be heard." She hoped to parlay her work in the state and national party into a message that she would have immediate influence in the House, and the word "voice" connoted her aspiration to speak for the needs of San Francisco, perhaps especially for women voters.[12] Britt would be the special interest representative of the gay community; she, by contrast, would be a player who could argue more effectively on behalf of all San Francisco, including the interests of its gay community. For the second time, Pelosi made the argument that she was at once an outsider who would bring a fresh perspective and an insider who was sufficiently well connected to get things done.

There were two dimensions to the contest between Pelosi and Britt. First, it was a competition between a white woman and a gay man, freighted with identity politics. Second, it was a case study in raw power politics. Pelosi sought to marginalize Britt while at the same time promising to better serve the needs of his core constituency. She also did not shy from presenting herself as a housewife and mother and dressing her campaign in images of her family. If there were San Francisco voters who found little affinity with the gay community, they understood that they had another alternative in the race. Pelosi scrambled to a 36%–32% win over Britt on April 7, and on June 3 she easily won the runoff against the leading Republican.[13]

As she stood at the threshold of her House career, her experience at that point provides some insight into American politics. Although Britt had served on the San Francisco Board of Supervisors and Pelosi had not, she was clearly the more "establishment" candidate in this race. She had already played on the state and national stage. Her precongressional experience by far exceeded that of any recent Speaker, except perhaps Tip O'Neill.[14] Yet even with Sala Burton's imprimatur, Pelosi had to fight to win her first election. She succeeded by claiming that her national connections would pay dividends for her district *and* by arguing that she would be an outsider to the

Washington establishment. It was the same case she had made against Paul Kirk, and one that would resonate throughout her career. She would bring a western perspective to Washington politics. Why has this argument been so important for Pelosi? An answer lies in the underlying changes that were coming to define the New American Politics. The "old" liberalism associated with the New Deal and Great Society had lost its cachet with a majority of American voters. With the popular Ronald Reagan in the White House, conservatism was ascendant. Pelosi could hardly turn her back on her liberal values or her liberal constituency, but she sought to reframe liberalism in order to get past (or around) ideology. Liberalism needed to find a new vocabulary and a new voice.

WASHINGTON

Pelosi arrived in Washington as the most junior member of the House of Representatives, but she was far from being the least influential. She carried into office a network based on a lifetime of friendships and connections, buttressed by substantial service to her party and its elected members. How would she translate these assets into effectively representing her constituents and shaping public policy? Her legislative craft is captured by these adjectives: relentless, passionate, entrepreneurial, pragmatic, and coalitional. In developing that craft, she wanted to define herself and not allow others to define her, and in the process put to rest any "party girl" or "airhead" images that might have survived in her political opponents' minds.[15]

Legislative Craft

In the first decade of her service as congresswoman, Pelosi pursued an agenda that was ideologically liberal, focused on her San Francisco district, and in support of core Democratic Party positions. She was in favor of human rights, opposed to unrestricted free trade, prochoice, and an environmentalist. These positions situate her squarely in her San Francisco district and explain why since her first race she has not been seriously challenged again. Take, for example, her work in the area of HIV/AIDS, an issue of critical importance to the gay community nationally and in San Francisco. Britt could have no reasonable grounds to complain that Pelosi was inattentive to her constituents. Her fight on behalf of AIDS victims was the subject of her first speech on the House floor and was sustained subsequently. She pursued increased funding for AIDS research and treatment, aid to cities impacted by the problems of AIDS victims, protections for their rights, and insurance coverage and housing support for them. She criticized the Clinton administration when it decided against federal funding for a needle exchange program. When the Republican Congress sought to cut funding for AIDS research, she sponsored an amendment to restore the funds.[16]

She was equally determined in her fight to create a trust to govern San Francisco's Presidio, an old military base overlooking the Pacific Ocean that was scheduled to be closed. She led a decade-long effort to ensure that it would be preserved in substantial part as parkland under the authority of the National Park Service. If her work on AIDS was passionate, her dedication to the Presidio Trust was relentless. In both instances, her technique was to build coalitions by reaching out to those who might otherwise have opposed her. In the case of AIDS, she stressed that a communicable disease might have widespread effects about which all Americans should be concerned. She emphasized the humanitarian dimension of the problem in order to win converts. In the case of the Presidio, she argued that a self-sustaining trust would save the taxpayers the burden of the expenses associated with base closure. Observers stress her achievement in obtaining bipartisan backing for an urban recreation area in America's most liberal city.[17]

Pelosi's name became identified with the issue of human rights in China, and in this she found herself in an odd alliance with religious and libertarian conservatives. In the wake of Tiananmen Square, Pelosi and her staff decided to make the issue a central component of her legislative program; two decades later it remains among her central commitments as Speaker. Initially, she tried to secure visa extensions for Chinese students studying in the United States who might be subject to persecution on their return. The George H. W. Bush administration favored granting Most Favored Nation status to China and maintaining positive diplomatic relations with Beijing. In the wake of Tiananmen Square, Bush sought to put quiet pressure on the Chinese government, sending national security adviser Brent Scowcroft as an emissary. Bush vetoed Pelosi's bill to extend student visas; the House overrode the veto, but the Senate did not. Pelosi pushed legislation to condition Most Favored Nation status on China's human rights record. In 1991, she took part in a delegation to Beijing and challenged protocol by displaying a sign commemorating Tiananmen. While the Bush administration argued that quiet diplomacy would be most effective in influencing the Chinese government, Pelosi argued that only legislative restrictions would force its hand.[18]

Prospects for a tougher Chinese policy seemed improved with the election of Bill Clinton, who had campaigned as a critic of the Bush administration's approach. Clinton signed an executive order imposing human rights conditions on trade policy with China. But within a year, the administration backed away from this policy and supported Most Favored Nation status renewal. This policy shift was in line with Clinton's developing emphasis on globalization as the centerpiece of American foreign policy. It also reflected the influence of business, including the technology sector, in increasing trade with China. The potential of the China market loomed large. Contemplating Clinton's final surrender to the new "China lobby," Pelosi lamented the influence of big business on American trade policy. "That's why the president changed his view," she said. "Because big business weighed in. They have enormous resources. They are willing to spend an unlimited amount. And the money not only speaks, the money rules."[19]

Pelosi's dispute with Clinton over the issue of trade with China was only one example of the tensions between the two Democrats. In 1993, she opposed his "Don't Ask, Don't Tell" policy governing gays in the military. She spoke out against his policy for expedited review of Haitian immigrants, fearing that it would lead to political persecution. She opposed legislation to restrict immigration of the HIV infected, while Clinton, reneging on a campaign pledge to end the ban, backed off from the issue. The following year, Pelosi stood against American participation in the International Conference on the Status of Women after the Chinese government imprisoned dissident Harry Wu. She implored the first lady not to attend, but Hillary Clinton went anyway.[20]

Perhaps the most striking conflict between President Clinton and Pelosi was on the larger issue of free trade. Clinton worked assiduously to obtain congressional approval of the North American Free Trade Agreement. To win wavering votes, he promised to implement an executive order enforcing labor and environmental requirements. Pelosi was alone among Bay area liberals in voting for the Agreement, and later she concluded that Clinton had not honored his commitments. She became an outspoken opponent of unrestricted free trade and opposed Clinton on the creation of the World Trade Organization. It is clear that she had come to view Clinton as unreliable.[21] Still, she recognized the pragmatic need to work with the president. He had, after all, done her a favor in naming her as chair of the party's platform committee at the 1992 Democratic National Convention. In 1996, she strongly supported his reelection in spite of her disagreements with him on trade and other issues.[22]

The Liberal

If there is one word that best describes Pelosi's record in the House it is "liberal." Tip O'Neill once bragged that he had supported federal funding for research to help midgets grow. Pelosi was no less abashed in her belief that government was the source of public good. In a 1996 interview, she said: "I pride myself in being called a 'liberal.'" Representing one of the most liberal districts in the country, she was free to stand firm for her own liberal values, but she was willing to compromise when necessary.

> I don't consider myself a moderate. But I certainly reach out to them. We have to have the votes. Sometimes you don't have the votes even on the Democratic side and you have to reach out to the Republicans. There are plenty of reasons to vote against every bill that comes up here. You vote for nothing if you are an absolute, 100% purist—you would vote for no bill.

For Pelosi, legislation is the art of the possible. The pragmatic legislator gets what she can, and then lives to fight another day.

> And how do you get votes? You get votes by giving votes, get votes by educating people to what you are trying to achieve and if there is something in your proposal that they couldn't accommodate, you had to see if that was part of your bottom line, if it was not something you could live without. You can deal with it later. There's always tomorrow, after all.[23]

Etched in Pelosi's unabashed liberalism and in her sometimes tense relationship with the Clintons is the fundamental political dilemma that has marked her political career and its times. Bill Clinton was associated with the New Democratic "third way." He had chaired the DLC. He was from Arkansas and represented a variant of southern populism that bore some similarity to that of Jimmy Carter. Clinton's political art lay in his ability to preempt Republican policy positions.[24] This centrist approach called for blurring the lines between Democrats and Republicans. It was anathema to Pelosi, whose politics was firmly grounded in her liberal ideology. Clinton's approach became especially important after the Republicans took control of the House in 1995. Newt Gingrich had led the Republicans to victory by pursuing an ideological and confrontational politics, rejecting the accommodating style of Republican leader Bob Michel. Clinton's compromises may have been in his interest, but they often betrayed core Democratic positions and served to constrain congressional Democrats. Pelosi was willing to compromise when necessary, but she always saw compromise as a step toward achieving her ultimate policy goals rather than as an alternative to them.

Acquiring Influence

Such an incremental approach would be served by the accretion of influence, and so we must ask: How did Pelosi go about acquiring influence in the House? From the beginning, she sought to build relationships. One venue was a weekly dinner group composed of a spectrum of mostly liberal Democrats originally convened by Congressman Marty Russo of Illinois and often hosted by New York congressman Tom Downey.[25] Participants were members who lived in Washington during the week and kept their primary residences in their home districts. They sought camaraderie and relief from the unyielding demands of public office in a zone of private friendship. Pelosi slipped into the spot Sala Burton had occupied and became herself an occasional host of these dinners, at which her freezer, according to a regular, was always well stocked with chocolate ice cream.[26]

Pelosi forged friendships in other ways. Her defense of Pennsylvania congressman Austin Murphy in the face of ethics charges won her the respect of Murphy's Pennsylvania colleague John Murtha, the chair of the Appropriations Defense subcommittee. He would become a key ally in her rise to the speakership. She availed herself of the many contacts she had made during her years as a national committeewoman and even drew on friendships her father had forged decades before.[27] Her work on AIDS, China, and other human rights issues enabled her to develop relationships within and across party lines.[28] Because her initial assignment to the House Banking Committee was not directly related to some of her policy priorities, she had to reach out to a diverse range of members. Her characteristic approach was to seek as many cosponsors as possible for a bill, casting a wide net. She also did favors for members, ranging from simple courtesies such as introductions at caucus meetings to more substantial assistance such as sponsoring fund-raisers in San Francisco.

Moving Up

Pelosi began to rise in the House power structure. She launched a two-year effort to win a coveted seat on the House Appropriations Committee, where she further cemented her relationship with Murtha. She eventually became ranking member of the Foreign Operations Subcommittee. In 1995, she was appointed to the House Select Intelligence Committee, eventually becoming its longest-serving Democrat. Taken together, these two assignments gave Pelosi a firm foundation in foreign policy and an ability to leverage influence through the appropriations process. She consistently demonstrated her ability to deliver for her constituents, while gaining the latitude to play on the national and world stage.

Pelosi served as a deputy whip and a member of the House Ethics Committee. The ethics process had become thoroughly politicized in the late 1980s and early 1990s as House Republicans, led by Gingrich, brought charges against Speaker Jim Wright and attacked the "corrupt" culture of the Democratic majority as evidenced by scandals at the House Bank, Post Office, and Restaurant.[29] Wright was accused of a variety of violations of House rules, including the allegation that he had received inappropriate royalties on sales to special interest groups of a book he had written. This scorched earth tactic resulted in Wright's resignation in 1989 and contributed to the defeat of his successor, Tom Foley, in the 1994 elections, in which the Republicans captured the House for the first time in forty years. Cast into the minority in the 104th Congress, the Democrats sought retribution, using the ethics process to attack Gingrich. Eventually, eighty-four complaints were filed against the Republican Speaker. In the end, all were dropped but one: that he had abused the Internal Revenue code when his non-profit Progress and Freedom Foundation had funded a course he had taught, the contents of which his accusers claimed had been essentially political in character.[30] The effort against Gingrich was led by Democratic whip David Bonior of Michigan; Nancy Pelosi took the point for the Democrats on the Ethics Committee.

If Pelosi's legislative work had shown her to be a staunch liberal and an effective coalition builder, her activity on the Ethics Committee revealed that her partisan instincts, sown in Baltimore and cultivated in California, were sharp. She had a deep respect for the House and its institutional norms and believed that Gingrich did not. In January 1996, two Republican members of the Ethics Committee publicly stated that Gingrich would be found guilty of no charges that might prevent him from serving as Speaker. Pelosi was enraged. Gingrich had in fact agreed to accept censure and to pay a $300,000 fine for misleading the Committee, but the Committee's rules on confidentiality prevented Pelosi from publicly challenging these statements. To Pelosi, Gingrich was not fit to serve as Speaker, given the nature of the charges against him.[31]

By 1998 Pelosi had established her identity as a member of Congress. She had become widely known as a staunch liberal, dedicated to her causes. She was also known as a shrewd legislator, able to reach compromise on important issues. She had made her voice heard to the benefit of her constituents. And she had shown that she had the gumption for a political fight. She had, in her first decade of service, established a record of accomplishment that exceeded that of most recent Speakers.[32] Yet in 1998, few would have put her on any list of future Speakers. She had made it from the kitchen to the House, but she had not made the more difficult transition from rank-in-file member to party leader. She would now.

INTO THE LEADERSHIP

Even as she built her legislative portfolio and reputation, Pelosi had continued to do what she has always done better than others: raise money for the Democratic Party and its candidates. In the process, she forged relationships with new members. She held fund-raisers on behalf of Democratic challengers and incumbents. She raised money for the DCCC. On two occasions she turned down Democratic leader Dick Gephardt's request to chair the DCCC; but as one member put it in a confidential interview, no matter who chaired the DCCC, it was often Nancy Pelosi who often brought in the money. Her willingness to support challengers and members was not ideologically conditioned. Her only concern was that Democrats win.

As her star rose within the Democratic Caucus, Pelosi was sometimes asked about her aspirations. She consistently denied leadership ambitions. Her commitments, she would say, were to her constituents and her issues. Having grown up in the home of a big-city mayor, she was disinclined to seek that office in San Francisco. In the House, other California members such as George Miller and Vic Fazio stood ahead of her in line for party leadership. Published commentary and private accounts vary in their estimation of Pelosi's true ambitions. Some suggest that Pelosi harbored leadership ambitions from the outset, but she denied it.[33] Ambition, however, was in her bloodlines and character. She had, after all, gone straight for the position of DNC chair when no one had given her much chance of success.

Hat in the Ring

Analytically, the seed of Pelosi's ambition is less important than its fruit. For when she did decide to seek party leadership, she did so in an unorthodox way. Vic Fazio's announcement of his retirement from the House in November 1997 launched a dialogue within the California delegation about who among them might be advanced for party leadership. The obvious choice was George Miller, the most seasoned among the delegation's liberals. Miller, however, was not interested. During the spring and early summer of 1998, members close to Pelosi encouraged her to become their candidate. A canvas of members indicated that she had a good chance to win. Some of our informants claim that Pelosi was at first resistant; others believe that she had been angling for leadership from an earlier point. Whatever the provenance, her decision to seek a leadership position was made clear at a dinner held in July 1998 among a circle of her closest colleagues. She decided to seek the position of Democratic whip.[34]

This decision was extraordinary in two respects. First, the position of Democratic whip was not open; David Bonior was the party whip and was not at that time aiming to step down or out. Pelosi was not proposing to challenge Bonior. How does one go about campaigning for an office that is not open? Second, Pelosi intended to skip over the "lesser" party offices for which female members had historically competed. She would not stand for caucus chair, vice chair, or secretary. She had earned her spurs in candidate recruitment, in fund-raising, and on issues important to the party, and she had no need to settle for a lesser party position. Her plan was to announce her intention to seek the position of whip in the next Congress—assuming that the Democrats would win the majority, Dick Gephardt would become Speaker, and David Bonior would become floor leader. She was seeking to establish an inside position on the chance that the Democrats might resume their majority.

Maryland congressman Steny Hoyer had lost to Bonior in the race to become whip in 1994 and contemplated another run should Bonior elevate to floor leader. Hoyer and Pelosi had a very long history, going back to their service as interns for Maryland senator Daniel Brewster in 1963.[35] Pelosi had supported Hoyer against Bonior in 1994. He was understandably surprised, then, when she called in August 1998 to tell him of her plans. Pelosi circulated a letter to House Democrats announcing her intention, and the longest leadership race in House history was on. Through 1999, Pelosi and Hoyer jockeyed for position. Pelosi made it clear that this was the beginning, not the end, of her leadership ambition. As she told one reporter, "Think of me in terms of a majority whip or whatever comes after that."[36]

To the uninitiated, and sometimes even the cognoscenti, House leadership races are mysterious ventures. They are deeply political, as each member calculates his or her interest. They are also deeply personal, as candidates draw on and seek to foster relationships with their colleagues. Networks of personal relationships are typically grounded within state delegations, through regional networks, or through the congressional apparatus, that is, the committee system, party organization, or informal groups. Precisely because they do involve both political and personal elements, leadership races can be destabilizing, both before and after the election. During the race, candidates and their supporters are constantly gauging the sentiments of their colleagues, calculating, and seeking advantage. Afterward, the losing candidates and their supporters sometimes lick their wounds, harbor resentments, and look to the future for new opportunities. Since these elections are by secret ballot, members' commitments are uncertain, and it is not unusual for two candidates to claim and believe they have a majority of committed votes. It will then be said that the loser cannot count, and the loser will believe that someone lied.

Many members, including Hoyer, resisted the prospect of an extended competition for whip. It seemed odd to campaign for a position that was not known to be available. Still, the Democrats did hope to capture the House, and aspirants to the leadership had to confront the fact that Pelosi had already launched her campaign. They had to keep pace or be left behind. She began with a series of dinners, building out from her core group of supporters. The purpose was to introduce her in a leadership context and to enable her to present her analysis of what ailed House Democrats and her vision for the future. She continued to raise money for the DCCC, for individual members, and for challengers. She used her own PAC (PAC to the Future) to disburse contributions. To expand her influence, she also briefly created a second PAC called Team Majority. The National Legal and Policy Center filed a complaint with the Federal Election Commission alleging that Pelosi's two PACs were being intentionally used to circumvent long-established contribution limits, in effect allowing contributors to "double up" their donations. The second PAC—a clear violation of federal election laws—was quickly shut down. She hired a full-time political strategist. She worked her various networks, including the Appropriations Committee. Recognizing the need to attract support among conservative Democrats, she asked Murtha to head her campaign. And she made personal contacts with most of the Democratic members.

The Case for Leadership

What case did Nancy Pelosi make on behalf of her leadership ambition? She promised to reinvigorate the Democratic caucus with a new vision of leadership. She argued that the party's electoral prospects depended on active and aggressive leadership that would challenge Republicans. She reprised her 1985 DNC argument that she represented a "western" perspective that was innovative and in tune with the times. She appealed to her colleagues in the California delegation and on the Appropriations Committee. She appealed to liberal Democrats on the basis of her unyielding liberal record. And she appealed to female members to support her in a historic "first."

Above all else, Pelosi promised to fight to restore the Democrats' majority. In making her case she took sides on the key strategic schism within the Democratic Caucus, a position that would come to define her approach to leadership and differentiate her from Hoyer. The Democrats had been traumatized by being thrust into the minority in 1995 after forty years in control of the House. Their competitions for party leadership had in the past given scant attention to the skills and strategies that would be needed if they were to retain or regain the majority. Faced with the new Republican monolith, the Democrats' first instinct was to assume that the GOP majority was somehow a fluke and that the voters would quickly correct their 1994 mistake. But by the late 1990s, it was apparent that the Democrats would have to find a way back into power.

At the center of this effort was their party leader, Richard Gephardt. Since his first election to the House in 1976, Gephardt had been among its most respected and effective members. His early career had been marked by a pragmatic turn against Great Society liberalism, emphasizing fiscal responsibility and a practical focus on government programs. As he had moved into the leadership in the late 1980s, he had shifted from the center toward the left, especially on trade and labor issues. His district had trended Republican, and after 1992 he never won 60% of the vote. Thus, while he was liberal on some issues, he was more moderate on others. In the 106th Congress, for example, he had liberal ratings of 83% in 1999 and 84% in 2000, rather moderate by the standards of the Democratic Caucus. On key votes on the estate tax, gun control, GOP-labeled partial birth abortion, and the Cuban embargo, he had voted with the Republicans.[37]

Gephardt had centralized strategy and message in his minority leader office and set out to move the party to the political center to compete for swing congressional districts. He convened a group of up to fifty to sixty Democrats (about a quarter of the Democratic Caucus) many of whom met in his office every afternoon at five o'clock to discuss strategy, tactics, and message. He wanted a message to reinforce the party's electoral strategy, and he wanted the party on message. These deliberations focused on how the House should be run and the need for bipartisanship. A new strategic plan emphasized extensive consultations with the Republicans and a fair deal on committee ratios. This focus on bipartisanship was grounded in practical considerations and reflected the increasing number of moderates in the Democratic Caucus. With the power of the committee chairs diminished by the retirement of "old bulls," this strategy, with the expectation of a narrow Democratic majority, anticipated the need for that new majority to forge coalitions with moderate Republicans.[38]

This approach stressed the need to *compromise* with a future Republican minority and the belief that bipartisanship would be the key to both gaining and maintaining Democratic control of the House. Interestingly, the main drafter, Congressman Ben Cardin of Maryland, occupied Thomas D'Alesandro's old House seat and ended up as the manager for Hoyer's whip campaign. Where did this leave Nancy Pelosi? Gephardt, Cardin, and Hoyer wanted to move away from Pelosi's signature issues, such as the fight over China's trade status; but the absence of a woman in the Democratic leadership created obvious problems. Pelosi was quick to point out the advantages of having a woman in the leadership, stressing that it would be a "feather in the cap" for the House Democrats.[39]

Pelosi challenged the centrist strategy Gephardt had developed while seeking to take advantage of her gender. These two issues defined the Pelosi-Hoyer race. Hoyer argued that Pelosi was too liberal for the job and that her staunch liberalism and San Francisco base were inconsistent with the message the Democrats were trying to promote and the strategy they hoped to implement as the majority party. Pelosi argued that she had earned the opportunity for higher leadership in the fund-raising trenches and it was time for the caucus to elect a woman to its top leadership. She also contended that the party could not regain or exercise power unless it stood for its principles.[40] As she put it in early 2000, "I'd caution Democrats not to compromise on issues that will only produce incremental changes that will help Republicans."[41]

Opportunity Knocks

The 2000 election set in motion events that would result in Pelosi winning the Democratic whip job but not as she originally planned. As the election approached, both Pelosi and Hoyer claimed the allegiance of a substantial number of Democrats. Unknown was the number of votes that would be needed and, indeed, if the race was going to happen at all. Unfortunately for Hoyer, Pelosi, and their Democratic colleagues, the voters did not cooperate and returned the Republicans to power. The Democrats picked up six seats in California (due in part to Pelosi's efforts) but lost seats elsewhere and ended up with a net gain of only two.[42] While the 2000 election did not produce the Democratic majority Pelosi had been counting on, it did presage better things to come for her. Her work in raising money and promoting candidates enhanced her position in the caucus, especially since there would be an additional half-dozen Democrats from California. She felt the pain of Bush's Electoral College victory over Gore as much as any Democrat; but a unified Republican government would later provide a target-rich environment for Democrats.

The closely contested presidential election was accompanied by Republican gains in governorships and state legislatures, including those of Michigan, where a Republican governor, working with a Republican legislature was poised to implement a redistricting plan designed to cause the Democrats as much pain as possible. The plan put two Democratic incumbents, Lynn Rivers and John Dingell, in the same district and David Bonior in a district that leaned Republican. Interestingly, Pelosi sided with Rivers against the powerful Dingell, simply because "she was for me and he was not."[43] Facing an uphill fight to hold onto his House seat, Bonior decided in August 2001 to leave the House and run for governor of Michigan. Although his official resignation would not take effect until January 2001, the race to replace him was now officially on. Pelosi and Hoyer both ran typical campaigns. They sought private commitments and public endorsements from members. They made the rounds of the various caucuses. They sent letters to members and made personal phone calls. They enlisted surrogates to round up votes. They each claimed to have the votes necessary to win. Only one of them could be right.

On October 10, 2001, Nancy Pelosi defeated Steny Hoyer by a vote of 118 to 95 to become the Democratic whip. Her election was accurately reported as a historic event as a woman broke into the top leadership in Congress for the first time. On that, all could agree. Beyond that, interpretations varied. Hoyer had offered more centrist leadership and drew regional support from the South and the East and ideological backers among Blue Dogs and New Democrats. While he and his supporters had sought to associate Pelosi with the "old" liberalism of the Democratic Party and him with the "new" Democratic approach, Pelosi had offered a different construction. The categories of old and new Democrat were already passé, she claimed. The real difference was between the entrepreneurial style of the West versus the calcified approach of the East.[44]

After the whip election, she sought to interpret her victory, defining it in terms on which she could predicate her subsequent leadership. Hoyer, the loser, offered a pragmatic interpretation, attributing her success to her substantial advantage within the large California delegation and among female members. This election, he said, had been all about region and gender. Pelosi offered a construction of new and old that hinged on style, tactics, and attitude rather than ideology or gender. The election was "about the new; it's not about male or female."[45] But what was new about it if not the fact of her gender? Her interpretation was a calculated move to distance herself from the image of the liberal San Francisco Democrat. The liberal-conservative divide, she said, was an "old formula that overlooks the Bay area's entrepreneurial spirit."[46] That entrepreneurial spirit would, she argued, help Democrats win back the House. What the Democrats needed was less *positioning* and more *organizing*. Elections are not won in caucus meetings in Washington; they are won in the local vineyards, vine by vine, grape by grape. Fund-raising, organization, and candidate recruitment matter more than the party leaders' voting record.

Pelosi's argument was met with some skepticism among Hoyer supporters, who argued that she would send the wrong message to swing voters. One lawmaker said, "A woman from California who is a liberal, from my point of view, casts the wrong image for where the party wants to be…. We want to be in the Center."[47] As whip, minority leader, and Speaker, Pelosi would have to deal with this underlying tension between the Blue Dog, New Dem wing and the progressive wing of the caucus.

Analyzing the Results

Why did Nancy Pelosi defeat Steny Hoyer? The answer to this question is the cornerstone of the later, larger question of how she became Speaker of the House. The whip election postmortems offer one important element of an answer to both questions: "she is also a prolific fund-raiser, a talent that both her adversaries and her allies say helped propel her to victory."[48] As one account documented,

> Pelosi, one of Capitol Hill's most prodigious fund-raisers, gave more than $1.1 million to fellow Democrats through her personal campaign fund and her leadership committee—PAC to the Future—during the 1999–2000 campaign cycle, according to an analysis by the Washington-based Center for Responsive Politics. That makes her the biggest Democratic donor and the overall third-highest political donor to party causes and federal candidates—outmatched only by Republican Speaker of the House Dennis Hastert and GOP Majority Whip Tom DeLay, who each contributed $1.3 million, the study says. In contrast, Pelosi's rival yesterday in the contest for the Democratic No. 2 post, Rep. Steny Hoyer of Maryland, contributed $927,000, making him fifth among Democrats, the study showed.[49]

In chapter 4, we explore in greater depth her overall fund-raising through her PAC, for the DCCC, and on behalf of individual members and challengers. We also look in greater depth at her disbursement of funds. Here, it will suffice to note that in the 2000 election cycle, Pelosi was generous to both members and challengers in competitive races but also showed largesse to her winning coalition with many smaller symbolic contributions to electorally secure members who would support her election to whip.

The bases of Pelosi's rise to power extended beyond her fund-raising to other factors, including her ability, her gender, her region, her committee assignments, and her personal network. What set her apart from her competitors as a female contending for a leadership position was the fact that *she* brought together this particular matrix and capitalized on it to win the whip race. Still, it is hard to ignore the importance of her fund-raising in advancing her career. She, of course, did not want her accomplishment to be defined by money any more than she wanted it to be defined by gender or ideology. In fact, she often deplored the influence of money in politics even as she excelled at raising it. The inescapable reality, however, was that the entrepreneurial spirit of the West was all about winning elections in the first place—and elections are not won without money.[50]

Aside from the fund-raising factor, the underlying political dynamic should not be overlooked. There were more liberals than moderates or conservatives in the Democratic Caucus. By moving to the center, the liberal majority would concede power to the moderate and conservative minority and accept its general policy prescriptions for the party. It seems more logical, however, for a liberal majority to elect liberal leaders and then ask them to work pragmatically with more moderate and conservative members to secure their districts. Viewed in this way, Pelosi emerged as the most viable candidate from the party's left wing. She did so because of her efforts on behalf of members, but also because she had demonstrated a willingness to reach out to moderates and conservatives, some of whose votes she won. In addition, she represented a larger state; the margin between her and Hoyer was not far distant from the difference in the sizes of the California and Maryland delegations. Finally, there was considerable sentiment that the caucus, which in 2001 comprised 20% female members, needed a woman in its leadership. Texas congressman Martin Frost's defeat of Rosa DeLauro for caucus chair had left the caucus with an entirely male leadership, and some members thought this needed to be corrected.

Promotion to Leader

Pelosi was elected Democratic whip just one month after 9/11. She formally took office on January 15, 2002. She was elected Democratic floor leader on November 14, 2002, just ten months later. In between these two House leadership elections, the Democrats lost seats in the 2002 congressional elections. This was the fourth consecutive election in which Dick Gephardt failed to lead his party back into power. He was a capable leader, widely respected among his peers, including Pelosi, and the two leaders worked well together. But Pelosi and Gephardt did not agree on fundamental elements of policy and strategy. He accepted the premise that the Democrats should not move too far to the left if they wanted to regain control of the House, while she believed that they needed to carve out clear policy differences from the Republicans. He had run for president in 1988, and it was widely anticipated that should the Republicans retain their majority in the 2002 elections, he would leave the House to launch a presidential campaign.[51]

No issue better manifest the leadership difference than that of Gephardt's support of the American invasion of Iraq and the congressional use-of-force resolution. This vote, just a month prior to the 2002 election, reflected the choice the Democrats had made in electing Pelosi as their whip. Gephardt joined every major Democratic presidential aspirant in voting for the war resolution and joined with President Bush in celebrating it. Hoyer also voted for it. Nancy Pelosi voted against it and carried a clear majority of House Democrats along with her.[52] This was a defining moment for Pelosi. On the most important vote of this Congress, as important a vote as Congress ever takes, she opposed the centrists. While they won the vote, she won the Democrats. The risks were obvious. In the election, the Republicans now ran against Democrats who had voted with Pelosi against the use-of-force resolution. While the opposition party normally gains seats in off-year elections, in 2002 the Republicans gained six seats. The short-term effect of the 2002 election was to enlarge the Republican majority and consign the Democrats to at least two more years in the minority. Pelosi stood against the resolution on principle and took a political risk. If the war were to unfold as the administration anticipated, House Democrats might be found on the wrong side of history.

Electoral Disappointment 2002

The Democrats' losses in the 2002 elections could hardly be blamed on Nancy Pelosi. The party had picked up seats in California, and she had campaigned vigorously in all parts of the country. She had raised millions for the party and had worked assiduously to support its candidates in 2002. "She . . . works tirelessly, crisscrossing the country to drum up votes and dollars. Pelosi's aides say she raised between $7 million and $8 million for the 2002 campaign through appearances in 30 states and 90 congressional districts—many of which are much more conservative than her own."[53] In one 72-hour span, she "flew 3,678 miles, traveled 14 hours in rented vans, shook more than 600 hands, visited six congressional districts, raised more than $50,000 for fellow Democrats, and visited three grandchildren."[54] While all party leaders campaign for members and raise money, Pelosi's pace was exceptional and reflected her basic approach to party leadership: it was necessary to make a majority before she could lead it.

In spite of her efforts, many Democrats still harbored doubts about having her as their leader. She had further defined her liberal image by her position on the war. In this context, first Martin Frost and then Tennessee congressman Harold Ford, Jr., took her on in the 2002 Democratic leader election. Ohioan Marcy Kaptur, a moderate from the Rust Belt and the senior woman in the Democratic Caucus, entered the race at the last minute to offset the dominance of the East and West coasts in caucus leadership, but lacking support she withdrew before the vote and backed Frost for his "more cautious, pragmatic strategy."[55] Harold Ford focused specifically on the Iraq resolution in presenting his case against Pelosi:

> One area of stark contrast between my opponent and me is Iraq. Rep.
> Pelosi opposed the president and voted against the resolution. I worked
> with Republicans and Democrats to pass a narrowly tailored resolution and
> joined Democrats and Republicans in voting for it. Ultimately, congressional
> support helped the administration negotiate a strong resolution that won the
> unanimous approval of the U.N. Security Council.[56]

Frost, Ford, and Kaptur were not alone. The Republicans salivated at the
prospect of the liberal Pelosi as the Democratic leader. "Go, Nancy!" GOP
lobbyist Ed Rogers said, laughing. "In no way does she help them become
a national party. She's a liberal, San Francisco Democrat who has a host
of positions that are anathema to Southern, middle-of-the-road voters."[57]
Pelosi appeared happy to join the Republicans in a debate over values and
to define the differences between the two parties rather than blur them.
"We must draw clear distinctions between our vision of the future and the
extreme policies put forward by the Republicans," she said; "we cannot allow
Republicans to pretend they share our values and then legislate against those
values without consequence."[58]

Implicit in Pelosi's argument was a critique of Gephardt's leadership. She
believed that the party had taken the wrong lessons from its experience in
the minority. The mantra of the centrists was to move to the middle. Yet the
Republicans had won the House by moving to the right, and its leadership
was monolithically conservative. If the majority was to be found in the center, why had they succeeded? Pelosi's answer was that the Republicans had
been more effective tacticians than the Democrats. What was needed was
not a policy shift but a more effective political apparatus. Instead of criti-
cizing Gephardt's approach, she spoke of the need to "build on" his record.
Yet it was clear that he had failed to lead the Democrats back to power, and
she believed that the problem lay in organization rather than message.[59] In
fact, even as Republicans salivated at the prospect of wrapping Democratic
electoral prospects around her image, she plowed forward. Her conception
of leadership was operational rather than ideological. As one account had
it, there were really two Nancy Pelosis. One was the "latte liberal" from San
Francisco the Republicans sought to lampoon; the other was the pragmatic
politician who knew how to win.[60] To the question of which Pelosi would
lead, she offered the latter conception.

> People who ask it don't understand what leadership is.... What's important
> is: Can you rally the troops? Do you have the knowledge to make the right
> judgments? Do you have a plan and the ability to attract enough supporters
> to make it happen? It isn't about your voting record.[61]

As their new leader, Pelosi would now be tested, and the criterion was clear. Could she lead the Democrats to the majority? Some doubted her capacity to lead or the wisdom of her new strategy. A *New York Times* editorial expressed doubt about her ability to convey the party message to the public, saying that she has not "been much of a powerhouse on television."[62] Not surprisingly, the *San Francisco Chronicle* offered a more positive assessment: Democrats "must not be afraid to make the case against a rush to war, ill-advised tax cuts, assaults on the environment or other Bush initiatives that many centrist Americans might oppose—if the president's policies were exposed to full and vigorous debate. Nancy Pelosi is the right leader for this critical challenge."[63] These two editorials defined divergent perspectives on Pelosi's ability to unite the Democrats, articulate the party message, and win control of the House. Pelosi offered her own riposte: "I can take the hit, but the fact is that I was elected for a reason. The reason is that I bring strong credentials in legislation, strong political credentials to be a political leader as well, and that's what I will do for the House Democrats."[64]

WINNING

The voice that will be heard would now speak for the House Democrats. "Never again," said Pelosi, "will the Democratic Party go into an election without a Democratic message saying who we are, what we stand for, and what we will fight for."[65] While Pelosi now had new stature, her powers were quite limited. The Republican majority stifled the Democratic minority, and voice was about the only tool she had. When President Bush proposed yet another round of regressive tax cuts, she put forward a Democratic alternative that offered rebates to middle-class taxpayers, an extension of unemployment benefits, and assistance to the states.[66] Recognizing the limits of her power, she said that "institutionally, the only leverage we have is the voice of the American people. That's why our challenge is so much greater now to get the word out as to what the differences are between the parties."[67]

Taking on Bush

The Democrats pursued a message strategy of promoting their tax program while attacking Bush. They offered a three-point critique of the president: first, suggesting a "credibility gap" between Bush's "compassionate conservatism" rhetoric and his actions that favored the rich; second, noting that the Bush tax cuts did little to address the country's pressing need for more funding for homeland security and domestic needs; and third, charging that the huge budget deficits would undermine the economy and reduce employment.[68] The Democrats were more united in their opposition to Bush's economic program than they were united on a plan of their own. "You're always going to have discord when you have this many people running and trying to get their message out," said Pelosi's communications director, Brendan Daly; "we are trying to build unity and consensus."[69] House and Senate Democrats sought to coordinate their message operations, which were brought to a new level of intensity. If anything, they ran a danger of speaking with too many voices.

The war in Iraq continued to divide the Democrats. The Bush administration had used its war on terror to put them on the defensive. Having won congressional authorization for use of force, the administration sought to press its advantage in 2003. Pelosi had spoken out consistently against the war, and she spoke for the majority of Democrats, who opposed it. Her critics feared that she would carry the caucus to the left—but here we see the first manifestation of Pelosi's approach to party leadership. While she opposed the war and spoke out against it, she did not make it a matter of party orthodoxy. "They [the Republicans] try to convey that image of the Democrats as weak on defense. I don't think we should take that. There is no party position on the war, much to the dismay of our grass-roots constituents."[70] In April 2003, when the Republicans brought to the House floor a resolution praising President Bush and declaring support for the troops, Pelosi's approach became clear. The resolution had passed unanimously in the Senate, but in the House hard-core war opponents refused to go along. Pelosi, seeking to protect her caucus from any suggestion that it was not supportive of the troops, supported the resolution, even though, as she put it, "I am devastated by the fact that we are going to war."[71] She sought to persuade all Democrats to support the resolution, even while telling them that they could vote their consciences. For her part, she did not vote her conscience but cast a pragmatic vote in favor of the resolution. She voted *against* the war in October of 2002; she voted *for* the troops in 2003.

Balancing Left and Right

Pelosi's approach to the caucus and her own voting record assumed greater importance because of her much higher visibility. As the first female party leader, she attracted wide public attention and with it the danger that the Democrats would be branded with the label of San Francisco liberalism. This was not simply a matter of appearances. Polls in 2003 showed that the public trusted the Republicans on national security by a margin of two to one over the Democrats.[72] Centrist Democrats insisted that the party needed a muscular national defense posture. Antiwar Democrats ran the risk of appearing soft. Yet they were deeply and sincerely opposed to the war, as was Pelosi. Asked about the apparent rift in the party, she said: "The Democrats are where they are. One at a time, one at a time. This is a vote of conscience, as war is for everyone."[73] As is sometimes the case, Pelosi's syntax garbled her message, which was that Democrats must be patient, recognizing their lack of institutional control and their internal divisions.

Pelosi's approach was at odds with the energized left wing of the Democratic Party. The year 2003 witnessed the blooming of "netroots" politics in Howard Dean's candidacy for the Democratic presidential nomination. This new form of campaign activity harnessed the communication power of the internet to traditional local organizing into an inter-connected network of like-minded activists. The netroots initially connoted a mostly left-of-center phenomenon that offered ideological enthusiasm, technological sophistication, and generational change. They embraced Nancy Pelosi's core strategic concept: the Democrats had to offer an alternative to the Republicans. They reflected her lifelong commitment to organization and mobilization as the keys to political success. They shared her ideological commitments and her distaste for George Bush, agreed with her on the Iraq War, and manifested her core belief that the path back to power lay in energizing voters. Yet they presented a conundrum for her. She needed their energy and enthusiasm, but she could not allow the left-wing netroots to control the Democratic Party's agenda or guide legislative strategy in the House.[74]

Pelosi understood that the path back to power lay in *conservative* districts. To the left wing of the Democratic Party, the DLC was a group of Republican fellow travelers, willing to sell out the core principles of the party. The netroots appeared to believe that it was not necessary to win seats in the South; the DLC appeared to believe that the way to win seats in the South was for the party to be like the Republicans. She thought Gephardt and the DLC had set the right goal but the wrong strategy. She had a different idea: take on the Bush administration where it was vulnerable, recruit candidates who could win in swing districts, rally the party base for fund-raising and energy, and present a clear set of alternative policies on issues on which the various elements of the party could coalesce.

Fortunately for Pelosi, the Republicans cooperated by offering policies the Democrats could rally against. An interesting example was the Republicans' Medicare prescription drug bill. Polls showed that the soaring cost of prescription drugs was a major concern for voters, and the Republicans wanted to deny the issue to the Democrats. In offering the largest expansion of the welfare state since Medicare was created in the 1960s, the Republicans were guided by free market principles and influenced by the insurance and pharmaceutical lobbies. They produced a bill that sought to contain premiums through market competition but did little to control prices. To restrain costs, the bill provided for a coverage gap designed to discourage use but left consumers with little protection. The Republicans also declined to pay for the huge new program, piling it onto the national debt instead.

The Republican bill offered a target of opportunity for Pelosi; this was a bill that all Democrats could oppose. Liberals like herself would oppose it because it was too stingy, and conservatives would oppose it because it was fiscally irresponsible. Most Democrats felt that more should be done to address the underlying problem of skyrocketing drug and insurance costs. For Pelosi, the best strategy was to simply say no to the Republicans' bill and force them to produce a majority from among their own ranks. The vote would be a difficult pill for them to swallow, so to speak, because most Republicans were against expanding benefit programs and many were against deficit spending.[75]

Pelosi was successful in holding the House Democrats together, and in November 2003 the Republican leadership was forced to hold the final vote on the Medicare bill open for three hours in order to twist enough arms for passage. Their tactics opened a fresh public relations front for the Democrats, who castigated Speaker Hastert and Republican leader Tom DeLay for being heavy-handed. The Republicans made themselves vulnerable to the same kind of criticism they had deployed against the Democrats in the 1994 elections. The Republicans had committed several sins. They had excluded the Democrats from conference deliberations. They had rushed the 1,100-page bill to the floor without the normal 24-hour layover, giving members only an hour to review it. They had held the vote open in violation of House rules.[76] And they had used coercive tactics to change Republican members' votes.[77]

By the end of 2003, Pelosi was winning praise from both liberal and conservative Democrats. She performed a careful balancing act between tough and healing talk. Sometimes she threatened defecting members' committee assignments and other perks; most often, she did not punish or exclude them. Instead, she sought to convince the Democrats that their real interest lay in electing a House majority rather than in cutting deals with Republicans. She worked hard to win the loyalty of centrist Democrats and sought to protect them by keeping the focus off of such hot-button social issues as gun control and abortion. Conservative Democrats stressed that "she listens," in contrast to their expectations. Sometimes criticized for placing too high a premium on loyalty, she responded by saying that there is a difference between rewarding those who have supported you and punishing those who do not (offering carrots but not sticks).[78] This formula appeared to work, as the Democrats attained nearly 90% party unity in 2003.[79]

Electoral Disappointment 2004

In 2004, Pelosi turned full firepower on Bush and the House Republicans.[80] If Democrats could agree on nothing else, they were determined, one might say desperate, to win control of the House, and anxious to go on the attack. Events conspired to assist them. The war in Iraq appeared to spiral out of control. The scandal at Abu Ghraib prison was followed by an outbreak of sectarian violence. The American death toll continued to rise. Bush's approval ratings declined. Pelosi's attacks on him were harsh and direct; she called him an "incompetent leader" who "lacks the judgment, experience, or knowledge to make good decisions." The emperor "has no clothes," she said.[81] While the war dragged on, the Republican leadership essentially shut down the House. During the summer of 2004, the House was typically in session only two or three days per week, and few important bills were brought to the floor.[82] The absence of substantive legislation offered two payoffs to the Democrats. It enabled them to challenge the "do nothing" Republicans, and it allowed them to avoid internal divisions. In fact, the Republicans played right into Pelosi's hands. Her main argument in seeking the leadership had been that the Democrats needed to offer a clear alternative vision. She was now free to hammer Bush and the House Republicans without risking division within her ranks. Indeed, even as the Republicans ground the legislative process to a halt, Pelosi enjoyed tremendous support from Democrats. Democratic Party unity reached its highest point in decades.[83]

As the 2004 election approached, Pelosi was convinced that the Democrats would gain a majority in the House.[84] But as polls showed Democratic presidential nominee John Kerry losing ground to President Bush, Democratic hopes for the House began to fade as well.[85] Pelosi continued to challenge the administration on the Iraq War, claiming "It is clear this administration didn't know what it's getting into [sic], or else it misled the American people."[86] In the end, the voters decided to stick with Bush and the House Republicans. Bush defeated Kerry by three percentage points, and the Republicans gained five House seats. In the election's aftermath, the Democrats undertook the usual postmortems with predictable results. The centrist Democrats claimed that the losses confirmed their long-standing view that the party needed to move to the right. Pelosi sought to keep the focus on President Bush and congressional Republicans. "The president won't be able to blame anyone, because the Republicans have full control," she said, vowing to make sure that the American people knew it.[87]

Pelosi did not think she needed a new strategy; she simply needed better effort. Her mantra was money, message, and mobilization. She believed that winning elections was largely a matter of effort. To assist her in implementing her electoral strategy, she appointed Illinois congressman Rahm Emanuel as

DCCC chair. Emanuel, a former White House aide to President Clinton, was known for being shrewd, relentless, and abrasive. Pelosi admired Emanuel's "reptilian" qualities, a cold-blooded determination to do whatever was legal and necessary in order to win.[88] Pelosi and Emanuel launched an exhaustive effort to target districts, recruit candidates, raise money, and hone message. Their strategic premise was simple: given the unpopularity of the war, the Democrats should keep on the offensive.

They also faced the choice of a new national chairman. In the wake of the party's electoral setback, this position would assume new importance. Pelosi had, of course, trod this ground before in her own quest to become DNC chair in 1984 under the similar circumstances of a lost presidential election. At that time, she had run as the outsider against the establishment candidate, Paul Kirk, arguing then that a fresh approach was needed, and that she could make that happen. This time, former Vermont governor and presidential candidate Howard Dean presented himself as the change candidate, advocating a new generational and technological approach to politics via the internet. Despite the similarities between Dean's appeal and her own DNC race, Pelosi opposed Dean and favored former Democratic congressman Tim Roemer of Indiana. Roemer brought national security credentials as a member of the 9/11 commission, and Pelosi argued that he would be an effective spokesman for the party. This argument did not prevail against Dean's straightforward appeal to state party leaders, saying that he would put DNC resources at their disposal, and Dean was easily elected. Pelosi's support for Roemer offers another example of her frequent impulse to help her friends and not her enemies. The third candidate in the race was former Democratic whip Martin Frost of Texas. Frost had challenged Pelosi for Democratic Leader in 2002. After his seat was redistricted by Texas Republicans, he was defeated in 2004. Pelosi would not support Frost and did not want to support Dean. This left only Roemer. For the first but not the last time, she rode a losing horse.[89]

Republican Implosion

Bush took a curious lesson from the results of a close election. Declaring it a mandate, he announced an ambitious legislative program whose centerpiece reform of Social Security would allow private investment accounts for the first time. Pelosi quickly pounced, rallying congressional Democrats against the concept of privatizing Social Security. As the most important decision she made as minority leader, this strategic choice is worth analyzing. Recall that after the 2002 elections, she vowed that the Democrats would never again enter an election without a clearly articulated party message. The Democrats had erred in not staking out their own positions in contrast to the Republicans. She was now under considerable pressure from Republicans and many Democrats to produce a Democratic Social Security reform plan, yet she refused to do so. Even though the public was convinced that Social Security faced a crisis, Pelosi stood firmly on the proposition that "the Social Security system is our program." She aimed to defend the status quo against Bush's privatization plan.[90]

If the Democrats had proposed a Social Security plan of their own, the Republicans would have attacked it. Instead, the Democrats sold the idea that the Republicans were out to gut Social Security rather than save it. The Republicans had nothing to attack and much to defend. In spite of Bush's national tour to promote his plan, it was stillborn; Pelosi had organized over 1,000 town hall meetings across the country to rally support against it. By the end of February 2005, Bush's grand second-term vision and its center-piece had crumbled.[91]

The strategy of letting the Republicans commit hara-kiri required their cooperation. Little could Pelosi have foreseen how cooperative the Republicans would be. The 109th Congress produced one political fiasco after another for the GOP. In January and February 2005, the DeLay scandal was in the news. Majority Leader Tom DeLay was indicted in Texas for violating state campaign finance laws. To protect him, the Republicans sought to alter House rules to permit an indicted member to continue to serve in the leadership. They were forced to back down on the rules change, but Speaker Hastert sacked the Republican chair of the Ethics Committee, Congressman Joel Hefley of Colorado, who appeared willing to find against DeLay. In the end, DeLay was forced to resign as majority leader and then decided to retire from the House. And there were other scandals. California congressman Duke Cunningham was convicted of federal bribery charges. Ohio congressman Bob Ney went to jail for accepting gifts from lobbyist Jack Abramoff in exchange for legislative favors. Abramoff entered the hoosegow as well. In the fall of 2006, Congressman Mark Foley of Florida resigned amid allegations that he had sent inappropriate emails to male pages.

The Republicans also had legislative troubles. In March 2005, they rammed through a bill to force the federal courts to take up the Florida case of Terri Schiavo. Polls showed that over 70% of the public disapproved of the action. In April, they were unable to enact a budget resolution. When they did succeed, they often pushed bills that were easy for the Democrats to attack. An energy bill offered more tax breaks to the oil and gas industry. A budget resolution providing for steep cuts in Medicare reimbursements passed 214 to 211. The Central American Free Trade Agreement passed by 217 to 215. An oil refining bill passed 212 to 210 after a 40-minute vote. These votes were marked by the heavy-handed tactics in which the Republican leadership specialized. By the fall of 2005, public opinion had begun to turn against the Republicans, and even the heavy hand no longer seemed to work. They were forced to drop a plan to open drilling in the Arctic National Wildlife Refuge and pulled a budget reconciliation bill when they could not twist enough arms to pass it. Meanwhile, the war in Iraq produced higher American casualties each month. Congressman Murtha of Pennsylvania, a leading Democratic defense hawk, turned against the war and called for a withdrawal of American troops. His opposition both reflected and contributed to public disapproval of the war.

Playing Offense

Pelosi's instinct to go on the attack, first manifested in her approach to Social Security, led the Democrats to the correct political strategy. In fact, her play-book for the 2006 election cycle borrowed substantially from Gingrich's approach in 1994. She sought to nationalize the election and turn it into a referendum on Bush and the House Republicans. Gingrich had run against Bill Clinton and the alleged institutional corruption of the House Democrats, ensconced in power too long. But he had also offered a substantive policy vision, the Contract With America, that promised a redirection of American politics. Pelosi faced two limitations in emulating that aspect of the Gingrich game plan: if the Democrats had a governing philosophy, it was likely too far out to the left; and Pelosi was not herself a persuasive spokesperson for the party. Indeed, since the Republicans were sure to run against her, she needed to keep as low a profile as possible. Thus, the Democratic version of the GOP Contract—"Six for '06"—was a rather bland menu of poll-tested proposals that would provide few targets for the Republicans.[92] The Democrats promised to implement the 9/11 commission's recommendations, further subsidize college student loans, raise the minimum wage, broaden stem cell research, reduce Big Oil subsidies and invest in renewable energy, and authorize Medicare to negotiate prescription drug prices. This platform provided the Democrats with talking points without forcing them to defend risky ground and answered the concern that the party could not win by simply attacking the Republicans. As Pelosi put it, "you can't beat something with nothing."[93] But perhaps you could beat something with not very much.

The Six for '06 agenda, like the New Direction Congress theme into which it fed in the 110th Congress, was the gloss on a campaign strategy that involved two more foundational elements. The first was organizational, a continuation of the approach Pelosi had taken since entering the leadership—continuous fund-raising, recruitment of candidates who have a chance to win, obsessive attention to details, a rapid-response communications operation. The second was substantive: attack Bush and the Republicans relentlessly. As Pelosi later put it, "we went outside Congress and got help from professionals in the corporate world who told us, 'You're No. 2 and you want to be No. 1. You have to take down No. 1.' "[94] Pelosi recognized that the Republicans would pursue the reverse strategy—to take down No. 2, that is, her. She carefully calibrated her public exposure, campaigning in all parts of the country but not in districts where candidates needed to distance themselves from her and the national party. Sure enough, Republicans ran commercials against her in several congressional districts, in one case alleging that she would advance a "homosexual agenda."[95] The strategy was flawed, in that Pelosi was not well known to the American public and President Bush was. The Republican attacks gained no traction, and the Democratic candidate won in several swing districts in which such ads had run. The lesson was clear: No. 2 can run against No. 1, but No. 1 is stuck with its own record.

POISED FOR POWER

On November 8, 2006, the voters elected 233 Democrats to the House, and Pelosi was poised to become the first woman Speaker and the highest elected female officeholder in American history. To reach this pinnacle of power, she had to face many challenges. She had to overcome the impression that she was not a serious politician. She had to confront the characterization that she was simply another San Francisco liberal. She had to convince voters and members of the House that a woman could be successful in a leadership position. She had to win elections. Her path was neither short nor easy. Along it, she was able to define her political persona rather than allowing it to be defined by others. Her congressional opponent had called her a "party girl." A labor leader had called her an "airhead." Republicans had called her a "San Francisco Democrat." Yet she had managed to transcend these caricatures.

Her rise to power coincided with a period of extreme and sometimes vitriolic partisanship in American politics. Her career had been set against the backdrop of the Reagan presidency, the Democrats' historic loss of the House in 1994, and the effects on the House of the Gingrich revolution and twelve years of Republican control. Her emergence as party leader was situated in the context of the several related political transformations that we call the New American Politics. One was ideological, reflecting the decline of New Deal and Great Society liberalism and the rise of a new conservatism. Another was institutional, reflecting altered power relationships and cultural norms in the House. A third was technological, reflecting the rise of cable news and the twenty-four-hour news cycle and the evolution of the internet and the new politics it made possible. A fourth was generational, as the Greatest Generation began to pass on, the baby boomers moved into their prime years, and Generation X matured. A fifth was demographic, as the make-up of America's population changed dramatically and the role of women in American society was fundamentally altered. And a sixth was political, as hyperpartisanship sapped vitality from the national spirit.

Speaker Nancy Pelosi, as she would soon be called, was a participant in and a product of these several trends in American political life. Now, however, she would have at her disposal something she had never really had before: power. As Speaker, she would have real power under the rules of the House and the Democratic Caucus. She would have a say in shaping the national agenda. The question then became: How would she use her power?

Chapter 3

Power in the House

The titular Democratic leader of the House...should become the operating head of the legislative apparatus. There his power would be observable and responsible, and therefore accountable.

—Former congressman Richard Bolling (D-MO) (1968)

Nancy Pelosi's election as Speaker of the House was a transformative moment in American history. The meaning of that moment could not be fully revealed, however, until Pelosi began to wield the power she had won. In the attention that was quite appropriately given to the historic nature of her accomplishment in being elected Speaker, there was less focus on how she might govern. The foundational premise of her political career had always been that she would bring a fresh "western" and "entrepreneurial" approach to politics and government. That was how she had campaigned to become DNC chair, for her seat in the House, and for leadership of the Democratic Caucus. By self-definition, she would pursue a leadership style well suited to a new kind of political environment in which old conventions would give way to new ideas, strategies, and tactics. Yet the office to which she had been elected was as old as the Constitution and defined by organizational arrangements nearly as enduring. What new things were possible?

In this chapter, we analyze Pelosi's leadership of the House in the 110th Congress in relationship to her organization of the Democratic Caucus, her efforts in consensus building among Democrats, her attitude toward Republicans, her use of her power under the rules of the House, in policymaking, and in crisis management. The picture that emerges from published accounts and our informants is that of a Speaker who goes to extraordinary lengths to build bridges across the caucus divides and to foster consensus within it. This Speaker is willing to apply the levers of power when necessary in order to achieve her objectives, primary among which are to maintain and enlarge the Democratic majority while passing legislation that furthers policy objectives on which most Democrats can agree. To accomplish both of these goals, she has relied on three integrated strategies: control, compromise, and sequencing. By employing all three, she has aimed to position the Democratic Party on ground the majority of Americans will share, to minimize threats to members in marginal districts, and to move policy incrementally. We conclude our analysis by considering a prominent alternative to strategy, the improvisation that characterized the government's response to the financial crises of 2008.

ORGANIZING THE HOUSE

Speaker-in-waiting Pelosi faced crucial decisions as she contemplated how she wanted to organize her Democratic majority and write the rules for the 110th Congress. She had to consider how to organize the House Democrats to enhance their cohesiveness and legislative effectiveness, how best to integrate new members with an eye toward ensuring their reelections, who to appoint to or support for the various party leadership positions and committee assignments, and needed modifications to the House rules. She had two months to accomplish these tasks.

In considering these decisions, Pelosi could draw on a lifetime in political experience and on the specific examples of the Democratic and Republican Speakers with whom she had served. The speakership she had won was in important respects a different institution from the one Tom Foley and Jim Wright had known. Gingrich and the Republicans had shattered the old system and made the committees subservient to the party leadership. Pelosi had also observed that the Republican machine had eventually ground to a halt. If opportunities were afforded by an enhanced speakership, there was also a dangerous temptation to drive too fast.

Assembling the Leadership Team

Pelosi holds organization to be her first passion, and now she had the chance to organize on a large scale. A minority party leader has organizational responsibilities but little true institutional power. The Speaker of the House has both. The decisions she made tell us a great deal about her approach to power and the ethos that guides it. Three principles appear to have guided her decision-making: competency, loyalty, and diversity. Her challenge lay in assembling a leadership team that would integrate all three. She believed in putting people into positions for which their talents fit them. She would reward those who had been loyal to her. And she wanted the party organization to reflect the party's diversity. The application of these principles proved tricky, however, as they sometimes pointed in different directions. She aimed to create a team that would help her bring the caucus together while keeping it loyal to her.

Her first decisions addressed the party leadership structure. Emanuel had earned his claim to a higher party position by virtue of his successful leadership of the DCCC. He had recruited many of the new Democratic members and worked tirelessly for their campaigns. He had also helped reelect at-risk members from marginal districts. He was experienced and media savvy and had a strong constituency in the caucus. He was unlikely to challenge Steny Hoyer for the position of majority leader, but he contemplated a race to become Democratic whip. Here, loyalty ran up against the principle of diversity. Congressman James Clyburn of South Carolina, the incumbent chair of the Democratic Caucus, sought to become just the second African-American member in the party's higher leadership ranks. Pelosi wanted a place at the leadership table for the Congressional Black Caucus, some of whose members were disgruntled about her previous committee assignments. To avoid a contested whip race, she convinced Emanuel to seek the position of caucus chair instead of whip, promising him an enhanced portfolio in that position. Emanuel agreed, and Pelosi had defused a potential race that might have divided the caucus.[1] To round out her leadership team, she named Congressman Xavier Becerra of California assistant to the Speaker, providing a voice at the leadership table for Hispanic and progressive members.[2]

Her adroit handling of the third- and fourth-ranking leadership positions rendered her late-breaking decision to back John Murtha in a challenge of Steny Hoyer for majority leader all the more surprising. Murtha had been elevated in prominence by Pelosi as the party's voice in opposition to the Iraq War. In June 2006, he informed Pelosi that if the Democrats took the House, he would run for majority leader. He had managed, it will be recalled, Pelosi's campaign against Hoyer in the long battle of 1998–2001. He was instrumental in bringing some moderate and conservative members to her side. He had put a safe face on the Democrats' opposition to the war. This publicly visible role was unusual for Murtha, the quintessential congressional backroom operator. Apparently, he enjoyed the attention and concluded that he had gained sufficient support to challenge

Hoyer. Still, his was an improbable candidacy. Murtha had spent his entire career in the appropriations trenches, where he was known as a deal-maker and earmark specialist. He called Pelosi's lobby reform proposals "total crap" in the midst of the majority leader race. He was recognized as an expert in defense policy but not as a policy generalist. Aside from his opposition to Iraq, there was little to suggest that he would be an effective spokesperson for the House Democrats. While Murtha would balance the leadership ideologically, Hoyer had strong support among moderates and conservatives as well.

Pelosi, recognizing that a campaign by Murtha for leader would divide the Democrats during the vital months leading up to the election, persuaded him to defer active campaigning until after it was over. It was, therefore, all the more striking when she announced her support for him and campaigned on his behalf in the days leading up to the caucus vote. She not only embraced him but advocated vocally on his behalf, even suggesting that members' committee assignments might be affected by the choice. It was not entirely unprecedented for a party leader to become involved in a competitive race for the number two slot. Tip O'Neill worked behind the scenes in 1976 to help Jim Wright defeat Phil Burton.[3] Republican leader Bob Michel actively supported fellow Illinoisan Ed Madigan for GOP whip in his 1989 race against Gingrich. And Gingrich himself was known to have tacitly supported Pennsylvanian Bob Walker in the whip race he lost to DeLay in 1994. While party leaders do sometimes take sides, more frequently they choose not to do so. They know that their preference will alienate one candidate's supporters and is no guarantee that their preferred candidate will win. To publicly oppose a member who has strong support in the caucus simply puts the Speaker's own support at risk. A Speaker would only take that risk if he or she felt very strongly that one candidate was better suited to the position than the other or felt that the other candidate was a person with whom he or she could not work.

These considerations did not appear to apply here. While some tension apparently survived from the long race for whip between the two, Pelosi and Hoyer had worked together for three years. When Pelosi ran for leader in 2002, Hoyer did not challenge her. Hoyer was, by most accounts, better suited to the job than Murtha. Still, Pelosi got behind Murtha in a losing effort. In the end, Hoyer prevailed by a vote of 149 to 86. Pelosi offered as her reason for supporting Murtha that she thought he would be a more effective opponent of the Iraq War.[4] This seems implausible, since a Speaker would surely make such a crucial decision on the basis of a broader range of considerations. In fact, Murtha's efforts to force Bush's hand on the war in February 2007 met with resistance within the caucus, an indication that Murtha's political instincts were not well honed.[5]

Published postmortems and confidential interviews with observers suggest that her decision to back Murtha in this race was a reflection of her first principle: loyalty. In Pelosi's world, loyalty counts for a great deal. Hoyer had been her adversary and had on occasion strayed from Pelosi's party line as whip. Murtha had been loyal to her, and she reciprocated by supporting him. She was apparently encouraged in this inclination by some of her closest supporters in the Democratic caucus. Loyalty, of course, is a two-way street. Pelosi would give loyalty, and she expected loyalty in return, especially within her leadership group. Her loyal supporters spent almost three years competing with Hoyer's loyal supporters in the whip race that launched her leadership career. It would seem quite natural, in this context, for the Pelosi team to want to have a strong loyalist as majority leader rather than an erstwhile opponent. As Representative Michael Capuano of Massachusetts put it, "the bottom line is that Nancy has decided what team she wants.... What members have to ask themselves is whether they want a unified leadership team or a fractured leadership team."[6]

Our interviews indicate that Pelosi was also led to believe that with her support, Murtha had the votes. If so, the outcome reflected poorly on someone's capacity to count, a skill Pelosi valued highly. Here, though, her error appears less in a faulty vote count than in a decision to take on a fight she might easily have avoided. Four days prior to the November 16 vote, her staff was indicating to reporters that she would not become involved; yet on the same day, she announced her support for Murtha.[7] Had she remained neutral, Murtha's defeat would not have been absorbed into her reputation. Newspaper accounts suggested, and our informants agree, that Pelosi's embrace of Murtha was a misstep, if for no other reason than, as one member put it, "she lost." Other commentators were more critical. "It's easy to go from tenaciousness to stubbornness, and that is what we've got here," held congressional savant Norman Ornstein.[8] Knowing that Murtha might lose, Pelosi was perhaps convinced that his defeat would not strike a damaging blow to her leadership. She would move on.[9]

Emerging from the caucus meeting with a triumphant Hoyer by her side and an evidently chagrined Murtha standing in the background, she announced, "Let the healing begin!" By some measures, Hoyer emerged from the Murtha race stronger than he had been before. He had lost a whip race to David Bonior in 1994 and a second whip race to Pelosi in 2001. Now, he had won a competitive race for floor leader against the active opposition of a popular new Speaker. He could now count on the support of 149 Democrats who had voted for him in a contested election. He had his own constituency. He also had a future, and by all accounts he decided to put the floor leader race behind him in order to work for the good of the party and to ensure his own standing among his colleagues. Tensions between Hoyer and Pelosi would continue, but the two would also prove capable of working together. In fact, Hoyer served as an important bridge to the more conservative members of the caucus.

We learn a great deal in this case about Speaker Pelosi. She does not encounter many criticisms from among House Democrats, but one sometimes hears that she is "loyal to a fault." No doubt, this case informs that sentiment. The fault would appear to lie in broaching unneeded conflict out of a sense of loyalty. Leadership races have often poisoned the House. The fallout from the Wright-Burton-Bolling-McFall race for Democratic leader in 1976 was still felt a decade later, even after Burton had died. The infighting in the Republican leadership started the day their majority first organized in 1994 and lasted throughout their twelve years in the majority.[10] Pelosi's view, as suggested to us by one of our confidential informants, is that "leadership races happen." Someone wins and someone loses, but once the race is over, everyone moves on and the "healing" begins. Loyalty means helping your friends and opposing your adversaries. Everyone understands the rules of the game among professional politicians. It's strictly business, nothing personal. This is hardly a new or entrepreneurial attitude; rather it is the essence of the old-style urban machine politics into which she was born.

Organizing the Committees

With the leadership team in place, Pelosi turned her attention to committee assignments. Here we see further evidence of the complex challenges facing a Democratic Speaker, especially one who assumes the power to make committee appointments. To better understand these challenges, some background on the committee assignment process will prove useful. When the Democrats took control of the House in 1911, after the revolt against Republican Speaker Uncle Joe Cannon in 1910, they decided to give the power of committee assignments to the Democratic members of the Ways and Means Committee. This arrangement remained in place for 65 years—until the reforms of the early 1970s, when committee assignments were transferred to the Democratic SPC, chaired by the Speaker. Under Speakers O'Neill, Wright, and Foley, the Democratic SPC functioned as a sort of influence market: key power holders on this committee would bargain among themselves to promote favored candidates. Speakers would sometimes intervene on behalf of members from their state delegations and other allies. When the Democrats were thrown into the minority, this bargaining system was continued under the direction of Minority Leader Dick Gephardt. When Pelosi replaced Gephardt as minority leader, she made final decisions on nominations to the major policy committees: Ways and Means, Appropriations, and Energy and Commerce.

On becoming Speaker, Pelosi decided that she would make all Democratic committee assignment nominations, subject to the ratification of the Democratic SPC and the Democratic Caucus. Pelosi thus became the first Speaker, Republican or Democrat, to be in direct charge of committee assignments in over a hundred years.[11] Speakers had resisted this power for good reason: they had not wanted to deal with the inevitable political fallout from disappointed expectations, and with few exceptions they had seen no personal stake in committee memberships. Pelosi had a different view. She wanted to be in a position to reward loyalty in order to build her power base and to ensure diversity in committee appointments.

Immediately, she faced a difficult decision: should she appoint Congresswoman Jane Harman of California as chair of the House Intelligence Committee? This was the culmination of tension between the two Californians that had escalated since Pelosi had been elected whip. Here, all of Pelosi's principles came into play: competency, loyalty, and diversity. Harman, who had first been elected to the House in 1992 and was among the more conservative Democrats in the California delegation, had staked out expertise on national security issues as a member of the Intelligence Committee. In 1998, she had abandoned her House seat to run for governor of California. She was defeated, but in 2000 Gephardt prevailed on her to run for her old House seat with a promise to reinstate her seniority on the Intelligence Committee. When Gephardt left the House in 2002, Pelosi honored his commitment and made Harman the ranking member, in the process putting her ahead of Sanford Bishop of Georgia and Alcee Hastings of Florida, both African-American members. Pelosi rewarded Bishop with a spot on the Appropriations Committee, but this episode had rankled members of the Congressional Black Caucus (CBC).

By 2006, Pelosi and Harman had reached a parting of the ways. Published accounts suggested that Harman had been too prominent (in Pelosi's judgment) in supporting the Bush administration's counterterrorism policies, appearing on national talk shows twice as often as Pelosi.[12] The relationship between Pelosi and Harman had never been close. In 1998, Pelosi initially supported Leon Panetta for the Democratic gubernatorial nomination in California and shifted her support to Harman only after Panetta declined to run. Harman was also more conservative than Pelosi. Intending to continue the Democratic assault on the Bush administration's national security policies, Pelosi preferred that the chair of the Intelligence Committee not defend them.[13]

Having decided against Harman, Pelosi faced an additional problem. The next ranking member of the Intelligence Committee was Hastings, who had been elected to the House in 1992 after having been impeached and removed from his prior position as a federal judge. This was hardly the image Pelosi wanted to convey, and she decided against nominating Hastings. The Black Caucus did not look kindly on her bypassing him for the top job on the committee. Pelosi next considered the third-ranking member, Silvestre Reyes of Texas, and Congressman Rush Holt of New Jersey. Media accounts reported sentiment that Holt was the better qualified, but Pelosi went with Reyes. She could defend her decision on the basis of Reyes's seniority (even though she passed over the more senior Hastings) and enhance her standing among Hispanic members. Her decision to bypass Harman and Hastings framed one dimension of her decision to avoid a race between Rahm Emanuel and Jim Clyburn for whip. With Clyburn as whip, the CBC had a high-ranking member in the leadership. Reyes became the only Hispanic committee chair.

Pelosi's handling of the Intelligence Committee assignments was only the most visible manifestation of her approach to staffing the committees. Historically, the Democrats had relied almost exclusively on seniority in determining the chairs of committees and subcommittees. Pelosi continued to respect seniority in most instances, but her committee assignment nominations for new members were made with a view to their district and reelection needs, their areas of interest and expertise, and equity across state delegations and the various demographic categories of the caucus. A number of at-risk freshmen for example, Heath Shuler [NC], Jason Altmire [PA], John Hall [AZ], and Harry Mitchell [NY], ended up with subcommittee chairships) as did a number of relatively junior women. (We will have more to say about women in the committee system in chapter 6.) Transfers for continuing members were heavily influenced by honoring seniority and balancing the diversity of the caucus. In the end, Pelosi apparently emerged from the committee appointment process without rebellion or open criticism from her caucus. She appears to have been able to advance the interests of more junior members without upsetting more senior members, including the several CBC members who became committee chairs.

Another key issue was term limits. Under Speaker Gingrich, the Republicans had imposed a three-term limit for committee chairs and a four-term limit for the Speaker. Later the Republicans dropped term limits for the Speaker, but those for committee chairs were retained. Senior Democrats opposed term limits when they were in the minority, but now Pelosi included it in the House rules, amid some confusion. Some Democrats, claiming that when they voted on the new rules they were unaware that the term limit had been incorporated into them, vowed to revisit the issue in the future. For the time being, however, Pelosi had taken an important step toward institutionalizing the power of the speakership relative to that of the committees.[14]

Diversity

Pelosi led a Democratic Caucus that was diverse, with respect to both demographics and ideology. Its ideological spectrum was perhaps less broad than in decades past, due to the movement of southern, conservative seats to the Republicans, but was still far more diverse than the Republican Conference. Indeed, the Democrats were only able to regain the majority by winning in more conservative districts. Faced with the fact of this diversity, Pelosi framed it as a virtue, emphasizing it both rhetorically and institutionally. She was determined that the distribution of committee assignments and chairships reflect the diversity of the caucus. At the same time, because she wanted to avoid the kind of politicking that had characterized the Republican Conference, she decided that seniority should normally be honored in the nomination of committee chairs. Pelosi's efforts to attain diversity were quite successful. According to an analysis by CQ Weekly,

> women chair 27 panels—four full committees and 23 subcommittees—or 22 percent of the 125 total panels in the House. And women hold an identical 22 percent of the membership in the Democratic Caucus. Blacks, Hispanics and Asian-Americans, meanwhile, hold seven committee and 30 subcommittee chairmanships, or 30 percent of all the gavels—and members of these ethnic minorities hold 28 percent of the caucus seats.[15]

Pelosi also ensured that the California delegation was nurtured: by one account, "the state's 34 House Democrats account for 14 percent of the caucus membership, and this year 18 percent of all the House chairmanships."[16] Tending the California garden while promoting loyal supporters continued to be a Pelosi staple. In June 2008, she nominated Congresswoman Doris Matsui of California, an Asian American, to a seat on Energy and Commerce. Matsui had been elected to the House in 2005 to succeed her late husband, Bob Matsui, a Pelosi loyalist who had served as her first DCCC chair. Doris Matsui was opposed by Donna Christensen, the delegate from the Virgin Islands, an African American. The Energy and Commerce seat had opened when African American Albert Wynn of Maryland lost his House seat in the Democratic primary. Christensen had the support of the Congressional Black Caucus, which wanted to retain its representation on this powerful committee. Pelosi's close confidant Anna Eshoo was the only Californian on Energy and Commerce. Pelosi's selection of Matsui was based on state delegation and personal loyalty. And by controlling appointments to the Democratic SPC, she sustained her choices for committee assignments. The vote on the SPC was 30 to 7 in support of her nomination of Matsui.[17]

The Select Committee

Pelosi made one other important decision in organizing the committees of the 110th Congress. She decided to appoint a select committee on energy independence and global warming, anticipating that these concerns would become a major political issue for the Democrats in the run-up to the 2008 elections. She also was firmly committed to addressing the problem of global warming as a policy matter. She faced a practical problem, however. Legislation addressing global warming would fall under the jurisdiction of the Energy and Commerce Committee, chaired by John Dingell (D-MI), who was a powerful protector of automobile industry interests. He had also been a strong supporter of Steny Hoyer, in retribution for Pelosi's support of Congresswoman Lynn Rivers when Dingell and Rivers had been pitted against each other in the 2002 primary. Confronting a powerful and resourceful chairman who was a known political adversary, Pelosi sought a detour for her global warming initiative. She charged all committees of relevant jurisdiction to take up the issue of climate change; and then she appointed a select committee to focus specifically on it.

The House Select Committee on Energy Independence and Global Warming would have had full legislative powers under Pelosi's original proposal, including the power to hold hearings, issue subpoenas, and draft legislation. Pelosi wanted to raise the visibility of global warming as an issue, and she wanted to be able to shape legislation without being hamstrung by Dingell's attachment to Detroit. Her transfer of Energy and Commerce jurisdiction to the select committee was a direct challenge not only to Dingell but to the jurisdictional claims of all standing committees. If the Speaker could circumvent one committee in this manner, she could circumvent them all. Dingell was joined in his protest by such Pelosi loyalists as Henry Waxman of California, who had served for years on Energy and Commerce and was now the chair of the Oversight and Investigations Committee. Faced with rebellion in the ranks, Pelosi compromised with Dingell for the first, and not the last, time. The new committee, chaired by Ed Markey (D-MA), would have the power to conduct hearings on the issue but no power to report legislation to the floor; and it would go out of business on October 1, 2008. This episode demonstrated a limit to Pelosi's power. She got her select committee only after agreeing to neuter its legislative powers. When the House moved to draft energy legislation, it would move through Energy and Commerce, and she would have to deal with John Dingell.[18]

BUILDING CONSENSUS

In organizing the House Democrats, arraying committee assignments, and setting the rules under which the House would operate, Pelosi juggled several considerations. These included her desire to assert central leadership, her need to strike an appropriate balance within the Democratic Caucus, and her obligation to ensure fair treatment of the minority. All of these organizing decisions were preliminary to the ultimate challenges of furthering consensus in her party by building coalitions and making policy. Her approach to these vital tasks gave definition to her conception of her role as Speaker and revealed the extent and nature of her grasp of the demands of office.

Pelosi's Position in the Democratic Caucus

To set the context of her approach, we begin by analyzing her strategic position in the House and in the Democratic Caucus. As we have stressed, one key component of the New American Politics is party polarization. Commentators have often observed—and political scientists have empirically demonstrated—that the House in the 110th Congress was as polarized as other recent congresses. One measure of this polarization is the scores devised by political scientists that we presented in table 1.1. In addition, the *National Journal*'s scoring shows that only five Republican members in the 110th Congress's first session were more liberal than a Democrat.[19] (In other words, 231 of 236 Democrats were more liberal than any Republican.) The *Journal*'s scores for 2008 were similar, showing only six Republicans more liberal than a Democrat.[20] Another indicator of the extent of polarization is the level of party unity attained by each party when voting in opposition to the other. The Democrats attained a record 92% party unity in both 2007 and 2008; the Republicans were not far behind, recording 85% unity in 2007 and 87% in 2008.[21] Because of the high degree of party polarization and unity, Pelosi, like Republicans Hastert and Gingrich before her, would be forced to find most of the 218 votes needed to pass important legislation within her own party's ranks when push came to shove.

As we observed in chapter 2, Pelosi began her House career from a position securely based among liberal Democrats. Pelosi is Speaker and Martin

Frost and Harold Ford are not because liberals are in the majority in the caucus. But the Democratic Caucus remained diverse, and she needed to reach out beyond her base in order to build legislative coalitions. There are over 400 informal caucuses in the House. Within the Democratic Caucus, the most significant in terms of numbers are the Progressive Caucus, the New Democrats, and the Blue Dog Democrats. Other important caucuses, such as the CBC and Congressional Hispanic Caucus (CHC) overlap with them. These three caucuses cover the ideological spectrum from left to center to right. The progressives are traditional liberals. They favor redistributive economic policies, they support trade unions, and they strongly criticized the Bush administration's foreign policy. The New Democrats (sometimes called New Dems) are centrists aligned with the DLC's "third way." They take an interest in economic, trade, and technology issues, reflecting President Clinton's approach to governing: mend it, don't end it. They are often characterized as "business-friendly" Democrats. The Blue Dogs are fiscal conservatives; many of them represent rural districts. Many are also cultural conservatives, although the main glue that ties them together is their commitment to fiscal responsibility, that is, balanced budgets. They are the staunchest advocates of pay-as-you-go (PAYGO) budget rules.

Networking

As minority leader and now as Speaker, Pelosi reached out to centrist and more conservative Democrats. She sought to govern by developing a consensus within the caucus rather than simply seeking to advance her own policy preferences. Her outreach efforts had tangible results. Several Blue Dog members are strong Pelosi allies. She has advanced many of them to major committee assignments.[22] Perhaps most important, she insisted that the PAYGO requirement the Blue Dogs favor be written into House rules. Legislative proposals affecting revenue decrease or outlay increase must be offset by revenue increases or expenditure reductions, so as to avoid increasing the federal deficit. Any bill or amendment that violates PAYGO is subject to a point of order on the floor that the chair is obligated to sustain.[23] After PAYGO had been in effect through the 1990s, the Republican majority had removed it from the rules in 2002. The Democratic minority, led by the Blue Dogs, had pressed to reinstate it, but the Republicans resisted imposing it on tax cuts. With Pelosi's support, PAYGO was put in place for the 110th Congress.

This outreach to the Blue Dogs was only one aspect of her effort to build consensus within the caucus. Acutely aware of the Democrats' tenuous hold on their majority, she knew that control hinged on their ability to hold on to the seats gained in the 2006 election in previously Republican-held districts. The Republicans had targeted 61 Democratic seats in districts President Bush had carried in 2004. A large number of these had been freshmen. As we saw in chapter 2, Pelosi and Rahm Emanuel had led the Democrats to their majority by recruiting candidates who suited the districts they hoped to win. This resulted in a freshman class that was substantially more conservative than the caucus median, many of whom were substantially at risk in the 2008 elections. To hold the newly won seats, it was necessary to bring the new members into full participation in the legislative process, give them opportunities to sponsor key legislation, protect them against votes that might be used against them in 2008, and consult with them on a regular basis.

Toward these ends, Pelosi hosted these freshmen at a breakfast in her conference room every Wednesday when the House was in session. Working with Emanuel and the staff of the Democratic Caucus, she created a program she called "Frontline" to coordinate policy and message to support these at-risk members. Freshmen members were pushed forward during the early months of the 110th Congress, especially on reform issues. The Democratic class 2006 was more diverse than the Republican class of 1994 and accordingly less cohesive. Their diversity actually worked to Pelosi's benefit—in two ways. She did not have to face a unified freshmen class clamoring for dramatic changes she could not deliver; and she could work with each to help facilitate his or her reelection. By reaching out to the freshmen, she sought to integrate and socialize them into the caucus under her leadership.[24]

In addition to her outreach to organized caucuses and at-risk members, she sought to build bridges within the Democratic Caucus and among various constituencies in a variety of ways. She sought to reconstruct the relationships between rural and urban Democrats that had been the cornerstone of their coalition since the New Deal era. Her outreach to the Blue Dogs and her relationship with Agriculture Committee Chair Collin Peterson contributed importantly to this goal. When the CHC became upset with the House leadership for perceived slights of its policy concerns, Pelosi both castigated, when the CHC sought to block a rule on the Alternative Minimum Tax bill, and consulted, when it felt excluded from policy debate.[25] Pelosi's outreach to the CHC typified her approach. She ran the Democratic Caucus as what one observer called a "meet market."[26] Her days on Capitol Hill included numerous meetings: meetings to plan strategy, consult with members, plan meetings, debrief meetings, and so forth. She regularly attended the weekly meeting of the Democratic Caucus and met at least three times a week with her leadership team.[27]

These efforts are entirely consistent with emphasis scholars have placed on intraparty consultation in the postreform House.[28] We suggest that they are also entirely consistent with Pelosi's penchant for organizational detail, interpersonal politics, and pragmatism. Her exhaustive efforts to build consensus within the Democratic Caucus called forth an essential pragmatism that her liberal politics had not foreshadowed. It was natural for the Democrats to be led by a liberal member; it was necessary that their leader be committed to bringing all the elements of the party together. Of course, as much could be said of the Republicans, with this difference: the Republican strategy was always to play to their party's generally conservative base voters. This strategy turned into a self-reinforcing race to the right, abandoning the middle ground of American politics. The Democratic Caucus had edged toward the center in the 2006 election, and to retain power, its consensus would have to gather near the middle ground of national politics. To lead her caucus in that direction, Pelosi had to mollify the left while accommodating the right. As a first-trimester evaluation had it:

> Some Democrats worried that she would run the House as a San Francisco liberal with a "left coast" agenda and as a machine politician with a long memory for slights. But so far, Pelosi, who reached her first 100 days as Speaker on Friday, has defied those expectations. She has embraced a centrist agenda and built relationships with rivals.[29]

Our interviews confirm this impression: in the 110th Congress, Pelosi encountered more criticism within the Democratic Caucus from the left than from the right. She took more heat generated by the dashed hopes of liberals than the fears of conservatives. While Blue Dog Democrats say they have been pleased by Pelosi's outreach to them, progressive Democrats sometimes chafe at her willingness to compromise.[30] Pelosi has sought to reassure liberals with her rhetorical commitment to their agenda when speaking to groups such as Take Back America or the Center for American Progress.[31] At the same time, she has been willing to call them to task when they balk in following her leadership, even threatening their committee assignments.[32]

MANAGING THE FLOOR

In organizing the Democratic Caucus and arraying Democratic committee assignments, Speaker Pelosi sought to balance her desire for a loyal and centrally directed party leadership structure with the need to reflect and accommodate the diversity among House Democrats and the party culture it produces. As she considered House governance, she had to find a way to strike another balance, this time among three responsibilities: her institutional role as the Speaker of the House, her partisan role as the leader of its majority party, and her own personal and district-driven inclinations.

As we discussed in chapter 1, when the Republicans took control of the House in 1995 they promised to be fairer to the Democrats than the Democratic majority had been to them. In particular, they promised more regular use of open rules. The Republican leadership apparently believed that they could hold their narrow majority together by opposing amendments the Democrats would offer and by restricting time for floor debate, thus reducing the number of amendments. They quickly became disabused of such optimistic notions, discovering that holding their majority in line required them to structure floor alternatives just as the Democrats had done. Nonetheless, the Republicans contended that at least on one key procedure, they remained more generous to their opposition than the Democrats had been. The Democrats had on occasion denied the Republicans the opportunity to send legislation back to committee via a motion to recommit (MTR). The Republicans, now that they were in the majority, preferred to permit MTRs, while treating them as procedural votes requiring party discipline. At the same time, the Republicans broke new ground in that they sometimes excluded Democratic conferees from the process of House-Senate conferences.

Against this backdrop, Minority Leader Pelosi had proposed a "Minority Bill of Rights" in June 2004. She sought Speaker Hastert's support for a basic set of procedural guarantees to be afforded the minority no matter which party controlled the House. Included in her list of minority rights was its right to offer germane amendments (that is, open rules), adherence to a fifteen-minute limit on floor votes, a guarantee that bills would be held over for one day before being brought to the floor (so that members would have time to read them), an assurance that meetings between House and Senate conferees would be inclusive and transparent, and a guarantee of the MTR.[33] Pelosi's proposal addressed the complaints both the Democratic and Republican minority leaderships had made over the previous two decades. She sought to make an issue of Republican management of the House just as Gingrich had done in the years leading up to the 1994 election. In so doing, however, she set in place markers against which her own administration of the House could be gauged.

Special Rules

Her first actions as Speaker demonstrated little respect for the principles that she had advocated as minority leader. The Democrats had campaigned in 2006 on the Six for '06 legislative platform, an echo of the 1994 Republican Contract With America.[34] Pelosi had promised that the new Democratic

majority would deliver on its Six for '06 pledge within the first 100 legislative hours (in contrast to the Contract With America pledge to pass its bills
in the first 100 days of the 104th Congress). Six for '06 became the "First
100 Hours" agenda as the 110th Congress convened. The Democrats could
not afford to waste any floor time on Republican amendments, and Pelosi
wanted the flexibility to craft the bills that would gather maximum bipartisan
support without the distraction of pesky Republican proposals. Therefore,
she decided to bring the "First 100 Hours" package to the floor under closed
rules. Her strategy was successful. All of the legislation passed easily, winning
substantial Republican support with very few Democratic defectors.

Pelosi, Rules Committee chair Louise Slaughter and key members of
that committee said publicly that the Democrats had a sincere desire to
run a more open House than the Republicans had. In this, they were perhaps as well-intended as the Republicans had been in the heady aftermath
of their return to power in 1995; but soon, and inevitably, the Democrats
were forced to crack down on the Republicans, in part because of GOP mischief. On the very first bill brought forward under an open rule—H.R. 547,
the Advanced Fuels Infrastructure Research and Development Act—the
Republicans offered an amendment designed to allow them to make an issue
of the Speaker's use of a larger military plane than Speaker Hastert had used.
Pelosi's trip home was twice as long as Hastert's and required a plane that
had greater range and used more fuel.[35] The Republicans characterized the
bigger plane as evidence of arrogance of power and in the guise of concern
over an energy issue, devoted two full hours of floor debate to it.

This episode was only the first indication of the problems the Republicans
might seek to cause the Democrats under open rules. In June 2007, for
example, Republicans took advantage of open rules and other procedural
tactics to protest the Democrats' plan to defer earmarks in appropriations
bills until House-Senate conferees met to work out the final language. It was
apparent to Speaker Pelosi that managing her majority necessitated using
the Rules Committee to structure choices. This history of Democratic, then
Republican, and now Democratic majority party governance underscores
the need of the majority party to structure choice that will entail the use of
special rules.

Table 3.1, showing the majority parties' use of various categories of
special rules in the 103rd Congress through the 110th, reveals that the
Democratic majority in the 110th Congress was not greatly different than
its Republican predecessors. These Democrats used closed and modified
closed rules far more often than did the last Democratic majority in the
103rd Congress. Combining these two categories, the numbers are 18% for
the 103rd Congress versus 44% for the 110th. But the Democrats used closed
and modified closed rules slightly more often in the 110th Congress than

Table 3.1 Special Rules Used by the Majority, by Type: 103rd through 110th Congresses

Congress	103rd 1993–94		104th 1995–96		105th 1997–98		106th 1999–2000		107th 2001–02		108th 2003–04		109th 2005–06		110th 2007–08	
Majority	Democrats		Republicans		Republicans		Republicans		Republicans		Republicans		Republicans		Democrats	
Rule type	No.	%	No.	%	No.	%	No.	%	No.	%	No.	%	No.	%	No.	%
Open/mod. open	46	44	83	58	74	53	91	51	40	37	34	26	24	19	23	14
Structured	40	38	20	14	6	4	32	18	20	19	34	26	52	42	70	42
Modified closed	9	9	20	14	36	25	17	9	24	22	28	21	9	7	12	7
Closed	9	9	19	14	24	17	39	22	23	22	37	28	40	32	62	37
Totals	104	100	142	100	140	100	179	100	107	100	133	100	125	100	167	100
Self-executing	30	22	38	25	52	35	40	22	42	37	30	22	28	22	49	29

Source: Data for 103rd through 109th Congresses provided by Don Wolfensberger, director, Congress Project: Woodrow Wilson Center, Washington, D.C. Data for 110th Congress collected by the authors from U.S. House of Representatives, Committee on Rules, Rules Reported at http://www.rules.house.gov.

the Republicans did during their six majorities; the average of these rules for those six congresses is 39%. Structured rules were also used to serve the purposes of the majority party, typically restricting the options available to the minority. Fully 42% of the rules adopted by the Democrats were structured; only 14% were open or modified open. Finally, like the Republican majorities, the Democrats resorted to self-executing rules about a third (29%) of the time. Self-executing rules are used to ram through substantive legislative provisions in the adoption of the rule itself—another means of suppressing minority party options.

Motions to Recommit

While the Democrats' use of restrictive rules was essentially similar to the Republicans' practices, their approach to MTRs was decidedly different and offers insight into Speaker Pelosi's approach to party leadership as well as to differences between the Democratic Caucus and the Republican Conference. According to an explanation offered by the Rules Committee, "After the third reading of a bill (or resolution), but before the Speaker orders the vote on final passage of the bill (or resolution), a motion to recommit the bill, either with or without instructions, to the committee which originally reported it is in order. (Rule XVI and XVII) [sic] This motion is traditionally the right of the Minority and gives them one last chance to amend or kill the bill."[36] Historically, the MTR has taken one of three forms. The first is a straight motion "without instructions"; it effectively kills the bill by returning it to the committee of origin with no command that it be brought back to the House for further consideration. The second is a motion with instructions to the committee of original jurisdiction, commanding the committee to return the bill to the House "forthwith" having incorporated the instructed revision. The revised bill is brought immediately to the House floor without intervening motion. In this case, the MTR is in effect a final amendment to the bill. Third, an MTR with instructions may command the committee of original jurisdiction to return the bill to the House "promptly." Under this command, the committee has an opportunity to both incorporate the commanded instruction and make other changes in the bill aimed at gathering majority support. Typically, a bill recommitted "promptly" is unlikely to reemerge from committee because the committee majority will not support the commanded revisions.[37] The MTR is so fundamental to the rights of the minority that Thomas Jefferson included it in his *Manual of Procedure*, which remains the foundation of parliamentary procedure in the House of Representatives.

As we noted, the Republicans had treated all MTRs as procedural votes, expecting that their members would vote nay. Speaker Pelosi chose to treat MTRs as substantive votes, allowing members the latitude to vote the substance of the motion according to their policy preferences and political needs. Realizing that straight MTRs "without instructions" (effectively killing the bill) would likely draw a sharper partisan response from the Speaker, the Republicans chose to offer MTRs with instructions. Most Republican MTRs in the 110th Congress were "forthwith," but on occasion the Republicans drafted "promptly" MTRs in which, under cover of a general instruction to the committee of origin, they sought to incorporate language that would put Democrats on record as having voted on a substantive proposition, for example against a proposed tax cut. Seeking political advantage, the Republicans designated floor staff to draft MTRs on the fly and crafted motions designed to put conservative and moderate Democrats in Republican-leaning districts on the spot.

The Republicans offered 124 MTRs in the 110th Congress, of which 24 were approved. On five other occasions, the Speaker pulled bills because she feared losing a MTR vote.[38] Several of the 24 successful MTRs carried easily, as many Democrats decided to jump on board rather than fight. Some MTRs were hotly disputed and defeated, but on many of these a number of conservative Democrats voted yea, denying the Republicans the issue in their districts. When a conservative Democrat voted against an MTR, the Republicans were often quick to shoot out press releases highlighting his or her vote. The Democrats' Frontline team quickly responded in kind. Table 3.2 lists the 24 MTRs that passed the House during the 110th Congress. This compares to only 14 successful MTRs during the six Republican-majority terms. Among the 24 successful MTR votes in the 110th Congress, we observe that on 14, over half of the Democrats voted yea; these were bipartisan votes. An additional 6 successful MTRs won the support of at least 50 Democrats.[39] Among all 24 successful MTRs, only an Iraq War vote struck at the core of the Speaker's agenda. Even here, she allowed members to vote their conscience and district, thus protecting her majority.

Pelosi's approach to MTRs tells us a lot about her leadership strategy. By allowing the Republican MTRs to go forward and then allowing the Democrats to vote as they wished, she sought to undermine the Republican strategy. The leadership whipped (counted and sought to persuade members) very few of these votes and defeated almost all of the MTRs they actively opposed. Since members were able to vote their districts, none of these votes appears to have contributed to the defeat of an incumbent Democrat in the 2008 election.

Table 3.2 Successful Motions to Recommit (in Order of Margin), 110th Congress

Bill	Act Title	Date	Yea	Nay	D yea	D nay	R yea	R nay
H.R. 700	Amended Federal Water Pollution Control	3/8/07	427	0	230	0	197	0
H.R. 985	Whistleblower Protection Enhancement	3/14/07	426	0	229	0	197	0
H.R. 569	Water Quality Investment	3/7/07	425	0	228	0	197	0
H.R. 5811	Electronic Communication Preservation	7/9/08	419	1	227	1	192	0
H.R. 362	Science and Math Teacher Scholarships	4/24/07	408	4	218	4	190	0
H.R. 1585	National Defense Authorization	5/17/07	394	30	198	29	196	1
H.R. 2102	Reporter Federal Shield Law	10/16/07	388	33	193	32	195	1
H.R. 3524	HOPE VI Housing Reauthorization	1/17/08	372	28	190	28	182	0
H.R. 720	Water Quality Financing Act of 2007	3/9/07	359	56	172	54	187	2
H.R. 2316	Honest Leadership and Open Government Act of 2007	5/24/07	346	71	158	64	188	7
H.R. 2446	Afghanistan Freedom and Security Support	6/6/07	345	71	152	68	193	3
H.R. 1483	National Heritage Areas	10/24/07	344	71	153	71	191	0
H.R. 2740	Overseas Contractor Accountability	10/4/07	342	75	150	75	192	0

Bill	Title	Date						
H J Res 52	Fiscal 2008 Continuing Resolution	9/26/07	341	79	146	79	195	0
H.R. 1362	Accountability in Contracting	3/15/07	309	114	115	114	194	0
H.R. 1401	Rail and Public Transportation Security	3/27/07	304	121	105	121	199	0
H.R. 2634	International Debt Relief	4/16/08	291	130	97	129	194	1
H.R. 928	Inspector General System	10/3/07	274	144	80	144	194	0
H.R. 363	Science and Engineering Research	4/24/07	264	154	75	149	189	5
H.R. 1684	Department of Homeland Security Authorization	5/9/07	264	160	66	160	198	0
H.R. 1227	Gulf Coast Hurricane Housing Recovery	3/21/07	249	176	55	175	194	1
H.R. 1011	Virginia Wilderness Protection	10/23/07	236	178	48	176	188	2
H.R. 1851	Section 8 Voucher Reform Act	7/12/07	233	186	45	182	188	4
H.R. 2317	Lobbying Transparency Act	5/24/07	228	192	33	192	195	0

Source: Congressional Record, 110th Congress, 2007–8, http://www.gpoaccess.gov/crecord/

House-Senate Conferences

An additional dimension of procedural control lies in the bicameral relationship between the House and the Senate. Frequently the House and Senate will pass identical versions of the same bill. When the two chambers produce different versions there are two ways to reconcile them. Historically, the common practice has been to hold a "conference" between delegates from the House and Senate, who are called "conferees." The conference reaches agreement on a single text, the "conference report," which is then reported back to each chamber for a final vote on it, with no opportunity for amendment. An alternative method, evidently more cumbersome, is to simply pass the bill back and forth between the two chambers until the same version of the bill finally passes in each. This process, sometimes called "ping-ponging," avoids conferences and their possible complications.

The Republicans when they were in control of both chambers sometimes used the conference process but excluded the Democrats from meaningful participation. The official meetings of the conferees were merely pro forma, designed to ratify understandings the House and Senate Republican conferees had reached in informal negotiations. Democrats protested loudly, and Pelosi included a commitment to hold regular and meaningful conferences in her "Minority Bill of Rights."

Here again, once in power, she skirted the principles she had enunciated while in the minority. While conferences were not railroaded in the manner the Republicans had used, only a few were held. Table 3.3 shows that Pelosi's leadership continued the steady downward trend since the 103rd Congress in the percentage of bills reconciled through conference. The majority of laws (63–82%) in all of these congresses were cleared without amendment between chambers (i.e., the identical bill passed both chambers); (11–24%) were reconciled by amendment between chambers (ping-pong). The portion reconciled through conference, 13% in the 103rd Congress, descended to 2% in the 110th. This pattern indicates that Speaker Pelosi and Senate Majority Leader Harry Reid, as had the Republican majority, found it more useful to bypass conferences and rely instead on floor majorities.[40]

Fast-Track

Pelosi's most controversial assertion of power under the rules of the House occurred when she pulled the timetable out from under the Colombia Free Trade Agreement (CFTA), which raised larger issues relating to the separation of powers—an instructive example of her conception of

Table 3.3 House-Senate Conferences 103rd–110th Congresses (1993–2008)

Congress	Public laws	Cleared without amendment (%)	Amended between chambers (%)	Conferees appointed (%)
103rd (1993–94)	465	63	24	13
104th (1995–96)	333	70	17	13
105th (1997–98)	394	71	20	10
106th (1999–2000)	580	75	18	7
107th (2001–2)	377	77	15	9
108th (2003–4)	498	82	11	7
109th (2005–6)	482	82	12	5
110th (2007–8)	460	80	18	2

Source: Bart Jansen, "Capitol Hill's Conferences: Can They Be Revived?" CQ Weekly, January 5, 2009, 19.

the uses of her power as Speaker. The CFTA was among a small number of trade agreements negotiated by President Bush under the so-called fast-track authority, authorization for which had subsequently expired.[41] Under fast-track, the administration negotiates the trade agreement and then the House and Senate must ratify it on an up-or-down vote with no amendments allowed. President Bush was anxious to win congressional approval for CFTA because of his general pro–free trade philosophy; while American markets were already largely available to Colombian exports, this agreement was needed to open the Colombian markets to American exports. Democrats were, in general, suspicious of free trade agreements that might lead to outsourcing of American jobs, especially those that lacked strong environmental and labor requirements. The CFTA raised additional questions because of the history of political persecution of labor unions in Colombia.

Fast-track worked best when an administration consulted with Congress before submitting agreements for approval. An unstated expectation existed that Bush would consult with the Democratic leadership of the House and Senate on the timing of any CFTA vote. However, the fast-track statute set in motion a mandatory 60-day timetable for congressional action. Bush, seeking approval of CFTA as among the few remaining policy accomplishments available to his administration, submitted the agreement on April 7, 2008, setting the clock in motion. Speaker Pelosi had two problems in search of solution. First, a vote on CFTA would split her caucus and put some members at risk. Second, Bush had violated the implicit obligation to consult when he decided to submit CFTA without consulting with her.

Faced with this dilemma, Pelosi turned to the Rules Committee. Democrat Jim McGovern of Massachusetts, after consulting with Rules Committee staff and the House parliamentarian's office, proposed to Rules Committee chair Louise Slaughter that the House had the power to suspend, by majority vote, the timetable the fast-track authority required, because the authorizing statute specified that nothing in it compromised the constitutional right of each chamber to set its own rules. In other words, the fast-track timetable placed the House under a procedural obligation that could be waived by a majority vote. Of course, the entire purpose of fast-track was to force expedited congressional action, and the authority represented an inherent demand on a chamber's procedures. If trade agreements were subject to normal congressional procedures, they could be amended, and consideration could be prolonged. This would hamstring administrations in negotiating them. If the House or Senate could simply waive the timetable by a simple majority vote, then an essential element of fast-track would be undermined.

Pelosi embraced the Rules Committee recommendation. After meeting with the leadership and her caucus, she took a Rules Committee resolution to the House floor, where on April 10, 2008, the House passed H.R. 1092 by a vote of 224 to 195. There were 10 Democratic defectors, 9 of whom were Blue Dogs. Bush was furious, regarding the vote as essentially undermining Congress's obligations under the Free Trade Act. Pelosi saw it differently. For the first time, the Speaker had been able to gain procedural advantage over the president. As she saw it, she now had gained "leverage" against Bush that would be useful as his presidency wound to its end. As one informant put it to us, "Nancy Pelosi is not a cheap date. If Bush wants something from her, he now has to give something in return."[42]

POLICY-MAKING

All of Pelosi's efforts to organize the Democrats, control the floor, and build consensus within the caucus aimed ultimately at passing legislation. At her first meeting as Speaker with the Democratic committee chairs, she offered a metaphor to frame their approach to legislating. Think of us, she said, as authors of a book. We are to write the narrative of the 110th Congress, and each month will comprise a chapter. How will our story end? What will the last chapter say? How do we build the plotline, chapter by chapter, to reach the conclusion we envision? Just as a plot must have structure, the legislative process must have strategy. Both must be coherent in order to succeed. What would their strategy be? she asked.[43]

We find Pelosi relying on three essential strategies: control, compromise, and sequencing. Traditionally, Democratic Speakers had remained aloof from the detailed process of drafting legislation, leaving that work to the committees. The leadership's responsibility was to move committee bills on the floor. Then the Republicans, after attaining their majority, had often chosen to bypass the committees, and the leadership had been deeply involved in drafting legislation. Pelosi wanted to return to regular order, with committees assuming the principal responsibility for bill writing. Yet she also wanted to ensure that the pace of legislation was consistent with her substantive priorities and strategic vision. To illustrate, we discuss her initial legislative agenda, her approach to agricultural and energy legislation, and the series of votes on the Iraq War.[44]

Control: The First 100 Hours

Pelosi's effort to govern by exercising control began with the Democrats' Six for '06 First 100 Hours legislative agenda. As noted, this initial agenda resembled in concept but differed in substance from the 1995 Republican Contract With America. Both were poll tested for political appeal, but the Contract was both more ambitious and less realistic. It included a constitutional amendment to put term limits on the House, tort reform, cuts in welfare, internal House reforms, tax cuts, and other GOP staples. The Democrats' legislative program aimed at the center of the electorate and included a variety of popular proposals that many Republicans would find difficult to oppose. Table 3.4 summarizes the First 100 Hours legislation. To fund these priorities, the Democrats proposed repealing tax benefits for the oil industry.[45]

As we have shown, Pelosi began her speakership by violating regular order. The bills were drafted by the leadership in consultation with the committee chairs but were not subject to the normal committee process. Instead, the leadership brought the bills directly to the Rules Committee and then to the floor under closed rules that barred Republican amendments. While the Republicans complained about their lack of input and inability to offer amendments, in fact many Republicans voted for these measures precisely because they were widely popular. They straddled the middle of the House, as is evident from the final passage votes (see table 3.4). Clearly, the Democrats had struck center ground in their initial legislative program, and they won praise for a "qualified success."[46]

Table 3.4   First 100 Hours Legislation, January 2007

Bill	Title/description	Date	Vote	Republicans Yea	Democrats Nay
H.R. 1	Implementing the 9/11 Commission Recommendations Act	1/9/07	299–128	68	0
H.R. 2	Fair Minimum Wage Act	1/10/07	315–116	82	0
H.R. 3	Stem Cell Research Enhancement Act	1/11/07	253–174	37	16
H.R. 4	Medicare Prescription Drug Price Negotiation Act	1/12/07	255–170	24	0
H.R. 5	College Student Relief Act	1/17/07	356–71	124	0
H.R. 6	Creating Long-Term Energy Alternatives for the Nation Act	1/18/07	264–163	36	4

Source: Office of the Clerk, U.S. House of Representatives, http://clerk.house.gov/evs/2007/ ROLL_000.asp.

Compromise: Agriculture

With the passage of the First 100 Hours package, Pelosi began to build consensus in the Democratic Caucus while shearing off Republicans—an easy task with these popular bills, less so with more controversial legislation. There are two ways to gather a legislative majority: to bring forward widely popular legislation or to build consensus through compromise. On the farm and energy bills, Pelosi followed the second path, deeply immersing herself in the committee process.

The 2007 farm bill (reauthorizing federal agricultural programs including crop subsidies) was a classic example of coalitional politics. Historically, Democratic majorities were nurtured by the urban-rural coalition forged in the crucible of the New Deal. City members would vote for farm programs; rural members would vote for urban programs.[47] This nexus was sanctified in the food stamp program, which was placed in the Department of Agriculture in order to ensure support from rural lawmakers. At the core of any agriculture bill are commodity price supports, which are the quintessence of distributive politics: peanuts, sugar, corn, wheat, dairy...name the commodity and it is a part of the congressional logrolling. Since urban members are not natural constituents of agriculture bills, why should they embrace price supports if they have the effect of driving up costs for consumers? The answer has been: because they will get something in return.

In 2007, that return was an enhancement of food stamp benefits, a demand of progressive Democrats. The geography of the Congressional Progressive Caucus is essentially bicoastal. There are few farm state progressives today. Pelosi had a long-standing aspiration to restore the urban-rural alliance in the Democratic Party. She also had a constituency stake on the farm bill, because fruit and vegetables (the California agricultural staples) had been excluded from some federal support programs.[48]

Federal farm programs have a checkered history. Originally designed to preserve high-quality food at a reasonable price for consumers, they were always defended on the Jeffersonian ground that it was important to preserve the way of life of the independent farmer. But in recent decades, as the vast majority of farm acreage became subject to corporate or other non-resident ownership, farm subsidies designed to assist the family farm came to deliver the bulk of their benefit to absentee personal or corporate owners. Stories were rife of wealthy suburbanites financing their homesteads by keeping agricultural acreage out of production. In 1996, the Republican Freedom to Farm Act sought to wean agriculture from crop subsidies; but in 2002 a Republican Congress worked with the Bush administration to pass the most lucrative farm subsidies in American history.

Unlike Gingrich, Pelosi had no interest in doing away with commodity subsidies, although she was sympathetic to liberals' demands to reform the programs. She was primarily interested in preserving her majority, finding consensus on the farm bill, and including benefits for California fruit and vegetable growers. To accomplish her goals, she needed to broker compromise between urban progressives and rural conservatives. She might draw some rural Republican votes, but she needed urban Democratic votes to ensure passage of the bill. The Blue Dog Democrats would, of course, insist that the bill satisfy the PAYGO requirements. But of the 25 members of the House Agriculture Committee, 20 were Blue Dogs. They would seek offsets but could be counted on to support the bill. It was the progressives who might walk, and they wanted reform.

She had evinced a strong desire to proceed under regular order, allowing the committees to do their work. While she had bypassed the committees in passing the First 100 Hours legislation, she allowed the Agriculture Committee to proceed in regular order. But she worked closely with Chairman Collin Peterson as the committee developed the bill. She assured him that if the bill contained sufficient reform to satisfy progressives and fulfilled PAYGO requirements desired by Blue Dogs, she would protect it against amendment on the House floor.[49] Winning progressive support for the measure proved challenging. In the end, Pelosi brokered a compromise that was built into the special rule governing the bill. Our interviews suggest that the final agreement on the farm bill was secured at a late hour, when Pelosi, after meeting with progressives, told Peterson that an enhanced food stamp benefit (including a pilot program for fruits and vegetables) was necessary or else the bill would fail. Peterson agreed. In order to ensure the deal, Pelosi instructed the Rules Committee to include the compromise as a self-executing amendment in the rule itself. The resulting rule, H.Res. 574, was complex and had the effect of locking in the compromises she and Peterson had struck, incorporating into the bill amendments supported by the leadership and allowing a limited number of Republican floor amendments, all of which failed.[50] The rule was adopted on a near party line vote of 222 to 202, a Republican motion to recommit failed 198 to 223, and the farm bill passed 231 to 191.[51]

Compromise: Energy Legislation

Pelosi's work on the farm bill was facilitated by a close working relationship with Peterson and a distributive policy domain that fostered compromise; there were many deals to be struck. Her work on energy legislation also required compromise and deal-making, but this time confronting a more hostile committee environment, that of the Energy and Commerce Committee chaired by John Dingell. Recall that she had sought to circumvent or pressure Dingell with the creation of the House Select Committee on Energy Independence and Global Warming. Her challenge was not, however, posed only by the personal power of Dingell; it was defined by the various and conflicting interests at play in the energy policy debate.

She was fast out of the box with H.R. 6, the Clean Energy Act of 2007, authored by Congressman Nick Rahall of New Jersey. Aimed to shift tax incentives from nonrenewable to renewable energy sources, the Rahall bill was introduced on January 12, 2007, and passed the House on January 18, 2007, by a vote of 264 to 163. At the same time, Pelosi charged Dingell to produce by June 2007 a more comprehensive energy bill that would begin to move the country toward energy independence and a lower carbon imprint. Climate change, she believed, should now trump the nation's reliance on carbon fuels.

Essentially, Pelosi and other progressives wanted to remove tax incentives for fossil fuel production and shift the cost savings to incentives for renewable sources: wind, solar, and biofuels. They also wanted to impose requirements for use of renewable sources in producing electricity. Renewable energy proponents offered the twin concepts of Renewable Portfolio Standards (RPS) and Renewable Energy Credits (REC). The RPS would require utilities to produce a percentage of their electricity from renewable sources. The REC were to be traded in a system that would allow utilities in states with abundant renewable energy resources to sell credits for their production in excess of the minimum standards to utilities in states that did not have such resources. This plan would force utilities in the gas and coal states to buy credits or undertake the expense of developing alternative sources. The other major component of the new bill was the revision of the corporate average fuel economy (CAFE) standards for motor vehicles, which Pelosi wanted to see substantially increased in order to reduce fuel consumption and carbon emissions.

The players in the energy game included the automobile industry, centered in Dingell's Detroit, the oil patch (Louisiana, Texas, and Oklahoma), the coal states (especially West Virginia), biofuel interests in the Great Plains, environmentalists, and southern states where alternative energy sources are scarce. These interests were represented by powerful members of Congress. In the House, Congressman Rick Boucher of West Virginia, chair of the Energy and Commerce subcommittee on Energy, advocated for coal interests and, like Dingell, opposed Pelosi and the environmentalists. Thus, when Pelosi indicated, as she often did, that energy legislation was her most important priority as Speaker, she was taking on powerful interests that were entrenched in the committee system.

Dingell's initial committee bill was designed to fail. It incorporated a provision that would have superseded California's strict tailpipe emissions law and proposed weaker CAFE standards than Pelosi wanted. Pelosi engaged in an extensive bargaining process with Dingell and Boucher. Neither embraced her ambitious goals for addressing climate change. Within the Energy and Commerce Committee, Dingell also sought to accommodate oil interests and their principal advocate, ranking Republican Joe Barton of Texas. In June 2007, Dingell and Pelosi appeared to reach a compromise, with Dingell agreeing to remove the California emissions preemption Pelosi opposed and Pelosi agreeing to defer CAFE standards to subsequent climate change legislation. She was optimistic that a bill could be passed by July 4, 2007, symbolizing an important step toward energy independence and a cleaner environment.[52]

Passage of the energy bill would not come quickly or easily. Dingell was unable to reach consensus within the committee and ended up working with Pelosi to produce two new bills: H.R. 3221, the Energy Policy Act, and H.R. 2776, the Renewable Tax Incentives Act. These bills gathered together the substance of several independent bills addressing aspects of energy policy. The primary vehicle was H.R. 3221; significantly, Pelosi was its author, a clear indication that she had taken ownership of the issue. The two bills were brought to the floor under a self-executing rule that incorporated the deals Pelosi had struck. After a marathon 72 hours of steady negotiations, she won passage of both bills. On August 4, 2007, H.R. 3221 passed by a vote of 241 to 172 and H.R. 2776 passed by a vote of 221 to 189. A Republican motion to recommit H.R. 2776 that effectively rewrote the bill in the direction of more oil and gas production was defeated by a vote of 169 to 244.[53] Finally, the House incorporated H.R. 2776 into H.R. 3221, creating an omnibus energy bill.

As the House worked its way through these various bills, the Senate had taken up the House-passed H.R. 6 and turned it into a comprehensive energy bill of its own design. The Senate bill included CAFE standards that had been deleted from the House bill and had higher standards for the transition to renewable fuels. It did not, however, include three key elements of Pelosi's climate change strategy that were central to her plan to limit greenhouse gas emissions: the RPS, the Renewable Energy Electricity Production Tax Credit (PTC), and the repeal of tax incentives for oil and gas production. The RPS would have implemented an emissions trading regime that imposed cost on states that did not have ready sources of renewable energy (requiring their firms to purchase energy credits from those in states that did). The PTC and the repeal of oil and gas tax incentives would have shifted the bias in the tax code away from fossil fuels and in the direction of renewable energy sources.

Since the House and Senate had passed different bills, Senate Republicans opposed to the legislation were able to block a House-Senate conference.[54] Instead, the House took up the Senate version of H.R. 6 and amended it to include the key elements of H.R. 3221, adding more demanding CAFE standards. When the amended H.R. 6 was sent back to the Senate, however, it failed to attain cloture. Bush had threatened a veto, and the Republicans rallied to defend his position. Seeking 60 votes, Senate Majority Leader Harry Reid stripped out the RPS provisions and modified the tax provisions. Once again, the Senate failed to attain cloture. Finally, on December 13, 2007, Reid agreed to remove both the RPS and most tax provisions, and H.R. 6 passed the Senate by a comfortable 86 to 8. The House approved the Senate bill on December 18, and the president signed the bill into law the following day.[55] Pelosi had won back the CAFE standards she had lost in the House, but she had lost the heart of her plan to move the country toward renewable energy sources. Still, she claimed it as a victory for environmental and energy policy change, while promising to revisit renewable energy.

This case study demonstrates both the strength and the limitations of Pelosi's position. She was able to move an energy bill through the House that Dingell did not like but supported. By stripping the CAFE standards from the House bill, Pelosi offered Dingell something he could take back home to Michigan. By including the alternative energy provisions, she gained leverage on the Senate. The final bill omitted the taxes on the energy industry she had sought as well as the two main alternative fuels provisions at the heart of her "new direction" energy policy. But the bill included the higher CAFE standards and incentives for biofuels, two important policy objectives. This was a partial victory, but a victory nonetheless. She understood that this legislation would not solve the climate crisis; and she had succeeded only on terms that were acceptable to Dingell. Still, she had turned an important page in the novel of the 110th Congress, and the passage of the energy bill suggested that the politics of energy and climate change may have taken a permanent turn.[56]

Sequencing: Iraq War Votes

The Iraq War best illustrates Pelosi's third strategic conception, sequencing— its capacity and its limits. The Democrats had ridden to power on the back of public disapproval of the war and its prosecution by the Bush administration. By November 2006, public support for the president and the war had substantially declined. Only a third of Americans supported the war, about the same number as approved of the president's performance.[57] The liberal base of the Democratic Party was angry and energized and now demanded congressional action to bring the war to a speedy conclusion. Pelosi had been among the most ardent critics of the war from the beginning, but now she had to balance the demands for a quick withdrawal from the left wing of the caucus and the cautious attitude of its more conservative members. With a thin House majority of 232 to 203, she could afford to lose only a handful of Democrats on any Iraq War measure. Just how many would depend on the degree of solidarity in the Republican ranks.

Pelosi knew that the House would be forced to consider both a supplemental appropriation to fund the war in early 2007 and further decisions on war funding later in the year. The most passionate war critics preferred no funding for continued combat operations; other war critics demanded a timetable for American withdrawal as a condition of further appropriations. Some conservative Democrats favored an American withdrawal but not legislated timetables. Others believed in deferring to the president on issues of war and peace. Within the Republican Conference, antiwar sentiment was increasing due in large part to growing opposition to the war in GOP districts. A few Republicans opposed the war on principle. These divisions within and between the two legislative parties were set against the backdrop of the Vietnam War and the way it had defined the foreign policy perspectives of Democrats and Republicans for a generation. The peace wing of the Democratic Party had favored disengagement from Vietnam and regarded that war as a historic blunder. Many Republicans believed that the Vietnam War had been "lost" when the Democratic Congress cut off funding for military operations in the wake of the Paris Peace Accords that brought the war to an initial end in 1973. Since Vietnam, Republicans had gained political advantage by accusing Democrats of "cutting and running" and being weak on national defense issues subsequently. They regarded the Reagan administration's muscular approach to the Soviet Union as having brought about the end of the "evil empire" and were unwilling to see America "lose" another war.

Thus, Pelosi faced a complicated set of calculations. In order to satisfy the demands of the progressives in her party, she had to legislate in the direction of an end to the conflict, but without losing conservative Democrats. She could not afford to put her "majority makers" at risk or allow the Democratic Party to again be branded as weak on national defense and hostile to the American military. How then, to oppose the war while supporting the troops? How to win votes without losing the next election? Her strategy called for a series of votes that could win passage in the House while building the pressure on House Republicans. She hoped that events in Iraq and continuous pressure on House Republicans would crack the opposition and provide a sufficiently bipartisan foundation to inoculate the Democrats against the charge that they sought to end the war by a partisan, legislative fiat.

In the fall of 2006, the bipartisan Iraq Study Group had recommended that the American mission shift from fighting insurgents to training Iraq troops. This new mission would be supplemented by a diplomatic initiative to reach an accord among the rival Iraqi factions. Rejecting this approach, President Bush accepted the recommendations of General David Petraeus and other military advisers to go in the opposite direction. Instead of shifting to a training mission, American troops would move from their sanctuaries to embed among the Iraqi population. The Petraeus plan called for an increase in American troop levels that was initially estimated at 20,000, but later increased to over 30,000. This new strategy became known as the "surge."

Confronting this situation, Pelosi planned a surge of her own, a series of votes that, she hoped, would build toward an eventual change in U.S. policy. The first step in the sequence was H.Con.Res. 63, a simple, 97-word statement of legislative sentiment opposing Bush's surge. This nonbinding resolution stood in stark contrast to a convoluted Senate version that ran for pages with various preambles and qualifiers. It simply declared the House on record as opposing the surge strategy. Given the recommendations by the Iraq Study Group and the increasing public opposition to the war, Pelosi hoped that this resolution would win a substantial number of Republican votes. She brought the resolution to the floor under a closed rule: either you were for the surge or you were against it.[58]

H. Con. Res. 63 was debated on the House floor February 13–15, 2008. Almost 400 members spoke for five minutes each declaring their positions on the surge and the war. Leadership sources stated publicly that they hoped to win from 20 to 60 Republican votes. Then, in the middle of the House debate, Congressman Murtha went public on the MoveOn.org website to announce the strategy he intended to pursue as the House Appropriations Committee took up the Iraq War supplemental appropriations bill the following month. Instead of setting a strict timetable for withdrawal, the House would impose on the administration a set of restrictions on troop deployments as part of the supplemental bill. These restrictions aimed at ensuring that the troops were sufficiently rested, trained, and equipped for their mission. In this way, Murtha said, it would be possible to effectively end the war without voting to do so directly. He believed the restrictions would be "troop friendly" and demonstrate Congress's commitment to their well-being. Murtha would oppose the war and support the troops, exactly as Pelosi wanted to do.

Apparently, Murtha did not consult with the Speaker or other members of the leadership team in developing these plans. The Republican leadership line (echoing the Bush administration) was made clear in the floor debates: the Democrats intended to end the war, and this resolution was the first step toward an ultimate surrender. The resolution, of course, was carefully crafted to avoid this implication. It said:

Resolved by the House of Representatives (the Senate concurring), That

(1) Congress and the American people will continue to support and protect the members of the United States Armed Forces who are serving or who have served bravely and honorably in Iraq; and

(2) Congress disapproves of the decision of President George W. Bush announced on January 10, 2007, to deploy more than 20,000 additional United States combat troops to Iraq.

About this language, Speaker Pelosi said: "We will vote on a straightforward proposition: do you support the president's plan or oppose it?" In response to which Republican leader, John Boehner, replied: "This resolution is the first step in the Democrats' plan to cut off funding for American troops who are in harm's way, and their leaders have made this abundantly clear."[59] Congressman Murtha's take? "Murtha dismissed that vote (on H. Con. Res. 63) as he promoted his coming plans.... 'This vote (on the war supplemental) will be the most important vote in changing the direction on this war.' "[60] Murtha's statements undercut Pelosi's strategy while consolidating Republican opposition to H. Con. Res. 63. When the vote was taken the next day, it carried by a vote of 246 to 182; 17 Republicans voted yea and only 2

Democrats nay. The Speaker had not won as many Republican votes as she had hoped, and the first vote in her Iraq sequence was essentially along partisan lines.[61] She would likely have to find the votes to pass the supplemental appropriations bill largely from among her own members.

Enacting of the war funding bill would prove even more difficult than enacting the antisurge resolution. Progressive Democrats wanted to provide funding only for an orderly withdrawal. Blue Dogs were divided, with some supporting the president, others seeking conditions on further funding, following Murtha, and still others supporting a timetable for withdrawal. Republicans would be more likely to support funding for the troops than to support Bush's war policy in general. Pelosi needed to reach 218 votes.[62] On March 8, 2007, she announced the Democrats' plan *before* the Appropriations Committee took up the bill.[63] She aimed to guide and constrain the committee process rather than to simply accept its product. This bill was a classic example of congressional logrolling. The progressives got a set of deadlines for withdrawal conditioned on the Iraqi government's progress in reaching benchmarks for self-governance. American troops would be home by fall 2008, according to the plan. Murtha got his restrictions on troop deployments, subject to presidential waiver. Blue Dogs got language imposing accountability for war contractors. Then there were the vote-seeking additions: $1.2 billion for the war in Afghanistan; $3.5 billion for veterans' health benefits; $735 million for children's health care (the State Children's Health Insurance Program [SCHIP]), agricultural subsidies, and additional Hurricane Katrina relief.[64] The "Pelosi Plan," the *Washington Post* said, was better designed to win the vote than to win the war.[65]

Precisely so. Pelosi was the general of House Democrats, and her objective was to hold her troops together. To do so, the leadership deployed all of its resources, including direct cajoling by the Speaker. The most obdurate members were the progressives in the Out of Iraq Caucus, whose opposition to the war was so visceral as to weigh against considerations of party loyalty. One chief deputy whip, Maxine Waters of California, refused to whip the bill for the Democrats. Barbara Lee of California, who had been appointed to the Appropriations Committee by Pelosi, was the only committee Democrat to oppose the bill. When the measure came to the floor on March 23, 2007, Pelosi and her leadership team ratcheted up their efforts. Pelosi posed the question in simple terms: will this be recorded as a victory for President Bush or as the beginning of the end of the war in Iraq? This argument, and leadership pressure, convinced enough wavering progressives to provide Pelosi with a 218 to 212 victory. Fourteen Democrats voted against the resolution, and two Republicans voted for it.[66]

Pelosi quickly offered her interpretation of the result: "We begin the end of the war."[67] Of course, this was not to be the case. The Senate produced its version of the Iraq War supplemental on March 29, and the final version was shipped to Bush on April 26, whereupon he vetoed it. Congress produced a revised emergency supplemental appropriations bill in early May. To satisfy the divergent views in the caucus, Pelosi initially offered two bills. The first bill required redeployment of the troops and was defeated 171 to 255. The liberals (including Pelosi) were able to go on record as against the war. The second vote was to fund the troops and included progress benchmarks. This bill passed by a narrow 221 to 205. After negotiations with the White House, the Senate returned the bill to the House with amendments that weakened the benchmarks by providing for a presidential waiver. The bill also included a variety of domestic spending priorities that the Democrats favored and the administration opposed, including the first increase in the minimum wage in a decade.

When the Senate version of the bill was reconsidered by the House in late May 2007, Pelosi again used her power to structure two House amendments. The first amendment provided for the range of domestic spending priorities the Democrats wanted, including Katrina relief. It passed 348 to 73, as even Republicans jumped on board. The second amendment provided for the funding of the troops with the weakened benchmark provisions. It passed 280 to 142, with opposition primarily from liberal Democrats. The president was required to make periodic progress reports to Congress, the first of which was to come in June. The Democrats' strategy was to use these reports as fodder for additional Iraq War resolutions over the course of the summer and fall and on into 2008. And in fact, the House did return repeatedly to the Iraq question in the 110th Congress. Table 3.5 displays the key Iraq votes, with Democratic defections categorized by ideology, revealing that Pelosi suffered defections on both her left and right flanks but was nonetheless able to maintain sufficient party unity to carry the war-limiting votes she supported in 2007. In 2008, however, the political dynamic changed because the surge was proving successful. Pelosi's sequencing depended on the assumption that the war would progressively worsen, thus putting political pressure on congressional Republicans and the Bush administration. In fact, the opposite occurred as the reduction in violence in Iraq and a decline in the number of American casualties gave Republicans breathing space. The last Iraq War vote in the 110th Congress occurred in January 2008 on the Department of Defense Reauthorization bill, which continued authority for the conduct of the war into the 111th Congress. Pelosi permitted that vote to go forward even as she voted against it. She did not have the votes to end the war, and it was time to get the issue out of the way so as not to complicate life for Democrats in the 2008 elections. Her sequencing of these votes had enabled her to build support for various war-limiting proposals, but the sequence ended when it was apparent that further votes would only erode her political position.

Table 3.5 House Iraq War Votes (February 2007–January 2008)

Date	Bill	Description	Yea	Nay	Democratic Nay			
					Total	Conservative	Moderate	Liberal
2/16/07	H.Con.Res. 63	Disapproving of the surge	246	182	2	2	0	0
3/23/07	H.R. 1591	Emergency supplemental w/timetable	218	212	14	6	2	6
5/2/07	H.R. 1591	Veto override	222	203	7	6	1	0
5/10/07	H.R. 2206	Emergency supplemental with benchmarks	221	205	10	1	2	7
5/10/07	H.R. 2237	Redeployment of armed forces	171	255	59	18	38	3
5/24/07	H.R. 2206	Emergency supplemental: House Amendment No. 1—domestic spending	348	73	1	0	1	0
5/24/07	H.R. 2206	Emergency Supplemental: House Amendment No. 2—war funding	280	142	140	0	21	119
7/12/07	H.R. 2956	Withdrawal deadline	223	201	10	7	3	0
7/25/07	H.R. 2929	Denying funding for permanent U.S. bases	399	24	0	0	0	0
8/2/07	H.R. 3159	Murtha: military readiness and rest	229	194	4	3	1	0
8/5/07	H.R. 3222	Department of Defense appropriation	395	13	12	0	1	11
9/26/07	H.J.Res. 52	Continuing appropriation	404	14	13	0	1	12
11/14/07	H.R. 4156	Emergency supplemental	218	203	15	7	5	3
1/16/08	H.R. 4986	National defense authorization act	369	46	42	0	4	38

Source: Compiled by the authors from Office of the House Clerk, "U.S. House of Representatives Roll Call Votes 110th Congress–1st Session (2008)," accessed at http://clerk.house.gov/legislative/legvotes.html. Ideological ratings taken from *National Journal* vote ratings at http://www.nationaljournal.com/2008voteratings. Ratings below 50 were categorized as conservative, between 51 and 70 as moderate, and above 70 as liberal.

Two patterns emerge in this set of Iraq votes. The first relates to substance. The close votes represented attempts by the Democrats to constrain President Bush and/or impose timetables or deadlines for U.S. withdrawal. The lopsided votes both provided Bush with the funding he requested for the troops. The second relates to politics. The Democrats were able to hold their slim majorities on a series of votes aimed at bringing the war to an end with almost no support from Republicans. On the close votes, Democratic defections occurred on both the right and left, yet Pelosi was able to hold her caucus together. Congress then passed funding bills with strong bipartisan majorities, thus protecting Democrats from the claim that they would not support the troops. The sole concession made by Bush was to a set of benchmarks and reporting requirements. He made no concessions on war funding itself.

Behind these votes lay a strategic calculation by the Democrats. They appeared convinced that the war was, in effect, lost and assumed that eventually Republican support for it would collapse. As Murtha put it in May, "By September, they'll come around, I think."[68] But the Republicans did not come around. In June 2007, the Democratic electoral base was restive, and congressional approval ratings were plummeting. A White House report detailing mixed progress on benchmarks propelled the House to a July 12 vote for an April 1, 2008, deadline, which died in the Senate. The August recess brought substantial pressure by antiwar groups.[69] In September General Petraeus testified before Congress, and the Government Accountability Office issued a report indicating that the Iraqi government had failed to meet most benchmarks. Even as the public's focus on the war intensified, congressional Democrats could not break through the Republican wall of support surrounding Bush. Faced with this reality, Pelosi and Reid shifted gears and focus, seeking some bipartisan ground on Iraq and giving more attention to domestic issues.[70]

In fact, the Democrats had caught themselves in a dilemma shaped by two factors. First, the constitutional system of separated powers favored the president, who only needed 40 of the 49 Republican Senators (given the support of independent Joseph Lieberman of Connecticut) to sustain vetoes of antiwar measures. Second, the surge was working, a possibility the Democratic congressional leadership apparently did not contemplate. American and Iraqi casualties declined, forcing Pelosi and other war opponents to argue instead that the Iraqi government was not making sufficient progress toward fulfilling the political benchmarks. Unfortunately for her, this argument did not resonate among Republican voters, thus buttressing Bush's support where he needed it most, among his party base. Confronting these realities, Pelosi could not prevent the death of more stringent antiwar legislation in the Senate, as Republican support for Bush solidified. As the first session of the 110th Congress came to a close, she had shifted attention away from Iraq to the more politically favorable ground of children's health insurance.

The series of Iraq War votes offers insight into Pelosi's strategic situation and judgment. She was caught between the expectations she had raised in appealing to war opposition in the 2006 election campaign on the one hand and her limited capacity to do anything about the war on the other. Her most ardent constituencies sought results she could not produce. Here we are reminded of the situation Speaker Gingrich encountered in leading his party to a House majority on the back of the budget deficit issue in 1994. He pushed for a balanced budget plan in 1995, which President Clinton was unwilling to accept, and he had banked on Clinton caving in. Pelosi had calculated that congressional Republicans would cave in on the Iraq War. The lesson seems plain: do not plan strategy on an assumption that your opponents will help you out. Republican backbone was, of course, girded by the success of the surge, offering a second lesson: do not count on realities that you cannot control; instead, anticipate that events will turn against you and plan for that contingency. Pelosi's sequencing strategy appeared to presume a snowball effect, what political scientists might call path dependency. By structuring a sequence of votes, she hoped to put pressure on the Republicans in hopes that they would finally break ranks. Sometimes, however, snowballs melt.

Pelosi's approach involved heavy stroking of members (one progressive confessed to 20 "therapy sessions" with the Speaker; another prayed with her), pork barreling (Katrina relief in a supplemental), anticipation (if we keep up the pressure, the Republicans will cave), and survival instincts (we've got to hold our majority). The last of these was preeminent. The Speaker needed to keep the party base in the House energized without jeopardizing the seats of the more conservative "majority makers." One tactic was to allow liberals to offer "end the war" amendments and resolutions, for which the Speaker herself voted while she realized they would be defeated. In the process, she declared an end to the Hastert doctrine that had paid obeisance to the will of the "majority of the majority." Announcing that she had "larger obligations," she was willing to accept legislative defeats if the seats of marginal members were preserved in the process.

CRISES

Our review of Pelosi's leadership in 2007 has highlighted three basic legislative strategies: control, compromise, and sequencing. The year 2008 was characterized throughout by a fourth approach, albeit one that can hardly be called a strategy: improvisation. Not surprisingly, her best laid plans of 2007 gave way to extemporizing in an election year. The extent to which the congressional agenda was dominated in 2008 by unanticipated events is nonetheless quite striking. Three factors drove Pelosi's improvisational agenda during the second session of the 110th Congress. First, she could not advance her agenda so long as the Senate was closely divided and President Bush wielded the veto pen. Second, 2008 was an election year, and her priority was to hold and enlarge her majority. Third, and most important by far, she faced the pressure of unexpected events: the weakening of the economy, the collapse of the subprime mortgage market, a spike in oil prices, the crash of the financial services industry, and the imminent failure of the Detroit automakers.

During the era of the New American Politics, Congress has addressed many vital public issues and cast many consequential votes. In October 1987, a collapse of the stock market led House Speaker Jim Wright to use extraordinary parliamentary maneuvers to enact an important budget bill. In 1990, 1993, and 1997, Congress acted responsibly to reduce the budget deficit, finally creating a budget surplus in 1998. In the aftermath of the attacks of September 11, 2001, Congress enacted important, if controversial, national security legislation and created the Department of Homeland Security. In 2003, responding to public demand, Congress created the largest expansion of the welfare state since the Great Society by adding a prescription drug benefit to Medicare. From 2002 and to the end of the Bush administration, Congress cast a series of difficult votes on the Iraq War. Thus, members of Congress and their leaders understood what it meant to take on a tough issue and to cast tough votes. Now they would be asked to do so again.

Stimulus and Housing

The first crisis wave hit Congress in January 2008. Faced with a deteriorating economy, Bush sought an economic stimulus package from Congress. Accordingly, Pelosi worked on a bipartisan and bicameral basis with treasury secretary Henry Paulson, John Boehner, and Senate majority leader Harry Reid to enact one. Pelosi and Boehner worked out the details of the bipartisan package in a late-night session with Paulson. Comprised mostly of tax cuts and rebates, the bill had passed quickly and with bipartisan support.[71] As the scope of the subprime mortgage crisis became clear in the spring of 2008, Bush again prodded Congress to act. This time, however, Republicans did not go along. Ironically, the legislative vehicle for the housing bill was H.R. 3221, the original vessel for the Speaker's energy legislation. Since the substance of H.R. 3221 had been incorporated into H.R. 6 by the Senate, the bill remained before the Senate and available for refurbishing. In April 2008, H.R. 3221 was reborn as the American Housing Rescue and Foreclosure Prevention Act.[72] The bill provided for a federal bailout of Fannie Mae and Freddie Mac, offered tax incentives for home purchasers, facilitated municipal purchases of foreclosed homes, and provided authority for lenders to work out renegotiated mortgages with borrowers, among other provisions. In late July, the Senate-drafted bill reached the House, where Pelosi engineered its passage in a series of four major votes. Republicans voted for one amendment 95 to 94 but voted nay on the other three amendments by overwhelming margins (154 nays, 159 nays, and 149 nays). Pelosi lost only four Democratic votes across all four House votes on the bill.[73]

Thus, the first two key congressional actions on the economy reflected the ideological fault line between the two parties. Democrats were willing to vote for both tax cuts and federal interventions to bolster the economy, as a whole, and the financial markets, in particular. Republicans were quite happy to vote for the tax cuts but recoiled at the prospect of a greater government role in rescuing the mortgage market. In the first case, Pelosi worked closely with Boehner to fashion the bill; in the second case, she led the Democrats to nearly unanimous support in the face of overwhelming Republican opposition. Having succeeded by two very different strategies to stimulate the economy and rescue the home mortgage industry, Pelosi might have felt that her crisis management was at an end. It was not.

Bailout

On Thursday, September 18, 2008, Treasury Secretary Paulson and Federal Reserve chairman Ben Bernanke sought an emergency meeting of the Democratic and Republican leadership of Congress to present to them information regarding a looming crisis in the financial markets in the United States and around the world. Their depiction of the situation was dire, leaving the legislators stunned by the magnitude of the crisis. The national and world economies faced imminent financial collapse.[74] The subprime mortgage crisis in the United States, with which the government had been reckoning through much of 2007, had spread to and beyond the banking system as the entire financial derivatives market teetered on the brink of disaster. The highly leveraged and largely unregulated network of collateralized debt obligations, mortgage investment securities, and credit default swaps was about to come crashing down. A collapse of the financial markets would freeze credit in the so-called real economy. Firms would be unable to borrow to stock inventories or make payrolls. Banks would be unable or unwilling to lend to each other. Customers might seek to withdraw funds from savings accounts, leading to runs on the banks as not seen since the 1930s. Huge corporations such as Countrywide Mortgage Company, the investment firm Bear Stearns, and IndyMac Bank had all gone bankrupt. Soon, the investment house Lehman Brothers would join their ranks. The government stepped in to rescue insurance giant AIG because it was adjudged too large to fail—that is, its failure would have a catastrophic effect on the economy. Unless Congress acted immediately to authorize the Treasury Department to intervene in the financial markets, Paulson and Bernanke told Congress, the country would be thrown into financial chaos.

The initial impulse of both the Democratic and Republican leadership was toward bipartisanship, less from a spirit of comity than a fear of political consequences. Already that year, Congress had enacted measures to deal with financial crisis: the economic stimulus package in a largely bipartisan fashion and, on a more partisan basis, the legislation intended to ease the housing crisis. The Democratic and Republican leadership set out to forge a bipartisan compromise bailout for Wall Street, but this time bipartisan ground proved hard to find. On Sunday, September 21, Secretary Paulson presented to the congressional leadership a three-page proposal that would have provided authority to the treasury secretary to expend up to $700 billion to purchase toxic securities, with neither congressional nor judicial oversight. In effect, the Bush administration was saying "Act now; trust us!" The congressional leadership, on a bipartisan basis, was willing to do the former but not the latter. A week of intense bipartisan negotiations ensued, during which Pelosi and Republican leader Boehner appeared to be cooperating, going so far on Wednesday, September 24, as to issue a joint statement announcing an imminent agreement. The following day, Bush convened a White House meeting attended by the joint congressional leadership and the two major party presidential nominees (Democrat Barack Obama of Illinois and Republican John McCain of Arizona) for the purpose of anointing the rescue plan. To the surprise of other participants in the meeting, Boehner announced that the package was not acceptable to a majority of House Republicans in its current form. Under pressure to act, Pelosi and Boehner nonetheless decided to bring the bill to a House vote the following day, Friday, September 29. It failed by a vote of 205 to 228, with Democrats voting 140 to 95 in favor and Republicans voting 65 to 133 against. The Dow Jones Industrial Average sank 777 points.[75]

What had happened? Recriminations abounded in the aftermath of the House defeat of the bailout. Democrats blamed the Republican leadership, which had won the support of only a third of its members. Republicans sought to place the blame on Speaker Pelosi's somewhat partisan floor speech in support of the bill. Both parties blamed Bush and the White House for a lack of leadership and effective lobbying. Where, really, did the responsibility lie? It appears that Pelosi's initial instinct was to see this crisis as requiring a bipartisan response similar to the economic stimulus legislation that had been enacted earlier in the year. The general rule of thumb for bipartisan deal-making on tough votes (as illustrated, say, by congressional pay raises) is the 50–50 rule, whereby each party's leadership is expected to produce support from at least half of its members. These become "bipartisan" bills not, as is often the case, because they are noncontroversial but precisely because they are extremely so. In this case, Congress was being solicited by a Republican administration emphasizing the severity of the crisis. In these circumstances, Pelosi would have expected Boehner to produce 100 Republican votes. Since Boehner and GOP whip Roy Blunt were projecting only about 80 Republican yeas, the Democrats would need about 140 votes to reach a majority. The Democrats would have to carry the Republican president's bill. In the event, Pelosi produced her votes, but Boehner and Blunt could not produce theirs.

Analysis of the vote shows that Republican opposition came from among the most conservative members and those facing tight election contests. Democratic opposition came from among the party's most liberal members and those whose seats were in jeopardy. With public opinion running strongly against the bill (media reports had constituent phone calls and emails in some districts running 99 to 1 in opposition), there was little political incentive for at-risk members to cast a tough vote. Fully 19 of 34 the Democratic Frontliners and 21 of 24 members of the Republicans' similar Regain Our Majority program voted against the bill.[76] Many of these at-risk members were situated closer to the center than to either tail of the House ideological distribution. When their votes were joined to those of the ideological extremes, the center could not hold. As one account had it, "the center had collapsed in favor of a coalition of far-right and far-left zealots."[77]

Pelosi's floor speech on behalf of the bill became an issue.[78] In it she had placed the blame for the financial crisis squarely on the Bush administration, saying:

> Madam Speaker, when was the last time someone asked you for $700 billion. It is a number that is staggering, but tells us only the costs of the Bush Administration's failed economic policies—policies built upon budgetary recklessness, on an anything goes mentality, with no regulation, no supervision, and no discipline in the system.[79]

She went on to acknowledge those she said had worked in support of the bill, naming Paulson and key Democratic members of the House but not naming or mentioning her counterparts in the House Republican leadership.

Curiously, the Speaker and Majority leader Steny Hoyer had reversed traditional roles in speaking on behalf of the bill. Usually, the majority floor leader,
a party official, rallies his or her members, and the Speaker, a constitutional
officer, later closes debate with a bipartisan appeal to conscience. In this case,
Pelosi's diatribe had come first, and Hoyer had followed with a far more bipartisan statement. Republicans were quick to blame their inability to produce
the votes on her floor speech, but this was (and soon became recognized as)
disingenuous. No Republican had switched to nay in pique against Pelosi. Still,
she had handed a talking point to the Republicans just when they most needed
one—because most of the blame for the bailout defeat fell quickly on their
shoulders.[80] Boehner had offered assurances to Pelosi that the Republican
leadership could produce 80 votes; in the end, they got only 65. If Pelosi was
upset and defensive, Boehner and Blunt were described as "dazed."[81] "Anarchy
Reigns over GOP" one headline read.[82] It appeared that Boehner and Blunt
had less influence in the Republican Conference than the younger conservatives on the lower rungs of the leadership ladder.

Should Pelosi be faulted for this systemic collapse, or her role in it?
Assuming, as we reasonably should, that responsibility for the lack of
Republican support falls squarely on the Republican leadership, Pelosi would
have been required to come up with the additional votes needed for House
passage of the original bill from among those progressive Democrats who
voted against it. Once it was apparent that the Republicans were unable to
produce their quota of votes, Pelosi gave up, saying out loud on the House
floor: "That's it. We're finished." Pelosi's critics held that she should not have
brought the bill to the floor without knowing for sure that she had the votes
to pass it.[83] Given the exigent circumstances, however, she had little choice
but to bring the bill to the floor expeditiously. Still, she did not push hard for
Democratic votes. Jim Clyburn's team did not whip the vote, and according
to one observer, "before the vote Hoyer and Pelosi had this weird message of,
'I'm voting for it, but we're not asking for your vote.'"[84] Pelosi was clearly relying on the Republican leadership to produce enough votes to ensure passage
of the bill. In her eyes, the bailout was a Republican initiative that demanded
substantial Republican support.

We conclude that Pelosi was ill advised to lapse into partisan rhetoric in
a situation that called for as much comity and consensus as the House was
capable of producing. But the House was not capable of producing much, and
Pelosi's speech was a reflection rather than a cause of the problem. Thoughtful
postmortems took the defeat of the bailout bill as a sign of "leadership breakdown" and a "political meltdown" reflecting a lack of capacity for institutional
leadership in the government.[85] It is well to remember, however, that the
defeat of the initial financial bailout bill did not lead to its permanent demise.
A week later, the Senate attached its version of the bill to a House-passed

tax bill providing the annual respite from the Alternative Minimum Tax for middle-income taxpayers. Pelosi had managed to get the bill through the House by providing offsets to satisfy PAYGO rules in order to please Blue Dog Democrats. Democratic Senators had made a solemn oath to the Blue Dogs that they would adhere to PAYGO. That commitment was quickly swept aside, and the Senate loaded the bill with $150 billion in new spending over and above the $700 billion in the financial rescue package. The Senate passed this bill on October 1 on a bipartisan vote of 74 to 25. The bill then returned to the House, where it passed on October 3 by 263 to 171, with a majority of Republicans still voting in opposition. Pelosi's floor statement this time was a model of bipartisan decorum. Thus, at the end of the day, Pelosi got not only the bailout package but also the Alternative Minimum Tax bill she had supported. But she was able to do so only because the Senate was able to hold the center ground and to succeed where initially the House had failed.

Detroit

The passage of the financial bailout in October was not the end of crisis management. After the November elections, Detroit came calling for a rescue package for the Big Three automakers. By then, the economic situation appeared even worse than it had in September. The demise of Ford, Chrysler, and General Motors threatened to send an economy that was now in a confirmed recession spiraling into a depression. Pelosi wanted to provide the requested assistance via federally guaranteed loans, taking the money from the Troubled Assets Relief Program (TARP) that had been set up in the financial bailout legislation. The Bush administration wanted to supply the money from a pool of loan guarantees previously provided to the automakers to facilitate the transition to more fuel-efficient vehicles. As usual, most congressional Republicans were skeptical of any federal bailout of failing private enterprises.[86]

This time the House went first. Overcoming her initial reluctance, Pelosi pushed through a bill that acceded to Bush's insistence that the funds be taken from the existing "green" funding already provided to the industry.[87] Pelosi had, perhaps, learned a lesson in an earlier fight over offshore drilling (which we discuss in chapter 4): cut your losses before they hurt.[88] In a reversal of fortune, however, the Senate was unable to reach an agreement that would attain cloture. The auto bailout died in Congress, leaving Bush with no recourse but to provide bridge funding to the industry from the TARP fund, as Pelosi had originally proposed. Once again, the government had failed to respond to an emergency, and once again it had found a way to patch together a temporary solution. Improvisation worked where planning failed.

But why did these two bailouts take different paths? Why did Pelosi fail in her initial effort to pass the TARP legislation (relying instead on the Senate to move a bill she could pass in the House), and succeed in passing the auto bailout (even though the bill died in the Senate)? The answer goes to the constituencies of the two political parties. The TARP bill was seen by many Democrats as providing taxpayer money to irresponsible Wall Street finaglers. It lacked support among the liberal Democrats comprising the majority of the Democratic Caucus. The auto bailout was perceived as assisting unionized blue-collar workers. Both liberal and conservative Democrats could support it. The vote on the auto rescue was largely along party lines, with Democrats supporting 205 to 20 and Republicans opposing 32 to 150.

This suggests that Pelosi is most effective, even in a crisis, when she can appeal to the natural instincts of her majority. Her staunch partisanship is an asset when confronting issues that rally her party base; it can be a liability when the situation requires bipartisan cooperation and concessions from both sides. This is a manifestation of the role of the Speaker in the era of the New American Politics.

SPEAKER PELOSI IN THE 110TH CONGRESS

Our survey of Pelosi's use of power in the 110th Congress has sought to suggest its diverse range. In concluding this discussion, we want to emphasize what—from her perspective—must appear its seamless integration. Reporters, commentators, and political scientists are in the business of describing and analyzing political phenomena, disaggregating that which is inherently indivisible. Speakers confront reality in whole cloth and must draw together the various threads of power into a single tapestry. While deferring to our concluding chapter a fuller development of Speaker Pelosi's conception of power, we pause to consider the lessons of the 110th Congress.

To do so, we employ a strategy she herself has followed: backward mapping. Just as she asked her committee chairs to think about their ultimate goal and work backward to their present point of departure, we can consider Pelosi's ultimate objectives and trace her path toward attaining them. Her first priority was to retain and if possible enlarge her majority in the 2008 elections. To do so, she needed to attain objectives potentially in tension. Whereas the Democratic majority needed to establish a legislative record to take to the country in November 2008, it was vital to protect the "majority makers" from casting votes that might jeopardize their reelection prospects. To her left, Pelosi saw a liberal caucus majority that was eager to advance its policy goals; to her right, she saw a group of members representing more conservative constituencies. Her challenge was to structure legislative choices to attain sufficient progress on a party agenda to satisfy the caucus and the public, while avoiding putting members at risk.

To accomplish this, she sought to lead by caucus consensus. But consensus among Democrats is not, to say the least, a naturally occurring phenomenon. The Democrats are a diverse group that could not be held together by ideological congruence or leadership sanctions. Instead, she had to use her power to build consensus. Deferring to seniority allowed her to avoid fights over committee assignments. Occasional exceptions rewarded loyalty or contributions to party welfare. Her application of House rules and procedures aimed at agenda control for the purpose of protecting members from difficult votes or denying the Republicans opportunities for political mischief. When it was clear that the Democrats had to proceed on policies she and other progressives opposed, as in funding the Iraq War, she allowed legislation to move forward even as she voted against it. When bipartisan coalition building offered the prospect of advancing Democratic policy objectives, she facilitated it.

Pelosi needed to prove that House Democrats could govern and to put Republicans and the Bush administration on the defensive. Where she had a popular issue that Democrats would solidly support and Republicans overwhelmingly oppose, she pushed hard. The best example was SCHIP, an expansion of which she pushed through the House, was ratified by the Senate, and was vetoed by President Bush. In 2007, she made sure that the trains ran on time, passing all appropriations bills. In 2008, she concluded that there was no reason to pass appropriations bills on terms Bush would accept when they could defer spending decisions until the 111th Congress in the expectation that a Democratic president would be there to sign them.[89]

The Speaker of the House is not omniscient but is the only person who is witness to the full spectrum of strategy. The best outside chroniclers can hope to attain is an approximation of the Speaker's situation and an appreciation of its complexity. From our vantage point, Speaker Pelosi, in the 110th Congress, proved adept at orchestrating the complex policy processes of the House with control, compromise, sequencing, and improvisation. We believe that Dick Bolling, who called for a commanding Speaker in 1968, would be pleased to observe Pelosi's conduct of office. But the speakership today involves an external role Bolling did not anticipate.[90] As Pelosi dealt with internal House governance and legislation, she also worked tirelessly to recruit candidates and raise money for Democratic campaigns and to speak on behalf of her party and her personal priorities. We turn our attention to that subject in chapter 4.

Chapter 4

The Outside Game

Money is the mother's milk of politics.

—Jesse Unruh, Speaker of the California Assembly, 1961–68

If you don't know where you are going, you will wind up somewhere else.

—Yogi Berra

Don't the powers that be know my campaign slogan was "The Voice That Will Be Heard"? How can I not be heard?

—Nancy Pelosi (1987)

Speakers in the era of the New American Politics attend to far more duties than those defined by the Capitol environs. Their role demands a greater involvement in two key areas: elections and political message development. Speakers are the fulcrum of the "permanent campaign" that has come to characterize the House during this era.[1] As the epigraphs to this chapter suggest, successful Speakers must master campaign fund-raising, organize with a clear sense of direction, and find a voice that will resonate beyond the Beltway.[2] Since Tip O'Neill was elected Speaker in 1977, some scholars have characterized this more prominent public role of Speakers as the "public speakership."[3] O'Neill was thrust into the public limelight because of his high-profile opposition to President Reagan. Not all of his successors have matched O'Neill's visibility or his approval ratings, yet Speakers who have neglected to reach out beyond the Beltway have done so at their peril.

In this chapter, we assess Pelosi's electoral role and message operation, beginning with its early evolution during her service as minority leader and then tracing its evolution since she became Speaker. She led the Democrats to an electoral revival, and her communications team has been technologically savvy and disciplined. She is the chief campaign fund-raiser of her party—she raked in at least $26 million for the DCCC alone in the 2008 cycle—and its leading spokesperson, having made more House floor speeches than any other Speaker in recent history.[4] She lives and breathes the mantra she has instilled in her closest political advisors—message, mobilization, money, and management. Nonetheless, her public persona and speaking style expose some of her limitations, which have been the targets of criticism and sometimes misogynist caricature. Future Speakers, we believe, will recognize the high bar her performance as electoral strategist has set but also will take note of her vulnerabilities as party messenger. In choosing subsequent party leaders, future members of Congress will attend to the lessons learned from her speakership.

ELECTORAL STRATEGY

The seeds of Pelosi's mastery of the New American Politics were sown in the ashes of the Democrats' defeat at the polls in 2004. The prospects were grim. President Bush had been reelected to a second term. The Republicans had increased their margin in the House by three seats to hold a 29-seat edge over the Democrats (232 to 203), beginning a second decade of GOP congressional control. Senate Democratic leader Tom Daschle of South Dakota had been unseated, while the GOP had swept six open Senate seats in the South. The architect of this victory and Bush's political consigliere, Karl Rove, boasted: "Today conservatism is the guiding philosophy in the White House, the Senate, the House, and in governorships and state legislatures throughout America. Liberalism is edging toward irrelevance."[5]

Unfortunately for Rove, someone forgot to tell Nancy Pelosi that her party and her impulses were irrelevant. The woman whose own rise to the speakership would depend on proving Rove wrong set to work to reverse her party's fortunes. How well did she succeed? Four years later, after the November 2008 elections, she was being touted as "the most powerful Speaker in a generation" with "no rivals within her own leadership ranks."[6] Dramatic victories in 2006 and 2008 first secured the Democrats a House majority for the first time in 12 years and then widened the party's margin. Across these two elections, 55 seats switched from GOP to Democratic control under Pelosi's leadership. At the outset of the 111th Congress, her Democratic Caucus enjoyed a 76-seat margin over their Republican rivals, the largest party majority since the 103rd Congress in 1993.[7] We attribute Pelosi's electoral success to her leadership, energy, total engagement, and integration of campaign and legislative operations as Democratic leader. To say that she is a hands-on leader understates the case. Along the way, she also enjoyed some luck.

In the past, Speakers have stood at some remove from active campaign participation. Sam Rayburn was known to have kept a cash drawer on which he could occasionally draw, but he delegated the real work of campaign organization to members such as Lyndon Johnson.[8] John McCormack was not an active campaigner, and while Carl Albert made more campaign appearances than McCormack, Albert's involvement was minimal in comparison to the political role Speakers have come to play today. Institutionally, the party campaign committees functioned to some degree autonomously from the party leadership. The Republicans elected the chair of the National Republican Congressional Committee, making it a formally autonomous element of the party leadership. Democratic Speakers appointed the chair of the DCCC but did not normally get directly involved in its operation.[9] Things would be different with Nancy Pelosi as leader.

Transforming the DCCC

A turning point for the Democrats occurred in the early 1980s. Reagan had swept the Republicans to a Senate majority for the first time since 1956, and O'Neill's House majority had dwindled to a margin of merely 26 seats. Anxious to replenish his troops, O'Neill appointed a young California congressman, Tony Coehlo to chair the DCCC. Coehlo became a founding father of the New American Politics. He developed a systematic plan for candidate recruitment and fund-raising. He put the squeeze on business PACs that had been historically inclined to support Republicans, telling them that if they wanted a seat at the table of the enduring Democratic majority, they had to put some skin in the game. While Coehlo was building the coffers of the DCCC, individual party leaders began to raise money through their own leadership PACs. They would then contribute to member and challenger campaigns in order to earn chits for subsequent leadership elections. Speaker O'Neill made campaign appearances according to a schedule set by Coehlo, and Majority leader Jim Wright appeared on behalf of candidates and members at their request—a practice now expected of leadership aspirants in both parties. Ambitious members formed leadership PACs and contributed to their colleagues' campaigns.

The majority party has a natural advantage in the dollar chase, so to level the playing field, Pelosi's fund-raising capability was an important consideration when the Democrats elected her their minority leader. Gephardt got more involved with the DCCC after the Democrats were thrust into the minority in 1996, but he also had presidential ambitions that shared space with his party obligations; his schedule often took him to Iowa and New Hampshire. Pelosi, harboring no presidential ambitions, made it her primary mission to reclaim the majority and become Speaker, and she was totally engaged in the effort. She understood Jesse Unruh's admonition and knew that when many millions were needed to compete in districts across the nation, neither party could rely on a single annual fund-raising dinner that might produce $1 million in contributions. She perfected fund-raising in the New American Politics.

As minority leader, she was careful, in her selection of DCCC chairs, to choose those who could meet the party's particular but evolving needs. Her first appointee was the late Robert Matsui, a quiet, studious lawyer whose advice was critical in laying the groundwork for a new fund-raising regime under the Bipartisan Campaign Reform Act of 2002, commonly known as the McCain-Feingold law. This law fundamentally altered fund-raising by increasing the amount of money an individual or PAC could contribute to individual candidates and party committees and eliminating so-called soft money contributions to the national parties.[10] This matrix of possibilities required particular attention to compliance, even as the Democrats sought to close the funding gap with Republicans. In the immediate aftermath of the law's passage, some described it as the "Democratic Party Suicide Bill," and in the first quarter of 2003, Republican campaign fund-raising exceeded the Democratic Party's efforts fourfold.[11] Matsui's job was to figure out how Democrats could operate and thrive within the new McCain-Feingold policy parameters. The 2004 electoral cycle was challenging for the DCCC, but the party emerged with a new fund-raising strategy that reflected Pelosi's vision. Figure 4.1 shows the transformation of DCCC fund-raising under her leadership.

As Figure 4.1 shows, the DCCC was initially hurt by McCain-Feingold limitations but made several important adjustments. It came to depend heavily on the contributions from the members themselves or the leadership PACs. The giving shifted its geography to a greater role for California donors, clearly fertile territory for Pelosi, and a lesser role for lobbying interests inside the Beltway. Whereas Coehlo was sometimes accused of pulling the House Democratic Party to the right because of money he raised from business interests, Pelosi seems to have avoided that problem by locating wealthy donors across a broader spectrum.[12] The mix of industry contributors changed, with unions most notably disappearing as a major source of party contributions (although they would continue to make independent expenditure on behalf of Democratic candidates). The resulting approach was to wean the DCCC from its reliance on a limited number of big donors and put in place a new business model based on fund-raising in equal shares that aspirants had raised and contributed to party campaign coffers. While the Republicans had made important exceptions to the seniority rule at the outset of the 104th Congress, they generally adhered to seniority during the 104th Congress through the 106th. During the 107th to 109th, this changed, and candidates for committee chairships were interviewed by the Republican steering committee. The primary variable explaining committee chair selection during these two congresses was the amount of money successful applicants for the positions had raised.[16] While this approach aimed to promote and reward party fund-raising, it was unstable because it fostered competition. Perhaps the most publicized example of this method of proceeding was the 2005 competition between Jerry Lewis (CA), Ralph Regula (OH), and Harold Rogers (KY) for the chairship of the Appropriations Committee. Hastert and the other GOP leaders selected Lewis in part on the basis of the fact that he had raised more money for the party than his two opponents.[17]

Pelosi followed a different approach. She did not demand contributions in exchange for chair positions or auction off coveted posts to the biggest fund-raiser as the Republicans had done. In making committee chair appointments in the 110th Congress, she honored seniority in every case except that of Harman and valued diversity as a primary goal in her committee appointments. Published accounts report that several Democratic committee chairs did not pay their dues to the DCCC until contacted by the Speaker. Some members, in fact, failed to meet their fund-raising targets, and Pelosi visited no direct penalty on them for falling short.[18]

Pelosi emphasizes the collective fortunes of the party in supporting the overall campaign effort. Indeed, some rank-and-file members have also refused to kick into the DCCC coffer, preferring instead to transfer funds directly to colleagues. Pelosi's response to noncontributors has not been directly retributive. That is not, we are told, how she works. She does, however, have a long memory and calls on it when the occasion for favored treatment arises in the future. The difference between the Republican pay-to-play approach and Pelosi's may not be readily discernible. Whereas the GOP fostered direct competition between members and made fund-raising a prerequisite for plum committee assignments, Pelosi sets targets and celebrates those who exceeded them.

Recruiting Candidates, Winning Elections

When Democrats fell short in their efforts to retake the House in 2004, Pelo redoubled her focus on bringing her party back from its minority status. if heedful of Yogi Berra's aphorism, she knew where she wanted to go—in

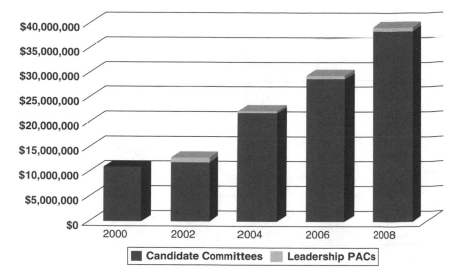

Contributions to DCCC from Candidates & Leadership PACs

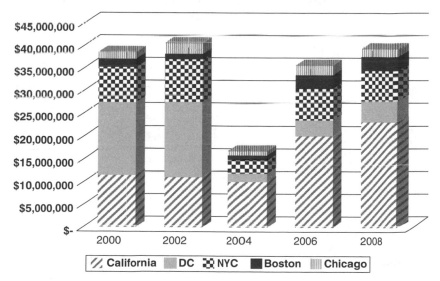

Contributions to DCCC by Region

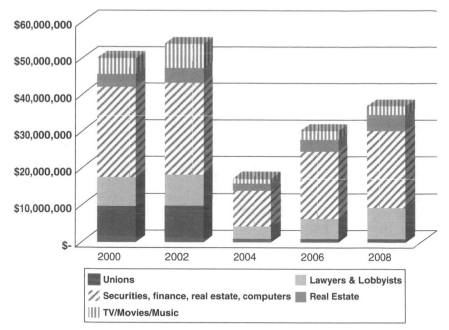

Contributions by Industry to DCCC

Figure 4.1   Changing Mix of DCCC Contributions under Pelosi's Leadership (2004–9)

Source: Opensecrets.org. The Center for Responsive Politics, "Democratic Congressional Campaign Committee 2000–2008," http://www.opensecrets.org/parties/totals. php?cmte=DCCC&cycle=2010, accessed July 22, 2009.

from large donors, the grassroots, and dues from the members of Congress. To facilitate grassroots contributors, online fund-raising efforts became central to the DCCC operation.

To accomplish the plan, Pelosi traveled extensively, combining fund-raising meetings with policy outreach events that identified potential new contributors and broadened the party's constituencies. She visited 30 states in the 2006 cycle and 28 states in the 2008 cycle.[13] These events were entirely characteristic of their species: larger dinners to attract more moderate contributors and private receptions for the fat cats. Traveling the country as she did to host and lend star-power to these fund-raisers, Pelosi sought to build a network of supporters. She asked the host members to introduce her to influential people in the district. She sought private meetings with those whose experience, information, or ideas might educate her about both public opinion and public policy. Thus, for Pelosi, the campaign swings were never simply about money; they were also about organization, networking, and public policy.

Internal Fund-raising

To raise money from members, the Democrats put in place a kind of tariff structure. Pelosi called personally and regularly to remind Democratic members of their expected contributions to the DCCC, a practice she continues to follow. Member tariffs take into account the differences in district wealth and member opportunities as chairs or subcommittee leaders with access to fund-raising sources. The baseline tariff expected from members was $125,000. The largest dues were owed by committee and subcommittee chairs, especially those serving on the three most powerful committees: Ways and Means, Appropriations, and Energy and Commerce. Members from relatively prosperous constituencies might be asked to contribute more than those representing poorer districts. Safe-seat members might be expected to contribute more than members representing more marginal districts. To cite an example, one Appropriations Committee member was asked to raise $250,000 in direct contributions to the DCCC and another $250,000 via his campaign committee that could be distributed to individual members (member to member). To facilitate this fund-raising, Pelosi did not simply demand contributions from members; she made herself available to help raise the money. If, for example, a subcommittee chair or member of a power committee had a substantial tariff to the DCCC, Pelosi would travel to the member's district to help raise the money. A Pelosi appearance at a local fund-raiser might yield tens of thousands of dollars in direct contributions to the DCCC credited to the member.

Willing largess to the DCCC did not go unnoticed. For example, the candidate Debbie Wasserman Schultz gave $100,000 to the DCCC in 2004, helped to raise $11 million as a sitting member in the 2006 election cycle, and found herself as a junior member with an Appropriations subcommittee chair when the Democrats took over in 2007.[14] By contrast, laggards supporting the campaign effort are singled out to the rest of the caucus with a gentle but pointed message so as to "encourage them to be a part of the team."[15]

Pelosi has imposed no direct penalty for noncompliance, and her internal alignment of committee chairs did not reflect a "pay-to-play" system similar to the one Republicans employed during the later years of their majority. Under pay to play, committee chairships, subcommittee chairships, and committee transfers were based in substantial part on the amount of m

the majority. She turned to Illinois congressman Rahm Emanuel, known for his "take no prisoners" style, to lead the DCCC and the party back to power. Emanuel has been given great credit for the Democrats' victory in 2006 (burnishing his credentials for future leadership office), but he was in fact the junior partner on the campaign team. Pelosi and Emanuel started with the pragmatic assumption that to secure a House Democratic majority, the DCCC would have to recruit, welcome, support, and protect moderate and conservative Democrats in districts typically friendlier to Republicans. Emanuel made it his business to recruit candidates who could win and to reject potential candidates who offered poorer prospects. He was relentless in suborning the candidates he sought. When the former NFL quarterback Heath Shuler of North Carolina expressed concern that he would not have time for his parental duties if he entered politics, Emanuel made it a point to call him when he (Emanuel) was on his way to pick up his own children after school.[19] This strategy paid off in 2006 when, among 42 newly elected Democrats, 29 were elected in districts previously held by Republicans. These new members would, however, pull the caucus to the right. At the end of the 110th Congress, 15 Democrats had party unity scores below 85%; among these, 10 were freshmen.[20]

Once elected Speaker, Pelosi had to decide how extensive her involvement in the DCCC's campaign was to be. Previous Democratic Speakers, as noted, had chosen to delegate the campaign function to their appointed DCCC chairs. On the Republican side, the elected chairs of the National Republican Congressional Committee operated independently of—though in cooperation with—Speakers Gingrich and Hastert. Pelosi did not hesitate in abandoning these precedents. She regarded it as both her responsibility and her opportunity to retain control of the House Democrats' campaign strategy and organization. Key Pelosi staffers were already lodged in the DCCC; for example, since 2003 Pelosi's primary political strategist, Brian Wolff, had served a split appointment between her office and the DCCC, to ensure coordination between legislative and political strategy. In addition, former aide Jennifer Crider moved from the Speaker's staff to become press secretary to the DCCC in 2007. Wolff and Pelosi typically talked four or five times a day and shared a common political lexicon, including the trademark Pelosi phrase that was often repeated to her children: "Proper planning prevents poor performance."[21] Pelosi herself was immersed in every organizational aspect of fund-raising, candidate recruitment, and legislative strategy.

When Emanuel was elected chair of the Democratic Caucus, Pelosi asked him to take charge of the Frontline program to reelect the newly elected members who had brought the Democrats their majority. Integrating the legislative policy effort with campaign awareness, the Democratic Caucus staff mounted a rapid-response operation using press releases, talking points, and advertising to aid at-risk members in responding to Republican attacks in their districts. New members were given visible roles in sponsoring legislation and even in managing it on the floor. As we saw in chapter 3, Pelosi sought to protect these members by shielding them from risky votes and, on some occasions, giving them leave to vote their districts. She relied primarily on Emanuel as the voice of the Frontline members at the leadership table.

In order to expand the Democratic majority, Pelosi tapped Maryland congressman Chris Van Hollen to head the DCCC in the 110th Congress. With a reputation for winning tough campaigns and a smoother and more diplomatic demeanor than Emanuel, Van Hollen was Pelosi's pick not only to continue to enlarge the majority but also to maintain seats won in competitive or GOP-leaning districts.[22] Van Hollen had cochaired with Wasserman Shultz the Red-to-Blue operation run out of the DCCC, targeting vulnerable Republicans and open seats with the goal of expanding the Democratic majority. This operation had raised nearly $7.5 million in 2004 for 27 campaigns, raised nearly $22.6 million in 2006 for 56 campaigns, and worked for 63 candidates in 2008. The 2008 effort was successful in converting 26 seats previously held by the Republicans to Democratic control.[23]

Follow the Money

The lubricant for the Democrats' political machine was money, and Pelosi rode to power in no small part on her fund-raising ability, as we have already noted. Her success as a fund-raiser is legendary, but the overall magnitude of her efforts is hard to track. She maintains her own PAC, she raises money directly into the DCCC, and she appears at events or encourages donors to give directly to members. Among these sources, only the first is directly traceable through the Federal Election Commission. As she has risen in the leadership, the latter two—the more difficult ones to track—have become increasingly potent. Her staff estimates that she has raised around $135 million since being elected to the leadership. When she attends a function to solicit direct contributions to the DCCC, these contributions are not attributed to her in any official accounting. Nor is her work in "directing" contributions to members by "putting them in touch" with donors who might look favorably on them. In fact, this sort of fund-raising has always been central to Pelosi's strategy. Several of our informants, when asked to describe the history of their relationship with Pelosi, mentioned her early assistance in connecting them to potential donors. Published accounts stressed her claim to "have the biggest base of supporters, individual supporters, of anybody in the Congress."[24]

Two key questions can be asked about the Speaker's fund-raising efforts. Where did the money come from? Where did it go? To answer the first question, we conducted separate analyses of donations to either her personal reelection committee or one of her PACs during the election cycles of 1999–2000 through 2005–6. Her PAC to the Future operated continuously through the entire period of her party leadership. She also briefly created a second PAC called Team Majority, which, as noted earlier, she was forced to shut down because it clearly violated federal election laws that limit candidates to a single PAC. Candidates were asked to return these donations.

The data set contains a total of 5,596 contributions to her electoral accounts, totaling $10,602,006. Individuals made 3,547 contributions (63.4%), totaling $5,848,612; other PACs made 2,049 donations (36.6%), totaling $4,753,294. Clearly, her political base rests in the Bay Area, the source of 62.9% of all contributions. Her second base is in the D.C., area, where 15% of her contributions originated. She was also able to raise a significant amount of money across a broader geographic span: she raised 8% of her contributions in the Northeast, 6.8% from the rest of California, and 7.1% in the rest of the country. Over the years, the top five industry sectors giving to her various campaign committees has shifted slightly. In the earlier cycles, unions figured more prominently, whereas professionals and firms in the fields of law, securities and investment, health care, real estate, and insurance have become more generous donors in recent election cycles.[25] Since Federal Election Commission reports record the sex of each donor who has given $200 or more, it is possible to discern whether women figure significantly in Pelosi's fund-raising base. The answer is both yes and no. While women comprise only 36.2% of all individual Pelosi donors, they are on average more generous, with a mean donation of $1,752, compared to $1,590 for men.[26]

For a glimpse of her strategic thinking about funding candidates, her personal PAC provides the most traceability. We analyzed the pattern of donations made out of PAC to the Future over the four election cycles from 1999–2000 to 2005–6. In total, it disbursed $2,773,300 to 279 different candidates; some received donations in all four cycles, others benefited only once during this period. Several points are evident from our summary in table 4.1 of her giving from this PAC.

The pattern of her donations reveals a strategic politician who shifts her giving to reflect the political realities in which she is operating. As she evolved from whip candidate to minority leader and then Speaker, the sources of donations to her PAC shifted. In the later years, it was less of a force for campaign contributions; they dropped off markedly after the 2002 election. Clearly, her PAC became less central to her efforts as she hit the fund-raising circuit on behalf of individual candidates, raised money for the

Table 4.1 Donation Patterns from Speaker Pelosi's PAC to the Future (1999–2006)

Cycle summary	Characteristics of election contest:[a]	Number of races	Average donation
1999–2000	Competitive races	40	$9,174
Total donated: $738,300	• Incumbents	19	$8,605
	• Challengers	9	$9,444
No. of races: 100	• Open	12	$9,872
Average donation: $7,383	Noncompetitive races:	60	$6,189
	• Incumbents	27	$5,963
	• Challengers	21	$5,895
	• Open	12	$7,211
2001–2002	Competitive races:	41	$8,268
Total donated: $872,000	• Incumbents	17	$8,824
	• Challengers	7	$8,571
No. of Races: 115	• Open	17	$8,571
Average donation: $7,583	Noncompetitive races:	73	$7,232
	• Incumbents	51	$7,019
	• Challengers	9	$8,333
	• Open	13	$7,308
2003–2004	Competitive races:	24	$9,375
Total donated: $539,500	• Incumbents	10	$10,500
	• Challengers	7	$8,571
No. of races: 75	• Open	7	$8,571
Average donation: $7,291	Noncompetitive races:	50	$6,190
	• Incumbents	22	$7,500
	• Challengers	20	$4,225
	• Open	9	$7,222
2005–2006	Competitive races:	44	$8,034
Total donated: $623,500	• Incumbents	5	$9,400
	• Challengers	32	$7,391
No. of races: 83	• Open	7	$10,000
	Noncompetitive races:	39	$6,923
Average donation: $7,512	• Incumbents	16	$6,781
	• Challengers	12	$7,000
	• Open	11	$7,045

Source: Data from Federal Elections Commission, "PAC to the Future: Committee Reports—1999–2000 through 2005–6 cycles," http://query/nictusa.com/ cgi-bin/com_detail/ C00344234, accessed May 2, 2009.

[a] A competitive race is defined as one in which the Democratic candidate received 45–55% of the vote; all other races are considered noncompetitive.

DCCC, and encouraged the development of new fund-raising efforts such as the Red-to-Blue program, as noted. Because PAC to the Future was centered on San Francisco, she needed to move beyond its reach in order to raise the amount of money required in the competitive races the Democrats needed to win in order to attain and then retain their majority.

In the first two election cycles, our analysis reveals, a significant portion of her PAC resources went to incumbents, including those in noncompetitive races. We defined for this analysis a competitive race as one in which the Democratic candidate received 45–55% of the total vote, and all other races are considered noncompetitive. Thus in a competitive two-way race, a candidate might win or lose by a margin of victory of 10 percentage points or less. It is important to acknowledge that our definition of a competitive race comes only after the fact—the actual election results—which may not address the psychology of the incumbent, who may perceive a great deal of insecurity leading up to a November election. With that caveat, we note that in the 1999–2000 election cycle, Pelosi gave to 46 incumbents, including 27 whose victory margins averaged 32 percentage points more than their opponents. Again in the 2001–2 cycle, she gave to 68 incumbents, with 51 in noncompetitive races where the average margin of victory over their opponents was 42 points. We believe that this pattern demonstrates that these PAC donations were part of her efforts to rise in the Democratic leadership. Further, in 2001–2 and 2003–4 she gave to those who had been a big part of her winning leadership coalition, most significantly women and minorities. For example, in the run-up to the 2000 and 2002 elections, she gave to 20 different members of the Congressional Black Caucus. In the 2003–4 and 2005–6 electoral cycles combined, she gave to only three. Similarly, her contributions to safe-seat female incumbents were six in 2000 and eight in 2002, prior to becoming Democratic leader, and dropped to one in 2004 and two in 2006, after becoming leader.

We see a shift of strategy once she solidified her hold on the Democratic leadership. Donations to incumbents in noncompetitive races decline in number in the 2003–4 and 2005–6 cycles, though they do not disappear entirely. The donations to noncompetitive races remain a significant part of her giving, and we surmise that she may use her PAC to send a variety of signals, much in the way many people send holiday greeting cards in December. Some donations (like greeting cards) are expected as a matter of protocol, such as giving to other leaders (e.g. Gephardt and Bonior), especially when they move on to run for other offices. Some donations remind even her safe caucus members of her gratitude for their fealty (e.g. donations for the 2002 election to longtime friends and confidantes Louise Slaughter and Rosa DeLauro, both certainly secure in their districts). Yet other donations acknowledge members for some other symbolic purpose, such as recognizing the importance of a particular constituency like the Congressional Black Caucus and the Congressional Hispanic Caucus (e.g. six women of color received donations in 2000). Some donations defy any strategic or symbolic logic but may be an expected part of party business (e.g. successive donations in 2000, 2002, and 2006 to David Obey, a congressional veteran and now Appropriations Committee chair). Certainly, Pelosi spreads her donations broadly.

Clearly, after securing her leadership position, she focused increased attention on channeling money to incumbents who were at risk, challengers, and open seat candidates. These became a bigger part of her PAC giving after 2002, but there is evidence within her PAC giving history of the long-term goal of building a majority. To be sure, the donations to safe incumbents are on average considerably smaller than those aimed at protecting vulnerable incumbents and electing more Democrats in the most competitive open seats.

Perhaps more than anything else, her giving sets the example for others to follow. Loyalty is valued, but building and retaining a majority is paramount. All Democrats share in the benefits of being in the majority. Thus Speaker Pelosi expects other Democrats—members of the team—to contribute to their collective well-being.

CRAFTING AN IMAGE

The public speakership is not just a matter of electioneering. Political scientists have traced its institutional emergence to the postreform era of the late twentieth century, a time when Speakers were not as heavily engaged in electoral politics as Pelosi is today.[27] Previously, congressional leaders were selected more for their institutional stature and legislative skills; but more recently speakers have been expected to articulate policy positions beyond the Beltway, champion legislative achievements to a larger audience, represent the House in negotiations with the president, and be the public face of Congress. Speaker Gingrich, with his expansive aspirations to national leadership, was heralded by some as the epitome of this new development. Pelosi has gone to school on both his accomplishments and his foibles in crafting her own approach to the public role her office now demands.[28]

Image-making at its heart involves intense competition. On the one hand, a political leader tries to assert a favorable public persona, stressing qualities that are expected to resonate positively with the general public and especially voters. On the other hand, the opponents are seeking to exploit and caricature attributes about which the public is predisposed to think negatively. Increasingly, with the aid of focus-group-tested data, professional media consultants coach elected officials and advise professional partisans on strategies of image formation. This coaching in political communications comes with its own baggage, as the public becomes skeptical of manipulation by modern political tactics.[29]

Pelosi has understood that she has a stake in how the public comes to view her. She recognized that Gingrich had allowed himself to become caricatured by his political adversaries. The budget showdown in 1995 spawned the cartoon depiction of "Cry Baby" Gingrich and cemented the public's view of this tempestuous Republican. By contrast, Tip O'Neill's caricature consistently reinforced the public perception that he was a kindly Irishman of generous heart and good humor. An important aspect of Pelosi's image-making was the fact of her being the first female Speaker. We explore the gender aspects of her leadership in more depth in chapter 6. Here, we consider her grandmotherly presentation as but one dimension of her effort to shape her public image.

Baltimore Grandmother

As we saw in chapter 2, Pelosi has always had to contend with her political adversaries' attempts to frame her as a "San Francisco liberal." While these attempts had not prevented her from becoming the leader of the House Democrats or prevented them from winning a majority in the 2006 election, it has been in her interest to diminish her vulnerability as Speaker and avoid being stereotyped as a doctrinaire liberal. Therefore, she organized her investiture as Speaker as a sort of coming-out party and as political theatre designed to recast her own political image and that of her party and to reintroduce herself to the public, in part, as the daughter of an Italian-American Catholic family from Baltimore. According to noted scholar Kathleen Hall Jamieson, Pelosi engaged in a "strategic repositioning" designed to rebrand herself and the Democratic Party going forward to the 2008 elections.[30] We agree that her "strategic repositioning" was directed at immediate political objectives as Jamieson suggests, but we think it also reflected a deeper contemplation on Pelosi's part of the contribution a more centrist image might afford to the prospects for attaining more ambitious policy goals. She had a unique opportunity to define her own image because she was not widely known to the public before she became Speaker. First impressions are often lasting, and she did not wish to become a liability to the newly elected Democrats who would become her "majority makers." This attention to image making proved prescient as indeed she would become the target of many Republican attempts to identify her as a radical liberal.

The image she crafted is complex, parsed from the disparate parts of her background. The "Baltimore Pelosi" is not only a devout Catholic schoolgirl but also the daughter of a tough big-city mayor who knew how to count votes and track favors. She would be the old-fashioned deal-maker and political pragmatist who knew how to work the political process to achieve results, to make deals on both her left and right, and to solve problems which require government action. The "San Francisco Pelosi" would not be a latte-loving Speaker who gazed down on the American people from her castle on a San Francisco hillside; rather, she would capitalize on the Bay Area's proximity to technology and entrepreneurship to incorporate a thoroughly modern image of innovation, internet sophistication, and transparency.

In terms of her role as Speaker and as the first woman to hold the office, she had the opportunity to define herself in a way that would make it more difficult for her most ardent critics to challenge. Since few doubted her toughness, she could afford to be the "grandmotherly Pelosi" who watch-fully tended her brood and shared praise and credit with her members. As images go, several assets worked in her favor. She and her college sweetheart, Paul Pelosi, married in 1963 and raised five children, who in turn produced eight grandchildren. With a devoted husband and an attractive extended family, this stylish, well-tailored grandmother presented a profile that was intended to deter those who would seek to attack with mud and sticks. Well known for her sartorial sense, Pelosi could present herself as having a classy feminine side along with a firm maternal command over her caucus without concern for being framed as either weak or domineering.

As the public face of the House and its Democratic majority, however, Pelosi confronted a problem. Her speaking style can be somewhat stilted, scripted, and awkward. A 2006 appearance on *Meet the Press* was panned for just these reasons.[31] To be sure, House Speakers have not always been rec-ognized for their rhetorical skill.[32] Hastert was hardly loquacious. Moreover, women in politics have often faced criticism of their public speaking pre-cisely because their voices do not fit the expected norms. Pelosi has a char-acteristic way of speaking that her high visibility tends to exaggerate. For example, she loves alliterations. Her mantras "Money, message, mobiliza-tion, and management," "Proper planning prevents poor performance," and "Know people, know policy, know politics too" are just three examples. She tends toward a clipped, staccato delivery and the use of catchphrases about political and legislative strategies such as "move the ball forward," "sequenc-ing," and "leveraging," along with exhortations to her troops toward "focus, purpose, and action." She likes to repeat phrases for emphasis in a drum-beat fashion.

In having a characteristic speaking style, Pelosi is no different than any-body else; we all come to adopt particular ways of thinking and speaking.

Speakers, like most people, are pretty much set in their manner by the time they reach the pinnacle of American politics. But not all private vocabularies are well suited to public presentation. Recognizing the need to communicate more effectively, Pelosi proceeded as she always does, by hard work. She worked with communications consultants to improve her skills. She gained more experience as the demands of the speakership thrust her more regularly into public view. As she gained experience, her performance improved, and her confidence increased. It is surely not coincidental that she did not hold regular press conferences during the first nine months of the 110th Congress but held them regularly thereafter. This was the sign of a Speaker more comfortable in her role and more confident of her speaking ability.

Backlash

While the first woman Speaker chose to accentuate the kinder and gentler female image of grandmother, devoted wife and mother, and capable politician, House Republicans, conservative pundits, and political experts lashed back. The criticism was of a type, mixing partisan criticism of her politics and policies with frequent misogynist commentary on her dress, family, or appearance. The House Republican campaign committee began running ads featuring Pelosi in swing districts they hoped to capture in the 2008 elections. This strategy had failed in 2006, but the Republicans apparently believed that, as Speaker, Pelosi provided a clearer target. The Republican National Campaign Committee sought to link conservative Democratic incumbents to the "San Francisco liberal" once again. Attacks by conservative operatives were more crude. The GOP pollster and media guru Frank Luntz was quoted as saying "I always use the line for Nancy Pelosi, 'You get one shot at a facelift. If it doesn't work the first time, let it go.'"[33] Luntz's critique of Pelosi's facial appearance (while offering no evidence that she has had a face lift) fit a familiar double-bind for older women who get criticized if they look tired and aged and criticized even more if they try to preserve a youthful appearance. Bloggers Michelle Malkin and Matt Drudge, among others, posted unflattering pictures of her.[34] Pelosi's critics mixed attacks on her image and on her policy preferences, and much of the commentary was sexist (a topic to which we return in chapter 6).

The "liberal" tag followed her everywhere, but other attacks attempted to characterize her as privileged and out of touch. One such example was the Republican National Committee's criticism ("Pelosi Power Trip: 'Non-stop' Nancy Seeks Flight of Fancy") of the size of her military jet for cross-country travel, which we discussed in chapter 3. Another case in point occurred as gasoline prices were headed toward record high levels in the spring of 2008. House Republicans seized upon her verbal slip-up on a *Larry King Live* interview in April 2008 as evidence she was "shockingly out-of-touch with cost of the Pelosi Premium on hard-working Americans." In the interview, she misquoted the price of gas as $2.56 gallon when it was actually a dollar higher; however, the full sequence of the quote demonstrates that she thought she had said $3.56 per gallon.[35] (We discuss her handling of the gas crisis later in this chapter.) In 2009, when the debate over health care reform heated up, many conservative bloggers and protesters again portrayed the Speaker as out-of-touch and found a new moniker for Pelosi— "Nazi Nancy." The super-heated rhetoric reached a peak when the National Republican Congressional Committee distributed through the social networking media Twitter a video clip featuring an actor playing a ranting Hitler in praise of Pelosi.[36] Suffice it to say that the high profile of Speaker Pelosi has attracted a rhetorical onslaught more akin to sports bar rants than to civil discourse.

COMMUNICATIONS

Establishing her political persona and improving her communications skills were important steps, but these only served as foundations for doing the real work of the public Speaker: meshing political, legislative, and communications strategies. The coordination and organization of politics and policy not only furthers the Democrats' electoral interests but also suits Pelosi's own leadership style of knitting together a diverse team with herself as its principal organizer.

In the past, both the Democrats and Republicans situated party message functions outside the Speaker's office. The Democrats assigned responsibility for developing party policy positions and related message to the chair and staff of the Democratic Caucus. During the O'Neill era, the caucus would produce policy position papers, and prepare issue briefs and talking points for members. A daily series of "one-minute" speeches was coordinated and delivered at the beginning of each legislative session; some of these were written by caucus staff, others by the staff of the Democratic SPC, others by members themselves. These short speeches delivered a "message of the day" that during the Reagan administration was often reactive to White House pronouncements.

In the GOP, Conference chairs John Boehner and J. C. Watts were responsible for the dissemination of the party message, coordination among the communications directors on the members' staffs, and national outreach to the network of conservative activists and the Republican infrastructure.

Staple Republican tactics included their message of the day, blast faxes (messages simultaneously faxed to large numbers of recipients), outreach to minority groups, and, importantly, efforts to cultivate conservative talk radio. The Conference staff coordinated and assigned members to appear on network talk shows, prepared issue briefs for members to read while traveling to their districts, and organized conferences and forums focusing on Republican issues. Speaker Hastert continued this arrangement with the Conference.

As Speaker, Pelosi was determined to control the message for the Democrats. As we discussed in chapter 2, Gephardt and Pelosi as Democratic leaders assumed more control over party message and communications, and Pelosi continued that effort. As the first woman to become Speaker, she took center stage in the klieg lights. She thus had the potential to marry high public visibility with operational control of political operations and communications strategy; she was the first Speaker so situated.

Special Constituencies

During the 110th Congress, with a relatively narrow majority, Pelosi's political operation continued to work on multiple fronts. The goal was to govern in such a way that Democrats could be poised not only to expand their majority but also to secure the White House and Senate dominance. Outreach to minorities was handled through liaison with the CBC, the CHC, and the Congressional Asian and Pacific Islander Caucus, often with a specific staff member appointed by the Speaker. Staff were assigned to communicate with niche audiences, sometimes unexpected ones such as veterans. Using blogs, district meetings with veterans, special visits to Veterans Administration health-care facilities, and reports touting legislative initiatives, Pelosi pointed out shortfalls in Bush's funding of veterans programs and built new alliances with veterans' organizations.[37] Outreach to religious groups was organized by whip Jim Clyburn, an ordained minister. The Frontline project to reelect vulnerable Democrats was headed by Emanuel and run out of the Democratic Caucus. At her website, the Speaker has also showcased the work of seven different "communities," highlighting her own programs and covering various racial and cultural minorities, women, the young, and the lesbian, gay, bisexual, and transgendered constituency. All of these web-based outreach efforts have included periodic press releases, photos of her meeting with this group and that, YouTube clips on congressional topics of interest, and linkages to advocacy groups and opportunities to act or contribute to the Speaker's efforts.

An example of one of the more developed and multifaceted of these outreach endeavors can be seen in her efforts to reach younger voters. She organized among members the 30 Something Working Group, staffed by her office and featuring its own website. During the 2006 election cycle, the group sponsored what was called Rap, Rock 'n Roll Radio Row to communicate the impact on young workers of President Bush's privatization plan for Social Security. Teaming with professional athletes and musicians, the 30 Something Working Group organized debates and voter outreach efforts on college campuses around the country. This demographic and ideological outreach was complemented by a specific focus on at-risk members and potential takeover seats. In January 2008, Pelosi took part in an online chat on global warming with students at San Francisco State University as part of a nationwide event touted as the largest teach-in, in history. More than 40 additional members participated with thousands of young people at some 1500 high schools, colleges and universities in discussions of strategies to combat climate change, including enhanced public transportation, increased use and development of renewable energy, and cap-and-trade legislation.

Staffing

At the staff level, Pelosi made an important decision to redeploy a significant portion of the policy staff that Gephardt had assembled to focus principally on message and communications. Message would be centralized in the Speaker's office, extending a comprehensive communications strategy and operation in the speakership to a new level. As recently as 1971, Speaker Albert had become the first to appoint an official press secretary, assigning the duties to a junior member of his staff. Subsequently, Democratic Speakers had hired former reporters or trusted congressional aides to facilitate their interactions with the House press corps, promoting their message as the party message.

When the Republicans took control of the House in 1995 they were led by a Speaker who had attained great national visibility. Gingrich sought to translate his renown into influence by actively seeking media attention. His press secretary, Tony Blankley, occupied a prominent desk right outside the Speaker's office. Given Gingrich's high and controversial profile, Blankley was often on the defensive, fending off criticism and seeking to redirect press attention to the issues on which the Republicans hoped to legislate. Blankley was not in charge of the overall GOP communications effort, which was run out of the Republican Conference.

Hastert's personal relationship with the press was dramatically different. After the controversy that engulfed Speaker Gingrich and contributed to his political demise, the Republicans settled on Hastert in part because of his nonexistent public profile. He did not want or seek public attention and sought to operate as the quintessential insider, allowing other Republican leaders (prominently Tom DeLay, first as whip and then as floor leader) to serve as the public face of the party. Hastert's two press secretaries, John Feerehy and Ron Bonjean, faced the challenge of advertising and activating a sometimes reluctant Speaker.

One measure of the meagerness of previous Speakers' press efforts was the brevity of the daily press interactions. Speakers Rayburn, McCormack, and Albert met with the press for five minutes before the House went into session each legislative day. O'Neill, desiring a greater media presence, extended this to fifteen minutes. His second press secretary, Chris Matthews (who later attained visibility as a journalist and television commentator) distributed written statements and fact sheets to the press and spent much of his time in telephone conversations with media commentators and journalists, aggressively pushing the Speaker's message. Speaker Gingrich initiated a regular half-hour televised press conference, hoping to emerge as an alternative voice to President Clinton. Coming at precisely the moment when he was coming under fire from Democrats making allegations of his ethical misconduct, the press conferences quickly degenerated into fencing matches between Gingrich and the press corps, and he quickly terminated them. Hastert did not renew them.

For her communications effort, Pelosi turned to Brendan Daly, a media relations veteran with experience on the Hill and in the Clinton administration (the White House trade office and the Peace Corps) who came from a long family line of newspaper journalists. He joined Pelosi's inner circle of staff advisers in 2002 as communications director. When she became Speaker, the media operation expanded from a traditional focus on the "front door" news outlets (e.g. traditional mainstream professional news reporters) to include the "back door" of citizen-produced news and commentary (e.g. blogging and social networking in the new media). Daly, credited with being the Speaker's "spinner," plays defense in daily interactions with her critics and antagonists and offense in reaching out to friendly reporters or posting the Speaker's own messages. These have included Youtube broadcasts of Oversight Committee hearings, which garner play hits in excess of 100,000. The media practitioners on the Speaker's staff pay aggressive attention to both old and new media, and Daly is at the center of the operation, aided by a substantial staff.[38] As we have mentioned, the Speaker also has implemented a weekly televised press conference which is rebroadcast on CSPAN.

The Media Environment

The Speaker's media and outreach efforts are based on an understanding that citizens and voters are increasingly getting their news not from mainstream media but from the internet.[39] Managing the news environment is now a 24/7 dynamic, with hour-to-hour news deadlines, a continuous need to generate cable television and blogosphere updates, and new opportunities for targeted messaging and mobilization through YouTube and the netroots. Speaker O'Neill faced major national papers such as the *Washington Post*, *New York Times*, and the *Boston Globe*, the three broadcast television networks, and specialized outlets like the *Congressional Quarterly* and the *National Journal*. Speaker Pelosi now must contend with not only these but also cable networks, including CNN, Fox News, and MSNBC, and a panoply of international broadcasters. She must also deal with the around-the-clock commentary of talk radio, internet publications such as *Politico*, a host of alternative and specialized media (including two newspapers devoted to Congress), the blogosphere (including the most heavily trafficked—Huffington Post, Daily Kos, Talking Points Memo, Think Progress, Drudge Report, Hot Air, and Crooks and Liars), and finally late-night comedy faux news shows (prominently Jon Stewart's *Daily Show* and Stephen Colbert's *Colbert Report*).[40] Speaker Pelosi's operation strives to reach all of these outlets, recognizing both the need to generate "buzz" in the blogosphere and the realities of the "echo chamber."

This concept requires some clarification. According to our sources, "echo chamber" is a phrase Pelosi often uses. Her communications staff is entirely familiar with it. The term was first coined in 1998 by public relations strategists for Philip Morris, which sought to blunt claims linking smoking with cancer through a counter-campaign of "favorable information to resonate with and from various sources in order to increase its credibility with the target audience."[41] Scholars Kathleen Hall Jamieson and Joseph N. Capella applied the term to political discourse in a study examining how Republicans have sought to disseminate their message in a network of conservative media outlets.[42] Focusing on selected high-visibility conservative venues, such as Fox News and the Rush Limbaugh radio broadcast, Jamieson and Capella concluded that the Republicans' goal was to stimulate their base and, in the fashion of an echo, to return the sound to its point of origin. The strategy was to have conservative messages reverberating through different media so as to create an "echo chamber" that would reinforce a shared viewpoint and help to buttress and arm members of the conservative base to respond to opponents' arguments. Gingrich deployed the strategy in the 1990s, and in the 2000s Karl Rove perfected it as a way to win elections by turning out more base voters. They believed that in a polarized electorate, there was no political center to which they could appeal.

The Democrats' deployment of the metaphor may be different from that ascribed by scholars to the Republicans. Realizing that it would be necessary to win seats in conservative districts, Pelosi could not afford to simply rely on a network of liberal media outlets to stimulate the left; it was also necessary to promote the party message beyond the party's base. Thus, her goal was to communicate through as many venues as possible—liberal media outlets, mainstream national media, and local media around the country. To extend the metaphor, she sought a larger echo chamber that extended beyond the mainstream of her party. To make the party's case to a broader range of voters, it was necessary to stress facts as well as ideology. Staple elements of her media operation were traditional press releases, fact sheets addressing various areas of public policy, and "in the news" reprints of news articles recirculated from a wide range of media outlets.

Pelosi also recognized that traditional media sources were rapidly being supplanted by alternative information and opinion outlets. Scholars have yet to unravel fully the direction of influence and the complex interactions between the traditional news professionals and the largely volunteer blogosphere. The infancy of the research reflects the exploding growth of the blogosphere. Some factors are understood, however. First, journalists, opinion leaders, and political elites read blogs to take advantage of the early warning system—a kind of canary-in-the-mine signal from one's opponents or a means of launching trial balloons among one's supporters. This discourse has tremendous potential to shape the framing of stories when they do hit the traditional media.[43] At the same time, bloggers see their power mainly deriving from their ability to bypass traditional media gatekeepers; to confront and influence them, if necessary to "crush" or neutralize, their advantages, and then to mobilize true believers.[44] That attitude plays itself out in sometimes coarse and angry posts.[45] Most political blogs and internet communities are organized along ideological lines, with little crossover linking left- and right-wing opinion.[46] Therefore, as the blogosphere has expanded, public officials and campaign operatives have come to see blogs and other internet tools as vital weapons not only in communication but also in political mobilization and warfare.[47]

Results

Pelosi has been focused on this diverse media environment from the beginning. From the Speaker's office, a daily log of media contacts—circulated to top staff—tallies the fact sheets, speeches, one-minute floor speeches, member interviews, and press conferences being coordinated under Daly's watchful eye. The media outlets recorded in the four weeks of logs we reviewed reflect the full range of the New American Politics media environment into which Speaker Pelosi seeks to extend her voice. In a typical week, the staff is coordinating bookings of more than 20 members on talk radio, nationally syndicated cable television shows, and local television broadcasts. The Speaker herself makes time for interviews with media outlets as diverse as *Rolling Stone, Larry King, GQ, CNN en Espanol*, MTV (with editorial participation from the *Washington Post, Associated Press, Reuters,* and *Politico*), the *New York Times, Good Morning America*, and Jon Stewart's *Daily Show*. She has also appeared quite frequently on the major television news programs and has sat for extended interviews with leading broadcast journalists. Such appearances were rare for her predecessors.

Pelosi has become certainly the most media-accessible Speaker in history. In the first few months of her speakership, the mainstream media returned the favor with extensive coverage. Political scientists Karen Kedrowski and Rachel Grower, in a content analysis of three major national newspapers, the three network television news programs, and CNN, found that Pelosi generated two to four times the news coverage of any of her predecessors except Gingrich.[48] Their analysis extended only from the 2006 election through the first two months of the 110th Congress, which were compared to a similar period for six other former speakers and Senate majority leader Harry Reid. Among these news outlets, Pelosi received almost twice as much coverage as Reid (817 stories compared to 433). During this period of his speakership, Gingrich had the most media visibility (2,454 stories), which coincided with his daily press conferences and aggressive presentation of himself as the national spokesperson for the GOP. His high visibility also reflected great media interest in the first Republican Speaker in 40 years. Media attention can cut in both directions, positive and negative. As soon as he perceived a hostile media environment, he dropped the daily press briefings, and he provided only selective access later in his speakership.

As one of the most visible congressional leaders in history, Pelosi has drawn media attention in unusual ways. One indicator of her visibility is the two adult biographies and five biographies for young readers that were written about her during the 110th Congress.[49] She also published her own book, *Know Your Power: A Message to America's Daughters*. These books, some filled with chatty details about the Pelosi household and others focused on her pioneering political career, are prompted by her historic role as the first woman speaker; but it is a remarkable contrast that among other postreform Speakers only O'Neill and Gingrich have been the subject of adult biographies and none has been the subject of a juvenile biography. All of the previous postreform speakers have penned their own memoirs, some with co-authors.

Pelosi's communications operation reaches out to new media entrepreneurs and social media communities such as Digg, which featured her in its first Digg Dialogg, in which users could submit questions and then vote for their favorite questions to pose to the interview guest. The Speaker has posted to Momsrising.org. Exclusive interviews are extended to celebrity bloggers, and staff float policy ideas with friendly bloggers to get an early read on public reactions. A staff of three, headed by Karina Newton, tracks the blogosphere and plans Pelosi's forays into it. The goals of all of this activity are as follows: first, to take advantage of new technologies to democratize and make politics personal in ways that Sunday morning news talk shows cannot; second, to promote an aura of accountability and transparency in congressional workings; third, to maintain a rapid-response effort that competes to frame issues in ways most favorable to the Democrats' agenda; and finally, to take advantage of the changing technologies that are rapidly transforming how people get news and information.[50] It helps that Pelosi understands the lexicon of Silicon Valley and the dynamic nature of changing technology—a dynamism that infuses the worldview of a good part of her constituency and has also fueled her embrace of an innovation agenda. She became the first member of Congress to start an individual YouTube account, to participate in a Digg-It interview, to create work space in the Capitol for alternative media—Bloggers Alley and Radio Row—and to carry on a fake feud with comedian Stephen Colbert. As part of the launch of Congress's new YouTube hub, Pelosi okayed a cat's eye-view video of the Speaker's office, which then turned into the popular internet spoof of "rickrolling" (i.e. the abrupt online link to pop singer Rick Astley's music video). And yes, this Italian grandmother of eight has a Facebook account and is on Twitter.

In terms of visibility in the blogosphere, Pelosi rivaled President George W. Bush and the presidential candidates through much of 2008. Figure 4.2 compares the number of mentions of Pelosi in the blogosphere (obviously not all are friendly) with those of other congressional leaders and the president during a six-month period from the late spring through the fall of 2008. The number of blogosphere references to Speaker Pelosi was three to four times that of her congressional colleagues and similar to that of President Bush.[51]

MESSAGE AND MESSENGER

Pelosi has striven to perfect a message and be heard as the voice of the Democrats. To understand the content and style of this public effort, we analyzed the most visible portions of her communications and outreach operation: the 79 floor speeches, 50 press conferences, 60 other speeches, and

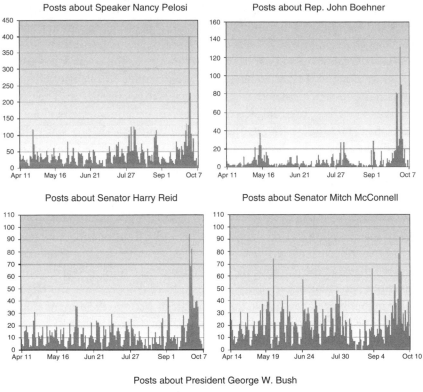

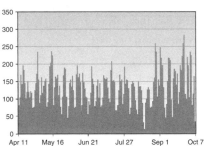

Figure 4.2   Daily Blog Posts about Congressional Leaders and the President (April–October 2008)

Note: The y-axis, which tracks the volume of daily blog posts, varies considerably for each of the individuals above with Pelosi having the largest volume, followed by Bush. The others trail significantly in terms of number of posts per day.

Source: Technorati.com, "Bloggers Central: Chart/posts containing...", http://technorati.com/chart/pelosi?compare=pelosi&chartdays=180, accessed October 7, 2008.

1,504 press releases the Speaker's office issued from January 2007 through the November 2008 election. In the first few months of 2007 she held irregular press conferences, but in September 2007 she began a schedule of weekly press interactions.[52] Over the course of the 110th Congress, her office issued 941 press announcements (not including 373 scheduling releases), 73 fact sheets, and 117 reprises of favorable media commentary titled "In the News." Approximately 200 video clips, mostly from C-SPAN and featuring floor speeches or oversight hearings, were posted through Youtube to various sites, including her own website, according to her staff. This output makes her the most prolific "public speaker" in history.

Probing more carefully into this public speakership, we want to assess, not merely describe, Pelosi's message and outreach efforts. In this regard, we see evidence that she has achieved consistency and discipline in the communications effort. To do that, she first has had to get her fractious caucus to make strategic choices about messaging. Then she has had to execute that message through the tools available to her. Finally, she has had to balance her predilections as a tough partisan with the institutional imperatives of leading the entire House.

The challenge for any Speaker is to allocate scarce personal and institutional resources to shape public policy and to frame policy efforts in the most favorable way to benefit her party in the public's mind. In chapter 3, we discussed Pelosi's mastery of the internal workings of the multi-ring circus that is the U.S. House. Here we focus on her messaging effort to compete in the public arena beyond the Beltway. In considering the message she wanted to convey, she needed first to establish the identity of the Democratic Party. To win elections, a political party needs to offer the voters something in which the party believes and then hope that the voters will come to believe in it as well. As her leadership campaigns presaged, she wanted the Democrats to be Democrats, not quasi-Republicans. She also wanted to capitalize on the evident public hunger for change, to present to the voters not only different policy prescriptions but also a sense of renewal. This required her to sustain a focused message, which was branded the New Direction Congress.

During her rise to leadership House Democrats engaged in a robust debate over whether to move more to the center or to position themselves closer to their party's left wing. Pelosi's election marked a triumph of the left, but she recognized that the House Democrats could not anchor their message on the left wing of the political spectrum. Positioning the Democratic minority to seize the majority and governing a diverse caucus with a narrow majority necessitated that she be pragmatic and strategic in reframing and delivering her party's message. How could she both stress a distinctive Democratic brand and appeal to swing voters?

Reframing

Understanding that she had to settle on a message capable of uniting the various elements of the Democratic Party, she turned for help to University of California linguistics expert George Lakoff, whose book *Don't Think of an Elephant!* had captivated thousands of Democrats with the argument that they were losing the issues debate to the Republicans primarily because of a lack of understanding of the importance of language and framing.[53] Lakoff's "thin paperback became as ubiquitous among Democrats in the Capitol as Mao's Little Red Book" was in China during the Cultural Revolution.[54] In it, he proposes, in effect, that progressives fight fire with fire and challenge the Republicans in the war of words. He argues that the two different political views of the nation held by conservatives and progressives reflect different moral understandings of the family: the strict father model and the nurturant parent model. Each has its own emotive vocabulary and linguistic frames. Progressives, he argues, need to reframe public discourse (not move to the right) in more nurturant terminology to appeal to swing voters. The language of nurturance and care was no stretch for Pelosi, the mother and grandmother whose career was anchored in advocacy around issues of AIDS/HIV, human rights, and preserving the environment for the next generation and beyond.

Reframing is not a new idea. Social scientists acknowledge the impact that frames—central organizing concepts—have on cognitive processing and public understanding of issues; and political scientists have analyzed how interest group issue framing, media content, and policy decisions interrelate.[55] Political scientist E. E. Schattschneider observed in 1960 that interest groups and advocates compete to frame public policy debates expansively or narrowly in order to affect media coverage, mobilize or contain public opinion, and ultimately influence decision-makers.[56] Political scientist Murray Edelman argued cogently to an earlier generation of students and scholars that symbols matter in politics. More than a decade ago, sociologist William Gamson showed how media discourse with its metaphors, visual images, moral appeals and other symbolic devices shaped the way that working class citizens talk about politics and political issues.[57]

If political scientists had already "framed" framing, so to speak, it was the Republicans who first applied these scholars' concepts in practical action. In 1994, GOP political consultant Luntz orchestrated the Republican Contract With America. Intellectually bolstered by both bachelor's and doctoral degrees in political science, Luntz conducted polls and focus groups to find the right language for the Republicans to use to "sell" their message to the American people.[58] In Luntz's vocabulary, every increase in federal revenue proposed by a Democrat was to be called a tax increase; the few suggested by Republicans were "revenue enhancers." Luntz relabeled the estate tax the "death tax," coined the term "partial birth abortion" to describe the procedure medical professionals call "intact dilation and extraction," and relabeled oil drilling "energy exploration." Republican politicians jumped on board the Luntz wagon. George W. Bush built his political career on the term "compassionate conservatism," which retrospectively proved devoid of meaning. He put his spin on world political geography by lumping three rogue regimes into an "axis of evil." He named his campaign against Al Qaeda a "war on terror," creating a pretext for the use of extraordinary executive power under the Constitution. The influential conservative intellectual Richard Weaver titled one of his books *Ideas Have Consequences*.[59] And indeed, ideas are communicated through words.

Democrats had tried before to repackage their agenda. In 2004, House Democrats crafted a pamphlet declaring their core values and proclaiming a "new partnership for America's future."[60] With the help of "branding expert" John Cullinane, the presentation of the six values—"prosperity, national security, fairness, opportunity, community and accountability"—was followed by a laundry list of familiar policies. In addition, Pelosi drew on the thinking of marketing guru Jack Trout, another of the experts called in to advise her caucus.[61] Trout characterizes marketing as warfare, suggests the need for simplicity in message, and offers the admonition that successful products "differentiate or die" in the competition.

Not everyone agreed that the problem confronting the Democrats would be solved by the selection of the right words. From the center, Rahm Emanuel and Bruce Reed of the DLC called Lakoff "flat-out wrong" and called for a plan of "big ideas," not just words.[62] On the left, commentator Marc Cooper castigated the Lakoff thesis, arguing that only a "jackass" could believe it was possible to defeat the Republicans by means of a mere change in vocabulary.[63] Progressive critics also called for a policy agenda based on ideas but not necessarily the ones centrist Democrats proposed. To the progressives, the agenda needed to represent more than "Republican Lite."

The difference between Emanuel's and Pelosi's strategic approaches reflects the underlying dynamic within the Democratic Party in the era of the New American Politics. Centrists like Emanuel believed that the Democrats needed to develop big ideas that would appeal to the center of the electorate. The liberal base of the party believed that they already had big ideas and simply needed more effective marketing. The DLC emphasized refashioning the Great Society; the progressives wanted to fulfill its promise. Meanwhile, Blue Dogs thought the Democrats should balance the federal budget.

This divide was not only ideological but also cultural and generational. The grassroots of the old Democratic Party had been hard-soled organizations whose shoe leather helped bootstrap a chronically underfunded political party. The labor unions and public interest groups were traditional political organizations with membership lists, dues structures, hierarchical organization, and bylaws. The renewed base of the Democratic Party was now the netroots: a conglomeration of ad hoc adherents that often did not meet the dictionary definition of "organization." They were "horizontal" rather than "vertical" (i.e. decentralized and not hierarchical), self-renewing, flexible, and as resistant to the staid ways of the old Democratic Party as they were to the institutional inertia they associated with "business as usual" in Washington. These new political activists came together in cyberspace through outfits such as MoveOn.org and venues such as the Daily Kos. They wanted more progressive policies, and they wanted a more open, accessible, and participative government. In the latter respect, they were the legatees of the 1960s movements embracing civil rights, women's liberation, the environment, and consumer protection and, of course, opposing the war in Vietnam. They were a thousand small donations rather than deep pockets, fingers on the keyboard more than boots on the ground.[64]

The New Direction Congress

Pelosi's search for a new vocabulary was in fact an attempt to bridge this strategic divide within the party. And who could better craft such a message than a daughter of Baltimore and the doyenne of Silicon Valley? The concept of the New Direction Congress was her solution. In order to grasp its utility, one must consider not only the associated substantive legislative proposals (which we discussed in chapter 3) but also the language in which the concept was expressed.

Under the rubric of the New Direction Congress, Democrats proposed the legislative initiatives offered as the First 100 Hours package, born from the Six for '06 campaign pledge. As table 4.2 suggests, the messaging morphed from Lakoff's suggested 10-word philosophy for progressives. The 10-word liberal philosophy lacked the familiarity and popular understanding of the conservative philosophy, thus the Democrats added specificity. The Six for '06 frame then provided an initial vehicle for more specific ideas, and the New Direction Congress frame in turn presented a corresponding set of broader goals in fairly innocuous bullet points. The label "New Direction Congress" offered simplicity and differentiation—the 110th Congress would not be the old Republican version—even if the initial agenda was short on the specifics of direction. Many from the Progressive Caucus found the message effort under-developed and too vacuous, far short of a governing philosophy and lacking a clear embrace of stances they wanted such as a commitment to end

Table 4.2 From Lakoff's 10-Word Philosophies to Reframing for a New Direction Congress

Lakoff's summary of conservatives' philosophy	Lakoff's summary of progressives' philosophy	The Six for '06 First 100 Hours legislation	Pelosi's framing of the "New Direction Congress" goals
Strong defense	Stronger America[a]	Implement 9/11 commission recommendations	Real security—at home and overseas
Free markets	Broad prosperity	Increase minimum wage	Prosperity—better American jobs, better pay
		Cut student loan interest rates	Opportunity—college access for all
Lower taxes	Better future	Repeal big oil subsidies; invest in renewable fuels	Energy independence—lower gas prices
Smaller government	Effective government	Promote stem cell research	Affordable health care; life-saving science
Family values	Mutual responsibility[b]	Lower Medicare drug costs	Retirement security and dignity
		Implement PAYGO budget discipline and ethics oversight	

Sources: George Lakoff, Don't Think of an Elephant! (White River Junction, VT: Chelsea Green Publishing) 2004, p. 94; Nancy Pelosi, A New Direction for America, http://www.speaker.gov/pdf/thebook.pdf, accessed October 3, 2009; and Democratic Caucus, U.S. House of Representatives, 100 Hours Legislation, http://www.dems.gov/index.asp?Type=B_PR&SEC=%7B449BBE79-704A-423C-AF88-6D9DF9D987D8%7D&DE=%EBADF72A3-AEB7-4946-9831-183B47B00B55%7D, accessed October 3, 2009.

[a] By "Stronger America," Lakoff refers not just to military resources but to U.S. strength in the world, our economy, educational system, environment and communities.

[b] By "Mutual responsibility," Lakoff defines mutually supportive and caring families and communities.

the Iraq War, a fix of the alternative minimum tax, immigration reform, and progress on poverty and economic inequality. Comparing the conservatives' and the progressives' messaging, *New York Times Magazine* writer Matt Bai observed:

> Look at the differences between the two. The Republican version is an argument, a series of philosophical assertions that require voters to make concrete choices about the direction of the country. Should we spend more or less on the military? Should government regulate industry or leave it unfettered? Lakoff's formulation, on the other hand, amounts to a vague collection of the least objectionable ideas in American life. Who out there wants to make the case against prosperity and a better future? Who doesn't want an effective government?[65]

The die, however, was cast, and the 110th Congress became the New Direction Congress, at least in the Democrats' vernacular. By 2008, the message had demonstrated an elasticity and resilience that could embrace a changing political environment. The logo displayed atop regular updates entitled "A New Direction for America" now displayed a number of catch-phrases—"Defend our country," "Strengthen our families," "Preserve our planet," "Grow our economy," "Restore accountability." Who could argue?

The New Direction Congress concept also provided rhetorical consistency to the House Democrats' progress reports and frequent reminders that the "old direction" was the responsibility of the Bush administration or the Republicans in Congress. For example, shortly before the November 2008 elections, the Democrats released a status report, "A New Direction for America," claiming credit for a host of initiatives on energy, green jobs, benefits for veterans, and college affordability, while laying blame squarely on the GOP, noting:

> The New Direction Congress has enacted into law key legislation to rebuild our economy, strengthen our national security, care for America's children and families, protect our planet, and restore accountability—with significant bipartisan support more than 70 percent of the time. More progress was prevented by the failed ideology and the continued obstruction of the Bush Administration and his allies in Congress. A New Direction for America is still needed.[66]

On Message

Having been a prominent architect of this messaging effort, how well has Pelosi fulfilled her role as messenger? Has she stayed on message? How have events intruded, or not? Our analysis shows that she has been fairly disciplined in her focus on the major issues and is an advocate who mixes policy and partisanship in the leadership of the House. Stylistically adopting a competitive and confrontational approach, she reflects both her Baltimore street-fighting political roots and the advice of marketing expert Trout with his promotion of a philosophy of marketing as warfare. The empirical evidence for these conclusions comes from our analysis of 1,504 media releases and 189 speeches by Pelosi (79 floor speeches, two State of the Union responses, 50 press conferences, 32 public speeches, and 26 joint public appearances). The media releases were coded for issue, policy or partisan content, type of release, and the primary voice in the message. About one-third (511) of the 1,504 media messages were scheduling announcements, routine House business, or nonsubstantive congratulatory notices; thus we have focused most of our analysis on 993 substantive media releases.

Our content analysis of the media releases and speeches focused on several variables. For both speeches and media releases, we utilized the topical issue codes developed by the Policy Agenda Project at the University of Washington.[67] Primary and secondary issues were coded, particularly for speeches or press conferences where the Speaker covered more than one topic. Any media release with specific and explicit partisan content (e.g. blaming actions of President Bush and the House GOP or claiming credit for the Democrats) was coded as "partisan" in nature, as opposed to media messages that focused strictly on policy explanation or analysis or details. (Speeches were also coded along stylistic dimensions.) We discuss the gendered dimension of Pelosi's style in Chapter 6. Here, we are most interested in a competitive-confrontational speaking style as contrasted with facilitative-conciliatory style, because this dimension captures the degree of combativeness in her speeches.[68] Where she used both styles or neither style could be discerned, a dominant style for this dimension was not assigned. Table 4.3 reports the issue content and style of all these communication efforts.

As table 4.3 suggests, the Speaker maintained a focused messaging operation during the 110th Congress, though some issues in the New Direction Congress got more play than others. Four issues comprised more than 70% of the media releases: (1) the economy, including the first stimulus package, mortgage crisis, and financial meltdown; (2) the Iraq War; (3) foreign policy and military matters other than Iraq; and (4) energy independence and climate change, the Speaker's signature personal priority.[69] In her speeches, the same four issues, plus health care and the debate over SCHIP, accounted for more than 68% of the primary speech topics. In spite of the Democrats' identification of retirement security as part of the New Direction Congress, retirement and Social Security issues were notably absent. All of the issues provided fodder for partisan point-scoring, but some messages took on a

Table 4.3 Issue Content, Partisan Tone, and Style of the Speaker Pelosi's Media Releases and Speeches

Issue[a]	Number of media releases (% of total)[b]	% media releases coded as partisan	Number of speeches (% of total)[c]	% speeches coded as "competitive-confrontational"
The economy, budget, taxes	218 (22%)	54.6%	29 (15.3%)	34.5%
Iraq War	180 (18.1%)	83.3	22 (11.6%)	68.2%
Foreign policy, military affairs	128 (12.9%)	32.8	33 (17.5%)	27.3%
Government operations	78 (7.9%)	75.6	6 (3.2%)	33.3%
Civil rights, women's rights	30 (3.0%)	20.0	13 (6.9%)	7.7%
Health, SCHIP	78 (7.9%)	51.3	22 (11.6%)	59.1%
Energy independence, environment	172 (17.3%)	64.5	23 (12.2%)	43.5%
Labor, employment, immigration	18 (1.8%)	44.4	5 (2.6%)	0%

Source: Calculations and coding by the authors of speeches and press releases from Speaker Nancy Pelosi Website, News Room, "Press Releases." Accessed at http://speaker.gov/newsroom/pressrelease_archive.

[a] $N = 993$, in categorical analysis of partisan versus policy media messages; the differences between issues is statistically significant (Pearson chi-square $= 127.563$(a), df $= 8$, $p = .000$).

[b] $N = 189$, in categorical analysis of competitive-confrontational speeches compared to facilitative-conciliatory speeches, the differences between issues is statistically significant (Pearson chi-square $= 58.423$, df 16, $p = .000$).

[c] Media releases and speeches on other topics are not represented in this table. A total of 91 media releases (9.2%) and 36 speeches (19%) were on other topics.

more partisan tone than others, with again the most notable—and statistically significant—being the Iraq War; government operations, including many of the House committees' oversight hearings and investigations into the Bush administration's activities; energy issues; and health care. On these issues, more than half of the releases were coded as partisan. Foreign policy and military affairs, along with civil rights issues, drew less partisan media messaging; among these topics, less than a third of the releases were coded as partisan.

Table 4.3 also shows that Pelosi does not pull her rhetorical punches. The characterization of a speech as competitive-confrontational required multiple verbal jabs or partisan point-scoring to establish its overall tone; categorizing a media release as having explicit partisan content could reflect a single partisan claim or allegation.[70] As a result, the percentage of speeches coded as competitive-confrontational is lower than the coding of partisan content in media releases. Overall, however, one out of three of her speeches was coded as competitive-confrontational, while her press conferences took on that style almost half (46.9%) of the time. The sharper rhetoric contained in press conferences is probably attributable to the types of questions posed by reporters attempting to highlight party differences and partisan maneuvering. The question-and-answer format also presents the Speaker when she is most unscripted, offering potential danger (an important example of which we address in chapter 5).

Not surprisingly, the agenda of issues took on a volatility driven by events and legislative activity. Figure 4.3 illustrates how the dominant issues played out over the period from January 2007 to the November 2008 election. While media messaging spiked on the topic of health care in October 2007 as the SCHIP bill was approved by the House, healthcare issues virtually disappeared as a battle front in the messaging war until July 2008, when Congress overrode Bush's veto of the Medicare Improvements for Patients and Providers Act. Foreign policy and votes on the Iraq War produced bursts of media activity throughout the period. In 2008, as the Speaker pushed her climate change priorities and the housing market began to crater, the economy and energy issues dominated the agenda.

Over the course of the 110th Congress, partisan rhetoric intensified. Figure 4.4 shows how the balance between policy-only media releases and partisan releases shifted from 2007 to 2008. Certainly part of the shift toward more partisanship may be attributed to the approaching election period. In 9 out of the 12 months of 2007, the media releases with a policy focus outnumbered those with a partisan tone, but in 2008 partisan releases outnumbered policy releases, often by margins of two or three to one. The party policy differences and the spike in gas prices

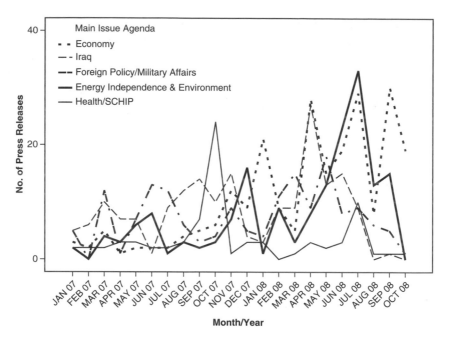

Figure 4.3   Issue Changes in Speaker Pelosi's Media Messaging in the 110th Congress (January 2007–November 2008)

Source: Speaker Nancy Pelosi, "Newsroom: Press Releases," http://www.speaker.gov/newsroom/pressreleases, accessed multiple times from January 2007 to November 2008.

proved a combustible mix. In all, 97 (approximately 56%) of the 173 media releases on energy independence were issued between May and September 2008—56 (32%) of them in June and July alone. The energy debate offers a good window on the message wars, so we offer an account of it here.

Crisis at the Pump

The partisan war over energy intensified in the summer of 2008 and offers an object case in the vicissitudes of political messaging. Pelosi had made the environment and climate change the major substantive policy focus of her speakership. These issues necessarily impinged on energy policy. She found herself confronting a White House controlled by two men with backgrounds in the oil and gas industry. They offered a ripe target for her messaging operation. In May 2007, the Speaker's office, in one of its releases, offered an

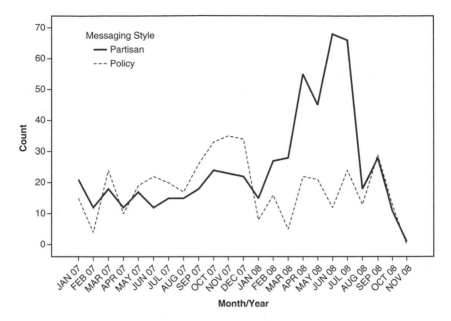

Figure 4.4   Changes in Partisan Tone of Speaker Pelosi's Media Messaging in 110th Congress (January 2007 to November 2008)

Source: Speaker Nancy Pelosi, "Newsroom: Press Releases," http://www.speaker.gov/newsroom/ pressreleases, accessed multiple times from January 2007 to November 2008.

accusation that the Bush administration and Republicans were lining the "pockets of Big Oil" and failing to protect consumers from "those who are cheating America's families by artificially inflating the price of gasoline."[71] Gas prices were, at that time, hovering around $3 per gallon.[72] Fourteen months later, they had spiked to over $4 per gallon, a historic high in the United States.

Sensing a chance to rescue what at that time appeared to be very bleak prospects for the November elections, Republicans proposed to increase domestic oil production by opening the Arctic National Wildlife Refuge and currently protected areas of the continental shelf to more oil exploration and extraction. "Drill baby drill" became the GOP mantra. Pelosi was determined to head off these efforts and offered four arguments in response. She pressed the point that any access granted to currently protected areas would not bring supply on line for several years. She argued that any increase in domestic supply would be easily offset by the ability of the Organization of the Petroleum Exporting Countries (OPEC) to reduce its own production in order to maintain higher prices. To provide immediate price relief at the pump, she advocated release of fuel from the nation's Strategic Petroleum

Reserves. And she contended that the major oil companies already owned leasing rights to millions of acres of public lands that were not in production. "Use it or lose it" became her refrain.

The Republicans counterattacked relentlessly. They invented a new gasoline "price index," the "Pelosi Premium," suggesting that somehow the Speaker was responsible for the spike in gasoline prices in 2008 because she opposed expanded oil exploration and production in environmentally sensitive areas. The House Republican Conference produced an attack video that many GOP congresspersons posted to their websites or personal blogs. Conservative bloggers came out in force; some tagged her as "Captain Planet" Pelosi and "Mafia Princess" Pelosi.

She fought back. In an interview with CNN's Wolf Blitzer on July 17, 2008, she attributed the skyrocketing gas prices to "two oil men in the White House and their protectors in the United States Senate."[73] She went on to broaden her criticism of the president: "You know, God bless him, bless his heart, president of the United States, a total failure, losing all credibility with the American people on the economy, on the war, on energy, you name the subject."[74] The Speaker's office issued a release with the title "Top Ten Questions for the House GOP on Energy" describing the GOP's energy plan as "none of the above" and listing 13 nay votes by a majority of congressional Republicans on energy measures.[75] She was prepared to take the negative publicity on behalf of her vulnerable members, but pressure to do something about gas prices was building.[76]

She defended her power, saying that she would not "hand over her gavel" to the Republicans just because they wanted a vote on drilling. Her goal, she said, was to do nothing less than to "save the planet."[77] Yet she realized that the Republicans would be silenced only by giving their members something on which to vote. She packaged a set of proposals surrounding her "use it or lose it" requirement for the industry. Realizing that the Republicans would offer a drilling amendment if given the chance, she brought the bill to the floor under Suspension of the Rules, allowing no amendments and requiring a two-thirds majority for passage. It failed. Over the August 2008 recess, a rump group of safe-seat Republicans held a "floor debate" calling for increased production. Of course, the House was not in session, but in the darkened chambers with no C-SPAN coverage, the Republicans packed the floor and galleries with staffers and were relentless in their pursuit of publicity for this stunt. At home, members learned that their constituents were very unhappy indeed about the price at the pump.

On returning to Washington, Pelosi realized that the tide of public opinion had turned against her. She indicated that she would be willing to consider a vote on expanded offshore drilling as part of a more comprehensive energy package. By September, in the face of pressure from at-risk members of her caucus, her emphatic defiance of the GOP charges was transformed into pragmatism, as Democrats agreed to allow the moratorium on offshore drilling on the outer continental shelf to expire. In spite of her intensive effort to shape public opinion by flooding the echo chamber with scores of press releases, fact sheets, media appearances, blog postings, and floor debate, Pelosi was watching her party's lead in the polls fritter away. The generic ballot poll, which had run steadily in favor of the Democrats, saw the Republicans narrow the Democrats' lead to three points.[78] Events had overcome her elaborate message operation.

Then she got lucky—if one can say that the imminent collapse of the U.S. and global economies can be called a lucky thing. In spite of careful positioning, intense tit for tat, and strategic calculations, the framing wars are sometimes won or lost on circumstances and luck. The financial crisis that erupted in September 2008 sucked all of the energy from the energy crisis. Almost simultaneously, and in parallel with the spreading financial crisis, the inflated gasoline prices began a precipitous drop and by mid-December were at their lowest levels since 2004. The "Pelosi Premium" as a rhetorical barb lost its sting. The question on voters' minds was where to place blame for the imploding economy. In retrospect, House Republicans found that their rhetorical device had failed them—it was confusing to the public and simply ran out of gas when circumstances changed.[79]

Political Messaging and Public Opinion

In the end, Pelosi and her Democrats, having chosen the New Direction Congress as their moniker, had branded their initiatives in a way that probably had little resonance beyond the Beltway but provided an overarching, if generic, claim. The accomplishments of the 110th Congress could be trumpeted as a "new direction" for veterans, families, Hispanics, the environment, you name it. At the same time, when House initiatives died in the Senate or were vetoed by the president, blame could be laid at the feet of the Bush administration or the Republicans. Backed by a sophisticated and coordinated—if at times frenetic—communications operation, Pelosi proved to be an effective and disciplined partisan who gave as good as she got and caught a break here and there to best the GOP in the messaging wars.

This is not to say that her efforts were rewarded with widespread public approval. Figure 4.5 traces the downward course of public opinion over the period of the 110th Congress. Approval ratings of Congress as a whole sank to new lows in the fall of 2008, reflecting public frustration with the financial crisis. The Speaker's own approval ratings rode a roller coaster of highs and

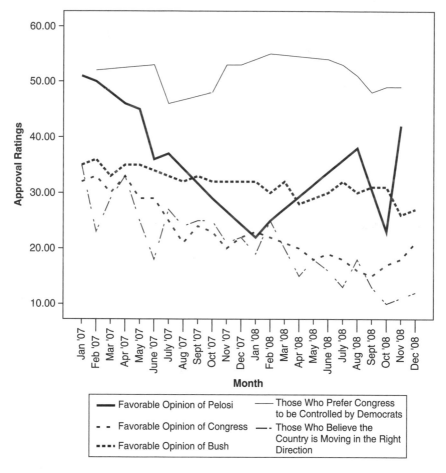

Figure 4.5   Public Opinion Polls during the 110th Congress (January 2007 through December 2008)

Source: PollingReport.com, "State of the Union" and "In the News: Political Figures," http://www.pollingreport.com/congress.htm, accessed January 8, 2009.

lows. She began her leadership of the House only partially known to the larger public. At the time of the 2006 election, the CNN/Opinion Research Corporation Poll found that 35% of its respondents had a favorable opinion of Nancy Pelosi, 24% an unfavorable opinion, and 23% had "never heard of" her. By February 2007, Rasmussen Reports found her the best known congressional leader and the only one whose favorable ratings outstripped the unfavorable: she polled 49% favorable and 40% unfavorable.[80] A year later, the Harris Poll showed her approval rating had dipped to 25%. In August

2008, the CNN/Opinion Research poll produced a 38% favorable and 37% unfavorable assessment of the Speaker. The percentage of respondents who had "never heard of" Nancy Pelosi had dropped to 11%.

We offer additional consideration of public attitudes toward Pelosi in chapter 7. Here we simply ask: Are such polls a measure of the Speaker's communications effectiveness? As political scientists John Hibbing and Christopher W. Larimer point out, dissatisfaction with Congress plays into the ideological self-interest of both the Left and Right.[81] No doubt, as the 110th Congress progressed, public opinion of its performance plummeted. From the left, the failings of Congress to pass its legislative agenda were laid at the feet of the Bush administration. From the right, critics asserted that the majority Democrats were a "do-nothing Congress." Another interpretation of congressional approval ratings, however, is that they capture the public's more general mood about whether the country is headed in the right or the wrong direction; and on the issues, Figure 4.5 shows that generally the public gave higher marks to the Democrats than the Republicans in the run-up to the 2008 elections. In reality, Hibbing and Larimer note that evaluations of Democrats and Republicans in Congress tend to move in tandem and that partisanship is relevant but not central in the face of the public's lack of understanding of the legislative branch.

What, then, can we say of the Speaker's efforts to communicate a message on behalf of the House? All of her extensive communications efforts failed to prevent a decline of public confidence in Congress, but perhaps this slide would have been worse in the absence of the all out messaging operation. On one key test, Pelosi succeeded quite well. The Democrats picked up a net of 21 seats in the 2008 House elections. This result suggests that Pelosi was effective in the partisan dimension of the Speaker's dual role—and to her partisan instincts we now turn.

PARTISAN WARRIOR

No one doubts Pelosi's credentials as a fiercely competitive Democrat. She once said (in 1992) about President George H. W. Bush: "George Bush is a hypocrite. He's such a jerk. He says he'll do anything to get re-elected. That alone ought to disqualify him. These people have to go."[82] Pretty harsh words, one might think, for any member of Congress to use to describe the president of the United States. As Speaker, Pelosi was not much easier on the "compassionate conservative" son than on the "kinder, gentler" father. In 2004, she described President George W. Bush's failures in Iraq by telling reporters: "The time has come to speak very frankly about the lack of leadership in the White House. So the emperor has no clothes. When are people going to face the reality? Pull the curtain back."[83] Her words prompted Republican leader Tom DeLay to charge that her "partisan hatred" of President Bush was "putting American lives at risk."[84] Democrats countered that the GOP reaction bordered on McCarthyism.

Pelosi's partisanship is deeply ingrained. In her autobiography, she relates a telling story from the 1960s. After a long and frustrating search for a home in San Francisco that would accommodate the large and growing Pelosi family, she found a house that was just right for them. She refused to buy it, however, when she learned that its prior owner was a Republican who was moving in order to join the Nixon administration.[85] Early in her congressional career and prior to assuming a leadership position, she exercised her sharp tongue on several occasions: she charged that independent counsel Kenneth Starr was acting as a "grand inquisitor" and "engaging in a witch hunt" in the Clinton-Lewinsky scandal, and she labeled former Speaker Gingrich a "hypocrite" and a "coward."[86] In a May 15, 2006, press conference, she was asked to comment on the House Republicans' campaign agenda on families and whether it would appeal to moderate voters. She responded: "I wouldn't have the faintest idea. What I see coming out of there is disarray, chaos, dissatisfaction, and uncertainty about the future."[87]

Pelosi's remarks are by no means a one-sided partisan phenomenon, and she has been the target of vitriolic Republican attacks. In the run-up to the 2006 election, the GOP featured her in some television and radio spots, direct-mail pieces, and candidate debates with the warning that a vote for a Democratic congressional candidate was a vote for Speaker Pelosi. Then majority whip Roy Blunt (MO) called the prospect of Pelosi becoming Speaker "just plain scary." In his nationally syndicated ABC radio program, Fox News commentator Sean Hannity exhorted GOP voters to action, saying "there are things in life worth fighting and dying for and one of 'em is making sure Nancy Pelosi doesn't become speaker."[88] Bloggers joined the fray; one predicted that a "doomsday scenario [of presidential succession] would become even more of a nightmare because of the new Speaker."[89] With no shortage of hyperbole and venom, the blogosphere posited a liberal Pelosi agenda of land grants for illegal immigrants, a federal program for subsidized transgender surgeries, and a cosmetic center equipped with tanning booths and Botox on Capitol Hill.[90]

She responded in kind. In an interview with Lesley Stahl of CBS's *60 Minutes*, she defended her characterization of her Republican colleagues as "immoral" and "corrupt" by commenting: "Well, actually, when I called them those names I was being gentle. There are much worse things I could have said about them."[91] If her words were startling, she went on to explain the realities of the contemporary Washington D.C. political life:

You know, we're professionals. We're professionals. You could go through a long list of things his [Bush's] surrogates have said about me. I know they have to do what they have to do, and they know I have to do what I have to do. And what I have to do is make a distinction in the public that's between the Democrats and the Republicans in order to win. This isn't personal.[92]

The intensity of partisan sparring continued as she took hold of the speakership and grew into its rigors. In a May 15, 2008, press conference, she was asked about President George W. Bush's speech in the Israeli Knesset wherein he criticized Senator Barack Obama and other Democrats who, he said, wanted to negotiate with terrorists and radicals. She responded:

You know, we have a protocol for the custom informally around here that we don't criticize the President when he is on foreign soil. One would think that that would apply to the President, that he would not criticize Americans when he is on foreign soil. I think what the President did in that regard is beneath the dignity of the office of President and unworthy of our representation at that observance in Israel.[93]

Pelosi's rhetorical barbs have a broad reach.[94] She can on occasion be dismissive toward the press. For example, at the same press conference, she was asked about the 2008 Democratic presidential contest and her own electoral priorities:

Questioner: You had quite a heated phone conversation with Harvey Weinstein, a strong Clinton supporter, about support for House candidates. You said that is your big priority. Are you concerned at all about the division here?
    Ms. Pelosi: What was my big priority?
    Questioner: Reelecting House Democrats.
    Ms. Pelosi: Yes, yes; I'm sorry. I didn't hear what you said. I was thinking you were talking about children, health care, education, homeownership when you said my biggest priority.[95]

So Nancy Pelosi is a very partisan politician. The real question is whether the Speaker acting as a partisan communicator may at times conflict with the institutional obligations of the speakership. She is not the first Speaker to lead the partisan charge or be subjected to the slings and arrows of the opposition party. Her raw antipathy for the Republican Party is shared by many Democrats, and the Republicans show little love lost toward the Democrats. Furthermore, a Speaker of either party cannot expect to be successful in today's hyperpartisan environment by hiding from public view and the criticism that comes with it.

In the era of the New American Politics, there are no soft shoulders to take the hard edge off partisanship. Tip O'Neill and Republican leader Bob Michel were regular golfing partners. Republican Speaker Nick Longworth and Democratic leader John Nance Garner shared a ride to the Capitol every day. Democratic Speaker Sam Rayburn and Republican leader Joe Martin patronized the "Board of Education" (after-business-hours gatherings in a hideaway office in the House), where they shared bourbon and branch water with members of both political parties. Pelosi prefers chocolate rather than bourbon, but we do not hear of her having such a friendly personal relationship with any of her Republican counterparts.

A strongly partisan Speaker is a natural byproduct of the New American Politics. Pelosi must, however, balance her sometimes harshly partisan rhetoric with her goal of sustaining support in the electorate for her party and its policy positions. A good Speaker is able to locate the center of gravity in American politics and to lead her legislative party, irrespective of her own predilections; but straddling the political center becomes much more difficult when political discourse is soured by partisan rhetoric. Pelosi may need to, in her words, "establish the difference between Republicans and Democrats in order to win," but as Speaker, she must sometimes bridge the differences in order to govern.

THE NEW DIRECTION

In this chapter, we have sought to trace the arc of the public dimension of Pelosi's speakership, that is, the dimension of her role that looks outward from the halls of Congress to the electoral process and public opinion. We suggest that these obligations are now central to the role of the Speaker in the era of the New American Politics. The days when Carl Albert could spend much of his time presiding over the House, or Tip O'Neill telling stories in the Democratic cloakroom, are gone. Pelosi has set a benchmark for future Speakers in developing and executing electoral strategy, in organizing and directing political communications, and in formulating and disseminating her party's message.

With respect to electoral strategy, the Speaker's first obligation is to win, hold, and enlarge her party's majority. Pelosi has been deeply involved in candidate recruitment and party fund-raising during each election cycle from 2002 forward. Hers has been a hands-on approach, exemplified in her choice of DCCC chairs, her continuous fund-raising and campaign travel, and her attention to candidate recruitment. Her organizational model has integrated the work of the DCCC and that of the Speaker's office. This approach has gone beyond coordination to reach control. This did not mean that she has been an asset to every Democratic member or candidate in every congressional district. To the contrary, her image as a "San Francisco liberal" has made her a liability in many conservative districts, some of which she could not step foot in without political risk. Still, she has traveled to all parts of the country and is far from a regional figure as the leader of the House Democrats.

In revamping the Democratic Party's message, Pelosi sought to underscore the essential difference between the new Democratic majority and its Republican predecessor. Dubbing the 110th the New Direction Congress, she tried to set up its central symbol as change. Whatever the Republicans had done, the Democrats would do differently. Policy differences were important, but their substance might be lost to public inattention without relentless promotion by the Democrats. Pelosi proved to be a disciplined and tireless advocate.

Pelosi has been determined to make sure that the Democrats do not repeat the mistakes of the Gingrich years. Her message strategy emphasizes a pragmatic approach to public policy, which is itself a change. She consistently counterpoises Democratic policies to those pursued by the Republicans, emphasizing that GOP policies favor entrenched interests, the wealthy, and the powerful, whereas Democratic policies favor average citizens, those who are struggling to get ahead, and those without voice in the political system. Yet, while Pelosi adopts a predictable liberal line, she deemphasizes ideology and stresses the concrete benefits the Democratic policies will provide for American families, especially children. As a woman, mother, and grandmother, she brings a credibility to these arguments that previous Speakers could not.

The results of the 2008 election proved the effectiveness of Pelosi's strategy. But branding is a tricky thing. While the New Direction rhetoric served the Democrats well in the 110th Congress, it might prove largely irrelevant in the changed environment of the 111th Congress with the Obama administration in power. Since congressional Democrats and President Obama all campaigned on a change in direction for the country, they have strong incentives to cooperate. But Obama, not Pelosi, will put his imprimatur on policy direction in the 111th Congress. Memorable "brand names" like the New Deal, the Great Society, and the New Frontier become presidential legacies with the help of a willing Congress, not because of the messaging operation of the Speaker. The danger for the Democrats is that they must govern, and whatever direction they take, the minority Republicans would be sure to offer an aggressive opposition. In the next chapter we explore Pelosi's leadership working with the Obama administration.

Chapter 5

Governing

The country must be governed from the middle. The country must be governed from the middle. I say that as being a proud progressive Democrat in the Congress of the United States and as Speaker of the House. The point is, you have to bring people together to reach consensus on solutions that are sustainable and acceptable to the American people.

—Nancy Pelosi (November 5, 2008)

On November 4, 2008, American voters went to the polls in record numbers to elect Barack Obama the forty-fourth president of the United States. In congressional elections, voters returned an 18-seat Democratic majority in the Senate (59 to 41) and a 78-seat Democratic majority in the House of Representatives (257 to 179).[1] House Speaker Pelosi had, for the second consecutive election, led her congressional party to a substantial victory. The Democrats were positioned to govern. Now the Speaker who aspired to save the planet would work with the president who aimed to change the world.

The new configuration of the government altered Pelosi's strategic situation. In the 110th Congress, with President Bush in the White House, she was still an opposition leader. While she was able to move important legislation in the House, much of her agenda was altered or failed in the Senate or fell prey to presidential vetoes. Her primary goals were to preserve and enlarge her House majority and to lay the groundwork for a Democrat to win the presidency in 2008. In the 111th Congress, the Democrats would be shooting real bullets, with an obligation and expectation to enact legislation addressing the many serious challenges facing the country. At the same time, her ability to set the House policy agenda would now be additionally constrained. She would continue to have to balance the varied interests and perspectives within the Democratic Caucus; and she would have to work with a Democratic White House determined to move its own policy agenda. Pelosi would now have to find a way to work with President Obama. Their many shared policy goals would facilitate their relationship; but their differing institutional interests and obligations would likely cause some degree of tension.

Early commentary stressed Pelosi's enhanced power position. Her larger majority would make it easier to assemble majority votes on key bills because she could allow more Democrats to take a pass if they needed to. Instead of having to position the Democrats against anticipated presidential vetoes, she would have the White House at her back in seeking to bring wavering members on board. Always the micromanager, she could now consolidate her power within the Democratic Caucus and in relationship to the Republican minority. "Pelosi's Power Reigns Supreme" held one account. "With the 111th, the Age of Pelosi Dawns" proclaimed another. Expectations were, to say the least, high.[2] In the shadows, however, Democratic members expressed reservations. Perhaps Pelosi might be getting too powerful.[3]

The 111th Congress presented marginal yet significant changes in congressional demographics. In the House, the Democratic gains in several districts were earned at the expense of moderate Republicans. The ideological separation between the two parties grew, due largely to the fact that the Republican Conference in the 111th Congress became more uniformly conservative. The larger Democratic majority now included new moderates but also new liberals; the liberal majority in the Democratic Caucus had become somewhat larger than before. The Republicans became more geographically confined to the southern and plains states, while the Democrats became more geographically diverse. Table 5.1 compares the geographic distribution among House Democrats in the 103rd Congress and the 111th. It demonstrates a clear shift in Democratic seats from the South and Midwest to the East and the West. It also shows the Republicans having gained ground mostly in the South. This greater diversity among Democrats complicated intraparty coalition building on energy policy, where regional interests are often more important than party affiliation. Consistent with the ambitions of the nation's first woman Speaker, Pelosi would now work with a larger number of female Democrats; fully 56 of the 73 women members are Democrats. Remarkably, the 111th Congress is now the oldest and longest tenured in decades. In the House, the average age of members is 57, the oldest since 1906, and the average tenure is 11 years, an all-time high.[4]

In this chapter, we first trace Pelosi's actions in organizing the House for the 111th Congress. Then we analyze her relationship with President

Table 5.1   Distribution of House Seats by Party and Region: 103rd, 110th, 111th Congresses

Congress	Party	East[a]	Midwest[b]	South[c]	West[d]	Total
103rd (1993–1994)	Democrats	57	61	85	55	258
	Republicans	42	44	52	38	176
	Other	1				1
110th (2007–2008)	Democrats	70	51	58	57	236
	Republicans	25	49	84	41	199
111th (2009–2010)	Democrats	77	55	62	63	257
	Republicans	18	45	80	35	178

[a]Conn., Del., Maine, Mass., N.H., N.J., N.Y., Pa., R.I., Vt., W.Va.

[b]Ill., Ind., Iowa, Kan., Mich., Minn., Mo., Neb., N.D., Ohio, S.D., Wis.

[c]Ala., Ark., Fla., Ga., Ky., La., Miss., N.C., Okla., S.C., Tenn., Texas, Va.

[d]Alaska, Ariz., Calif., Colo., Hawaii, Idaho, Mont., Nev., N.M., Ore., Utah, Wash., Wyo.

Source: Bruce Oppenheimer, "Barack Obama, Bill Clinton, and the Democratic Congressional Majority," Extensions, Spring: 11–15 (Norman: The Carl Albert Congressional Research and Studies Center), 2009.

Obama, from both a personal and institutional perspective. At the outset of the new administration, much attention was focused on Obama's professed interest in fostering a degree of bipartisan accommodation in Washington. We analyze bipartisanship's meaning and prospects. We then offer an assessment of Pelosi's strategic approach to governing in terms of partisanship and bipartisanship. We pause to consider the controversy that arose over her knowledge of the program set up by the Bush administration to use what it called "enhanced interrogation techniques" (EITs, i.e., "waterboarding" and other practices to inflict suffering on detainees in order to elicit information from them). Finally, we discuss the legislative record of the first session of the 111th Congress.

CONSOLIDATING POWER

The Leadership Team

In organizing the 110th Congress, as we described in chapter 3, Pelosi placed great emphasis on loyalty, going so far as to support John Murtha in his challenge to Steny Hoyer for the position of majority leader. Her reliance on loyalty appears to be both instinctive and strategic: it seems built into her political genes, yet it is clearly an expression of her strategic sense. Pelosi, as we have noted, has had ample opportunity to observe the effects of majority party leadership teams being torn by internecine strife. She wanted no part of such infighting among the members of her leadership team. In 2008, as in 2006, she wanted to avoid intramural fights over subordinate leadership positions. So she set out to consolidate her power by bringing order to the leadership. With Steny Hoyer and Jim Clyburn firmly in place as majority leader and whip, the key races were for the lower leadership offices.

In 2008, as in 2006, jockeying began with Rahm Emanuel. This time, however, the precipitating event was not his ambition to rise in the House but his decision to leave it to become President Obama's chief of staff.[5] This opened up the position of caucus chair, and Pelosi was once again confronted with the possibility of a dogfight. Congressman Chris Van Hollen of Maryland, the chair of the DCCC, wanted to follow his predecessor, Emanuel, to become caucus chair. Longtime Pelosi loyalist John Larson of Connecticut, the incumbent vice chair, wanted to move up to chair. Congressman Xavier Becerra of California declined Obama's offer of a cabinet-level position as U.S. trade representative, aiming instead to move up the leadership ranks to become caucus vice chair. He faced potential challenges from rising star Debbie Wasserman Schultz of Florida and moderate veteran Democrat Marcy Kaptur of Ohio. Congressman Joe Crowley of New York, a leader of the New Democrats, angled to become vice chair of the DCCC, a position Wasserman Schultz coveted, once she decided against a race for caucus vice chair.[6]

The flash point for this set of competing ambitions was the election of the caucus chair. Pelosi first persuaded Van Hollen to remain at the DCCC by offering him conjointly the position of Assistant to the Speaker (Becerra's old job) with an expanded portfolio in incumbent protection (a task that had been assigned to Emanuel as caucus chair in the 110th Congress). This cleared the path for Larson to become caucus chair and Becerra to become vice chair. To satisfy the ambitions of Crowley and Wasserman Schultz, Pelosi exercised the wisdom of Solomon, splitting the position of DCCC vice chair in two; Crowley became vice chair for fund-raising, Wasserman Schultz for incumbent protection.[7] Accepting Crowley back into her fold, Pelosi had once again avoided major fights over leadership positions, and once again she was ensured a loyal leadership team.

The Committees

When it came to electing committee chairs, however, a historic fight did occur with, we assume, Pelosi's tacit approval. She had sought since 2002 to get John Dingell out of her way. Now her ally, Henry Waxman of California, challenged Dingell for the chairship of the powerful Energy and Commerce Committee, through which the Obama administration's health and energy policies would pass. Speaker Pelosi and Majority Leader Hoyer remained officially neutral during this race, though it was well understood that Pelosi was for Waxman and Hoyer for Dingell. Perhaps she had learned the lesson of the Hoyer-Murtha race in 2006; a Speaker is wise to remain neutral in contested elections that she cannot control. Hoyer, ever the broker, sought a deal by which Dingell would agree to serve only one more term as chair of Energy and Commerce and Waxman would withdraw from the race. Both men rejected the proposal. When the Democratic Steering Committee met to make its committee chair nominations, Waxman won, 25 to 22.[8]

The Waxman-Dingell contest had its roots in four interrelated factors. The first was grounded in policy. Waxman had been a staunch advocate of energy conservation and climate change policies throughout his 30-year congressional career; Dingell had steadfastly supported the Detroit auto-makers. Pelosi's effort to create the House Select Committee on Energy Independence and Global Warming in the 110th Congress had been clearly an attempt to circumvent Dingell's power. Now, Waxman wanted to boot Dingell directly from the chairship. The second factor was institutional. The Democrats had accepted the Republican policy of term-limiting committee chairships amid considerable grumbling by senior members. The attachment to seniority was strong and deep in the caucus. Waxman's challenge was not simply to Dingell; it was to the principle of seniority itself. Dingell gained support among black members who believed that their most secure path to power was via the seniority system. The third factor was geography. Waxman represented the huge California delegation; Dingell was buttressed not only by the Michigan delegation but also by the network of districts that were reliant on the auto industry around the country. The fourth factor was money. Waxman had worked diligently during the 2006 and 2008 election cycles to cultivate support among new members by contributing to their campaigns. Most of them repaid him with their votes.[9]

On November 20, 2008, Waxman won the Democratic nomination as chair of Energy and Commerce by a vote of 137 to 122. Media accounts attributed his margin of victory to a better organized campaign, as well as to the support of Californians (including Pelosi) and newer members. Dingell's support (presumed to include Hoyer) was drawn from among Rust Belt members, the Congressional Black Caucus, Blue Dog Democrats, and other moderates. Postmortems suggested considerable unease among moderates at the prospect of a gathering liberal cyclone, among blacks now less secure in their seniority claims, and among oil-and-gas-state Democrats who had reason to suppose that Waxman would push policies unwelcome in their constituencies. Some members were simply loyal to Dingell or had

respect for his stature as the dean of the House.[10] Interestingly, other committee chairs quickly jumped on the Waxman victory as proof that term
limits were not needed. If, they argued, a committee chair is doing a good
job, we should keep him on; if not, he will be vulnerable to a challenge.[11] In
adopting new rules for the 111th Congress, term limits for committee chairs
were eliminated.

While Pelosi avoided getting caught in the middle of this fight, she was
surely pleased by the result. Anticipating an aggressive push by the Obama
administration on energy and health policy, she wanted to avoid the neces-
sity of cutting deals with Dingell as she had had to do on the 2007 energy
bill. While conventional wisdom had formed around the notion that the
financial crisis would force Obama to temper his ambitions, the president,
Rahm Emanuel, and Pelosi concluded that in crisis lay opportunity. Their
best opportunity to forge real change would come during the first year, certainly during the 111th Congress. It would prove difficult enough to form
winning coalitions on energy and health legislation in any event, all the more
so if Dingell controlled the helm of Energy and Commerce.

Furthermore, Dingell's ouster subtly bolstered Pelosi's power. The
Republican majority leadership had dominated the committee chairs,
bypassing seniority, interviewing candidates for the jobs, and imposing term
limits. For Pelosi to proceed in a similar way would have raised hackles in
the caucus, but she could rely on the fact that the caucus majority is reliably
liberal. If moderate committee chairs feared challenges from more liberal
members, they now had evidence that their fears might be well grounded.
A wink from the Speaker might be all it would take. Pelosi got the best
arrangement: Dingell gone without her appearing to have forced him out.
And the California delegation's power was substantially enhanced.[12]

In fact, Pelosi was in the process of developing a new relationship between
the Speaker and the committee chairs. During the House's feudal era, from
1911 until the reforms of the early 1970s, the committees were for the most
part autonomous of the party leadership. Vestiges of that arrangement lin-
gered under the Democratic majorities even as the speakership accrued more
power in the 1980s. Under the Republican majority, the leadership brought
the committee system to heel. Pelosi sought to strike a balance. On the one
hand, she believed that Congress required an effective committee system to
do its daily work. She valued regular order. On the other hand, she aimed
to be a powerful Speaker who took an active hand in the policy issues that
interested her or affected her party's political prospects. She needed to strike
the right balance between committee autonomy and leadership control.

In doing so, she has a major advantage: arguably, the most experienced
and talented set of committee chairs in the recent history of the House.
Pelosi has established strong relationships with all of them—including,

of course, close allies such as George Miller at Education and Workforce, Henry Waxman at Energy and Commerce, and Louise Slaughter at Rules, but also including other liberals such as Charlie Rangel at Ways and Means, David Obey at Appropriations, and Barney Frank at Financial Services, and moderates such as James Oberstar at Transportation, John Spratt at Budget, Ike Skelton at Armed Services, and Collin Peterson at Agriculture. These chairs know that their job security relies importantly on maintaining good relations with the Speaker. She, in turn, is pragmatic enough to know that she needs a positive working relationship with the committee chairs in order to attain her policy goals.[13]

The Rules

In addition to eliminating term limits on committee chairs, the Democrats adopted another key rule change for the 111th Congress, this time addressed to the Republican minority. As we indicated in our discussion in chapter 3 of the controversy over MTRs, in the 110th Congress, the Democrats allowed the Republicans to use MTRs, and Pelosi generally allowed members to vote their districts. Twenty-four MTRs were adopted. While these motions appear to have done little to either alter legislation or jeopardize Democratic members, they were an irritant. The most annoying were the "promptly" MTRs. The language in this type of MTR, because it requires returning the bill to committee (rather than immediately amending the bill), can be much looser and more politically charged.

Some examples will illustrate. In June 2007, Congressman Jerry Lewis of California, the ranking Republican on the Appropriations Committee, offered an amendment to the Treasury Department appropriations bill to "make clear that the funding provided to the IRS in this bill is only available to administer, implement, and enforce existing tax laws…. This motion will prohibit the IRS from implementing new taxes, protecting the American family and our economy."[14] The idea that the House could, in an appropriations bill, limit the ability of the IRS to collect taxes legally imposed in other legislation was, of course, preposterous. To vote against this MTR would, however, be portrayed by the Republicans as a vote in favor of tax increases. In August, Lewis was up to mischief again, offering an MTR to the Housing and Urban Development appropriations bill that would prevent the use of any federal funding for the employment of illegal aliens.[15] One member proposed an MTR to amend a Natural Resources Committee bill to include a provision to allow private citizens to carry guns on federal lands. Another proposed language on an Education and Labor bill affecting gasoline prices.[16] Since "promptly" MTRs are unlikely to ever return to the floor in the manner proposed, these votes of record were purely political. To prevent them, the Democrats specified that in the 111th Congress, all MTRs must be reported back to the House "forthwith."[17]

UNIFIED GOVERNMENT

The election of Obama altered the playing field for Pelosi. With Bush in the White House, her tasks were to oppose him and preserve her majority. Majority preservation remained her most fundamental obligation, but now she would have to work with a president of her own party. This presented new challenges for her. Her response reflected her experience, her position, and her strategic calculations.

Speakers and Presidents

The Speaker is, of course, the leader of one chamber in a bicameral legislature that has coequal status with the executive under the U.S. Constitution. Because the Speaker has both institutional and partisan obligations, it should not be assumed that alignment with the party controlling the White House automatically produces cooperation across the constitutional fault line between the legislative and executive branches. The Speaker's first obligation is to her constituents, her second is to her members, and her third is to her president. Speakers have historically sought to work cooperatively with their party's presidents, even on occasion with presidents of the opposite party; but they have also come into conflict with presidents of both parties.

For example, in the 1950s Speaker Rayburn worked with President Dwight Eisenhower on a range of legislation, calculating that it was better to cooperate than to confront. Speaker Albert supported the Nixon administration's foreign policy objectives, including Nixon's approach to the Vietnam War. John McCormack clearly saw his role as enacting Lyndon Johnson's Great Society. Tom Foley thought it his primary responsibility to move a Democratic agenda in cooperation with President Clinton but was undercut by Clinton's failed health care reform effort. The Democrats lost their majority, and Foley lost his seat. Speaker Hastert saw his role as moving George W. Bush's legislative program through the House. Thus, we see in these cases consistent intraparty cooperation and conditional cooperation across party lines.

Speakers and presidents have complicated relationships. For example, Tip O'Neill created a special committee to push Carter's energy bill through the

House (only to see it gutted in the Senate), and Carter moved a substantial amount of legislation through the Democratic Congress. Carter's congressional relations were always rocky, however, and O'Neill shared the disdain many liberal Democrats felt toward Carter and his White House team. Much has been made of the amicable relationship between O'Neill and President Reagan. The notion that they were friends after five o'clock is largely a myth: cordial yes, friends no. Reagan posed a threat to O'Neill's most fundamental beliefs, and O'Neill believed that it was he, not Reagan, who reflected the needs and aspirations of the American people. These two Irish politicians used a special commission to enact Social Security reform, and in 1986 Congress enacted a bipartisan tax reform bill. But for the most part, O'Neill sought to oppose Reagan. His successor, Jim Wright, moved aggressively to push a Democratic agenda on a lame-duck Reagan administration, with considerable success. Newt Gingrich saw himself as President Clinton's peer, offering television addresses to the nation and shaking hands with the president over an eventually unconsummated plan to reform campaign financing. After the government shutdowns of 1995–96, Gingrich lost traction, and by 1998 he was actively seeking to impeach Clinton. In the end, it was Gingrich who was driven from power.

This history suggests that the relationship between Speakers and presidents is conditional on circumstances. Party affiliation is a strong incentive to cooperation, but cooperation is not assured. If the president puts members of his congressional party at risk, it is incumbent on the Speaker to protect her members. Foley and Hastert did not do so and lost their majorities. Pelosi was, of course, in the House during the Clinton administration. She would draw on her own experience in understanding that as Speaker she must preserve the independence of judgment and action to protect her members. She also harbored less than fond memories of Clinton's "triangulation" strategy after the Republicans took control of Congress. Triangulation, to her, essentially meant selling out on the party's traditional principles in order to cut deals with the Republicans.

Pelosi and Obama

Still, Pelosi realized that the Democrats now had a long-awaited and historic opportunity to change the direction of public policy in America. As she often said, there were not major policy differences between the majority of House Democrats and President Obama. And there were many reasons to assume that she had favored Obama's candidacy from the beginning. While she had remained officially neutral during the long contest between Obama and Hillary Clinton, her closest congressional allies, George Miller and Anna Eshoo, were both firmly in Obama's camp. And Obama had carried Pelosi's district handily during the California primary.

It may come as some surprise, then, that Pelosi's first steps in the 111th Congress were to assert her independence from Obama on both policy and politics. Appearing on Fox News in early January 2009, she pushed for immediate repeal of the Bush tax cuts for families with incomes of $250,000 or more. Obama, having promised repeal, called for simply allowing the tax cuts to expire in 2010. Against the president's insistence that there be no recriminations for the conduct of Bush administration officials, Pelosi backed House Judiciary chair John Conyers's call for an investigation of controversial policies the Bush Justice Department had carried out. Expressing her disagreement with the president on Fox News was a declaration of independence and a shot across the bow of her conservative critics.[18] But she did not stop there. A month later, she appeared on MSNBC's Rachel Maddow Show to reiterate the call for accelerated tax increases for the wealthy and an accelerated American withdrawal from Iraq.[19]

These public policy declarations had a purpose. Speaker Hastert had earned a reputation as a Bush administration loyalist who expressed any dissenting views in private. In public, and in the legislative process, he viewed his role as that of point man for the Bush legislative agenda. Pelosi was determined not to be regarded as a "lap dog" for the Obama administration. Since she was in agreement with the president on most policy issues, she had to stake out her differences where she could and do so in a publicly visible way. She had her own reputation to protect, and her power. When Emanuel sought to "advise" her on his replacement as Democratic caucus chair, she told him bluntly to butt out. She also demanded to be informed about any contacts between the White House and members of the Democratic caucus. She was determined that the Obama administration not go behind her back in seeking to cut deals. Recalling the experience of the Clinton administration, "Pelosi 'is not going to allow Obama to triangulate her,' said a Democratic source close to the leadership. 'It's not going to happen to her.' "[20]

Public displays of independence could not, however, divert attention from the underlying solidarity of the Obama-Pelosi relationship. One aspect of Pelosi's approach to coordinated leadership has been to forge links at the staff level (as we described in chapter 4). She had established close collaboration at the staff level across all Democratic House leadership offices. It came as little surprise, then, when Obama hired Phil Schiliro, Henry Waxman's longtime assistant, to head the White House congressional liaison office, joining with Emanuel to form a formidable House alumni presence on Obama's staff.[21]

Coordinated staff. Political sympathy. Policy congruence. The evidence suggested that the White House and the House leadership would operate together like a well-oiled machine. The extent of skepticism is thus some-what surprising. In February, *Time* featured a story with the title "Obama vs. Pelosi: Can the President Work with the Democrats?"[22] A month later, a *Newsweek* title trumpeted "Obama's Pelosi Problem," suggesting that she would become the focal point of Republican resistance to the Obama agenda.[23] Both articles stressed the divergence in the strategic situation and political styles of the two Democratic leaders. Obama sought conciliation across party lines; Pelosi remained the "partisan battler" whose first obliga-tion was to her caucus and not to the administration's agenda.

While *Newsweek* alleged a degree of personal tension between the con-ciliating Obama and the controlling Pelosi, a degree of calculation may also have been involved. Both leaders are strategic politicians who try to think as many moves in advance as possible. Pelosi was well known for calibrating her strategies with respect to the House Democratic Caucus, the Senate, and the Bush White House. Now she recalibrated and concluded that if Obama wanted to appear to be the conciliator, he needed something on the left as well as on the right to conciliate. By pushing for more liberal policies than the president would openly embrace, she enabled him to sit down in the center of policy negotiations.[24]

But to the extent that Pelosi staked out a more liberal position, she ran the risk of alienating the moderates she had worked so hard to cultivate in the 110th Congress. In fact, party progressives and moderates swapped stances in the 111th Congress. As we noted, complaints about Pelosi in the 110th Congress often came from the political left. Liberals expected to real-ize more of their policy agenda than the Senate and President Bush would allow, and they took out their frustrations on Pelosi. Moderates rested in the knowledge that nothing too radical would be enacted under these circum-stances, and Pelosi protected them from tough votes. Now, with Obama in the White House and a large Democratic Senate majority, the possibility of a sharp move to the left seemed quite real. As moderates came under increas-ing pressure to support the Obama agenda, they began to push back. One response was to press for adherence to PAYGO rules in the budget process. Another was to appeal for regular order. To the extent that legislation would be developed in the committees, moderates would have opportunities to exert influence. Even freshmen moderates showed signs of independence.[25]

PARTISANSHIP, BIPARTISANSHIP, AND POSTPARTISANSHIP

Pelosi's strategic position in the House was affected by Obama's approach to governance. He won the presidency by promising to move beyond the partisan divide that had scarred American politics for a generation. In his primary contest with Hillary Clinton, he outflanked her on both the left and the right. Among progressives, he was viewed as the more authentic liberal. Among Democratic moderates and independents, he was viewed as the "postpartisan" conciliator. After his election he promised bipartisan outreach to Congress, and after his inauguration he sought good relations with both Republicans and Democrats. Yet there were always two dimensions to Obama's message. Alongside the postpartisan rhetoric was an aggressive challenge to the status quo. On the one hand, he had called for a postpartisan politics of national unification. "There is no red America and no blue America: there is only the United States of America" had been his mantra since his national debut in 2004. On the other hand, he frequently said: "one thing we know is that change never comes without a fight."[26] Obama often spoke of his reliance on Reinhold Niebuhr's belief that those who have power will not simply give it up.[27] Would Obama be the postpartisan conciliator or the feisty reformer? Could he be both?

His election was met with a spate of commentary stressing the former approach. "A New Era of Bipartisanship?" asked one commentator.[28] "Initial Steps by Obama Suggest a Bipartisan Flair," said another.[29] "Can President Obama Change the Way Washington Works?" asked a veteran observer.[30] "Can Anyone Bring America Together in an Era of Division?" echoed another.[31] The tenor of these commentaries was more one of hope than expectation. Recognizing the partisan character of the New American Politics that we have identified, commentators regarded the reach for bipartisan consensus as a "herculean task" that might lie beyond the evident capacities of the new president. If so, then we might expect to see President Obama searching for legislative majorities among Democrats rather than across party lines.

Public discourse confuses the concepts of "bipartisanship" and "postpartisanship."[32] The commentary we have just mentioned sometimes appeared to use the two terms interchangeably. In fact, there is an important difference. "Bipartisanship" refers to cooperation across party lines to enact specific legislation; it is often the politics of the deal, involving compromise. "Postpartisanship" appeals to the way public discourse is conducted. It seeks to move away from partisan and ideological posturing and toward pragmatic problem solving. In political theory, this is known as "deliberative democracy" and is set in contrast to ideological politics.[33] This distinction is related to another important dimension of postpartisanship: rhetorical tone. Obama thinks that how people talk to and about each other affects not only their capacity to focus in a pragmatic way on solutions to problems but also how they come to view each other. When he says that "there is no red America and no blue America, but only one United States of America," he suggests that Americans look upon each other as fellow citizens rather than as adversaries. He seeks to get past the cultural divisions that have defined the New American Politics, as we described them in chapter 1.

As the 111th Congress began, Pelosi adopted a more conciliatory tone, as the epigraph to this chapter suggests.[34] In an interview with *News Hour*'s Jim Lehrer, she said that she embraced Barack Obama's call for a new "spirit" in the government and the country. "Well, I welcome everything he is saying, because this is what many of us came here to do, the—again, the spirit of bipartisanship and civility."[35] Still, it is reasonable to ask what Pelosi means when she speaks of "governing from the center." Does she seek consensus among Democrats, governing from the center of the caucus? Or does she open the door to bipartisan cooperation, requiring compromise with Republicans?[36]

Barack Obama and Nancy Pelosi are of very different temperaments. He represents a new generation of postpartisans, while she is very much the product of the era of hyperpartisanship. Obama reaches out to his adversaries. She cherishes her loyal friends and has pushed her adversaries aside. He consistently stressed his desire to bridge partisan divisions; she has unleashed her harshest rhetoric against Republican opponents. We are aware of no verbal barbs by Obama, for example, that reflect the tone of the many partisan statements in Pelosi's rhetorical digest. Thus, President Obama intervened on behalf of Senator Joseph Lieberman and brought Hillary Clinton into his cabinet; Speaker Pelosi sought the defeat of Hoyer in his race for majority leader and tacitly supported Waxman in his defeat of Dingell for chair of the Commerce Committee.

Speaker Pelosi's various statements about bipartisanship and "governing from the center" are at odds with her highly partisan public image. She certainly was not stressing bipartisanship when George W. Bush was president of the United States. So well established was her reputation as a partisan competitor that friends and foes alike speculated on the meaning of her embrace of bipartisan, centrist rhetoric. Some Democrats thought she meant governing from the "center of the Democratic Caucus." Others suggested that it was a political feint calculated to soften her image now that the Democrats' governing position was secure. Republicans remained skeptical that Pelosi would alter her leadership approach but were happy to encourage any prospect of bipartisanship in the House.[37]

Some doubted that bipartisanship was either desirable or possible. Columnist Thomas Frank and historian Julian Zelizer weighed in against it. To the liberal Frank, bipartisanship simply meant making unnecessary concessions to conservatives. To the scholarly Zelizer, bipartisanship as a way of governing conjured memories of the old Conservative Coalition and its opposition to civil rights and other progressive policies. Political scientist James Morone suggested that the rhetorical emphasis did not matter, because bipartisanship so rarely happens in practice. Bipartisanship, he said, is a myth. Journalist Dan Balz explained why bipartisanship would be hard to attain in the 111th Congress. The Republican Party had become even more monolithically conservative as a result of the 2008 elections. Bipartisanship requires a number of centrists in both parties to provide the political space for accommodation. While the November 2008 elections produced more moderate Democrats than before, there were fewer moderate Republicans. With whom might Pelosi compromise on the Republican side?[38]

The skepticism among the pundits seemed justified when Pelosi abandoned the bipartisan rhetoric as she guided the major elements of President Obama's initial legislative program through the House by party-line votes. House Republicans voted unanimously against both the stimulus legislation and the first budget resolution. Yet Pelosi stuck by her guns, making two arguments. The first argument was procedural. Against the Republicans' claims that they had been excluded from meaningful participation in the development of the stimulus package, she issued a press release that described committee consideration of the legislation, the number of Republican amendments made eligible in committee and on the floor, and the specific Republican policy prescriptions that had been incorporated into the legislation.[39] Republicans, she claimed, complained about process but really had no policy alternatives to offer: "If you can't win on policy, then you go to process. If you can't win on process, then you go to personality."[40] Still, she insisted, the Republicans' procedural rights had been respected. Her second argument addressed the limits of bipartisanship. There are, she insisted, fundamental differences between Democrats and Republicans on major public policy issues. Republicans, she said frequently, are true to their convictions, and this is why they vote monolithically against Democratic bills.

> I believe that the Republicans are sincere in their vote against the (stimulus)
> bill. They do not believe in these investments in energy, health, education,
> infrastructure, and the rest. They don't believe in that. I don't think they
> voted politically. I think they voted what they believe. And President Obama
> and the Democrats had a different idea.[41]

As she put it in another interview: "If you can't find common ground, that doesn't mean that you're partisan. It just means that you believe in two different things."[42] These two arguments, one procedural and the other grounded in policy differences, serve to frame Pelosi's view of her obligations as Speaker. As the leader of the majority party in the House, she has an obligation to see its policy preferences enacted into law. As the Speaker, she has an obligation toward procedural fairness to the minority party. She has no obligation to bipartisan compromise for its own sake.

Thus, when challenged with the accusation that her rhetorical emphasis on bipartisanship and centrism was belied by her actual conduct, Pelosi returned to the solid ground of her institutional position. Having failed to garner even a single Republican vote on the stimulus after having (in her view) offered some policy concessions and procedural opportunities to the Republicans, she evoked her larger responsibilities as Speaker. According to an anonymous staffer, "what she realized with Obama coming in was that, yeah, we can go through this dance, but at the end of the day, this was going to be a tutorial for the Obama folks. They're (Republicans) all going to vote against you and then come to your cocktail party that night."[43] Pelosi stood her ground on policy and position:

> The debate on the recovery package is a clear manifestation of the differences
> between the two parties. Republicans ultimately could not accept our new
> direction for the economy, one with prosperity for the many, not the few.
> We gave them every opportunity for input. They wanted tax cuts, and we
> included them in the bill. They wanted a chance to mark up the bill, and we
> gave them 26 hours to add amendments in committee. Then they wanted
> amendments on the floor, and we gave them that. We're not afraid of debate,
> so we welcomed any ideas they had and accepted some of them. But when
> it came to the fundamental differences we have over economic policy we
> were not going down that path, and neither were they. In the end, many of
> their members did not even vote for their own alternative economic package,
> which is remarkable.[44]

Pelosi thus laid down clear markers of how she intended to handle her responsibilities with an enlarged House majority and a friendly administration. As Speaker, she acknowledged an obligation to a modicum of procedural fairness to the Republican minority. As leader of the House Democrats, she would seek to ensure that in the final analysis, the Democratic position would prevail. While she sought to take the edge off of partisanship with more conciliatory rhetoric, she had no intention of yielding policy ground to the Republicans on any important issue on which she could gather 218 votes for her position. And when necessary, she would take the partisan hits that were more often directed at her than at President Obama.[45] One such hit, however, she had not anticipated.

THE WATERBOARDING FLAP

On April 15, 2009, Obama made public four "torture" memos written by Justice Department lawyers during the Bush administration to provide a legal rationale for the use of EITs, a program Obama had discontinued.

These memos led to renewed calls for investigation into the Bush administration's policies and practices with respect to detainees under American control.[46] In response, defenders of the Bush administration claimed that members of the House and Senate intelligence committees had been briefed on the EIT program and had not objected to it at the time. This claim implicated Pelosi, who in 2002 had been the ranking Democrat on the House Select Intelligence Committee. When asked about her knowledge of the EIT program, Pelosi acknowledged attending a briefing by the CIA in September 2002. She claimed, however, that the briefing extended only to the legal justification of the program and had not indicated that it had already been implemented. She had first enunciated this position in 2007, and she stuck to this position in 2009.

On April 22, 2009, the *New York Times* reported the background of the EIT program, calling into question the adequacy of the legal analysis undergirding it.[47] The article specifically referred to a September 2002 briefing by the CIA of the chair (Porter Goss) and ranking member (Pelosi) of the House Intelligence Committee. The following day, when Pelosi was asked about the extent of her knowledge of the program at her weekly press conference, she said: "what they did tell us is that they had some legislative counsel—the office of Legislative Counsel opinions that they could be used, but not that they would."[48] Noting that her Republican colleague, Porter Goss, retained a different recollection of the briefing, she nonetheless insisted that her recollection was clear. Two days later, Goss published an op-ed piece in *Washington Post* declaring himself "slack-jawed" at Pelosi's interpretation of the briefing.[49] Pelosi had also asserted that as a member of the Intelligence Committee she was precluded from making any public statement about the briefing, at the time or later.[50] This claim elicited considerable skepticism in the media and led to renewed Republican attacks on Pelosi.[51] Even liberal blogs asked: "What Did Pelosi Know?"[52] Former vice president Dick Cheney was demanding release of other CIA documents that he claimed would prove that the EIT program had prevented terrorist attacks and saved American lives. Steny Hoyer called on the CIA to release all relevant information about the briefings.[53] The Obama Justice Department conducted an internal investigation of the Bush administration officials responsible for the so-called torture memos. It concluded that there was insufficient evidence to prosecute them for criminal conduct but that the investigation record should be made available to state bar associations for possible professional ethics inquiries.

In this charged political atmosphere, the CIA released a summary of 40 congressional briefings and hearing testimonies stretching from the initial briefing attended by Pelosi on September 4, 2002, to the most recent briefing on March 12, 2009. The individual briefing summaries indicated the nature and extent of the overall briefing on the EIT program that members of Congress had had and often included specific references to waterboarding and other EITs. Leon Panetta, the director of the CIA, stressed that the summaries were based in part on participants' recollections of events that were by now as much as seven years past; still, the compilation clearly suggested that Pelosi and other congressional leaders had been repeatedly briefed about the program. The initial briefing that Pelosi had attended (as reported on the summary) was described as follows: "Briefing on EITs including use of EITs on Abu Zubayda, background on authorities, and a description of the particular EITs that had been employed."[54] Pelosi and Porter Goss had both attended this briefing. Pelosi stated flatly that the CIA briefers had not disclosed that any prisoner had been waterboarded prior to that time; Goss claimed that the fact had been disclosed in the briefing.

Pelosi's attempt to distance herself from any complicit knowledge of the EIT program was understandable when taken from a purely political point of view. She was pushing for a "truth commission" or congressional investigation to uncover the scope and extent of the Bush EIT program. Now she was charged with having known about it from the beginning and not done anything to stop it. Her disavowal was further complicated by the revelation that her military adviser, Michael Sheehy, had informed her in February 2003 of the fact that prisoners had been waterboarded even prior to September 2002. By this time, Pelosi had become Democratic leader and was no longer a member of the Intelligence Committee. The new ranking member was Congresswoman Jane Harman of California. Harman and Sheehy had attended a February 5, 2003, briefing at which it was revealed that video tape recordings of the waterboarding existed and were to be destroyed. Harman wrote a letter to the CIA condemning waterboarding. When Sheehy informed Pelosi of the content of the CIA briefing, she took no action.

Thus, Pelosi perhaps knew in September 2002 and certainly knew by February 2003 of the EIT program; yet she said nothing publicly and took no action as a member of the congressional leadership to try and stop it. Faced with the CIA summary, Pelosi concluded that she had to respond. At a press conference on May 14, 2009, she read a prepared statement in which she stood by the claim that she had not been told that the EIT program had already been implemented at the briefing on September 4, 2002.[55] She acknowledged that she had been informed about the program in February 2003 but said she had taken no action for several reasons. First, Harman had already sent a letter. Second, a letter would not do any good, since it would not stop the program. Third, she was constrained from speaking publicly because of the confidentiality of the information provided to members of the Intelligence Committee.[56] In her new job as Democratic leader, Pelosi said, she was focused on winning control of Congress and the White House—the only sure means of ending the EIT program. She stressed this point repeatedly in her press conference and interviews.

With both Porter Goss and the Obama CIA claiming that she had been briefed on the program, Pelosi found herself in a difficult position. If she now recovered a memory, she would appear rather foolish. If, however, she continued to claim that she had not been informed about the waterboarding of Zubayda, then it could mean only one thing: the CIA had misled her and the committee by withholding information. How should she frame this contradiction to minimize the damage to her position?

In her prepared statement, she said:

> The CIA briefed me only once on some enhanced interrogation techniques in September 2002 in my capacity as Ranking Member of the Intelligence Committee. I was informed then that the Department of Justice's opinions had concluded that the use of enhanced interrogation techniques were legal. The only mention of waterboarding at that briefing was that it was not being employed. Those conducting the briefing promised to inform the appropriate members of Congress if that technique were to be used in the future.... We ... now know that techniques, including waterboarding, had already been employed, and that those briefing me in September 2002 gave me inaccurate and incomplete information. At the same time—this is exactly at the same time, September of 2002, the fall of 2002—at the same time, the Bush Administration was misleading the American people about the threat of weapons of mass destruction in Iraq.[57]

This statement elicited the following question from the press: "Madam Speaker, just to be clear, you are accusing the CIA of lying to you in September of 2002?" In response, Pelosi nodded her head and replied: "Yes, misleading the Congress of the United States. Misleading the Congress of the United States." And, the questioner asked, are they doing it again now? After all, Obama CIA director Leon Panetta had released the summary of the briefings. After some circumlocution, Pelosi got around to an answer to this question: "So, yes, I am saying that they are misleading, that the CIA was misleading the Congress."[58] In other words, the Panetta summary was itself a misleading rendering of history.

Here we have Speaker Pelosi under fire, undertaking a press conference specifically aimed at deflecting that fire by turning attention to the Bush administration's dissembling on the rationale for the Iraq War. The headlines she got were variations on this lead: "Pelosi Accuses the CIA of Lying to Congress." Panetta sprang to the defense of the CIA, standing publicly behind the accuracy of the briefing summary. Pelosi was forced to back off quickly. "We all share great respect for the dedicated men and women of the intelligence community.... My criticism of the manner in which the Bush Administration did not appropriately inform Congress is separate from my respect for those in the intelligence community who work to keep our country safe."[59]

Pelosi now lay under the heaviest barrage of criticism of her tenure. Gingrich, a specialist in congressional decapitation, called for her ouster. Conservative pundit Charles Krauthammer described her as "utterly contemptible." Without doubt, Pelosi had been "knocked off her game," just as the Democrats approached the heart of their legislative agenda.[60] Unsurprisingly, the criticism did not eschew misogyny. The Republican National Committee issued a video parody portraying Pelosi as somehow resembling the Ian Fleming character Pussy Galore.[61] Conservative talk show host Jack Quinn called Pelosi "that bitch," while another, Neal Boortz, declaimed: "How fun it is to watch that hag out there twisting in the wind." Even more mainstream conservative commentators such as Alex Castellanos and Mike Huckabee went after her dress and appearance.[62] More objective observers called this her first major stumble as Speaker, and a stumble it no doubt was.

We think that two lessons are to be learned from this episode, one about Pelosi and the other about her strategic situation. With respect to the latter, we think it is important to recognize the subtext of her statement. When Pelosi stressed that she had moved on to a leadership role in which her first obligation was to elect a Democratic majority to the House, she was explicitly reminding her Democratic members that they owed their power positions to her efforts. But she was also subtly reminding them that she had made a strategic decision in 2002 and 2003, and that decision was to avoid taking on the Bush administration's "war on terror." She had been a vocal opponent of the American invasion of Iraq; she did not want to appear weak in the fight against Al Qaeda. We should remember the timeline. In September 2002 when she received the first briefing, President Bush was launched on a full-scale public relations effort to prepare public opinion for the invasion of Iraq. This culminated in the passage of the war resolution in Congress in October. The Republicans gained seats in the 2002 election in November, following which Gephardt announced his retirement from the House. Pelosi was elected Democratic leader in December 2002. In February, when she was definitely informed about the waterboarding, Bush was on the verge of leading the country into war. This was the context in which Pelosi had chosen to remain silent on the EIT issue.[63]

We also are reminded by this episode of two personal qualities that have consistently characterized Pelosi's congressional career: she is a fighter whose first instinct is to go on offense, and she is sometimes an awkward communicator. In her press conference, both proclivities were joined. She sought to take the fight to President Bush and frame his administration's deceptions as the issue, but she ended up attacking the CIA. It is often remarked that Speaker Pelosi has a somewhat mechanical tendency to stay on message by the repetition of talking points. This practice is in fact a strategy she uses to corral her propensity to wander off message. In this press conference, she was so concerned to stay on message that she read her statement and then in response to questions sought to flip back through it so that she could respond to questions by rereading portions of it. That she was rattled was evident. When she was asked if the CIA had lied to her, she nodded her head emphatically, but then stuck with the word "misled" to avoid using the word "lied." She had allowed her statement to be abridged by a reporter's question. As one account had it, she had botched her own message.[64]

One thing was certain: the CIA flap was a big distraction for Pelosi and the House Democrats in pursuing their legislative agenda. Sensing danger, they rallied around her.[65] They sought to discount the significance of the issue (calling it "a tempest in a teapot"), to counterattack Pelosi's Republican critics, and to defend the plausibility of her case.[66] They claimed that the issue would not have an effect on members' reelection prospects and that the Speaker was in no serious trouble in the Democratic Caucus. Above all, the Democrats hoped to move on, in hopes that other matters would knock the story off of the front pages. They wanted to legislate.

LEGISLATING

President Obama and the Democratic-controlled 111th Congress were presented with an opportunity to reorient public policy in the United States. This was by no means the first time a Democratic president and Congress had a chance to make history. The comparisons are to Franklin Roosevelt in 1933, Harry Truman in 1949, John Kennedy in 1961, Lyndon Johnson in 1964, Jimmy Carter in 1977, and Bill Clinton in 1993. The record shows that Roosevelt and Johnson were able to move a substantial policy agenda with the help of huge congressional majorities and, in Roosevelt's case, a national emergency. Although Obama's congressional majorities were smaller, they were still robust, given the relatively high levels of party unity the congressional Democrats had attained. And, like Franklin Roosevelt, Obama faced a national economic crisis that created an opportunity to govern. His success was by no means assured, but in Speaker Pelosi he had an asset not available to his Democratic predecessors. Pelosi is a strong Speaker in an era of strong Speakers. The 111th Congress afforded her an opportunity to take her place in the front rank. In this section, we analyze her approach to legislating with the new administration.

Strategies

Pelosi had a stronger but a less free hand in developing legislative strategy with Obama in the White House. She would be asked to advance his legislative priorities, and her approach would be affected by his. In the early months of his administration, Obama revealed how he intended to proceed. In contrast to his two most recent predecessors, he declined to submit fully developed legislative packages to Congress.[67] Instead, he preferred to set clear priorities and broad goals and then allow Congress to develop the details. He aimed to avoid making his proposals the main target of opposition attack, and he wanted to build consensus in the process of developing legislation rather than after the fact. This is not to say that his administration was hands off. To the contrary, his team, led by Emanuel and Schiliro, were in close communication with congressional policy-makers. Obama also wanted to build public and interest group support for his policies. He would, of course, be the primary public face of his administration's policies; but the White House policy staff worked behind the scenes to build support among affected interests.

Obama had centered major policy-making in the White House rather than in the cabinet departments. Cabinet secretaries have a tendency to develop policy agendas of their own, and in the process of daily management of their department's programs, they often assume the perspectives of the interests those programs serve. Obama wanted to ensure that major policies were handled by experienced people who worked directly for him in the White House. He appointed a number of policy coordinators (dubbed "czars" in the press and by Republicans) as presidential advisers. Finally, he wanted to change the tone of the policy conversation by reaching out to Republicans. He hoped to win some Republican support for his policies or, when faced with GOP opposition, influence the manner of their opposition.

Obama also made strategic choices in the substance of policy. Instead of designing entirely new arrangements, he preferred to build on those that were already in place. This approach ensured that policy change would be incremental and created more bargaining space in which legislators could seek compromise and consensus. The public could be reassured that new policies would not abruptly overturn arrangements to which they were accustomed. The president also insisted on pursuing a range of major policy initiatives at once. He encountered skepticism among those who were concerned that the policy and political circuits would be overloaded, but he remained resolute. In part, he did not want to sacrifice any momentum his presidency had created; but this choice was also a strategic one. When there is only one major policy in play (for example, the Clinton administration's health-care reforms of 1993), everyone will shoot at it. When there are multiple policies on the field, opposition fire is scattered.

The Obama approach offered major advantages to Pelosi. She was known to like control and to micromanage policies that were important to her. In declining to send complete legislative packages to the Hill, Obama relieved her of the burden of defending something that was already proposed and provided her with more latitude in developing legislative strategy. At the same time, the Obama legislative program was far too encompassing for her to actively manage all of its elements. She would rely on the committee system to draft bills and build consensus behind them. Then, once the committees of primary jurisdiction had produced legislation, she would step in to negotiate the compromises necessary to secure passage on the House floor.[68]

A Fast Start

But not right away. Pelosi broke fast from the gate in 2009, just as she had in 2007, with a package of legislation ready to go. At the outset of the 110th Congress in 2007, she had violated regular order to push through her Six for '06 First 100 Days legislative package. As the 111th Congress got under way in 2009, with the Obama administration in power and the country caught up in a financial crisis, Pelosi once again violated regular order to push through several important bills, mostly on party-line votes. These bills fell into two categories. The first included Democratic priorities that had been thwarted by Bush and Senate Republicans in the 110th Congress. These included SCHIP, the Lilly Ledbetter Act, an omnibus appropriations bill funding the government for fiscal year 2009, and a supplemental appropriations bill. The second category included the Obama administration's response to the fiscal crisis. The centerpiece was the fiscal stimulus package; also enacted was legislation to improve oversight of TARP (a bill to address the housing crisis by relief to some homeowners facing foreclosure), and the administration's fiscal year 2010 budget proposal (via Congress's First Budget Resolution).[69]

The uniform House Republican opposition to Obama's stimulus bill and, later, to the Democrats fiscal year 2010 budget plan triggered the public commentary on bipartisanship that we discussed earlier. These bills embodied the change in policy direction the 2008 election had foreshadowed. They called forth a much more active role for the federal government in guiding the economy and a reprioritization of its budget. In the House, Pelosi was able to keep Blue Dog Democrats on board by promising future adherence to PAYGO requirements. The Democrats characterized their new priorities as, in Pelosi's words, "reflective of our national values." To Republican leader

John Boehner, these priorities represented "an audacious move to a big socialist government that pushes the nation's debt to dangerous levels."[70]

These party-line votes made the underlying reality apparent. The Democrats could expect little or no support from Republicans on any issue that touched on the fundamental interests or ideologies of the two parties. But Democrats had the votes to pass important legislation in the House even in the face of united Republican opposition. The implication was clear: Pelosi's first job was to build consensus within the Democratic Caucus. By bringing the Democrats together, she would be able to move legislation through the House. Pelosi and the Democrats' early success in legislating also altered the external interest group environment. If health-care providers, insurance companies, drug companies, big banks, utility companies, and energy companies were convinced that legislation would be enacted, their incentive would be to cooperate in hopes of attaining some of their legislative goals. House Republicans might find political advantage in opposition, but the affected interests could not afford to take the chance.

To ratchet up the pressure on the outside, however, progress would have to be made inside Congress. In the House, this meant that the committees of jurisdiction would have to move legislation to the floor, where the leadership would be expected to round up the votes for passage. This process would require a winnowing of legislative objectives in order to build majority support. Primary among the House's policy objectives would be consideration of health and energy legislation in the summer of 2009.

ENERGY AND HEALTH

In adopting the first congressional budget resolution, the Democratic majority made an important decision foreshadowing the end-game politics of energy and health legislation. They included a provision for using the process of reconciliation to pass health-care reform, but they did not do the same with energy legislation. Reconciliation is an option in the budget process that enables the Congress to bring government outlays within budget ceilings set in the budget resolution. Congress sometimes resorts to the reconciliation process in order to facilitate the passage of legislation that typically includes multiple provisions affecting the federal budget on either the spending or the revenue-raising sides. It is not typical to use the reconciliation process to move major policy legislation, but in this case it gave Reid a strategic option to deploy if necessary. Most significant to the strategic considerations of the leadership, a reconciliation bill cannot be filibustered on the Senate floor, so it only requires a bare majority vote to pass that body.[71]

Given that both health-care reform and legislation on energy and climate change are contentious, we might ask, why go for reconciliation for health-care reform and not for energy? Two factors appear to have been at play. First, health care was the more important priority. The goal of universal health care has been a central plank in the Democratic Party platform since the Truman administration. Any comprehensive health-care reform would need to address Medicare and Medicaid, and thus have a significant budgetary impact. Health-care reform also appears to be central to any long-term resolution of the long-term deficit problem facing the federal government.[72] Second, health care appeared the more attainable goal because it promised benefits to everyone through expanded coverage and lower costs. Energy fostered regional conflicts that would make it more difficult to muster a majority, beginning with the budget resolution itself. Using reconciliation on health care gave the Democrats leverage they might—or might not—need to push their legislation through the Senate. Energy legislation would require building a broader coalition from the start.

Prospects in both policy areas were enhanced by a significant shift in the interest group environment. Due in part to calculations of self-interest and in part to the likelihood that legislation would be enacted by the united Democratic government, industry showed an inclination to constructive participation. In the health arena, a variety of reform efforts had been under way since 2007. These included Better Health Care Together, an alliance of business and public interest groups, the Coalition to Advance Health Care Reform, a business group, and representatives of industry interests and reform advocates who joined in DividedWeFail.org, an initiative that included AARP, the Service Employees International Union, the Business Roundtable, and the National Federation of Independent Business.[73] These parties had come to recognize the need for reform in the face of skyrocketing health-care costs. The American health-care system had been built on the backs of employers, and employers were increasingly feeling the pinch. The system undermined American economic competitiveness, left millions of Americans uninsured, and produced relatively poor health outcomes for the average person. Against the backdrop of this ongoing dialogue, Obama consistently pledged to build on rather than radically transform the system. He hoped to build consensus rather than to challenge the status quo with a plan that could be caricaturized as "socialized medicine." Conservative advocacy groups such as the Americans for Prosperity Foundation and Conservatives for Patient Rights were quick to make this claim in a series of advertisements in the spring of 2009. Liberal advocacy groups, including Health Care for America Now and Obama's own grassroots organization, Organizing for America, weighed in on the other side.[74]

Energy offered fewer incentives for cooperation due to regional economic differences. Energy policy tends in the direction of a zero-sum game in which gains for some come at the expense of others. We saw in chapter 3 that Pelosi's renewable energy portfolio plan sank in the mud of regional disagreements. American energy is largely organized around fossil fuels: oil, natural gas, and coal. The nation is divided between energy-producing and energy-consuming states. Obama aimed to reduce American dependence on foreign oil, to reduce reliance on fossil fuels, to thus reduce greenhouse gases, and to build a new "green" economy. Some states have easier access to wind, geothermal, hydroelectric, or other alternative fuel sources. Reduced reliance on oil or coal hurts states that harbor them.

With both energy and health care, Pelosi had to balance five strategic objectives. First, she intended to support the President in his legislative efforts. Obama's success would mean success for Democrats. Second, she sought to preserve the prerogatives of the House institutionally and avoid falling victim, as she had in the 110th, to Senate or presidential preferences. Maintaining a strong negotiating position for the House would be critical in the inevitable end-game bargaining of the conference committee process. Third, as always, Pelosi was attentive to protecting her members and thus her majority in the House. She would be tested to find policy consensus within her diverse caucus, but the alternative would be to secure 218 votes and let electorally vulnerable members take a pass. Fourth, she had to be responsive to the strong policy preferences of the liberal majority in the Democratic Caucus, whose views she by in large shared. Finally, she sought to get new policy enacted into law, especially on these critical party priorities. Indeed achieving a new policy direction was the task she had set for herself. Unfortunately meeting each of these objectives would at times mean jeopardizing her ability to meet another objective.

Energy

The primary House venue for both health and energy legislation was the Energy and Commerce Committee, now chaired by Waxman. The importance of Waxman's dethroning of Dingell soon became apparent. With Dingell pushed to the side, Waxman and Energy Subcommittee chair Ed Markey of Massachusetts moved quickly to develop a climate change bill organized around a cap-and-trade system for controlling the release of emissions. With little prospect of gaining Republican support, the primary deal-making occurred among Democrats on the Energy and Commerce Committee. Markey worked closely with Rick Boucher of West Virginia, who chaired the Energy Subcommittee in the previous Congress and coauthored Dingell's energy bill.[75] The trick was to provide enough incentives, protections, and set-asides to bring wavering Democrats on board.

With Republicans arguing that cap-and-trade was a hidden tax increase for all American families, the Democrats had to be wary of embracing the concept, especially since it was far from clear that it could muster 60 votes in the Senate. Chris Van Hollen, DCCC chair, suggested deferring energy legislation until health care was enacted; he did not want his Frontline members to cast a hard vote only to see the bill die in the Senate. Waxman was insistent that the House take up both issues before the August recess. Even though centrist Democrats sought to delay the energy bill, Pelosi insisted that her "signature" issue go forward.[76] To win consensus within the committee, Waxman agreed to stretch out the timetables and lower the levels for emissions reductions. Cap allowances would initially be made available for free, thus reducing costs to industry.[77] On May 22, the bill cleared Energy and Commerce along a largely party-line vote. One key to Waxman's and Markey's success was the support of several corporations that "now see carbon controls as inevitable and would like regulatory certainty."[78] Motivating the industry's change of heart was a major U.S. Supreme Court decision acknowledging the statutory authority of the Environmental Protection Agency to regulate greenhouse gases. If Congress did not act, the Environmental Protection Agency would, and industrial interests assumed they could get a better deal from Congress.[79]

No sooner had the energy bill cleared Energy and Commerce than a revolt brewed among other committees. While eight committees could claim a piece of jurisdiction, it was Agriculture chair Collin Peterson and Ways and Means chair Charlie Rangel who were most insistent. Peterson, in particular, was prepared to oppose the bill unless the concerns of agricultural interests and rural Americans were addressed. Faced with a potential insurrection, Pelosi took control. She gave all committees with jurisdiction a June 19 deadline to mark up the bill. Peterson claimed to speak on behalf of 45 Democrats, enough to defeat the bill assuming nearly unanimous Republican opposition.[80]

At the end of June, the energy logjam in the House broke. Working around the clock, Waxman negotiated an agreement with Peterson that assuaged the concerns of Agriculture. Included was a provision to shift enforcement of land use and carbon offset provisions in the cap-and-trade program from the Environmental Protection Agency to the Department of Agriculture. This was a classic congressional gambit, trading structural control for policy authorization in order to reach compromise.[81] Agriculture was also given an across-the-board exemption from emission caps that would apply to other industries. When combined with the exemptions, offsets, and deadline extensions for compliance with mandatory emissions limits which Waxman already had conceded to get the bill out of committee, the resulting bill was perceived by most environmentalists as substantially weakened.

In a surprise move, Pelosi announced on Monday, June 22, that she would bring the bill to the House floor the following Friday, June 26. The leadership had made the decision to take the bill to the floor after Waxman and Markey reached agreement with Peterson. Her announcement launched an intensive effort by herself, other Democratic leaders, members of Energy and Commerce led by Waxman and Markey, and the Obama administration. Pelosi met individually and in small groups with Democrats, seeking their endorsement. She met with a group of 11 moderate Republicans whose votes she hoped to win. Through the week, the Democratic whip counts were consistently short of the 218 needed to ensure passage. The decision to take the bill to the floor was a major risk for Pelosi. A defeat might derail energy legislation for the entire 111th Congress. On the day of the vote, she scurried around the House floor to corral support. Unsurprisingly, her efforts were directed at progressives who found the bill too weak. She argued that it was necessary to keep the process going if anything at all was to be achieved. As the vote took place, she stood at the rear rail with two "if needed" yea votes at her side. They were needed. In the end, she prevailed by a vote of 219 to 212, losing 44 Democrats and winning the support of 8 Republicans.[82] She had passed her bill while preserving the political viability of many members, but had in the process been willing to see the bill weakened.

This was a remarkable victory for Pelosi. On its face, it evoked memories of Speaker Hastert's dogged efforts to push Bush administration policies through the House on narrow, party-line votes. But the comparison is superficial. Operating with a narrower majority, Hastert turned to heavy-handed methods to hold nearly every Republican vote in line. The accumulated weight of this strategy eventually sank his majority. Pelosi, working with a larger margin, wanted to pass the bill without jeopardizing her majority. While the final tally was close, Frontline Democrats were set free to vote their districts. Among the Democratic nay votes were 4 liberals and 40 moderates, many representing coal or oil districts. The eight Republican yeas came from districts with active environmental constituencies. She arranged to fly Congressmen Patrick Kennedy and John Lewis, both of whom had been absent for health reasons, in for the vote.[83] Pelosi had carefully calibrated the votes to produce just enough to win.

Pelosi and Hastert also differed in that she had made energy and climate her "signature" issue from the outset of her speakership. Hastert was usually pushing someone else's priority; Pelosi was often pushing her own. We described in chapter 3 the limited success she was able to achieve in the 2007 energy bill. She said at that time that it was only the first step in the process of creating a new national energy policy. Now she had taken the next major step. Even though the bill had been substantially watered down as the legislative process had its way, the House had passed a cap-and-trade bill that would move national energy policy in a new direction—if, that is, the House-passed bill could survive Senate scrutiny. This was far from assured. The Senate tips representation in favor of small states, and its rules empower individual senators. There were a substantial number of moderate Democrats who might resist even the watered-down bill that had passed the House. Even their larger majority did not ensure Senate passage. Having decided not to include energy legislation in reconciliation, the Democrats would need 60 votes to pass a bill in the Senate. Still, the House Democrats had set the table for Senate consideration, and the passage of the bill was widely recognized as a major achievement for Speaker Pelosi. As Democratic whip Jim Clyburn put it, "Nancy Pelosi was the whip on this."[84]

Health

Pelosi was able to pass the energy bill by cutting side deals to win votes. Health-care reform required a comprehensive approach to attain its goals of universal coverage, quality, and cost-control. Fundamental differences in philosophical approaches would prove difficult to bridge and the interest-group terrain would provide many obstacles. It became clear early on that House Republicans would provide no votes for any Democratic health care reform bill. Three House Committees drafted health reform bills: Energy and Commerce, Education and Workforce, and Ways and Means. While progressives dominated on the Education and Ways and Means Committees, moderates controlled the swing votes on Energy and Commerce. Progressives wanted a bill that would provide universal coverage and a public health option; moderates insisted that the bill be fully funded and were skeptical about a public insurance plan.[85]

The two more liberal committees produced draft legislation by early June. The going was tougher at Energy and Commerce, where Waxman pushed the Committee to report an expansive health-care reform bill with a public option. Meeting Blue Dog resistance on the cost of the plan, Waxman eventually reached a compromise that secured approval of the bill by the committee. In a deal supported by Pelosi and the Obama administration, Waxman reached an agreement with committee moderates in late July that the public option would not be tied to Medicare reimbursement rates (instead providing that the public plan's administrators would have to negotiate rates with health-care providers), and the bill also exempted small businesses from the its employer mandate.[86]

In the Senate, two committees drafted legislation. The Health, Education, Labor, and Pensions Committee (HELP) produced an ambitious bill in late June that mandated coverage and provided for a robust public alternative to the private insurance market. The Finance Committee engaged in a bipartisan effort by its chair, Max Baucus of Montana, and five other senators (Democrats Jeff Bingaman of New Mexico and Kent Conrad of North Dakota, and Republicans Charles Grassley of Iowa, Mike Enzi of Wyoming, and Olympia Snowe of Maine). While also proposing mandated coverage (with exemptions for small businesses), this "gang of six" discussed government-regulated health-care cooperatives as an alternative to a public health-care plan, and increasing the qualifying income level for government subsidies, in order to reduce costs. This would produce less coverage.[87]

As the summer wore on, conservative attacks on the Democrats' health-care proposals began to have an effect on public opinion. Republicans concentrated their attacks on the public plan option. Since a government-run plan would be subsidized by the taxpayers, the argument ran, it would always be at a competitive advantage, eventually driving private health insurers out of business. The American Medical Association, while claiming to support health-care reform in principle, weighed in against any public plan option tied to Medicare reimbursement rates in fear that it would shrink doctors' incomes. Rural hospitals claimed they could not survive on Medicare reimbursement rates. Fights loomed over both the structure of the bill and its cost. When the Congressional Budget Office evaluated a preliminary version of a Senate bill authored by Ted Kennedy and estimated it would only cover an additional 13 million people at a cost of $1.6 trillion over 10 years, the Republicans pounced.[88]

House and Senate Democrats were pushed onto the defensive. In mid-June, Obama launched a publicity offensive aimed at rallying public opinion behind his preferred policy options. Pelosi reaffirmed that no bill would emerge from the House without a public plan. She and Majority Leader Steny Hoyer increased their activity on behalf of the bill.[89] It seems likely that Pelosi's decision to bring the energy bill to the floor at the end of June was aimed at clearing the decks for health care in July.

As the August congressional recess began, momentum behind health-care reform seemed to be regaining. However, there were troubling signs. President Obama had asked for action in both chambers by the end of July, and neither had acted. In the Senate, the Finance Committee negotiators appeared nowhere near agreement. The August recess was the longest in years. With Labor Day occurring on September 7, members would return to their districts for a full five weeks of constituent interaction. The stage was set for a prolonged public relations battle between Democrats defending the developing health-care bills, and Republican opponents and their allies determined to go on the attack.[90] Conservative groups organized to attack the Democratic bills at town hall meetings held by representatives and senators in their districts and states. Claims circulated that the Democratic legislation created so-called death panels that would make end-of-life decisions for people. Republican critics claimed that everyone would eventually be forced into a government-run insurance program. The specter of socialism was raised. Democrats from conservative-leaning districts faced intense political pressure to oppose the Democrats' reforms. Some of the town hall discourse became vitriolic thus attracting the attention of the media.[91] Anyone paying much attention to the health-care coverage would have concluded that the August recess was a setback for the administration and Democratic congressional majority.

Responding to the recess onslaught, the Democrats sought to restart their drive for health care reform when they returned to work in September. President Obama's address to a joint session of Congress on September 10th set the tone for a renewed push. Refuting the most egregious myths, Obama called for legislation that would be deficit neutral and cost no more than $900 billion over ten years. When the Senate Finance Committee was unable to reach bipartisan agreement among the gang of six, Baucus proceeded to mark up the Finance Committee bill at the end of the month. In the House, the Democratic leadership engaged in extensive consultations with all members and factions in search of a formula that could command a majority of votes on the floor.

Speaker Pelosi was the central figure in the House. With three committee-reported bills on her table, she sought to forge them into a single legislative package that would meet the president's goals and around which she could build consensus among House Democrats. Her "meet market" approach to consensus building was on full display as she engaged in an extensive round of individual and small-group meetings with House Democrats. The external political environment was still threatening. In September, Gallup polling reported trust in the legislative branch at low levels and the electorate deeply divided over health care reform. Public disaffection with Congress was bipartisan, with both parties attaining new lows for the year, the Democrats at 36% and the Republicans even lower at 27%.[92]

But when the House members returned to Washington, something surprising occurred. Away now from the stormy town hall meetings and cloistered together in Capitol meeting rooms, the Democrats searched for common ground. Press accounts reported that both conservative and liberal Democrats were seeking accommodation.[93] In the details of the polling data were clues to the possibilities for compromise. While public support on broad questions pertaining to health reform was mixed, specific elements of the plan garnered more positive reactions. For example, in October, a poll by the Pew Research Center for the People and the Press found 34% favoring health care reform. But when asked, about specific elements of reform, the results were much more favorable: 82% favored a ban on insurance plans that limited coverage of pre-existing medical conditions; 66% favored individual insurance mandates (everyone would be required to carry health insurance); 66% favored employer mandates (employers would have to provide coverage or pay a penalty); 58% favored taxing the wealth to pay for reform; 66% favored medical liability reform. Importantly, 55% favored a public insurance plan to compete with private insurance companies.[94]

Given public support for key elements of health-care reform and the fact that the provision of a public option was consistently found to provide substantial cost savings (in the private system and to the federal government), Speaker Pelosi pressed for some variation of the public option that could gather a majority of votes. The bills that had emerged from the committees were relatively liberal. Now, however, the inclusion of a public option based on Medicare rates or on Medicare rates "plus 5%" consistently produced CBO estimates below $900 billion. Blue Dog Democrats, who had sought a lower cost plan but had also opposed a strong public option, were caught in a conflict of goals. Reducing federal deficits is the holy grail of Blue Dog politics, and liberal Democrats were quick to point out that the inconsistency in their position.

Pelosi pushed hard for her preferred "robust" public option. In September and October, she repeatedly insisted that the House bill would include a public option and argued that a plan tied to Medicare rates would be most cost effective. She also stated that several alternative policy models would meet the demand for a public insurance option to help restrain the private market. Determined to pass the strongest bill she could, Pelosi sought to advance the strongest version of the public option that could win on the floor. On October 29, Pelosi announced that she would bring to the House floor a bill that would include a public insurance plan requiring negotiated rates with health care providers.[95] The Speaker's bill was along the lines of the deal that Waxman had previously negotiated with Blue Dog members of the Energy and Commerce Committee. Pelosi's decision was made after an extensive whip counting effort, and in the end, her preferred robust public option fell a few votes short of the majority she needed.

But she was not done dealing. Announcing that the bill would be brought to the floor during the first week of November, Pelosi and her leadership team engaged in a continuous round of negotiations. President Obama invited groups of legislators to the White House to discuss their concerns. These negotiations were complex because the various constituencies sought substantive policy changes and not simply the sort of distributive concessions that marked the energy bill. The final hurdle came on the issue of abortion. The federal government had for decades included in health-related legislation variations of the Hyde Amendment prohibiting the use of taxpayer dollars for abortion services. Pro-life legislators now insisted that abortion services be unavailable under the public insurance plan and also to any insurance policy purchased in part with taxpayer subsidized insurance credits. Compromise language sequestering abortion premiums from public subsidies had been included in the bill negotiated in the Energy and Commerce Committee and was now included in Pelosi's base bill. Faced with 40 pro-life defectors, Pelosi sought further compromise language to be included in the final version of the bill. Pro-life legislators, backed by the United States Conference of Catholic Bishops, insisted on an amendment to deny abortion services to any participant in the exchange whose premiums would be subsidized by the taxpayers. Any woman seeking abortion coverage would not find it in the new insurance exchange.[96]

Pelosi struck another compromise and agreed to make an anti-abortion amendment to this effect in order on the floor. This amendment, offered by Michigan Democrat Bart Stupak, was one of only two permitted under the rule governing floor consideration of the bill. The other was the Republican substitute offered by GOP floor leader John Boehner. The Republicans were also granted a MTR which they used to propose a tort reform provision. Pelosi's final strategic decisions were very unpopular among liberal Democrats who sought a stronger public insurance plan and asked for a free-standing amendment for their preferred public plan. She also angered pro-choice members by allowing the Stupak amendment.

The effects of Pelosi's strategic bargaining were reflected in the number of key endorsements the final bill received. In the days leading up to the vote both the American Medical Association and the American Association of Retired Persons endorsed the bill. They were joined by dozens of health-care provider groups. With the agreement to permit the Stupak amendment, the United States Conference of Catholic Bishops tacitly embraced the legislation.

These decisions reflected Pelosi's fundamental pragmatism. While the bill brought to the floor was not the bill she desired, it was the most progressive bill that could win. And win she did. On Saturday, November 7, 2009 the House debated and cast a series of votes on the Affordable Health Care for America Act. The Stupak Amendment passed by a vote of 240–194 with one member voting present. The Republican substitute offering minimal reform was defeated 258–176, with Democrats voting unanimously in opposition. The Republican motion to recommit was defeated 247–187 with 13 Democrats voting with the Republicans. Finally, at 11:15 P.M. the House approved the bill by a vote of 220–215. The Speaker lost 39 Democrats and gained 1 Republican vote.[97]

According to one account, the Speaker's strategic decisions on the health care bill offered "... a lesson in the limits of power for House Speaker Nancy Pelosi—and in the immense challenge of managing disappointment on the left."[98] We think that Speaker Pelosi is all too aware of the limits on her power. The American constitutional system aims to place obstacles in the path of the exercise of power, and no officer of the government is more aware of this than the Speaker of the House. Her pragmatic approach testifies to her understanding that, even in a unified party government power is constrained. The similarity between the energy bill and the health care bill is striking. In both cases Pelosi was forced to concede ground to the center in order to gather a bare majority on the House floor. In both cases she won while absorbing defections by members representing more conservative districts. In both cases she won by negotiating with the various factions within the Democratic Caucus. In both cases she had to hold liberals in line in support of centrist policies. In both cases she received minimal Republican support. Notwithstanding the fact that she had moved to the center in order to pass the bills, she was attacked from the right as pressing a liberal, statist agenda. But in both energy and health policy, she moved legislation aimed at manipulating the incentive structure of the private market rather than replacing it or taxing it directly.

And she won high praise from her Democratic colleagues in the process. A principal theme of this book stresses the need for a House Speaker to build consensus within her party caucus because she is unlikely to find much support across the aisle. In chapter 7 we return to this theme as we provide our overall assessment of Speaker Pelosi. Here, though, we pause to observe the high praise given her across the ideological spectrum of the House Democratic Caucus and by her erstwhile opponents. Thus, we find her opponents on the abortion amendment, praising her for her leadership in allowing the floor vote on the Stupak amendment. Stupak himself praised Pelosi in his testimony before the House Rules Committee. Pro-choice Democrats who had argued bitterly, to the point of tears, against the Stupak amendment, stood proudly by Pelosi's side after the final passage of the bill.[99] We find John Dingell, whose defeat at the polls she had sought and whose ouster from his powerful committee chair she had encouraged, saying: "You, Madam Speaker ...we thank you for the extraordinary leadership which you have given us in bringing us to the point where we are today." Steny Hoyer, whose leadership career she had sought to end, attributed the Democrats' victory to "her focus, her vision, her tenacity, her energy."[100] Of course members say nice things about their leaders when they win a big vote, but a clue to Pelosi's leadership style lies in contrasting her after-action statements to the encomiums she received. Eschewing credit, she extended her praise to her leadership team, now calling it a partnership, and in particular to her old adversary, John Dingell.[101]

House passage of the health bill meant that the game would continue, and now would shift to the "other body," the United States Senate. As every member of the House, Democrat or Republican, quickly learns, the real enemy is not the other party, it is the other body, the place where House-passed bills often go to die. Cloture rules in the Senate require 60 senators to pass bills, and with a bare 60-vote organizing majority, Senate Majority Leader Harry Reid (D-NV) would be hard pressed to move either energy or health bills through a fractious Senate. These were the two signature issues on which President Obama had campaigned, and the fate of his administration would hang in the balance. But with the health bill, as with the energy bill before it, Pelosi had done her part. She had set the table for the Senate to act. She had given Obama a chance. She had passed landmark legislation in the House of Representatives. Whether she had overreached and put her majority at risk would be determined by the final legislative results and the outcome of the 2010 elections.[102]

HOW TO GOVERN

We conclude our discussion of Speaker Pelosi's leadership in the 111th Congress before its first session has been completed. At the time of writing, the fate of the major energy and health care bills, which we have analyzed to understand her approach to leadership under unified party control, have yet to be determined. Still, we can state that the House of Representatives passed a substantial number of important bills in the first session of the 111th Congress, as table 5.2 illustrates. The table presents selected bills that passed the House by December 16, 2009. The public law number is provided for those bills that were enacted into law by that date. We selected bills and resolutions that were substantively significant and embodied major elements of the Democratic agenda. Important legislation, including surface transportation funding, was still moving through committee in December. From the day of her election as Speaker, Pelosi had promised a "New Direction Congress." This legislation represents a return on that promise. Some of these bills comprise a direct policy reversal from the previous Republican administration and House majority. Several represent new policy in which the Republican majority expressed no interest. Table 5.2 also provides the final passage votes along with the number of Democratic defectors and Republican converts. We see that in some policy areas such as national defense and small business promotion, legislation moved with substantial bipartisan support. Overall the Speaker won the support of more Republicans than she suffered the loss of support among Democrats. On several important bills the Democrats were unanimously in support. This voting pattern offers evidence of effective party government.

Table 5.2 Selected House Legislation and Votes of the 111th Congress, First session (listed by date of House action through December 16, 2009)

Bill No.	Title	Yea	Nay	Dem Nay	Rep Yea
H.R. 12	Lilly Ledbetter Fair Pay Act (P.L. 111–2)*	256	163	3	10
H.R. 2	Children's Health Insurance Program Reauthorization Act (PL 111–3)	289	139	2	40
H.R. 384	TARP Reform and Accountability Act	260	166	10	18
H.R. 1	American Recovery and Reinvestment Act of 2009 (Stimulus) (PL 111–5)	246	183	7	0
H.R. 1106	Helping Families Save Their Homes Act (PL 111–22)	234	191	24	7
H.R. 1262	Water Pollution Control Act Authorization Amendments	317	101	0	73
H.R. 1388	Edward M. Kennedy Serve America Act (111–13)	275	149	0	26
H.R. 1256	Family Smoking and Prevention Act (PL 111–31)	298	112	8	70
H. Con. Res. 85	Congressional Budget Resolution	233	196	20	0
H.R. 1913	Local Law Enforcement Hate Crimes Prevention Act (PL 111–84)**	249	175	17	18
H.R. 627	Credit Card Holders Bill of Rights Act (PL 111–24)	357	70	1	105
H.R. 1728	Mortgage Reform and Anti-Predatory Lending Act	300	114	3	60
H.R. 2187	21st Century Green High Performing Public Schools Facilities Act	275	155	1	24
H.R. 2352	Job Creation Through Entrepreneurship Act	406	15	0	159
S. 454	Weapons Systems Acquisition Reform Act (PL 111–23)	411	0	0	0
H.R. 915	FAA Reauthorization Act	277	136	4	37
H.R. 626	Federal Employees Paid Parental Leave Act	258	154	5	24

(continued)

Table 5.2 Continued

Bill No.	Title	Yea	Nay	Dem Nay	Rep Yea
H.R. 1886	PEACE Act (Aid to Pakistan)	234	185	18	8
H.R. 2346	Supplemental Appropriations Act (Iraq & Afghanistan wars) (PL 111–32)***	368	60	51	168
H.R. 2647	Dept of Defense Authorization Act (PL 111–84)"	389	22	20	168
H.R. 2454	American Clean Energy and Security Act	219	212	44	8
H.R. 2965	Enhancing Small Business Research and Innovation Act	386	41	13	149
H.R. 2920	Statutory Pay-As-You-Go Act	265	166	13	24
H.R. 2749	Food Safety Enhancement Act	283	142	20	54
H.R. 3269	Corporate and Financial Institution Compensation Fairness Act	237	185	16	2
H.R. 3246	Advanced Vehicle Technology Act	312	114	1	62
H.R. 3221	Student Aid and Fiscal Responsibility Act	253	171	4	6
H.R. 3585	Solar Technology Road Map	310	106	0	63
H.R. 3854	Small Business Financing and Investment Act	389	32	0	139
H.R. 3692	Affordable Health Choices for America Act	220	215	39	1
H.R. 4173	Wall Street Reform and Consumer Protection Act	223	202	27	0

*This bill was merged with S. 181 to become the Lilly Ledbetter Fair Pay Act.

**H.R. 1913 was incorporated into H.R. 2647 which enacted the hate crimes provisions into PL 111–84.

***This bill also established the car rebate program known as "Cash for Clunkers."

Source: Office of the Clerk, "Legislation and Votes," accessed at http://clerk.house.gov/legislative/legvotes.html, and Library of Congress, Thomas, Public Laws of the 111th Congress, accessed at http://www.thomas.gov/bss/d111/d111laws.html.

As we saw in chapter 3, Pelosi had facilitated the Democrats' success in the 2008 House elections by allowing members to vote their districts when necessary. This pattern continued on the major energy and health bills. The Speaker also continued her policy, deployed in the previous congress, of allowing members to treat MTRs as substantive rather than procedural votes. The decision to remove "promptly" MTRs, discussed previously in this chapter, led to a reduction in the number offered by the Republicans. By November 7, 2009 the Republicans had offered 39 MTRs; during the same period in 2007, they had offered 55. Their success rate was similar. In the 110th Congress the Republicans prevailed on 24 of 124 MTRs or 19.35%; in the 111th Congress (through December 16, 2009) they had prevailed on 9 of 43 or 21%. Yet on six of these 9 MTRs a majority of Democrats voted with the Republicans, indicating that the leadership had not whipped against them. Pelosi's larger majority, her decision to remove "promptly" MTRs, and her willingness to let members vote their districts had minimized the effectiveness of this tactic.

Any assessment of the 111th Congress must address the major crises the government faced at the beginning of 2009. The Obama administration and the enhanced Democratic majorities in the House and Senate faced the most serious set of public policy challenges of any new administration since 1933. In addition to the financial crisis and the burden of two wars, the country now had to deal with the downside of having put off resolving its most difficult public policy problems for too long. Indeed, the government had made things worse by deepening its policy commitments without providing a source of revenue. Revamping policy in the areas of health, education, the environment, energy, immigration, and entitlements along with many lesser issues would require political skill of the highest order, even given a unified government under Democratic control. The last unified Democratic government (in the 103rd Congress) had failed. Under the unified Republican government of the 107th Congress through the 109th, the philosophy of the governing party and its uncompromising desire to hold power had led to substantial public policy paralysis. The second George W. Bush administration produced few significant public policy achievements.

At the outset of the 111th Congress, as we have seen, great rhetorical emphasis was placed on the notion that to address the major challenges, it would be necessary to gather bipartisan consensus. By the August recess, it was apparent that bipartisanship on some major policy issues was not to be found. Instead, one witnessed the Democrats marshaling majorities largely within their own ranks on financial services, energy, and health care legislation. To win these votes, the House Democratic leadership had bargained its way to a majority. In this effort they demonstrated great skill, justifying one lobbyist's characterization of Speaker Pelosi: "She's just a damn good inside pol…she protects her flock."[103] It remained to be seen, however, whether Pelosi's decision to push controversial bills through the House would win for her flock a renewed license to govern by the American people. This is the challenge confronting House speakers in the era of the New American Politics. We return to it in chapter 7. First, however, we analyze in more depth Pelosi's career and speakership from the perspective of her gender.

Chapter 6

Gender

I was different in those days: a dedicated Democrat and an effective party organizer, but not in any way a public person.

—Nancy Pelosi (1987)

I didn't run because I'm a woman, but because I can help us win the majority.... But the idea of a woman as whip is very powerful. It is an important signal to women that there is infinite opportunity.

—Nancy Pelosi (2001)

Think of me as a lioness—you threaten my cubs, you have a problem.

—Nancy Pelosi (2008)

Nancy Pelosi's own words trace the evolution of her career as well as a revolution in thinking about the role of women in politics.[1] Over the last 40 years, women have entered on to the center stage of American politics. The 2008 presidential election offered evidence of this fact. Along the way, women have had to navigate a political terrain presenting obstacles and opportunities as well as gendered advantages and disadvantages. Elected to the House during this transformational period, Pelosi like other women found advantage in downplaying gender differences. But today, as Speaker, she reflects a full range of gendered images.

The more prominent roles women have come to play in the nation's political life represent a significant aspect of the New American Politics. We have suggested that this new era in America's political development is characterized by a greater diversity in participation across various demographic categories. Yet the status of women in American political life has differed from that of other excluded groups. Women, after all, have comprised more than one-half of the population all along, and their situation has thus differed from that of marginalized minorities. Women have faced many of the same barriers, including outright legal discrimination and social prejudice; but their experience has been in the context of a gendered structure of economic and social opportunity that resides deeply within the mindsets of both men and women in the society. Historians who record the rise of President Barack Obama will parse the complexities of race as a dimension of the New American Politics. Nancy Pelosi's story is about the shifting fault line of gender in this new era.

Her rise to the speakership is all the more significant in this context. Her career reveals much about what has changed and the challenges that remain for women who would aspire to the highest levels of governing. At strategic points in her public career, she avoided talking about how being a woman shaped her rise to power. For a long time, she eschewed political candidacy in favor of the obligations and joys of motherhood. Later, as a party operative, she became the relentless organizer. Today, she wields unprecedented political power as a member of Congress. Her story illustrates many of the twists and turns confronting every woman pursuing a path into politics; but because of the magnitude of her ultimate success, hers is (so far) a unique narrative. In this chapter, we analyze the paradoxes of gender power that have played into the career of the first woman Speaker in an attempt to understand the transformation of American politics.

A GENDER FRAMEWORK OF ANALYSIS

Gender is central, not peripheral, to understanding Pelosi as a politician, though she herself would not always choose to acknowledge it. Gender is a constant in her personal identity and public self. Yet we suggest that she has not allowed her gender to define or limit her career, even as it has shaped the opportunities, norms, and the political strategies that have marked her success. Despite her public disavowals, she has displayed a form of ambition— private ambition—that is largely unrecognized in political science. We also argue that she has brought a distinctive voice to her new role, a voice that confronts and capitalizes on gender stereotypes. She has persistently articulated the legitimacy of the uniquely female experience of motherhood as preparation for and authority in political office. Her leadership style seems very consistent with how women lead in other settings. Most significantly, her approach as speaker is well suited to the contemporary Congress and the charged partisan environment in which she operates.

We frame Pelosi's career with three concepts: ambition, opportunity, and voice. These concepts represent important theoretical lenses familiar to those who study gender and politics. The debate over the underrepresentation of women in political office often focuses on the question of ambition.[2] Historically, political ambition was assumed to be antithetical to women's nature and best manifested in the ideal of "Republican womanhood," whose expression of political involvement and ambition took place through the nurturing of husbands and sons.[3] Well into the twentieth century, women were thought to lack political ambition, to be disinterested in public affairs, and to perceive the public sphere as a masculine domain. As scholars came to "discover" political women, they asked whether sexism or institutional arrangements thwart ambitious women.[4] Some wondered whether traditional gender socialization nurtures less ambition in women and gives them less encouragement to pursue political careers.[5] Other scholars argued that a masculine ethos pervades politics and discourages qualified women from acting on impulses of ambition.[6] Whatever the source, even recent scholarly work suggests that a gender gap in political ambition persists.[7]

In addition to the assumptions scholars have held about these differences between men and women with respect to the incentives toward political ambition, political scientists have understood ambition itself mostly as it is displayed by political men. Joseph Schlesinger first posited that a legislator's ambition may be "discrete" (the desire for a specific office with a defined term), "static" (the goal of making a long career out of a particular office), or "progressive" (the aspiration "to attain an office more important than the one he now seeks or is holding").[8] In addition to these three, Rebekah Herrick and Michael K. Moore found evidence of a distinct fourth form of ambition: "intrainstitutional," that is, the aspiration some legislators have to leadership positions primarily within the institutions they occupy.[9]

These forms of ambition may be inadequate to describe political women. The literature on women and politics suggests that women are drawn into public life by the desire to tackle issues and solve policy problems rather than to acquire a specific office.[10] Thus, their politics is focused not on officeholding but on task accomplishment. In addition, with the exception of discrete ambition, all of the modes assume a considerable length of life in politics; yet many political women come to public office later in life and are thus less likely to aim for long political careers. As we noted in chapter 1, Pelosi both came first to Congress and took over the speakership at older ages than had any of the other postreform speakers. What defined Nancy Pelosi's ambition and determined her rise to the top?

The opportunity structure for members to rise in House leadership has its own gendered patterns and dynamic.[11] Experts in organizations and organizational behavior suggest that leadership ladders are not gender neutral, and such experts employ a host of structural metaphors—trapdoors, sticky floors, and glass ceilings—to describe various types of obstacles.[12] Congress has had its own version of dead-end committee assignments, symbolic but largely inconsequential leadership roles, and a marble ceiling. Historically, women have often been excluded from institutional power positions or strategic mentorships. Their token numbers have limited their influence, and the relative shortness of their political careers has necessarily truncated their opportunities to rise in the congressional hierarchy. In short, access to positions of power has not been uniformly available to women in the institution.

The masculine ethos of Congress, and politics more generally, has been slow to change. In 1978, when congressmen were interviewed about the political skills of women, they openly disparaged their female colleagues, and both male and female members expressed pessimism about women sharing leadership power.[13] By the 1990s, however, women had begun to contest for congressional leadership positions—albeit still mostly lower ones—in significant numbers, and optimism about women's prospects was rising. Speaker Pelosi's strategic choices short-circuited some of the gender barriers that had previously confronted other women. Her success in securing the speakership must be seen in the context of the gendered opportunity structure. So we ask: how did Nancy Pelosi successfully navigate the gendered labyrinths of the U.S. House?[14]

Voice is the essential antecedent of political participation, power, and influence. For the suffragists, securing the franchise was the first essential step toward achieving the goal of being heard. But women's voice has historically been encumbered by the paradox of public- and private-sphere expectations. The public woman—the shrew, the witch, and the harlot—was scorned and punished for speaking, while the private woman was simply not heard. Kathleen Hall Jamieson characterizes this public-private dilemma as the double bind of "silence/shame" and considers it one of the key barriers to women in political leadership.[15] In its contemporary manifestation, this bind burdens women with a host of stereotypical expectations that can detract from the substance and impact of their words. Since "the essence of politics is talk," finding one's voice and being heard is no small matter.[16] As we noted in chapter 2, Pelosi in her first congressional race acknowledged this essential fact in her slogan "The Voice That Will Be Heard." Our analysis of her speeches and press conferences (in chapter 4) suggests that she has incorporated a nuanced understanding of women's political voice—both its perceived strengths and negatives—into her leadership style. She is also contributing a distinctive voice to political discourse by her willingness to invoke liberally images of motherhood, the home, the family, and even the fiercely protective lioness.

Our analysis of voice extends to aspects of leadership style and presentation of self. Women in politics have been routinely scrutinized by the media and voters regarding their personal appearance, wardrobes, and marital status; the three Hs (hair, hemline, husband) hold a special fascination with the public and the media. The recent experiences of presidential candidate and U.S. senator Hillary Rodham Clinton and GOP vice presidential nominee and Alaska governor Sarah Palin demonstrate that disparate media coverage of women is still prevalent.[17]

Pelosi's leadership of the House, as noted, reveals a Speaker who is intensely competitive and partisan. She is also highly effective at coalition building and collaboration, willing to share credit, and almost relentlessly pragmatic; she takes victories when she can, and when she loses she returns to fight another day for the policy priorities she holds.[18] Many of our informants perceive her as having a style that is well suited to the political imperatives of the House, the realities of her ideologically diverse party, and the political times, irrespective of her gender; but this style also comprises distinctive gendered dimensions. Thus, we finally ask: how has Nancy Pelosi navigated the gendered shoals of public leadership, and how has she crafted a leadership style and political voice to meet the particular constraints of her speakership?

AMBITION

Pelosi's career trajectory bears both similarities with and differences from those of other congresswomen of her era. Like them, she has confronted key barriers, ranging from blatant sexism to subtle institutional biases. However, she also has enjoyed political assets and encouragement of her political ambition that many other women have not. Hers is a story shaped by and understood in the context of the modern women's movement, even though her pursuit of public office was not birthed by it. Her early disavowal of electoral aspiration stands in contrast to the classic formulation of progressive ambition. We argue that Pelosi displays a form of gendered ambition that has been less well understood and appreciated: task ambition. Rather than focusing on the attainment of office as a fulfillment of one's personal ambition, task ambition uses political opportunities to accomplish specific objectives. For Pelosi, the task was always to elect Democrats who would support the progressive policies she had learned in the D'Alesandro household.

Schlesinger's notion of "progressive ambition" suggests a well-formed sense of successive career steps that can be acted on when the opportunity arises.[19] But the literature on gender and ambition points out that the intersection between ambition and opportunity may vary for men compared to women in politics. Virginia Sapiro, for example, made note of the higher likelihood of women to defer to family commitments while similarly situated men acted on their political ambitions.[20] Others identified additional differences. One is a greater reluctance of women to disrupt interpersonal relations for the sake of pursuing one's political path.[21] Another resides in women's need for additional encouragement or recruitment in order to act on political ambition.[22] A third is a greater emphasis on issues as important to the decision to run.[23] We see evidence of all three factors in shaping Nancy Pelosi's ambition.

Historical Barriers

The barriers to public office have always been formidable. Every political candidate whether male or female needs the financial wherewithal, the public stature expected of officeholders, and the freedom of action to mount a successful election effort. For women, the historic legal doctrine of coverture, whereby a woman's legal existence was "suspended during marriage," magnified all three hurdles.[24] Recognized in English common law, coverture described women's legal status in the original 13 colonies. Married women were proclaimed "civilly dead" with no separate economic, civil, or legal rights except through their husband's status. Coverture provided a rationale for women's exclusion from the voting booth and the public square as well as the marketplace. Over the past two centuries, as women gained political and legal rights, the binds of coverture disappeared, even while the less visible barriers remained.

The remnants of coverture have blocked women's path to political office even in the modern era. Prior to the 1960s, the most common path traveled by women to Congress was through "widow's succession," whereby women succeeded their late husbands who died in office. Some women completed a single partial term of office (e.g., Rep. Rebecca Felton [D-GA], Rep. Marian Clarke [R-NY]), while others served distinguished careers of considerable length (e.g., Senator Margaret Chase Smith [R-ME], Rep. Frances Bolton [R-OH]).[25] Widows essentially inherited their husbands' wealth and good name, while also gaining the freedom of action expected of a public official. Female officeholding through widow's succession helped pave the way for the entrance of women into Congress and allowed women to secure office without "running as a woman."[26] As the stewards of their husbands' political legacy, widows could claim a certain political expertise, as well as a mantle of legitimacy that other women could not. Four current congresswomen succeeded their late husbands, and 47 of the 242 women who have served in the House or Senate did so after the death of their husbands.[27]

The second most common path of women to politics has been by way of economic privilege or social and political connections that "constitute an elite status."[28] Irwin Gertzog notes that such characteristics have substituted for widow's status as credentials that provided "inexperienced [women] candidates with a cachet that helped them claim credibility."[29] Women parlayed their prestige, fortune, and sometimes glamour into political careers, including, for example, Congresswoman Helen Gahagan Douglas (D-CA), world-famous stage actress and wife of fellow actor Melvyn Douglas, and Congresswoman Clare Boothe Luce (R-CN), who was well known as a playwright, journalist, and publishing executive.

A special subset within this elite group is comprised of political daughters who, like wives, can claim special expertise and personal exposure to politics through their families. The first political daughter to run (1926) and reach the U.S. House on a second attempt (1928) was Ruth Bryan Owens (D-FL) — though without the blessing of her father, William Jennings Bryan.[30] (Owens' own daughter ran unsuccessfully for Congress in 1958 and in 1960.) Sons and daughters of political leaders have the advantages of name and knowledge of the family profession. For example, Congresswoman Ruth Hanna McCormick (R-IL) defended her credentials by saying: "I didn't run for office as a woman. I ran as the daughter of [Republican Party boss and U.S. Senator] Mark Hanna and the wife of Medill McCormick [of the *Chicago Tribune* publishing family] and therefore well-equipped for office by heredity and training."[31] That training included her first political speech on behalf of her father's presidential candidate, William McKinley, and work as her father's secretary in his senatorial office. Among current and recent women in Congress are several political daughters: U.S. senators Nancy Kassebaum (R-KS) and Mary Landrieu (D-LA) and congresswomen Rosa DeLauro (D-CT), Barbara Kennelly (D-CT), Lucille Roybal-Allard (D-CA), Susan Molinari (R-NY), and, of course, Nancy Pelosi. Linda Witt and her colleagues note that life in "the political pond" may be even more important for daughters than sons:

> Contemporary political daughters, whether they are supported by their fathers or not, exhibit considerable ease with politics as a result of their early familiarity with political life. Not only are the nuts and bolts of politics— campaigning, parades, leafleting—more familiar to them, they readily claim the label "politician" for themselves, a label many women who are elected to office find distasteful.[32]

Gertzog notes that in today's Congress, most women, much like the men, gain seats as strategic politicians—that is, typically, by using lower levels of office as springboards to higher ones.[33] They base their selection of political campaigns on the likelihood of success, a dispassionate political calculus of the competition, and an understanding that future success often depends on "claiming credit" or "advertising" their past legislative accomplishments.[34] Gertzog notes:

> Congresswomen who are strategic politicians have come gradually to replace, first, widows of congressmen, and, second, women whose principal resource was the sociopolitical and economic status of their families....It means that prior election to state and local office has become a more important component of the credentials women rely on to secure seats in the House.[35]

Contemporary Underrepresentation

Family pedigree, economic wealth, prior officeholding, and strategic sense contribute to success for political women but are also required of men who enter politics. What, then, explains the difference in their numbers in elected office? In pondering women's underrepresentation, political scientists have focused on ambition.[36] In the most comprehensive analysis to date, Jennifer Lawless and Richard Fox implicate the "gender dynamics of the candidate emergence process" and proffer a theory of gender and political ambition.[37] Among equally qualified men and women in the primary "eligibility pools" (i.e. law, business, education, and politics), these authors find, women are less likely to have considered running for office, and thus are also less likely to have expressed an interest in running for office or to act on that interest. At the critical stage of candidate emergence, women are not poised to make a move, and they are less likely to be recruited or encouraged to run.[38]

The source of women's reluctance lies in traditional gender socialization and its pervasive effects, say Lawless and Fox. They describe three ways gender socialization advantages men and holds back women. The first includes traditional family roles. These burden women with a disproportionate share of household and child-care duties, produce less encouragement from family and parents to think about political careers, and impose on women (but not typically men) the problem of balancing home with career obligations. Second, in an underlying "masculinized ethos" of politics, women are less often recruited or encouraged to run for office than their male peers. Finally, there is evidence of a "gendered psyche" among women candidates, who tend to see themselves as less qualified, to be less confident in the adequacy of their experience, and generally to doubt their qualifications.

Such findings are not new. Marcia Lee's 1974 survey of female local party activists found that these women did not see themselves as officeholders. They believed that running for office was not a "proper" activity for a woman to pursue and thought "most men would prefer women to contribute to politics in ways other than running for office."[39] While survey indicators of traditional gender socialization may be more nuanced or phrased in politically correct ways 30 years later, Lawless and Fox report "the enduring effects of traditional gender socialization that transcend all generations." They point to data as recent as a 2003 survey of 18- to 24-year-old undergraduate students that found female undergraduates 40% less likely than males to have considered running for office as a possible career path.[40]

Pelosi's Ambition

What, then, about the woman who would be Speaker? To be sure, her own narrative and the accounts of others suggest that Pelosi was reluctant to run and had to be persuaded to step into her first race as a candidate for public office. "I was always around politics, but I knew one thing: I never wanted to run for public office," she told a group of children in her office as part of the 2007 Take Your Child to Work Day.[41] In her autobiography, she writes of several occasions on which she expressed reluctance to run for political office. She deflected entreaties from San Francisco Mayor Joseph Alioto to consider running for local office. Later, she balked at efforts to recruit her to run for Congress. She turned down the opportunity to run for a congressional seat in 1984, when Congressman Phil Burton suggested she run for his brother John's congressional seat.[42] That seat was ultimately won by Barbara Boxer. In 1987, on being recruited again, Pelosi hesitated: "I was forty-seven years old, a mother of five, happily married, and never—not even once—thinking or wanting this to happen to me."[43]

Ultimately, it took a request by a woman who had replaced her husband in Congress, Sala Burton, to convince Pelosi to take the plunge. Burton called Pelosi to her hospital bed and entreated her to seek the venerable San Francisco seat long held by her husband, Phil Burton. Although Pelosi told Burton she would make the run, she still harbored doubts.

> So I went to Alexandra [the youngest Pelosi child still at home] and I said, "Alexandra, Mom has an opportunity to run for Congress. But since you're just—you have one more year in high school. If you don't think that's a good idea, then don't worry about it because I'm not invested into this. It would be easy for me just to say no." And Alexandra said, in the vernacular of the time, "Mother, get a life."[44]

Given her insistence that she never imagined running for office, Pelosi does not fit the model of a modern strategic female politician but best mirrors the prototypical economic or political elite. She enjoyed both political connections and economic comfort that allowed her to jump into a high-profile congressional race as a relative novice and triumph over several other "quality candidates," that is, candidates who had held previous elective offices.[45] Growing up in a political family immersed in campaigns and constituency casework and enjoying considerable family wealth, Pelosi possessed advantages that allowed her, as a first-time congressional candidate, to be competitive. By the time she ran for Congress, she had acquired an atypical (especially for a woman) network of heavyweight Democratic mentors—governors, U.S. senators, and national party leaders. She also possessed one of the single most important assets of a successful political woman: a wealthy and supportive husband. Paul Pelosi's financial success as a real estate investor and developer allowed him to generously support his wife's political career. She also inherited elements of the Burton political coalition of liberals, environmentalists, labor unions, and women.[46]

Pelosi herself gives enormous credit to the lessons learned growing up in her Baltimore home, where politics was the D'Alesandro family business and both her mother and father participated as full partners in the enterprise. As a political daughter, she had been doted on by her father, who served in the Maryland State House, the U.S. House, and then as mayor of Baltimore. As the youngest child and only girl in the family, she held a favored position. She was chosen to hold the family Bible for her father at his first mayoral swearing in, and she accompanied her father to many functions, including a dinner feting then U.S. Senator John F. Kennedy. Baltimore politics taught her the lessons of detailed organization, the importance of small favors that later translated into loyal support, and a passion for the values of the Democratic Party. The D'Alesandro household was immersed in politics. As she put it, "Our whole lives were politics. If you entered the house, it was always campaign time, and if you went into the living room, it was always constituent time."[47]

Though her father was the officeholder and patriarch of the family, her mother, Annunciata, was the center of this political world, overseeing the constituent service operation—the so-called favor desk. Pelosi's mother was the model of a political woman, a model Pelosi herself followed as a behind-the-scenes party activist in California before she accepted Sala Burton's challenge. When Pelosi describes her role in politics as an extension of her role as a mother and grandmother, she harkens back to her mother's example, as well as her own experience of organizing her family and household around the rhythms of successive campaigns and political party work.

In many ways, Pelosi's upbringing epitomizes the traditional gender socialization that Lawless and Fox find to be a major hurdle for other women, but her family life and education also provided unique assets that allowed her to step across the threshold of opportunity when she was thrust into the race for the Burton seat. Pelosi entered college before the wave of enhanced opportunities that came as women secured legal and civil rights and gained access to higher education in the 1960s and 1970s. Throughout the 1950s, the aftermath of war promoted a view of femininity emphasizing "that women were greater powers for good when exerting their influence on children and the home rather than competing with men."[48] Annunciata D'Alesandro knew these constraints firsthand—her budding career as an auctioneer was cut short and her aspirations to study law were upended because of the demands of raising six children and acting as helpmate to her husband's political career. Annunciata (or "Big Nancy" as she was known in the Little Italy enclave of Baltimore) wanted for her daughter those things that had been beyond her own reach and possibilities. It was she who insisted, over the objections of her husband, that Nancy be allowed to leave home to attend Trinity College, a women's college in Washington, D.C.

Pelosi's high school and college days provided a host of leadership experiences often denied to young women of that era. She attended the Institute of Notre Dame, an all-girls high school under the care and tutelage of the Sisters of Notre Dame in Baltimore, and served as vice president of student government. At Trinity, she was active in the International Relations Club and the Political Affairs Club.[49] Elsewhere, the number of women studying political science was in decline, and more generally academic settings had witnessed "the great withdrawal" of professional women.[50] But in the protected environment of a women's educational institution, the study of politics and practical leadership experience came with women as role models and without the stigma or limitations of coeducational settings.[51] Both Trinity College and the Institute of Notre Dame helped to launch prominent women politicians; Senator Barbara Mikulski graduated from the Institute, and both Congresswoman Kennelly and Kathleen Sebelius, former governor of Kansas and now Secretary of Health and Human Services, are Trinity alumnae.

After college, Pelosi followed the most traditional path for a woman, marriage and children. Between 1964 and 1970, five children arrived on the scene, and by 1969, Nancy and Paul Pelosi had moved to San Francisco, where the late 1960s and 1970s witnessed great political fervor and social activism—the civil rights movement, the Berkeley free speech movement, growing anti–Vietnam War demonstrations, mobilization for the Equal Rights Amendment and women's rights, and the nascent gay rights movement. But the realities of running a household with five small children and the difficulties in finding babysitters and household help left Pelosi sidelined from these social movements. Her main volunteer activity focused on Democratic Party politics.

From her Baltimore roots, she knew how to incorporate political activity into a household of children. While her political philosophy was not at odds with the liberal tides washing over San Francisco, Pelosi, unlike many other political women of her generation, was not a movement feminist whose launch into politics came as a result of consciousness raising and Equal Rights Amendment activism. She simply did what her mother had done before her: involving her family in the work of the Democratic Party.

After the failure to secure passage of the Equal Rights Amendment to the U.S. Constitution, the modern women's movement inspired many politically active women into electoral politics. Pelosi's personal path was rooted in party politics and bore little resemblance to that of some of her female colleagues, whose political careers were nurtured by the women's movement, as these examples illustrate. While Paul and Nancy Pelosi were getting married in 1963 and celebrating the birth of their first daughter in 1964, Patsy Mink (D-HI) was campaigning to become the first Asian-American woman in Congress; she would be a fierce advocate for women's issues. While Congresswomen Bella Abzug and Shirley Chisholm were helping to cofound the National Women's Political Caucus in 1971 and Patricia Schroeder (D-CO) became the first woman with young children to be elected to the U.S. House, Nancy Pelosi was beginning her volunteer work for the California Democratic Party and tending to her children. When Virginia Shapard (D-GA) in her 1978 congressional race faced charges by Newt Gingrich that she would neglect her children if elected, Pelosi was juggling her children's homework, carpools, and leadership of the Northern California Democratic Party.[52] When Harriett Woods, a 20-year political veteran of local and Missouri legislative politics, ran for the U.S. Senate in Missouri in 1982 and was rebuffed by party officials who preferred a "man for the job," Pelosi was starting her second year as chair of the California Democratic Party.[53] When Geraldine Ferraro was named the 1984 vice presidential candidate of the Democratic Party, Pelosi was recruiting 10,000 volunteers as state party chair and chairing the host committee for the Democratic convention in San Francisco. When Ellen Malcolm first organized EMILY's List to promote women candidates in 1985, Pelosi already had established a vast fund-raising network and established ties with prominent California politicians: the Burton coalition, lieutenant governor and personal mentor Leo McCarthy, and her neighbor, Dianne Feinstein.

While the most common route to public office for women of her generation led them through successive local and state offices to gain credibility, Pelosi's rise demonstrated a distinctive pattern of "progressive ambition" in a realm that she knew could be balanced with her commitment to home and family. Even her service as the chair of the California Democratic Party allowed her to involve her family in her party-building activities, sometimes taking the kids with her as she traveled the state. Yet consider this contrast. In the 1986 electoral cycle, just one year before her special election, women running in congressional contests averaged 15 years of officeholding experience at the state and local level; Pelosi had never ventured beyond Democratic Party office.

If she harbored ambitions for a more public life, Pelosi had to confront the "the liability of being Ms., Mrs. or Mommy."[54] Embedded in beliefs about traditional family roles is the premise that "women, across generations, are forced to reconcile career and family with political ambition in ways that men are not."[55] If she was a stay-at-home mom, a female candidate might doubt her credibility and experience. If she pursued an office, she might be criticized for neglecting her family. If she was single or childless, she might be the target of rumors about her femininity. If she waited until her children were grown and her career established, the door to a political career might have closed. In short, as a political woman, Pelosi had to confront a familiar double bind offering hard choices. She could upset traditional norms of gender decorum, risk being defined by her husband or significant male patron, or communicate that her personal ambition came before marriage vows and family obligations.[56]

Pelosi chose motherhood. She intertwined the burdens of family and household duties and party politics until her children were grown and independent. This passage from her autobiography shows quite clearly her detachment from the raging political currents of the Vietnam era, her commitment to her family, and her latent ambition to be something other than a housewife.

> Someone once asked me if I was restless during that time [1968 presidential election], and I said no, because that implies some level of discontent. And I was personally content because for me, there was nothing more exciting than having and caring for new babies.... Yet I always knew that I did not want to deal only with meals, the laundry, and the house forever. I still thought that I'd go to law school when the children were grown.[57]

When she did launch a campaign for a high-profile position in the race for national party chair, she faced criticism. She was queried about her children and family, dismissed for her lack of experience, and characterized in gender-stereotypic ways as "just a housewife," a "party girl," and an "airhead."[58] When she did enter her first congressional race, she again confronted the charges that she was a lightweight, a stay-at-home mom who could not be a serious congressional contender.

What do we learn about women and political ambition by analyzing Pelosi's career? While we do not question her own assertions that she never imagined a life in public office, she demonstrated remarkable task ambition, in a context she knew well. Combining party activism and family life, she built a remarkable and unique network of friends and allies while working to elect Democrats to office. Unlike many of her female contemporaries in the U.S. House, she did not cut her political teeth in the women's movement and did not follow the typical path of serving in a series of local offices of increasing visibility.

Four factors distinguish Pelosi from the women in Lawless and Fox's study of emerging candidates. First, she had powerful female role models and educational experiences that bolstered her confidence. Not the least of these mentors and role models was her mother, who made sure that Nancy had an education that would free her from the constraints of Baltimore's Little Italy and offer new opportunities. Sala Burton was another formidable female role model whose own congressional service and personal imprimatur served to launch Pelosi into public office. Second, Pelosi was clearly *recruited* for officeholding, a push not always available to other women. Burton's deathbed blessing bestowed a credibility and legitimacy on Pelosi that were unassailable. To be sure, there were powerful male elected officials in Pelosi's network, such as Leo McCarthy and Jerry Brown; but she was also helped through the door of opportunity by the influence and support of Big Nancy and Sala Burton. Third, Pelosi successfully navigated traditional gender and family roles in a way that allowed her to leap several rungs up the political ladder rather than start at the bottom. Her party work and family life were seamlessly interwoven, and her personal wealth and family connections produced an unparalleled network of national political leaders and patrons who were ready and able to repay their political favors when she chose to run for Congress. Finally, she benefited from running in a state and district that was already accustomed to seeing women in high-profile public offices. Dianne Feinstein, Barbara Boxer, and Sala Burton had cleared the path Pelosi would travel. The masculine ethos of politics, which other women would confront in more conservative political settings, was breaking down in San Francisco.

Paradoxically, Pelosi's exercise of ambition did not include "running as a woman" but took the route of an earlier generation of women politicians who had found that disavowing one's gender was safer. Linda Witt, Karen Paget, and Glenna Matthews credit Helen Gahagan Douglas, another California congresswoman, with being the first woman politician to "run as a woman" and call attention to her sex to illustrate her public policy concerns—the economic plight of the housewife during World War II.[59] Pelosi, by contrast, adopted a genderless message, not a feminist strategy. She was the "voice that will be heard," generically suggesting she possessed the powerful connections to make an immediate impact on congressional politics.

Though not intended to specifically describe Pelosi, Witt and her colleagues may have written the best description of the ambition that took Pelosi from Little Italy to the speakership:

Let us imagine for a moment we have a woman "keenly interested in politics" who wants what her brother has been bequeathed—a right to run for high political office, the right to be a leader, to be a participant not an observer in her own citizenship. She's stuffed envelopes and canvassed voters. She burns with, probably silent, ambition. Yet her most painful "skirmishes" still may be on the horizon. Those are the daily battles she has with who she has been told she is (daughter, wife, mother, woman) and all she is trying to be (power-wielder, candidate, politician, leader, daughter, wife, mother, woman).[60]

POLITICAL OPPORTUNITY

Ambition plays out against the backdrop of political opportunities that come and go. Not only does opportunity determine fortunes on the campaign trail, it shapes institutional careers once members of Congress arrive in Washington. Richard Fenno notes that members come to Congress with aspirations to make good policy, serve their constituents, or move up and acquire power in the institution.[61] Success at any of these goals requires resources, time, and opportunity, but in particular the acquisition of positions of power requires staying power and making good strategic choices when opportunity presents itself.

Opportunity structures are not gender neutral, because men and women do not come to an institution with equivalent resources with which to take advantage of available opportunities.[62] Setting aside for the moment the question of how much raw institutional sexism still exists in Congress in the twenty-first century, it remains true that men and women enter into political life with different life circumstances and constraints. It is no accident that opportunity structures, though inherently invisible and informal, are described with a host of very concrete words—glass ceilings, sticky floors, pink-collar ghettos, dead ends, mommy tracks, and critical mass.[63] These metaphors imply physical barriers and rules that treat men and women differently and unfairly. In fact, sexism operates in more nuanced ways, with no explicit rules—only norms, unarticulated values, and expectations, which can only be learned through mentoring and learning the unspoken culture of an organization. Alice Eagly and Linda Carli note that the metaphor of the glass ceiling is misleading; they prefer the metaphor of labyrinths of power, to suggest the twists and turns of navigating a profession, company, or institution. Pelosi herself frequently refers to the "marble ceiling" as a metaphor more suited to the difficult challenge she faced.

What are the key features of the U.S. House that have made navigating its structures of power so formidable for women? First, because most women come to political careers, on average, at an older age than men, the seniority system puts women at a disadvantage in climbing the leadership ladder or obtaining committee chairs. Second, because women have been a numerical minority in Congress, their token status has, until recently, left them marginalized in terms of power. Third, over time women gained access to the lower rungs of the Republican and Democratic leadership ladders, but this did not lead to access to the higher rungs. Fourth, the types of districts most likely to elect women to Congress present challenges, albeit different ones in the two parties, for women aspiring to leadership positions. Fifth, sexism is still a reality that shapes perceptions about women in leadership, even though its effects are diminishing. We explore each of these opportunity variables in more detail and then turn to Pelosi's strategic choices in navigating the congressional labyrinth of leadership opportunities.

Power Structures

Seniority has long been a valued norm of Congress. As a practical matter, however, women have generally lacked sufficient seniority to move into higher levels of leadership or to chair committees.[64] The usual opportunities to garner political favors, acquire power, and move into vacant positions have evaded women members because of their lack of seniority. Since the so-called Year of the Woman election in 1992, the number of women coming to the House has risen steadily, a phenomenon more apparent on the Democratic side of the aisle, and with it seniority has increased. Even so, as the 110th Congress convened in January 2007, only 12 women ranked in the top third (78 members) of Democratic Party seniority. Only four women chaired standing committees, including one of the "power" committees (New York Congresswoman Louise Slaughter as head of the Rules Committee), but that small number is the highest ever attained for women in Congress.[65] The last woman to head a House committee was Representative Jan Meyers (R-KS), who led the Committee on Small Business in the 104th Congress (1995–96). Under the Republicans, the declining importance of seniority and the transition to term limits for committee chairs did not aid women in the House.[66] No GOP women were selected to chair a full committee, even though term limits created 14 openings on the 19 major House committees in the 107th Congress and more openings in subsequent congresses.[67]

A second impediment for women lies in their sheer numbers, or rather lack of them. Until recently, the small number of women serving in the House left them relegated to token status. Management expert Rosabeth Moss Kanter described the token experience as subjecting the rare woman or minority in an organization to heightened scrutiny, stereotypic judgments, performance pressures, and the absence of powerful sponsors.[68] Organizational sociologist Janice Yoder, who studied the gender integration of male bastions such as military academies, added the insight that tokens often experience rejection, hostility, and resistance as intruders or newcomers.[69] In congressional leadership, for example, women have generally been relegated to low-level leadership jobs corresponding to their token status. Furthermore, there have never been more than two women in elected leadership positions of either party simultaneously.

Prior to Pelosi, no woman had ever served in the top party leadership posts of Speaker, floor leader, or whip. The general pattern of the postreform period through the early 1990s was that women ran largely uncontested for the positions of conference vice chair or secretary but were unsuccessful in efforts to move up to higher office.[70] For example, House members Mary Rose Oakar (D-OH), Lynn Martin (R-IL), and Shirley Chisholm (D-NY) were consensus choices for lower level positions who met with open competition and defeat in their efforts to climb the leadership ladder.

During the last half of the 1990s, the number and success of women in congressional leadership began to change. Both parties moved to create additional elected leadership positions, broadening opportunities for participation.[71] While only 9 women sought elected leadership posts from the 94th (1971–72) through the 103rd (1993–94) congresses, 16 competed for posts between the 104th (1994–95) and the 109th (2005–6). In 1998, Representative Jennifer Dunn (R-WA) became the first woman to run for a senior leadership post in her unsuccessful candidacy for majority leader. Also in 1998, Democratic women organized and lobbied then minority leader Dick Gephardt (D-MO) "to appoint more women to fill openings on powerful committees and to include more women in the leadership," after a statistical analysis revealed a predominance of women on committees like agriculture and science and a paucity of women on the powerful Energy and Commerce and Ways and Means committees.[72] Gephardt responded and created a new position of assistant to the minority leader and appointed to it Congresswoman Rosa DeLauro, an unsuccessful candidate for caucus chair.

But even while leadership opportunities were expanding, female aspirants faced more competition, increasing the probability of failure. Between 1975 and 2007, 61.7% of women candidates ran in contested leadership races, compared with 46.6% of men. During the period 1991–2007, as the number of women in Congress increased steadily, women were much more likely to run in contested races than men: 77.8% of Democratic women ran in contested races, compared with 44.2% of the men, and among Republicans, 68.2% of women faced opponents, compared with 58.0% of the GOP men. This level of competition reflected two realities: first, initial rungs of the leadership ladder, where women were most likely to compete, draw the most candidates; second, some positions (particularly on the GOP side of the aisle) tacitly became women's posts, drawing multiple female leadership contestants but producing relatively few new women leaders.

The fourth feature of the opportunity structure involves the types of districts that elect women. Most successful leadership aspirants enjoy electoral security, allowing them to focus their efforts and energies on the campaigns of their party members. Political scientists Barbara Palmer and Dennis Simon identify factors for both parties in the House that make some districts more likely to elect women than others.[73] The most women-friendly districts for Republicans tend to be less conservative, more urban, and more diverse than the typical Republican-controlled district. Thus, Republican women are likely to be more moderate, hence outside the mainstream of their party in terms of ideology. Similarly, Palmer and Simon point out, Democratic women are most likely to win in districts that are more liberal, more urban, more diverse, and wealthier than those where most of their male colleagues win seats. Democratic women are ideologically more likely to be liberal, hence positioned beyond the median rather than close to the mean.

As a result, women in Congress may be poorly situated to compete for leadership positions as "middlemen"—a term first coined by political scientist David Truman, who posited that congressional leaders were more likely to emerge from the ideological middle of their party.[74] Truman's original formulation did not contend with more partisan legislative environments and the greater ideological polarization evident in the New American Politics. Indeed, more recent research suggests that at least in the last four congresses, most leaders emerge from the extremes of their party—the left for Democrats and the right for Republicans—and few would be considered "chamber moderates" who are outside of their party's mainstream and closer to the other party ideologically.[75] Pelosi was tagged by her opponents as too liberal to represent the mainstream of the Democratic Party in her rise to party leader; but in fact, there were more liberals than moderates in the Democratic Caucus.

Hidden Sexism

Finally, the opportunity structure has its own manifestations of sexism. The biographies of congresswomen include frequent references to unequal treatment—exclusion from insider gatherings, assignment to powerless committees, and denial of privileges that are the norm for the men.[76] Congressional lore tells of milestones of integrating the Capitol facilities, from the cloak-room to the committee room to the dining room to the gym. Masculinity influences both the trivial—everything from the masculine titles of office-holders to the availability of members' bathroom facilities—and the more pernicious.

The most insidious assumptions derive from beliefs that women are less capable of rational decision-making, too emotional to be relied on, and thus not up to the job of legislating. Such assumptions get communicated when accomplished women members are noted for their young adult experiences as high school or college cheerleaders rather than their professional achievements (e.g., senators Kay Bailey Hutchison [R-TX] and Carol Moseley-Braun [D-IL]).[77] Or when a colleague queries a woman's ability to both serve in Congress and raise a family—to which Congresswoman Pat Schroeder (D-CO) famously noted: "I have a brain and a uterus, and I use them both."[78] Or when women encounter the experience of former representative Jill Long (D-IN):

> A colleague of mine complimented me on my appearance and then said that
> he was going to chase me around the House floor....I was offended and I was
> embarrassed. Sexual harassment is serious. It is not funny and it is not cute,
> and it is certainly not complimentary.[79]

Pelosi herself has been subjected to gendered criticism of her intellect. Comedian turned commentator Dennis Miller described her as a "Mary Kay dropout" and a "latter day 'Wacky O'—regurgitating the Democratic talking points that she had to learn phonetically because the word 'grasp' is not even vaguely in her vocabulary."[80] Miller's references linking physical attractive-ness and brain power are old-school sexism, what Jamieson had labeled the double bind of femininity-competence, whereby a woman might have one attribute (beauty or brains) but certainly not both.[81]

The disparate status of congresswomen in part reflects the second-class status of women generally in realms of public life, but the barriers in Congress are falling, as they have been throughout society. Nonetheless, more nuanced manifestations of sexism remain. Echoing the sentiments of other highly successful women in male-dominated professions, Pelosi commented:

> Sexism is all-pervasive in our society, getting less so in the next generation
> and the next generation is less prone to that. I don't make a big issue of
> it....I just deal with that by outperforming, outworking or just succeeding
> in what I'm doing and hoping to gain the respect of my colleagues for what
> I do. If they still have a problem with sex, that's their problem. I can't make it
> be my problem. I won't be held up by it.[82]

Pelosi's Path

Pelosi's path through the congressional opportunity structure combined both traditional and novel elements. She had enough seniority and political clout to be competitive, and she could take advantage of the changing demography of her caucus. As noted in chapter 1, she was older when she first came to the House than all of her predecessors, except Dennis Hastert. Her Democratic predecessors generally entered as young men, and had on average 26 years to move from rookie member to Speaker. With 19 years of service in the House, when she ascended to the speakership, Pelosi was no novice. As we discussed in chapter 2, she had acquired a reputation for policy success on issues (e.g. AIDS, the Presidio, China trade, and human rights) that were not the typical portfolio of an aspiring leader. What the issues did illustrate was some mastery of the craft of legislative strategy. As John Jacobs wrote in the *San Francisco Chronicle* of her transition from "party girl" to "Capitol Hill mover and shaker":

> Pelosi is a skillful politician. She has learned the inside game of congressional politics well. She gets to people before the rolls are called, quietly states her case and often gets their votes. If she doesn't succeed at first, she just keeps coming at them again and again until she does. It's not yet fair to compare her legislatively to Phil Burton, considered by many House insiders to be one of the most brilliant legislative strategists of the post-war era. But where he was coarse, single-minded and sometimes out of control, she is cool, reassuring, non-threatening.[83]

How did Pelosi overcome the gender traps that thwarted other congresswomen? Gender certainly played a role in shaping her decision to run and the coalition she assembled. Previously, women had generally run only for lower level leadership positions such as secretary or vice chair of their party conference. Pelosi eschewed the lower rungs of the leadership ladder that had become the starting point for other women. She also made the strategic choice to run for the whip position, which was technically not yet vacant but would become so if the Democrats regained the majority. This preemptive announcement avoided a challenge to an incumbent leader and gave her standing as the first candidate to announce; thus, she sidestepped a story line that would have her as a less senior woman attempting to unseat a more established man.

Her main position of power from which to launch her run for whip was as a member of the Appropriations Committee, where she had developed alliances with powerful male colleagues.[84] She also benefited from the changing demography of the Democratic Caucus. She could count on the support of the women—a growing bloc within the caucus—and her home state allies. The sheer size of the California delegation gave her clear advantages. And the women mattered; political insiders reported that 35 of the 44 House women Democrats backed Pelosi in the 2001 race for minority whip, a significant voting bloc not previously available to other female aspirants to congressional leadership.[85] In short, she took advantage in 2001 of her own political position within the caucus and its growing number of Democratic women.

She faced the advantages and disadvantages of a woman who represented one of the most liberal districts in the country. She not only was electorally safe but also had ready access to campaign resources her party needed to win back a majority. Her own electoral security was never in doubt, and she had worked tirelessly to raise funds from wealthy Californians to spread across the congressional landscape. As noted in chapter 2, her San Francisco roots gave some in the caucus pause and inspired her opponents to criticize her as not being in the mainstream. With the increasing party polarization in the Congress, leaders from the ideological extremes are more common than leaders who might straddle the ideological center of the chamber.[86] Thus, based on recent leadership patterns, Pelosi's position in the liberal wing of the Democratic caucus compared to Hoyer's position as a "chamber moderate" should have predicted the viability of her candidacy, if not for her gender. Some speculated that all of the emphasis on Pelosi being "too liberal" was more a smoke screen for those members who were uncomfortable with the total package—a liberal San Francisco woman.[87] Indeed, much of the media coverage reinforced the gender differences by reminding readers, as if it were not obvious, that Pelosi would be "the first woman in congressional history" to win the post, whereas "Hoyer was a boy wonder in the state legislature."[88] Hoyer was credited with being a "member's member," a construction that is seemingly ungendered but echoes the characterization "man's man."[89] No one pointed out the gender dimension of the whip's race in more colorful terms than former representative Patricia Schroeder (D-CO): "'Male, female, purple, whatever, she's the best candidate,' says Schroeder. 'The only negative is that she's a woman.' Asked to explain, Schroeder said the undercurrent in this race is what she calls 'the Bubba beat—the Bubba tom-toms—that the party needs somebody who can talk to Bubba.'"[90] Ironically, in the whip's race, John Lewis (D-GA) briefly flirted with the possibility of entering the contest by advocating for a minority face among the party leadership. Seemingly ignoring the gender diversity Pelosi brought to the leadership team, Lewis noted:

"The leadership should be a reflection of the makeup of the Democratic Party and the country. Right now, the...leadership is all white."[91]

When she sought to move up to party leader in 2002, similar claims were made, as we reported in chapter 2. More than half of the newspaper articles from major cities across the country covering her leadership races mentioned her significant prowess at fund-raising and campaign organizing yet raised doubts, in the tradition of the middleman theory, about her qualifications.[92] Journalist Carl Hulse offered this familiar observation:

> The competition was being framed as a choice between a woman from one of the party's anchor states who could reinvigorate House Democrats with new ideas and leadership style and a man who has tangled successfully with tough Texas conservatives. It presents lawmakers with a crucial decision on which candidate they think can shape a message and an agenda that can broaden the party's appeal to voters.[93]

These commentaries reflect the duality of Pelosi's candidacy. It could be framed equally well in terms of ideology or of gender. Hulse, like most journalists, incorporated both dimensions, going out of his way to notice that the more liberal candidate was a woman whereas the more centrist candidate was a male. Why did gender matter? Because gender matters. Ultimately, Pelosi was able to transcend both ideology and gender with her organizational efforts. She won *both because* she was a woman *and because* she was a liberal.[94]

Tolerating Sexism

To Pelosi's credit, and benefit, she has never made sexism an issue during her House career and has embraced instead an attitude that performance and organizational skill pay off in the end. To be sure, she had experienced sexism in Congress. Her first job in the congressional office of U.S. senator Daniel Brewster (D-MD) was to grace the front desk as the pretty receptionist with a last name familiar to Maryland citizens. Meanwhile, a young law student, Steny Hoyer, was the senator's legislative aide, working on meatier policy matters. The 1960s was an era when all workplaces treated men and women very differently, and congressional offices were no exception segregating women into handmaiden, secretarial roles and reserving more professional duties for the men.

Later as a member, Pelosi learned the powerful lessons of exclusion from positional authority and from agenda control. As one of only three women serving on the Labor, Health and Human Services Subcommittee of Appropriations, she put up with the frustrations of the seniority system and a committee chair, William Natcher (D-KY), who used his power to thwart women's health policy and reproductive rights.[95] Through careful analysis, political scientist Debra Dodson shows how ostensibly gender-neutral rules and practices sustained "the last vestiges of the old-boys' network" on the Appropriations Committee during Pelosi's service.[96] For example, women were often bypassed in the appointing of conferees, according to Dodson's data. Dodson's accounting shows how the three women Democrats achieved some policy successes and experienced first-hand the importance of a critical mass—three Democratic women were clearly more effective on Labor, Health and Human Services than one, two, or none.

Pelosi has also endured sexist commentary from her ideological opponents. In the period immediately before and after the 2006 elections, *Media Matters for America*, a web-based nonprofit center dedicated to monitoring, analyzing, and correcting conservative misinformation in the U.S. media, reported numerous media figures' attacks on Pelosi on the basis of her gender. For example, on Fox News's *Special Report*, Morton M. Kondracke called Pelosi "the Wicked Witch of the West." *New York Post* Washington bureau chief Deborah Orin-Eilbeck twice called Pelosi a "shrew." And MSNBC's *Hardball* host Chris Matthews asked political and social commentator Mike Barnicle if Pelosi was "going to castrate Steny Hoyer" if Hoyer was elected House majority leader. On a separate occasion, Matthews asked of her policy fights with President Bush: "How does she do it without screaming? How does she do it without becoming grating?"[97]

The sexist commentary was often inseparable from discussion of policy differences. While addressing the Conservative Political Action Conference (an annual gathering of grassroots conservatives) in 2009, radio talk show host Roger Hedgecock diverged from his remarks on the "fairness doctrine" to offer the quip "I've never met Pelosi's husband but I want to give the guy a medal."[98] Rush Limbaugh in a January 2009 broadcast countered Pelosi's advocacy of family planning with this birth control suggestion: "Put pictures of Pelosi in every cheap motel room in America today. That will keep birthrates down because that picture will keep a lot of things down."[99] In October 2009, when Pelosi weighed into the debate on appropriate troop levels in Afghanistan, the National Republican Congressional Committee mocked her as "General Pelosi" and suggested that Gen. Stanley McChrystal, the top commander in the field, "should put her in her place." Democratic women fired back, seeing the phraseology as "evidence they [the NRCC] long for the

days when a woman's place was in the kitchen."[100] Finally, nationally syndicated talk radio host Michael Savage ranted about congressional hearings on
interrogation techniques used at Guantanamo:

> It's why Congress has the lowest ratings in history. It's because of yentas
> like Jane Harman, yentas like Barbara Boxer, yentas like Nancy Pelosi, and
> the weakling half-men in the Democrat Party who are waving the white
> flag.... Do you know that the Al Qaeda members at Gitmo are treated
> better than the Nazis were. They are treated better than the Nazis were at
> Nuremberg. That came out yesterday. And that's because these yentas who
> are living in unreality, who don't understand the first thing about the world
> they're living in, but have rich husbands who put them in power with their
> money, so they could have a little hobby in between getting their nails done.
> They're the ones who are standing up and saying, don't waterboard, don't
> torture.... Go home. Get out of politics. Go play with your grandchildren. Do
> anything. Do anything, but get out of politics, you yenta.[101]

Faced with this raw sexism, Pelosi never made it an issue. Quite the contrary, she adopted a very graceful and feminine style that won her allies
across the ideological spectrum. She eschewed an in-your-face feminism
that some other women of her generation embraced. We might recall, here,
that Pelosi had not cut her political teeth as a movement feminist. She supported feminist objectives, but in her approach to politics she did not want
to be pigeonholed as simply a feminist. This was why she chose to avoid the
more confrontational style of more visible feminist colleagues. In her personal interactions with members of Congress, her hostess sensibilities gave
her a softer touch as she sought to secure the votes of her more conservative
male colleagues.

The lessons of embedded gender inequality in Congress have certainly
not been lost on Pelosi. She has clearly sought to open up the opportunity
structure to other women. Within the complex House and party rules governing committee assignments, House Democrats allow members to bid for
available subcommittee leadership slots on the basis of committee seniority
(or subcommittee seniority, in the case of the Appropriations Committee).
The bidding process is also overlaid with caucus politics, requiring a deft
balancing of the diversity of the interests of women, African Americans,
Hispanics, and Blue Dogs. As we discussed in chapter 3, Speaker Pelosi is
immersed in the process of recommending committee assignments to the
Democratic SPC, which formally approves the assignments. The Speaker's
confidants Rosa DeLauro and George Miller cochair the committee, with
Miller as cochair for policy and DeLauro as cochair for steering. In that
capacity, DeLauro works closely with the Speaker in making decisions about

nominations to committees as well as to subcommittee and committee chair assignments. These have on occasion involved seniority "skips" that have benefited of women members.[102]

On a few occasions, Pelosi has used her authority to reward and punish. The removal of congresswoman Jane Harman (D-CA) (described in chapter 3) was the most high profile, but Pelosi also advanced less senior members ahead of others; for example, sophomore congresswoman Debbie Wasserman Schultz moved ahead of several more senior members to become chair of the Legislative Branch Subcommittee of Appropriations, and the late congresswoman Stephanie Tubbs Jones moved ahead of three other Democrats to become chair of the Committee on Standards of Official Conduct. Table 6.1 illustrates the differences in women's committee presence before and after Pelosi became Democratic leader and suggests the way congresswomen have benefited from her mastery of the committee structure. While women in fact had less seniority overall in the 110th than the 107th, the number of women chairs doubled, and the number of subcommittee leadership posts held by women increased by one-third.[103] As evidence of achieving critical mass in the committee system, the number of subcommittees with three or more Democratic women almost doubled from 18 in the 107th Congress, before she became party leader, to 34 in the 110th. Similarly, under Pelosi's tenure, three or more Democratic women came to serve on almost twice as many subcommittees focused on women's issues (from five to nine).[104] Whereas Democratic women held five seats on the prestigious Energy and Commerce Committee under Gephardt's leadership, eight Democratic women served on the committee (seven on the Health Subcommittee, which previously had only two women's voices to weigh in on women's health issues), and Congresswoman Diana DeGette (D-CO) also served as committee vice chair in the 110th. Only one Democrat woman served on the prestigious Ways and Means Committee when Gephardt was party leader, whereas Speaker Pelosi promoted three Democratic women to the committee when the 110th Congress opened. Pelosi's personal priority—the Select Committee on Energy Independence and Global Warming—included three Democratic women.

The 111th Congress saw incremental change in the number of women in committee or subcommittee leadership positions. Four new Democratic women were elected in 2008 for a total of 56 (24% of the caucus). Pelosi promoted California Zoe Lofgren to the chairship of the House Ethics Committee, for a total of three women committee chairs, and women ended up with two more subcommittee leadership posts than was the case in the 110th.

In sum, Pelosi mastered the congressional opportunity structure by not taking a traditional approach to the leadership ladder but rather by strategically seizing a rare opportunity to stake a claim to leadership without challenging

Table 6.1 Advancement of Democratic Women in the Committee Structure before and after Pelosi's Election as Party Leader

	107th Congress	110th Congress
Number of women in Democratic Caucus	42 (19.8%)	52 (22.3%)
Average seniority position of women Democrats	51.9	58.4
Number of female ranking minority members or committee chairs	2 (10.5%)	4[a] (20%)
Number of female ranking minority members or subcommittee chairs	15 (17.6%)	20 (22.2%)
Subcommittees with three or more women	18 of 96 (18.8%)	34 of 87 (39.1%)
Women's issues subcommittees with three or more women[b]	5 of 12 (41.7%)	9 of 13 (69.2%)
Average seniority position of committee chairs (men/women)	10.2/37.5	19.4/28.5
Average seniority position of subcommittee chairs (men/women)	34.9/44.5	40.9/49.1

[a]Two of these women, both of whom chaired committees at the beginning of the 110th, died in office.
[b]This typology of women's issues committees comes from Michelle Swers, *The Difference Women Make: The Policy Impact of Women in Congress* (Chicago: University of Chicago Press, 2002).

Note: In the 107th Congress, Democrats were in the minority and thus the top Democratic position on any given committee was as ranking minority member. In the 110th Congress, Democrats were in the majority and served as committee and subcommittee chairs. These numbers do not include the House's nonvoting delegates who represent U.S. territories.

Sources: Jackie Koszczuk and Martha Angle, editors, *CQ's Politics in America 2008: The 110th Congress*, Washington D.C.: CQ Press, 2007, and *CQ's Politics in America 2002: The 107th Congress*, Washington D.C.: CQ Press, 2001, and Office of the House Clerk, "Official List of Standing Committees and Subcommittees," accessed at http://clerk.house.gov/committee_info/scsoal.pdf.

an incumbent. The changing demography of the House allowed her to take advantage of core constituencies—Californians, minorities, and women. She has used her power as Speaker and her attention to detail to remake the power structures of key committees. To the benefit of women, among others, she has embraced the diversity of her caucus as a virtue rather than a challenge.

THE IMPORTANCE OF VOICE

When Pelosi made her first speech as Speaker, she marked a new milestone in the role of women in politics. From outright prohibitions on speaking in public to center-stage politics, women's speech has developed certain characteristics that are distinctive and challenging. Pelosi seems to understand both the historic and emblematic opportunity she has to speak in a distinctive woman's voice. She has extended that voice by using feminine analogies that confront and confound stereotypes. For example, as the epigraph to this chapter suggests, she has made good use of the stereotype of the "lioness" as both maternal and fiercely protective of her brood.

How has Pelosi navigated gender stereotypes in her own speech, self-presentation, and leadership style? The answer is that she has confronted, confounded, and then recast those stereotypes to create a persona that is distinctly feminine, explicitly maternal, and intensely partisan. It is the sum of the parts that allow her to avoid the double bind of being either too feminine or too masculine in her persona. This Italian-American grandmother, lest anyone forget, is a tough partisan competitor wrapped up in an elegant Armani suit (a staple in her wardrobe) and is focused on bettering the lives of children.

Female Speech

Certain attributes have been ascribed to a feminine style of political discourse. These characteristics have been confirmed by a wealth of research that affirms their presence in political discourse.[105] First, political women frequently connect their experience with political judgments in concrete, not abstract, terms. Second, women give voice to the values of inclusivity and relationships. Third, women, more than men, conceive of the power of public office as an opportunity to "get things done" and empower others. Fourth, women officeholders tend to approach policy holistically or in big-picture terms, seeing a connectedness between different problems. Fifth, women officeholders tend to speak for women and champion women's particular issues in the public arena.

We explored Speaker Pelosi's consistency and effectiveness in delivering her message in chapter 4. Here we are more interested in the extent to which her speech has confronted gender stereotypes and contributed to her leadership style. To that end, women's speech has always involved difficult choices—double binds, as some have suggested.[106] To speak or not to speak. To speak with forcefulness but to avoid a tone that might be construed in gendered negatives as shrill, harsh, or domineering. To speak with compassion and sensitivity but to sidestep language that might convey weakness or soft-heartedness. To speak with authority in a world that has only recently granted women the status of authoritative speech. To speak as a woman in a world that has been dominated by masculinity. To act like a woman but compete like a man.[107]

The literature on gendered communications is extensive and suggests that women come to politics on the campaign trail with advantages and disadvantages.[108] Historically, voters have perceived women candidates as more honest and trustworthy, as more likely to understand the concerns of average citizens, and as outsiders and agents of change.[109] But women have also been perceived by voters as too inexperienced, too liberal, and too weak on economic and security issues. The gender advice passed along by campaign experts was to be "tough but caring." As Linda Witt and her colleagues wrote after the experience of the 1992 Year of the Woman campaigns:

> the most critical remaining problem for any woman candidate still is tacking the fine line of ambiguities and stereotypes that voters and tradition superimpose on her. She must craft a message and a public persona that persuades party, pundits, and public—and not necessarily in that formerly preordained order—that she can be as clear and independent a decision maker as any man, but more caring and trustworthy. Meanwhile like every woman venturing into male territory, the woman candidate has to maintain some level of the traditional altruistic and apolitical above-it-all demeanor expected of a lady, all the while beating her opponents in what sometimes seems the closest thing to a blood sport that is still legal.[110]

The same gender stereotypes get in the way when women are governing, and the relatively few women's voices often go either unheard or get distorted in that arena as well. When serving as one of a small minority, women officeholders feel responsible for bearing everywoman's burden and speaking on her behalf.[111] As Barbara Mikulski remarked when she was the sole female U.S. senator: "You feel that you are speaking for every woman in the world who has ever lived in the past, who currently lives today, and who will live into the third millennium."[112]

Appearance and Attire

Political women in the public eye endure greater scrutiny than men with respect to their appearance and dress, which may distract from their effectiveness as communicators. Congresswoman Susan Molinari (R-NY) recalled that her first ever floor speech in 1990 was remembered more for what she wore—a pants suit (previously not seen on the House floor)—than what she said.[113] The 2008 presidential election served as a stark reminder that a woman's wardrobe is still considered political news: the press went bonkers when Hillary Clinton appeared with a hint of cleavage on CSPAN-2 while on the Senate floor and Sarah Palin's clothing buying spree made headlines.

Pelosi has not escaped scrutiny of her wardrobe. Every major news outlet from the *Wall Street Journal* to the *New York Times* to traditional fashion media weighed in with an analysis of the Pelosi wardrobe following the Democrats' electoral victory in November 2006, during her swearing in as speaker, and with subsequent references to her attire. In an analysis of media coverage of the Speaker, almost one-fifth of the stories (154 out of 817) were framed in terms of her family, her historic first, or her characteristics and attire as a woman.[114] The competition among headline writers for the best turned phrases was fierce—"She'll Have to Turn the Other Chic" (the *New York Daily News*); "Suited for Politics... She's Already Winning Votes for Her Fashion Sense" (the *Baltimore Sun*).[115] The *New York Times* chronicled her wardrobe day by day in her first week on the job.[116] The conclusion of the fashion arbiters was unanimous: the "dowdy days" of Washington were over. But this is not mere fluff, the *Times* offered:

> Women in politics are the first to say that they give serious thought to their appearance because, like it or not, voters at home, powerbrokers on the Hill and the news media are all mindful of the slightest faux pas. It is wrong to look too risqué, they say. But isn't it retrograde to equate looking good with being empty headed?... The men have it much easier because, unlike women, they are seldom punished for fashion mistakes.[117]

The fashion authorities applaud Pelosi's sense of style. Pulitzer Prize–winning fashion reporter Robin Givhan commented in the *Washington Post*:

> Armani stands as a kind of professional armor. It is protective but soft. Tailored but a drape. It is the style of business dress that in the 1980s famously feminized menswear and brought masculine confidence to women's wear. An Armani suit, for a woman, is a tool for playing with the boys without pretending to be one.[118]

Givhan concluded that Pelosi appears "consciously, comfortably and authoritatively female" and ready to confront a decision no man ever faced, that is, "how a woman who will be second in line of succession to the presidency should look." Givhan went on to praise Pelosi for choosing a "neutral-colored, softly tailored power suit. One that is accessorized with style rather than rote references to love of country. She looks dignified and serious. And in this case, she also happens to look quite good."

The microscopic sartorial attention smacked of sexism to many, and certainly her male predecessors were never subjected to such scrutiny. But for political women, it is a reality of life that is well documented in the literature. The coverage was also not new to Pelosi, who had previously been featured in *Time*, *Newsweek*, *Elle* ("Nancy Pelosi Is a Babe"), *Women's Wear Daily*, and *Glamour*, where she was honored among the magazine's "Women of the Year." Not surprisingly, the harshest criticism of her appearance and voice came from right-wing commentators on television and talk radio. *Media Matters for America* took note of cracks suggesting the Speaker had had one too many facelifts or Botox treatments.[119] In the period immediately before and after the 2006 elections, the *Media Matters* reported numerous media figures attacking Pelosi on the basis of her gender or appearance.[120]

In spite of the sexist commentary, Pelosi has mastered a style that is feminine yet authoritative, authentic, and attractive. One biographer notes that unsolicited comments on her appearance were a common feature of his interviews with others.[121] Our research produced similar comments, always intended as compliments. One of our informants, for example, remarked that it was very helpful that Pelosi was so attractive and elegant; otherwise, he (yes, he) said, she would be constantly criticized for her appearance. While this might be taken as something of a left-handed compliment, it seems likely to be true. The media commentary we have reviewed would certainly have a different tone for a less stylish Speaker.

The Pelosi Presentation

Pelosi's personal presentation is, however, much more complex than all of this glamour commentary would suggest. It is a style that toggles at times between harsh partisanship and feminine graciousness.[122] This distinctive touch carries over into other aspects of her personal interaction with her members. She furnishes her office with fresh flowers each day and an ample supply of Ghirardelli chocolate, a dietary mainstay for this San Franciscan. Chocolate is her signature. When she offered up a dish of candy to children visiting her office for Take Your Son and Daughter to Work Day, it was vintage Pelosi. When she was running for whip, meetings of the inner circle always began with food, and not just any food but great food according to our informants. Ever the gracious hostess, her charm won over the members, even if her policy preferences or legislative achievements did not. As one of her critics wrote, "members were flattered by her attention. When she was campaigning [for whip], she would drop in on members unannounced, leaving chocolate and a friendly note if they were not around."[123] These touches humanize the Speaker in a way that blunts the edge of others' caricatures.

As leader of the House of Representatives, Speaker Pelosi has embraced her identity as a mother and grandmother. On several occasions, she has described her experience as a mother as perfect training for the speakership. She told journalist Elaine Povich, "Just as I do as a mother, as Speaker, I intend to do a great deal of listening. But, when necessary, I am not afraid to use my mother-of-five voice to ensure that I am heard."[124] Her mother-of-five voice is invoked as a signal that she intends to have her position not only heard but considered as House direction. But the maternal voice of authority is only one aspect of this Speaker.

Continuing the analysis of the content of her press conferences and speeches that we began in chapter 4, it is possible to characterize her speaking style with more precision. Within the 189 speeches, we discovered that children and families represent the most important theme in her public rhetoric. Her first and second swearing-in speeches contained all of the elements of the Pelosi feminine style and, ultimately, the Pelosi trademark leadership style. There were generic (obligatory?) calls for partnership, not partisanship, which might be expected from any Speaker. But Pelosi added some uniquely feminine flourishes. In both speeches, after congratulating and welcoming the new members of the House, she acknowledged the members' families, whose "love and support...make your leadership possible." For Pelosi, references to family come easily and frequently, as she connects her life experiences as a mother and grandmother to the job of Speaker. In her inaugural speech in the 110th, she made reference to her childhood in a "staunchly Democratic" Italian-American household in Baltimore as a formative part of the experience she brings to the House. There followed an acknowledgment of family, parents, husband, children, and grandchildren. And then, lest no one miss the significance of the moment, she extolled her history-making feat—"For our daughters and granddaughters, today we have broken the marble ceiling. For our daughters and granddaughters, the sky is the limit, anything is possible for them."[125] At her swearing in to the 111th Congress, similar patterns were evident.[126] She mentioned children and families 10 times in this short speech. She also reminded the members of the historic significance of her election as the first woman Speaker, and as she had done at her investiture two years prior, she ended her speech with a call to the children and grandchildren of House members to join her at the podium.

In analyzing the content of Pelosi's speeches and press conferences over the course of the 110th Congress up to the 2008 election, one learns that she links all aspects of the Democrats' policy goals to children and families. She refers to the "New Direction" in roughly 37% of her speeches but mentions children and families in 78% of them. Mentions of children and families appeared in 85% of her speeches about national security, 82% of her remarks on energy independence, 91% of her speeches referring to better jobs, better pay, and access to college education, 93% of her talks on health care, and 85% of her comments on accountability and honesty in government. Pelosi has used her voice as Speaker to remind us that it is the voice of the mother of five children and eight grandchildren. Who could make that case more convincingly?

In the coding of her public pronouncements, we find that she uses a speech style that combines both feminine and masculine characteristics.[127] As we noted in chapter 4, she is direct and often competitive (both masculine traits in communication patterns) as well as profuse in crediting others and acknowledging collaborative efforts (both feminine traits). She adopts a direct, authoritative, and commanding style in 94% of her speeches. More than half of her speeches (55%) combine both competitive and confrontational statements with conciliatory statements. Another third (34%) of her speeches are wholly competitive—assessing blame, drawing partisan distinctions, and contrasting party positions. The most feminine aspect of her speaking style is her emphasis on collaboration (79% of her speeches), as she lavishes credit and praise on others (Republicans and Democrats, but more often the latter). She frequently calls for bipartisanship but just as often lapses into sharp criticism of her adversaries. It is this duality of the female voice and the partisan fighter that perhaps best captures Pelosi's political persona.

WHEN WOMEN LEAD

To frame Pelosi's rise to power and service as Speaker during the 110th Congress, we sought to use concepts well established in the women-in-politics literature: ambition, opportunity, and voice. Previously, books about the speakership of the House have had nothing to say about the gendered dimension of the office or the role of gender in shaping the ambitions and careers of those who have come to serve in it. Studies of congressional leadership in general and of the speakership in particular have often rested on the assumption that Speakers are generic strategic politicians who act according to rational calculations of self-interest.[128] Those calculations are seen as being shaped by the institutional contexts in which they are made, which vary across time and circumstance. Thus, leadership studies stress the size and cohesiveness of party majorities, institutional norms, electoral incentives, and the like. These studies have not taken gender as a central variable affecting legislative party leadership, in part because there have been insufficient examples to consider, at least when it comes to the U.S. House.

We believe that Pelosi's career confirms much that has been posited about women in politics and the House. Certainly, her career has reflected the ingrained biases against women who seek leadership positions. Her decision to defer entering electoral politics until her children were grown is typical of many political women of her generation. The fact that she entered politics from an elite background also fits what we know about women in politics. Like other political women, she had to confront the double bind that asked her to be tough while remaining feminine and to avoid being too much of either. In all of these respects, she is a typical political woman.

But she has brought something new to the table. Political women have been channeled into one of several categories (perhaps appearing as caricatures.) Some political women seek to become "one of the guys." Others choose to be feminist agitators. Still others prefer to be accommodators, blending into the background. All of these choices play to or against the female stereotype. Pelosi has taken a different path. She has aimed to *combine* femininity and force, to take advantage of her gender when it is useful, to downplay it when it might prove a liability. In effect, she has sought to reverse the double bind, letting it work to her advantage.

Thus, she consistently downplayed the importance of her gender to her political prospects. She does not like to talk about sexism or her gender, preferring instead to simply say that she intends to do her job. She is the first woman Speaker, but that is not how she wants to be remembered; she wants to be remembered as a powerful and effective Speaker. When she engages in the "tough talk" we have described in this chapter and in chapter 4, she is "telling it like a man," so to speak. Her aim—often achieved, according to our informants—is for her gender to be forgotten in the performance of her duties. She wants to dominate the room. One of our informants reported a meeting at which the Speaker was forcefully leading a discussion around a table at which she had engaged everyone's attention. Something funny was said, and she leaned back in her chair (she had been thrusting herself forward) and laughed. At that moment, our interlocutor said, "I realized just how petite she is; I had not thought about it in a long time." This is the effect Speaker Pelosi aims to achieve.

But she also does not want anyone to forget that she is a woman and stands for the issues women care about. Her high style matches her high commitment to women's issues. She brings to the speakership a unique voice, invoking the language of children and families and embracing her maternal roles as part of her identity and style. She both confronts and capitalizes on stereotypes. She was always likely to be seen as a woman, and so she has capitalized on that image to emphasize that she is a "mother and grandmother"—as a way to soften the edges of the intensely competitive partisan she also is.

In conclusion, we affirm that this speaker, because of her gender, is different from her predecessors. Her path to power was distinguished by a distinctive ambition focused on the immediate and singular task of electing Democrats and securing progressive policies. Her opportunity structure was gendered, yet she rose to the top within it. Her voice is distinctive, in part because it is a woman's voice. Her style of leadership incorporates feminine aspects of collaboration, consensus building, and consideration of the diversity of her caucus. In suggesting these distinctive qualities, we do not deny (to the contrary, we affirm) that her rise to power and her conduct as Speaker is consistent with what we have come to know about the office in studying her male predecessors. But she is not just like them.

Chapter 7

Leadership

In most of these areas [of governance] the solution involves some short-term pain in exchange for long-term gain. But Washington has become incapable of that. Passing a pork-laden bill takes no time. Trimming subsidies, raising taxes or making strategic investments are near impossible.... Compromise is hard. No one gets all or even most of what they want. But in a vast, continental land of 300 million, people are going to disagree. No compromise means nothing will get done. And America will slowly drift down in the roll of nations.

—Fareed Zakaria

Luck is what happens when preparation meets opportunity.

—Seneca

In concluding our examination of Speaker Pelosi, we want to address the most important question our study broaches: the capacity of American political institutions to provide the leadership the country requires. There is ample evidence to suggest that the country faces a crisis of confidence in its leadership. The John F. Kennedy School of Government's Center for Public Leadership at Harvard University conducts a regular survey on the basis of which it calculates its National Leadership Index.[1] In 2008, the Center asked respondents whether they agreed with the statement "We have a leadership crisis in this country today." 80% agreed or agreed strongly. The Center then asked whether respondents agreed with the statement, "Overall, our country's leaders are effective and do a good job." 70% disagreed or disagreed strongly. The survey respondents showed least confidence in its national elective leadership. Respondents were asked to rate leadership in various sectors on a scale of 0 (none at all) to 100 (a great deal). Table 7.1 summarizes the results.

In table 7.1 we see that respondents have substantially higher confidence in non-elected than in elected leaders. Military, medical professionals, the clergy, and the Supreme Court sit atop the ratings, but even these institutions lie in the range of "a moderate amount" of confidence. Congress, the media, and the executive branch fall toward the bottom of the ratings. At stake in this era of the New American Politics, then, is not only the health of our political system but also the extent of public confidence in the quality of its leadership. The Speaker of the House is among the national leaders empowered by the nation's constitutional order, next in line to the presidency after the vice-president, and the leader of one of the two cham-

Table 7.1　National Leadership Index: Overall Confidence in Leaders (2008)*

Sector	Mean Confidence
Military	70.9
Medical	67.6
Nonprofit & Charity	61.4
Local Government	57.7
Educational	55.3
State Government	54.9
Religious	52.4
News Media-Traditional	46.0
Business	45.0
Congressional	42.9
News Media-Alternative	39.5
Executive Branch	38.1

*Question wording: "How much confidence do you have in the leadership of the following sectors, a great deal, a moderate amount, or none at all?" Scale = 0–100 (where, 33.3=not much; 66.7=moderate amount; 100.0=great deal).

Source: Seth A. Rosenthal, Todd L. Pittinsky, Sadie Moore, Jennifer J. Ratcliff, Laura A. Maruskin, Claire R. Gravelin, 2008–12–17, "National Leadership Index 2008," Cambridge: Center for Public Leadership, John F. Kennedy School of Government, Harvard University, http://content.ksg.harvard.edu/leadership/images/CPLpdf/nli_2008.pdf.

bers of the nation's legislature. We now turn to the question of whether the speakership is able to provide the leadership the country so desperately requires. Toward this end, we first assess Speaker Pelosi from the perspective of congressional leadership theory, comparing her conduct as Speaker to that of her recent predecessors. We then seek to situate the speakership in the New American Politics, explaining the constraints this era imposes on the office. We argue that Pelosi's low public approval ratings are a reflection of the era in which she serves. We conclude with a consideration of the factors that have shaped Pelosi's speakership, and the lessons they offer future Speakers.

ASSESSING NANCY PELOSI

Speaker Pelosi has been by many measures an effective leader of the House. Under her leadership, the House resumed legislative and oversight duties that had atrophied under the Republican majority. Regular order was, for the most part, resumed. Committees did their work. The House passed important legislation in a variety of areas of public policy. Democrats attained 92% party unity in both 2007 and 2008.[2] The 110th Congress, for which we have complete information, was harder working than its Republican predecessor. Table 7.2 arrays various workload indicators and shows that the Democrat-controlled 110th Congress spent more time in session, cast more votes, passed more legislation, and conducted more oversight hearings than the Republican-controlled 109th. The legislation in the 110th addressed some of the most critical issues facing the present generation—health care, the environment, energy independence, and financial recovery and economic well-being.

While we do not have complete data for the 111th Congress at the time of writing, the pace of work in the first session has been unrelenting. Of course an active Congress is not necessarily an effective Congress, nor is it by itself evidence of effective leadership. But the legislative record of the first session is substantial, as we saw in table 5.2. The House of Representatives moved major elements of a Democratic policy agenda that had been stymied by the Republican congressional majorities and the Bush administration. The accomplishments included the fiscal stimulus package to jumpstart the flagging economy, an expansion of health insurance benefits to children, the omnibus and supplemental appropriations bills, and other legislation to address the fiscal crisis and improve oversight of the bailout of financial institutions, credit card reform, an Iraq War supplemental, and other significant legislation. Speaker Pelosi's role has been critical to this record of productivity, but an assessment of her speakership to date requires a broader

Table 7.2 Workload Indicators, U.S. House of Representatives (2005–6 and 2007–8)

	109th Congress (2005–6)	110th Congress (2007–8)
Time in session:		
Legislative days	241	282
Legislative hours	1,917	2,266
Roll call votes	1,214	1,876
Measures passed:		
Substantive	131	210
Routine	512	758
Symbolic	440	890
Suspensions	922	1,616
Oversight hearings:		
Full committee and subcommittee	960	1,403
Appropriations	242	362
Iraq	84	193
Markups	345	432

Source: Sarah A. Binder, Thomas E. Mann, Norman J. Ornstein, and Molly Reynolds, "Assessing the 110th Congress, Anticipating the 111th," Brookings Institution report, January 2008, www.brookings.edu/papers/2008/01_uscongress_mann.aspx, accessed January 29, 2009.

canvas. To explore further Speaker Pelosi's leadership we first discuss it in the context of congressional leadership in theory.

Congressional Leadership in Theory

Political scientists have given considerable attention to congressional leaders, focusing often on the constraints under which they labor. Leaders are sometimes regarded as "agents" doing service to their "principals" (the members).[3] James MacGregor Burns argues that legislative leadership is inherently transactional, involving deal-making and coalition building. He contrasts this notion of transactional leadership with the transforming potential of executive leadership.[4] One school of thought regards legislative parties as "cartels" that, with their leaders, offer solutions to problems of collective action.[5] Another theory regards legislative leadership as essentially conditional, arguing that leadership "style" must be adapted to "institutional context."[6] Some political scientists have suggested that legislative leaders have the capacity to influence the behavior of members or at least to act independently of member preferences under some circumstances; but this kind of courage appears to be much the exception rather than the rule.[7]

Scholars seeking to describe and explain leadership behavior often assume that legislators are simply rational actors. Members of Congress are presumed to be motivated by specific career goals. To pursue them, they must continue to get elected. Thus, their first constraint arises from reliance on the support of voters, contributors, and campaign workers at home. Once elected, they seek advancement. They may seek to rise within the institution, to pursue specific policy goals, or to satisfy a progressive ambition by seeking higher elected office. Party leaders are motivated by multiple ambitions. They must, of course, continue to get elected themselves; but they must also seek and maintain a legislative majority so that they can exercise institutional control. Party cartel theory stresses the importance of majority maintenance to leaders' institutional obligations and sees legislative parties as responses to dilemmas posed by the need for collective action among a set of self-interested members.

How much power will party leaders have, and how will that power be exercised? Conditional party government theory suggests that party leaders will exercise more institutional power under conditions of high party polarization. In a homogeneous majority, party members are bound together in mutual interest to empower leaders with strong institutional control. Principal-agent theory argues that party leaders do the bidding of members when leaders, as agents, exercise the powers they have been granted by members who are their principals. But how should party leaders employ those powers? The literature describes a variety of mechanisms for intraparty communication and coordination that have developed as a response to the demands members place on leaders. Legislative leadership theory regards these mechanisms as expressions of rationally self-interested behavior.

These various theoretical explanations do not differ on the qualities they imply as essential to effective congressional leadership. Party leaders today are expected to work assiduously to cultivate consensus, bridge factions, assuage concerns, and rally support. Leadership is, as Speaker Jim Wright was fond of saying, a "license to persuade." To persuade, House Speakers must first listen. Speaker Gingrich's mantra "listen, learn, help, lead" was but one formulation of the basic point. Democratic leader Gephardt was sometimes called "Iron Ears" in recognition of his patience in hearing members out. As we have noted, Speaker Pelosi has run the Democratic Caucus as a "meet market" with heavy emphasis on intraparty consultation. Members have reported "therapy" and prayer sessions with her. This premium that she places on listening, consultation, and consensus also conforms to gender research, which suggests that collaborative leadership style is often demonstrated by women leaders.[8]

Collaborative skills are thus a normative requirement for effective Speakers in the era of the New American Politics. Scholars have suggested other standards against which leadership performance can be judged. If legislative leaders have a special responsibility for gaining, holding, and enlarging a congressional majority, then they might reasonably be expected to perform well the essential tasks of fund-raising, candidate recruitment, and conveying the party message. If citizens expect leaders to provide policy direction for the country, then they should look to them to set a legislative agenda. If their job is to win floor votes, then they should have skills in intraparty and/or bipartisan coalition-building. If a leader's personal image and popularity contributes to the attainment of these other goals, then they should look to her public persona and effectiveness as a communicator. All of these criteria might apply to the several leadership positions serving Congress; but the Speaker of the House has additional responsibilities arising from the character of the office.[9] The Speaker is, after all, elected by all members of the House and not simply the majority of her party caucus. As a constitutional officer, she has the obligations to represent (i.e. speak for) the House in the councils of government and, internally, to respect the rights of each member and of the minority party under the rules of the House. She also is responsible for ensuring that the House attends to the public's business and performs its various legislative duties. The House is a deliberative body, and the Speaker has an obligation to foster the conditions in which deliberation can take place. Thus, we may ask of the Speaker, distinctly among party leaders, if she has conducted her office in accordance with these constitutional and institutional obligations.

Speaker Pelosi in Practice

Nancy Pelosi, in general, has done quite well by these various criteria. Obviously, she led her party to a substantial victory in the 2006 election and expanded the Democrat's House majority in 2008. As we discussed in chapter 4, she was directly involved in developing political strategy, recruiting candidates, articulating message, and raising money. Her performance was not faultless. In the summer of 2008, for example, she stumbled in responding to the spike in oil prices and the price of gas at the pump. Misreading the public mood, she stood against the Republican demand for offshore drilling and saw the Democrats' advantage in the generic ballot polls temporarily dissipate (although it recovered during the financial crisis that followed). In 2008, as in 2006 (with respect to the Iraq War), she reaped the political benefit of adverse events, as the collapse of the financial markets turned the public toward the Democrats. But had she not done the spade work over several years to put in place the political infrastructure, she would not have been able to capitalize on the political opportunities that arose.

In setting the policy agenda and forging majority coalitions, she had some success. The Democrats were able to move a substantial policy agenda through the House. Some important legislation became public law, and a considerable number of measures were approved with the support of both Democrats and Republicans. This is not to say that Pelosi treated the Republicans with kid gloves. To the contrary, she found it necessary to utilize the powers at her disposal more often to advance her legislative goals. For example, as one study of the 110th Congress has argued:

> as the Congress progressed and the agenda became more controversial, opposition tactics in the House and frustrations with the Senate led the House Democratic majority to embrace many of the same unorthodox means (circumventing standing committees, writing closed rules, using the suspension calendar, waiving layover requirements, avoiding the conference process) that the Republicans had employed to advance their agenda.[10]

This recourse to what scholar Barbara Sinclair has labeled "unorthodox" law-making is now a stable feature of Congress in the era of the New American Politics.[11] It derives from the need of the majority party to advance its legislative program in the face of partisan tactics adopted by the minority party. Speaker Hastert once said that his obligation was to "get the job done."[12] Even though Speaker Pelosi specifically disavowed Hastert's "majority of the majority" principle, she found it necessary to adopt some of the same tactics in order to attain her party's political and policy objectives. This was especially true in confronting the various economic crises that commenced in the fall of 2008 and continued into the Obama administration in 2009. Even some Democratic committee chairs questioned the Speaker's commitment to regular order.[13]

The leadership habits Pelosi developed in the 110th Congress carried over into the 111th, in which she played a much stronger hand. Because she had more Democrats, she had more room to maneuver. Because the Democrats controlled the White House, she no longer had to worry about presidential vetoes. The larger Democratic majority in the Senate offered greater potential for the enactment of the Democratic legislation program. It is not surprising, then, that she immediately took advantage of her enhanced power position to drive an active legislative agenda. She violated regular order at the outset of the 111th Congress just as she had at the beginning of the 110th to push through a number of important bills. On the key issues of health and energy reform, however, she allowed the committees to develop legislation before engaging to broker the compromises needed to pass the bills. She thus demonstrated a strategic sense in the application of her institutional power.

A Speaker today has an opportunity to assume a very visible public role. As the experience of Hastert indicates, some Speakers can decline the limelight—but not Nancy Pelosi, who as the first female Speaker had little choice but to accept it. In fact, she has embraced the attention thrust on her and sought to turn it to her advantage. As we saw in chapter 4, her approval ratings have been more variable than those of Congress as a whole. She started with relatively high approval ratings and saw them rise and fall during 2007 and 2008. In October 2008, the NBC-*Wall Street Journal* poll reported her public approval ratings as very positive 7%, somewhat positive 16%, neutral 21%, somewhat negative 14%, and very negative 27%. Fully 15% of respondents could not identify her or had no opinion.[14] Congressional approval ratings were even lower: only 20% of respondents rated Congress either positive or somewhat positive in the fall of 2008.[15] Yet in the end it did not matter. Despite late efforts by the Republicans to make her an issue in the presidential election, there is no evidence that voters' opinion of her was a significant factor in the presidential or congressional races, in which the Democrats won a substantial victory.

In the first few months of 2009, congressional approval ratings spiked from January to March from 19% to 38% before falling back to 32% in April.[16] As the year wore on and debates over the economy, energy, and health care became more intense, congressional approval ratings fell further. While approval of the Democratic Congress remained higher than during the last two years of Republican control, Congress continued to labor under a skeptical public eye. In September, Gallup found 63% of respondents disapproving of "the way Congress is handling its job." Congressional Democrats received a 37% approval rating, while congressional Republicans lagged behind at 27%.[17] The Real Clear Politics average of generic ballot polls conducted in early October showed the Democrats with only a 4.4% margin over the Republicans.[18] Pelosi's poll ratings were stubbornly and consistently negative. *Pollingreport.com* summarizes the results of the *NBC-Wall Street Journal* polling on Pelosi from January to September of 2009. In January her approval ratings stood at 27% and her disapproval ratings at 46%. In May her ratings were 24% approve, 46% disapprove. By September, her numbers were at 27% approval, 44% disapproval, and embedded within those numbers was a striking gender story: among women the approval-disapproval balance was 31% to 36% while among men the approvals were dwarfed twofold by disapprovals and among older men the ratio was 22% to 56%.[19] Why have Pelosi's approval ratings remained much more negative than positive? Certainly the gender difference reminds us of the longstanding pattern of bias against women's suitability for politics which we reported in the first chapter. But more importantly, we surmise that Pelosi's visible partisan role alienated both Republicans (who would not like her in any event) and many independents (put off by the perception that she is a highly partisan leader). The Republicans chose to make her rather than President Obama the object of their attack on the new regime, further eroding her standing. In spite of the fact that this strategy had failed in both 2006 and 2008, Republicans decided to renew their attacks on Pelosi as a primary element of their 2010 election strategy.[20] In addition, as we discussed in chapter 5, she damaged her public image when she undertook an attack on the CIA.

Pelosi's relatively low public approval ratings are, we believe, a reflection of the New American Politics. In the hyperpartisan environment in which Congress and the speakership are now enveloped, any Speaker will earn approval mostly from the base voters of her party. Pelosi's exemplar, Tip O'Neill, consistently won approval from about half of the public and left office with a public approval rate above 60%. His high visibility and substantial support were buttressed by his ability to preserve an independent political persona even though he was an iconic liberal. As was also true of his nemesis, Ronald Reagan, even his adversaries liked him. Because O'Neill did not absorb every political battle into his own reputation, he was often able to walk away from a losing fight without a scratch. O'Neill and Reagan governed at the outset of the era we have described. The corrosive effects of the partisan wars had not become endemic. Today's leaders are caught in a far more polarized environment. As we have seen, Pelosi has often presented herself as a staunch partisan—one reason why she is Speaker today. In the era of the New American Politics, this likely sets a ceiling on her popular appeal.

Pelosi's leadership style plays into her low approval ratings. She is a political battler by nature. While she has sought to take the edge off of her partisan image by donning a grandmotherly one, her partisan opponents are not as easily fooled as Little Red Riding Hood. She is also a sometimes erratic communicator who has to exercise discipline to avoid straying off message. When that discipline breaks down, her natural impulses sometimes take over. The best example was the contretemps over the extent of her knowledge about the CIA's EIT program. At the height of this episode, some wondered if it could prove fatal to Pelosi's speakership. The fact that her caucus rallied to her side indicated that it would not. Recent history proves that a Speaker is at risk only when her members feel themselves at risk. Pelosi's liberal image was no threat to liberal Democrats, but might cut against moderate Democrats in swing districts. Republicans had hitherto made no headway in these districts by attacking Pelosi; the CIA flap gave them another opportunity.[21]

Speaker Pelosi has brought an assertive approach to managing her party caucus. She is a hands-on leader, deeply involved in every aspect of the party operation. She has made and influenced the key leadership appointments.

She has made the committee assignments. She has taken control of the party message. She has integrated the DCCC and the Speaker's staff. She is the party's chief fund-raiser. She has recruited candidates and appeared on their behalf in all parts of the country. She is the leading public face of the House Democrats. She has managed relations with the Senate and the White House. All along the way, she has continued to represent her constituents in San Francisco. This range of activity and involvement has required enormous reserves of energy. In all of our interviews, the most frequent observations about Nancy Pelosi addressed her energy and drive. The metaphor of the "Energizer Bunny" was often invoked. We never solicited or implied interest in this topic; informants simply volunteered the description. The Speaker's days typically start at seven o'clock (three days a week, after a three-mile power walk) and often end at midnight.[22] Members may receive calls from her at any hour of the day or night. Her energy can be measured not only by the length of her working day but also by her efficiency in using her time. Leadership and management often occur on the run. The rapid clicking of high heels is the signal of her approach. Staff members run to keep pace as she moves around the Capitol.

We know of no good empirical measures of the effort Speakers invest in their duties. Albert put in long and dutiful days and regarded himself as a hard worker. He spent much of his day actually presiding over the House and had nowhere near the span of control that Pelosi exercises. O'Neill would have characterized his own approach as relaxed, and he was never accused of working too hard. Gingrich once said that a fact of life for him was that he was always tired, yet he spent a lot of his time and energy traveling around the country in pursuit of his grand vision and did not always mind the store on Capitol Hill.[23] Hastert spent every weekend at home attending to his "honey-do" list, except when he was asked to travel for fund-raising or other political appearances. Absent any precise measure, we simply assert this as our opinion: Speaker Nancy Pelosi has exerted more time and energy in the single-minded pursuit of her objectives than any of her modern predecessors.[24] We believe that this level of energy is demanded of the job today.

Pelosi and Her Predecessors

How does Speaker Pelosi's performance compare to that of her recent predecessors? Her avowed role model is Tip O'Neill. There are some similarities between these two Democratic Speakers. Both have been the products of urban, ethnic politics of the eastern seaboard. Both have been strong partisans. Pelosi has sought to emulate O'Neill's ability to bridge the fault lines in the Democratic Caucus. Notwithstanding these common elements, the differences between Pelosi's speakership and O'Neill's strike us as substantial. Before becoming Speaker, O'Neill never demonstrated much interest in the craft of legislation. He served as a leadership loyalist on the Rules Committee, a committee assignment at the time that precluded all others. This gave him access to a range of legislative interests without the responsibility for actually writing bills. Pelosi built her career in the committee system before entering the leadership, and she has strong policy interests. O'Neill played only a tangential role in support of the DCCC. He would make campaign appearances at the request of its chair and helped raise money for the DCCC's annual fund-raiser, but he was not active in candidate recruitment, was not the party's leading fund-raiser, and—especially during the Carter years—was not the main shaper of party message. During the Reagan administration, O'Neill gained greater visibility as the highest elected Democrat; but even then, he shared the spotlight with other prominent Democrats. It was during this time, after all, that the DLC was formed precisely as an alternative to O'Neill's more traditional liberalism. By contrast to O'Neill, Pelosi was clearly the party leader in every aspect of political management, including the DCCC operation. She appointed Emanuel; he did not appoint her. She articulated the message, helped to recruit the candidates, and raised more money than anyone else.

While O'Neill's involvement in legislation was largely restricted to cutting deals at the end of the process, Pelosi often has been immersed in the details of key legislation from beginning to end. In this respect, she has continued but extended a pattern that was developed on the Democratic side by Speakers Wright and Foley, both of whom were more involved in legislation than O'Neill had been. During the 100th Congress, Wright set an agenda for the Democrats, gave reporting deadlines to committees, monitored key legislation through the staff of the Democratic SPC, and ramrodded the bills on the floor. Foley was practiced in the art of forging consensus through task forces and other venues for intraparty coalition building. Pelosi built on their example but extended her reach further into the legislative process, first by exercising the power of naming Democrats initially to committees. Under her predecessors, the SPC had served as the Democratic committee on committees, making nominations for all committee slots and chair appointments. Pelosi arrogated this responsibility, subject to ratification by the SPC and a vote of the full Democratic Caucus, becoming the first Speaker, Democrat or Republican, to wield such power since the revolt against Speaker Cannon in 1910.

In fact, the most interesting gauge of Pelosi's power is comparison not to that of her Democratic predecessors but to that of her Republican counterparts Gingrich and Hastert. Pelosi, it is clear, disdains Gingrich, holding him primarily responsible for the corrosion in House culture that has occurred over the past generation. Still, his speakership provides the most interesting parallels to hers. He, too, developed a party agenda, recruited candidates, articulated party message, and raised a lot of money. The Republicans' victory in the 1994 elections, after 40 years out of power, was of greater historical dimension than the Democrats' return to power in the 2006 elections. Still, both Gingrich and Pelosi led their parties back from the wilderness. There is, however, a fundamental difference between the two as electoral strategists. Gingrich was trying to win elections in districts that leaned Republican but had been held by Democrats for a long time. He thought, therefore, that he could recruit very conservative candidates— candidates who agreed with him—and win in these districts. Pelosi had to win back the majority by winning in districts that still leaned Republican. She had no choice but to recruit candidates who could win in those districts even if they differed from her philosophically.[25]

In governing, Gingrich and Pelosi have been saddled with different problems. He had to deal with a large number of conservative ideologues who sought a radical policy agenda. She has had to deal on one side with a liberal caucus majority that is anxious to move its policy preferences, and on the other side with a set of more conservative members who know they have to position themselves very carefully in order to hold their districts. He was anchored to the right. She is pulled in both directions. While her heart is no doubt with the liberal Democrats, a good Speaker is able to locate the place where 218 votes reside and to lead her legislative party there, irrespective of her own predilections.

There was a fundamental flaw in Gingrich's conception of the speakership. Conceiving of himself as the leader of a parliamentary majority, he saw no reason to deal with the Democrats. As the "prime minister" of the House, he considered himself on the same plane as the president of the United States, going so far as to speak to the nation after the first 100 days of the 104th Congress to report on his Contract With America. In alienating the Democrats at the same time that he sought the public limelight, Gingrich sowed the seeds of his own destruction. He made himself a target, and he gave the Democrats the incentive to shoot. All that was missing was the ammunition, which was provided by the House ethics process and his own missteps in dealing with the charges the Democrats, led by Bonior and Pelosi, brought against him.

Pelosi has gone to school on Gingrich's mistakes. She has sought to preserve the advantages of her high public profile while minimizing its liabilities. Instead of putting herself out front on every issue as Gingrich had done, she has given credit to committee and subcommittee chairs, her leadership team, and rank-and-file members for their legislative accomplishments. At the same time, she has sought to put a congenial face on the House Democrats by wrapping them in her own feminine image. Pelosi's actions have not been simply a matter of creating an image, however. The underlying reality, as we have seen, is that Speaker Pelosi has empowered her members and has to some degree returned the House to a regular order in which members can play a constructive role.

Here, a comparison to Hastert is interesting. Hastert was elected Speaker by the Republicans because he was the opposite of Speaker Gingrich. Gingrich was high-profile, hot, and alienating; Hastert was decidedly low-profile, more temperate, and friendly. On taking the gavel, Hastert said that he wanted to return the House to regular order. To him, this meant that the Republicans would work through rather than around the committees. It did not entail cooperation with Democrats, however, and the Republican machine under Hastert became even more imperious than it had been under Gingrich. With Tom DeLay riding herd on Republicans, first as whip and then as floor leader, the leadership largely ignored the Democrats. Hastert often likened himself to the high school wrestling coach he had once been, saying that his job was to lead the "team" by empowering its talented members.[26] Coaches are generally unsympathetic with their opponents.

Yet there are crucial differences between Pelosi's and Hastert's situations and notions of empowerment. The Republican leadership team was riven from the beginning under Gingrich and remained divided under Hastert. Dick Armey, the Republican majority's first floor leader, despised DeLay, and the feeling was apparently mutual. Hastert owed his election as Speaker to DeLay, and over time DeLay's power created problems for Hastert. The Republican team that Hastert wanted to empower was in important respects a fiction. Even though the Republicans were more demographically and ideologically homogeneous than the Democrats, they were divided by internal leadership factions. And because they had gutted the committee seniority system, Republican members had no path forward except through their alliances with party leaders.

Pelosi was determined to avoid schisms in the ranks of the Democratic leadership. Her first instinct was to do so by driving out her opponents: hence her support of Larson against Crowley, of Murtha against Hoyer, and later, tacitly, of Waxman against Dingell. When she had to deal with members who had independent stature and inclination, her second instinct was to work with rather than against them; thus her generally positive relationship with Hoyer, her cooperation with Dingell on the 2007 energy bill, and with Peterson on agricultural and energy legislation. When she has talked about empowering members of the Democratic Caucus, she has usually referred to those loyal to her, those whose help she needs, or those whose seats she wishes to protect. She has been able to rely, however, on the committee system as a safety valve to release pressure that would otherwise build within the caucus, aggravating potential tensions within the ranks of the party leadership.

Pelosi has also learned by observing Hastert's relationship to President Bush. In accepting the president's agenda as his own, Hastert was led into a quagmire. The Iraq War, the unfunded expansion of the welfare state with the Medicare Part D prescription drug bill, the attempt to privatize Social Security, massive federal deficits, Hurricane Katrina—all the dimensions of Bush's policies became embedded in the public image of the House Republicans. Hastert needed space to protect his members from the taint of Bush's unpopularity, but he had left himself no room to do so. Pelosi has sought to avoid this error by declaring her independence from President Obama at the outset. Still, with Emanuel and Schiliro running the Obama White House legislative liaison, Pelosi achieved a high level of strategic coordination with Obama that paid off in a robust legislative agenda.

Does Her Gender Matter?

Speaker Pelosi's position as the first woman to hold this high office invites this question. Our analysis suggests that her gender is an inescapable and relevant aspect of her rise to leadership and profile in office but is less relevant, in many ways, to her day-to-day management of the House. We say less relevant, not irrelevant. She herself downplays the effect of her gender on her conduct as Speaker. She wants to be seen as a Speaker who happens to be a woman and not as a woman Speaker. Yet she is perfectly willing to capitalize on the publicity her historic stature has visited on her. Speaker Pelosi often exhibits a leadership style that is consistent with findings in the literature that women tend toward more collaborative styles than do men. She also presents herself as a tough-minded and hard-nosed politician, fending off the double bind about which we wrote in chapter 6. In our interviews we went out of our way to ask: "Does the fact of Speaker Pelosi being a woman make any difference?" The responses to this question ranged from "Yes, absolutely," to "Well, in some ways," to "None whatsoever." After sifting the sentiments the respondents expressed when we asked them to elaborate, we have concluded that there is a widespread recognition of the historic nature of her speakership and the symbolic importance of her being Speaker. Mothers and daughters pose for pictures beneath the sign over the entrance to her hall of power that reads "Speaker Nancy Pelosi." When it comes to the daily give-and-take of politics and legislation, gender seems to matter a great deal less.

Still, we may say that across the range of what we call the "Four Ss"—strategy, style, substance, and symbolism—Pelosi's gender matters. With respect to strategy, women members formed a crucial component of the coalition that carried her to the leadership. With respect to style, she has deliberately cultivated a collaborative approach, characteristic of female leadership styles. With respect to substance, she has been unrelenting in connecting the widest range of issues to their impact on families and children; we think that no male Speaker would have done the same. And with respect to symbolism, she clearly represents the greater diversity of opportunity that we have associated with the era of the New American Politics. In all these ways, her gender matters.

Too Partisan?

The most frequent criticism of Speaker Pelosi is that she is excessively partisan. We discussed the issue of partisanship in chapter 5, and we return to it now as we complete our study. In October 2008, near the end of the 110th Congress, the Speaker's office issued a fact sheet that claimed credit for passing "over 230 key measures, more than 70 percent with significant bipartisan support."[27] Her measure of bipartisanship was the support of at least 50 Republicans. Included were a variety of bills and amendments addressing the economy and housing, the infrastructure and transportation, consumer protection, pay equity, education, tax relief, trade, civil and voting rights, health care, the national defense, veterans, the Iraq and Afghanistan wars, homeland security, energy, small businesses, technological innovation, child safety, labor, the environment and public lands, law enforcement, foreign affairs, and government accountability. All of these bills were substantive.

The Speaker's press releases are, of course, aimed to promote her image and spread her message. In this press release her claim is that the House of Representatives had a productive record in the 110th Congress, much of it accomplished on a bipartisan basis. These claims require further analysis. Political scientist Charles O. Jones has offered a useful typology of policy coalitions: partisan, bipartisan, cross-partisan, and copartisan.[28] A partisan pattern develops when a bill is developed and enacted by the majority party with little or no input from the minority party. A bipartisan pattern occurs when a bill is developed from the beginning with substantial input from both parties. A cross-partisan pattern occurs when one party develops the policy and then seeks sufficient support from the other party to enact it. Often, it is the minority party that reaches across the aisle for the margin of votes needed. A copartisan pattern arises from split institutional control, when party leaders are forced to compromise across the boundaries of the separation of powers.

Jones's conception of bipartisanship is thus quite demanding, requiring real cooperation between party leaders. In order to assess the degrees of bipartisanship of the 109th Congress through the 111th (to date), we compiled final passage votes. Drawing on Jones's concepts (but imposing our own definitions), we specify as bipartisan those votes that gather majority support in both party caucuses. We use the term "semipartisan" for votes meeting Pelosi's 50-minority member support threshold. Votes capturing fewer than 50 minority members we label as partisan. We excluded several categories of final passage votes. A substantial number of bills on Pelosi's list passed by voice vote; voice votes are presumably bipartisan but obviously noncontroversial, so we exclude them from our analysis. We also excluded measures passed under suspension of the rules because they require a supermajority and again normally involve less controversial legislation. We excluded appropriations bills because they often involve distributive coalitions no matter which party is in the majority. Table 7.3 arrays the remaining final passage votes.

The data offer the perhaps surprising finding that under both the Republican majority in the 109th Congress and Democratic majority in the 110th Congress about half of these bills were passed with bipartisan support. They also indicate that in the 110th Congress the Democratic majority proceeded in a marginally more bipartisan fashion than its immediate Republican predecessor, conducting slightly more bipartisan and semipartisan votes, and fewer partisan votes. The 111th Congress, however, has been substantially more partisan, with the percentage of partisan votes doubling

Table 7.3 Voting Patterns, 109th–111th Congresses (2005 to 2009)

	109th	110th	111th*
Number of bipartisan votes (%)	59 (49.8)	122 (51.3)	16 (24.2)
Number of semipartisan votes (%)	15 (12.6)	44 (18.5)	8 (12.1)
Number of partisan votes (%)	45 (37.8)	72 (30.3)	42 (63.6)
Total	119	238	66

*Through December 16, 2009.

Source: Calculated by the authors from Office of the Clerk, "Legislation and Votes," accessed at http://clerk.house.gov/legislative/legvotes.html.

and the percentage of bipartisan and semipartisan votes sharply reduced. We assume that this shift is due to three factors. The first is the larger Democratic majority in the 111th Congress, enabling the party to more easily proceed on its own terms. The second is the fact that the Democrats controlled the White House. The Obama administration's legislative program provided a strong incentive to move legislation. The third factor is the decision of the Republicans to uniformly oppose major elements of the Democratic agenda. While Pelosi had pursued the same strategy in the 109th Congress, recall that she had also allowed her "majority makers" to vote their districts in the 110th. The sharply reduced Republican minority in the 111th Congress, shorn of moderate members, found no conflict between principle and politics and so could afford to simply vote no. Allowing for Republican intransigence, we do not believe that the data in table 7.3 support a claim that the Democratic majority has been more bipartisan than the Republican majorities of the Bush years.

This conclusion squares with our overall impression of Pelosi's leadership. She is a highly partisan Democrat. But this, we believe, should not be surprising. The era of the New American Politics is unlikely to produce Speakers who are not strong partisans, especially confronted by defiant congressional minorities that refuse to cooperate as was the case with Democrats in the 109th and Republicans in the 110th. The question is, are Speakers effective in advancing party interests while paying due respect to the institutional norms that create the possibility of bipartisan accommodation when the public interest demands it? This raises the further question of whether Speaker Pelosi is too liberal to do so.

Too Liberal?

Nancy Pelosi is unabashedly liberal, and has been criticized as a liberal by Republicans (as one might expect) and also by moderate and conservative Democrats. In tracing her climb to power we explained that the most frequent criticism of her by her Democratic opponents had been that she was too liberal to effectively lead them to regain their majority. Once she became Speaker, however, those more centrist Democrats were surprised at the extent of her willingness to accommodate their views, and during the 110th Congress it was the liberal Democrats who were most dissatisfied with her inability to deliver on their agenda.

In the 111th Congress the ground shifted and so did the attitudes of liberal and centrist Democrats. Now that the party had the capacity to govern, the Blue Dog Democrats were going to be put on the spot as liberal Democrats pushed their preferred policy options. Pelosi thus faced a choice. Should she seek to move the liberal agenda, or should she continue to accommodate the conservatives? As we saw in chapter 5, her solution on the key issues such as energy and health was to seek the most liberal bills for which she could rally 218 votes. To do so, however, she had to accommodate centrist demands, substantially altering the legislation.

One argument that Pelosi made in support of pressing for more liberal bills was that she wanted the House to be in a stronger bargaining position with the Senate when it came time to reconcile bills in conference. Knowing that the House would have to cede ground to the more centrist Senate, she wanted to start out as far on the left as possible. This strategy ran a serious risk however. As we saw in chapter 3, the House and Senate rarely resort to conferences to reconcile legislation. Instead, they "ping-pong" the bills between the two chambers until the same version of the bill has passed in both chambers. If the House bills are too liberal to pass in the Senate, the real negotiations take place in the Senate and the House is often forced to swallow the result. This happened in the 2007 energy bill and appeared likely to happen on both energy and health legislation in 2009.

From this perspective, Pelosi would have been better served by a different approach in the House. By working with centrist Democrats to fashion middle-ground legislation, she would accomplish several objectives. First, she would avoid putting centrist Democrats from swing districts at risk. Second, she would pass bills with larger House majorities, perhaps picking up the votes of a few Republicans. Third, she would enable the House to be a more influential player in the end game with the Senate and White House because the House would be offering legislation that might actually pass in the other body. Fourth, she would end up with more legislation and fewer House-passed bills lying dormant in the Senate. By pressing for liberal bills, Pelosi effectively marginalized the House and allowed the Senate to be the real shaper of policy.

This centrist critique is quite plausible and is offered by those who would have preferred to have Steny Hoyer as their Speaker rather than Nancy Pelosi. He very likely would have taken this approach. However as we have noted, Pelosi beat Hoyer because there are more liberals than moderates in the Democratic Caucus. Any party leader must attend to her base of support among members. Pelosi had sometimes disappointed her liberal base and denied her own policy preferences in the 110th Congress in making pragmatic accommodations to party centrists. She continued to do so in the 111th Congress, but operating with a larger majority, she was able to make fewer concessions. Even so, liberals were angry with her when she decided to go with the more moderate health care policies than to drive over the cliff on the liberal bandwagon.

This analysis etches Pelosi's fundamental dilemma, which has trailed her House leadership career. Centrist critics want her to govern as if she were Steny Hoyer; liberals want her to govern as if the centrists were not an essential component of their majority coalition. Pelosi can do neither, so instead she seeks the most liberal legislation that can gather a majority of votes. This strategy leaves both her left and right wings dissatisfied, and may put centrist Democratic seats at risk. She gambles that this strategy will produce legislation that moves public policy incrementally in her preferred direction and preserves her majority in the process. Taking such gambles is what party leaders are called upon to do in the environment of the New American Politics.

Operating in that environment, Nancy Pelosi has brought strong energy, organizational capability, interpersonal skill, and determination to succeed as party leader where her recent predecessors failed. A congressional party leader, however, will on occasion be called on to offer leadership to Congress and to the nation that transcends the boundaries of intra-party or inter-party conflict. The epigraph to this chapter raises the important question whether in the era of the New American Politics our leaders are capable of responding to this obligation. It is to this question that we now turn.

THE SPEAKERSHIP AND THE NEW AMERICAN POLITICS

We are left to wonder about the capacity of American institutions to produce or permit the kind of leadership that serves the public good. Many thoughtful observers share Fareed Zakaria's concern that our political institutions may not be capable of the compromises demanded of the crises of our time.[29] Some, we realize, will doubt that such transcendent leadership is desirable, or even possible. To them, the world is always aligned into competing parties who do battle until one wins and the other loses. All politics, hence all public policy, is a partisan brawl. The intramural debate within the Democratic Party has been between those who believe that the party is best served by centrist policies capable of attaining bipartisan accommodation (the Blue Dog and New Democrat view) and those who believe that the goal is to win the fight on behalf of liberal policy goals (the Progressive Caucus view). As a strategic matter, Pelosi has occasionally worked with the former, but her heart and her closest associations are with the latter. Her template for addressing the great challenges the country confronts is not that of transcendent bipartisanship but rather of pragmatic legislative craftwork in a highly partisan environment.

We have identified five key elements of the New American Politics: partisanship, fund-raising, organization, technology, and diversity. We conclude that Speaker Pelosi embodies all five of these. In representing the diversity of the country and in proving so effective in raising money, organizing the Democrats, and utilizing technology, she is the prototype of the era. She is also strongly partisan, reflecting both partisanship's constructive and destructive elements. Speaker Pelosi, our informants have told us, reveres the House as an institution—just as O'Neill, her role model, did. Notwithstanding his image as an Irish ward-heeler, O'Neill was in fact a strong institutionalist, typically deferential to the committee chairs and supporting seniority without exception. He was accommodating to his own members and reasonably fair to Republicans. He had many friends among them, including Republican leader Bob Michel, a golfing companion. Despite Pelosi's desire to emulate O'Neill, however, there is no similarity between O'Neill's relationship to Michel and her relationship with Boehner. The relatively distant relationship between Pelosi and Boehner typifies what leadership relationships have become during the era of the New American Politics. Indeed, Pelosi had a much cooler relationship with Speaker Hastert, and Speakers Gingrich and Hastert were barely on speaking terms with Democratic leader Dick Gephardt.

Both Gingrich and Hastert also thought of themselves as devoted to the House as an institution, but their conception of that institution differed from that of old-timers like O'Neill and Michel. Gingrich and Hastert saw the House in essentially parliamentary terms, believing that it ought to be governed by partisan majority. In seeking to restore more regular order to the House, Pelosi recognized the key role of the committee system and deliberately stepped away from that conception, as we have seen. Yet we have no doubt that Pelosi is and will likely remain a highly partisan Democrat. Whatever accommodations she may reach with Republicans along the way will come about because she has calculated that it is in her party's interest to do so. This is not surprising. The Speaker of the House is elected by the majority of her party caucus. When the parties are polarized along ideological lines, as they have been during this era of the New American Politics, they will elect leaders who reflect their majority faction. Neither a conservative Democrat nor a moderate Republican will get elected to party leadership under these conditions.

The best that can be hoped for, then, is a Speaker who has the ability to effectively manage her legislative majority while working where possible to lessen the tensions between the two parties. Here, the Democrats may actually have an advantage over the Republicans because their caucus is more diverse, ideologically, demographically, and regionally. Elected by a more homogeneous base, Republican Speakers are naturally encouraged to play to it. Democratic Speakers, in seeking accommodation within their own party's ranks, create space to include some Republicans, issue by issue. Republican Speakers, seeking to win with a "majority of the majority," preferred not to deal with the Democrats unless absolutely necessary. Pelosi, as in the example of the 2009 cap and trade energy bill, worked hard to win the votes of the handful of Republicans whose votes enabled her to pass the bill.

The qualities demanded of Democratic and Republican Speakers in this era of the New American Politics are thus technically similar but strategically different. Any effective Speaker must be able to integrate and manage the various components of party governance. These range from political functions, such as candidate recruitment and fund-raising, to legislative functions such as party organization and policy-making. A Speaker can no longer simply take her majority for granted, defer to the committee system, rely on automatic mechanisms such as seniority, or leave the branding of the party to others. The skills required are that of a political organizer, policy wonk, public relations expert, and institutional savant. The physical demands are enormous.

Republican and Democratic Speakers serve different electoral and congressional constituencies, and these differences shape the context in which they lead. Most House members have been elected in noncompetitive districts in which the primary election determined the general election outcome. The Democratic Party, however, is more coalitional, the Republican Party more ideological. While both parties are more ideologically homogeneous in the era of the New American Politics than they were a generation ago, the Democratic Party still must straddle greater ideological, geographic, and demographic ground. Republican constituencies tend to be more demographically and ideologically monolithic. As a result, Republican members are tethered to their party's base voters, a decided minority in the electorate. To govern, the Republican leaders exercised control over their conference by logrolling its members. This was the primary reason why the number of earmarks tripled on their watch and the public debt exploded. They distributed benefits to constituents, but their party base (and their ideology) would not allow them to raise taxes. Ironically, this irresponsible fiscal policy eventually cost them support among their own base voters contributing to their losses in 2006 and 2008.

Democrats have a different problem. Because of the diversity in their party caucus, Democrats must find accommodation. Because their majority margin has been won in districts previously held by Republicans, they cannot move too far to the left without jeopardizing their control of the House. At the same time, the liberal Democratic majority in the Democratic Caucus quite naturally wants to follow its policy instincts. Leading the caucus from the left, Speaker Pelosi's strategic challenge is to move policy in a progressive direction without fracturing the caucus or putting its majority at risk. Rather than to pursue tight leadership control, as the Republicans did, her task is to orchestrate the caucus to bring harmony from its normal cacophony and thus requires leadership skills of a high order.

This internal challenge is exacerbated by the external conditions imposed by the New American Politics. The incessant message war, the permanent campaign in all of its aspects, the new media, the diversification of the electorate, the utilization of new technologies—all of these elements put stress on Congress as an institution. Pelosi's effort to navigate the external environment has been more extensive than any previous Speaker. But the relentlessly partisan echo chamber wears on her ideologically divided caucus and makes it especially difficult to reach across the aisle to work with those whose aim is to wrest power away.

Incessant partisan acrimony has, unfortunately, come to define the speakership in the era of the New American Politics. Pelosi entered the House in 1987 just as Wright's tenure as Speaker began. Her career has spanned four speakerships prior to her own, each in its own way unsuccessful. Wright was forced to resign the speakership and his House seat because of the ethics charges that Gingrich brought against him. His successor, Foley, wanted to restore comity to the House, but the partisan rancor continued, and he became he first Speaker since the Civil War to lose his House seat as the Democrats lost their majority in 1994. The leader of the Republican Revolution, Gingrich, faced a coup attempt in 1997 and a challenge from Appropriations Committee chair Bob Livingston of Louisiana in 1998. Gingrich resigned from the House. His successor, Hastert, became the longest serving Republican Speaker, yet he had to deal constantly with the impression that DeLay was the real power in the House and the reality that DeLay seemed to believe that as well. Under Hastert's leadership, the Republicans eventually lost their majority; two years later, he resigned from the House, and the Democrats captured his seat. These Speakers have all been intelligent men who aimed to serve the country and their congressional party well. None of them, however, was able to navigate the rough seas the office has been forced to weather. Except in her approval ratings, Pelosi thus far appears to be succeeding where her predecessors have failed.

To hold power and to ride herd on the Democrats may not be enough, however. Enormous challenges lie ahead in setting policy for the decades and generations to come. The country faces an enormous unfunded policy deficit (the money needed to pay for its current policy obligations). A broken health-care system, unsustainable social welfare programs, an untenable energy model, a persistent immigration problem, a sagging public infrastructure, ineffective schools…these are only the most prominent of the challenges confronting the nation. It seems unlikely that they can be resolved without achieving some public consensus. Consensus in this regard is more than just a matter of winning elections and controlling policy; it is a matter of public education and reconciliation. It calls for leadership. Whether the speakership of the House of Representatives is the office that can provide that leadership is an open question.

THE OUTLIER

We have indicated that, so far, Pelosi has been a very effective Speaker of the House. Of course, with disapproval ratings hovering near 50%, we realize that one-half of the American people do not regard her so favorably. Public perceptions, favorable or unfavorable, are grounded in personal taste and political ideology. Pelosi also has her critics within the House Democratic Caucus among members who would prefer to be led by a more moderate Speaker. We do not seek to persuade those who do not like her that they should. Our task is to situate Pelosi in the context in which she has come to serve. At some future point, scholars will be able to render a more definitive judgment than we now can. We believe we can say something about her adaptation to the demands of the speakership today. Thus, we close this study by offering a Darwinian interpretation. Speaker Pelosi is a capable leader whose skills have so far proven better adapted to the environment of the New American Politics than those of her predecessors Wright, Foley, Gingrich, and Hastert. Her adaptation might be viewed as analogous to the process of genetic mutation. She carries the genes of the ethnic, ward politics of a Baltimore mayor and his politically active wife, but she has transformed herself and survived as a leader on the front lines of the new politics. She plays the old politics of personal loyalty and partisan commitment, yet she also has mastered the new politics of fund-raising, technology, and media relations. Her organizational and collaborative skills are well adapted to the demands of the House in this era. The woman and the moment have met.

In his recent book *Outliers*, Malcolm Gladwell examines "the story of success," that is, the factors that enable those who are successful to become so.[30] Contrary to the commonly accepted notion that success is born of native talent, Gladwell argues that two other factors play a more important role: preparation and opportunity. Taking his examples from a broad spectrum of human activity, he suggests that the real key to developing one's skills is simply practice—long hours of practice. He is specific about the amount of time that it takes to get good at something: 10,000 hours. We share Gladwell's view that the willingness to work hard—to practice that much—is a necessary but insufficient trait. The opportunity structure of a successful career in music, sports, business, or (we add) politics requires not only intensive effort but also the chance to capitalize on its results.

Like other highly accomplished individuals Gladwell describes, Nancy Pelosi has built on a lifetime of practice to become the political leader she is. Her training began at her father's and mother's feet and has extended through an adulthood of active involvement in politics. She often stresses her experience as a housewife and mother as informing her leadership style, and we do not dispute the claim. We suggest, though, that in the larger

context of the New American Politics, it was her practice in political organization, fund-raising, and coalition building that really prepared her to
become and serve as Speaker of the House. Effective institutions are those
that develop talent and filter those who have it into positions of responsibility. Rayburn, the most iconic Speaker of the twentieth century, was schooled
in the institutional life of the House from 1911 until he became its Speaker
in 1941. He was molded to the institution he was called on to lead, and
when he arrived at the top he was prepared. Gingrich entered the House in
1978 and became its Speaker in 1995. But to get there, he sought to blow
up the institutional barriers he thought had blocked the Republicans from
power. When he became Speaker, he had only abstract theories on which to
rely. Pelosi's path to the speakership started before she became a member, in
her work on behalf of the California Democratic Party, the DNC, and the
Democratic Senate Campaign Committee. As a member, she was an active
legislator, a leading fund-raiser, and a party operative. She developed the
skills required of the office along her path to it. When she got there, she was
ready. Seneca had it right: preparation met opportunity.

And opportunity usually involves some amount of luck. The reason Pelosi
is Speaker and Gephardt is not is due substantially to the fact that the political stars were not aligned for a Democratic victory during his service as
Democratic leader. Pelosi herself was unable to lead the Democrats to victory in 2004, and had she failed again in 2006, her leadership career might
have been brought short. Events in Iraq contributed as much or more to her
success than anything that the Democrats did on the campaign trail. Having
won power in the House, she proved adroit in maneuvering the Democrats
to a favorable position in the 2008 elections. But she was unable to accomplish most of her main policy objectives until Obama's coattails gave the
Democrats unified control of the government. While Pelosi appears to have
preferred Obama to Hillary Clinton as presidential candidate, she can hardly
take credit for his meteoric rise to power. And what might Pelosi's prospects
have been with Hillary Clinton in the White House? At a minimum, her
time on the stage as the nation's highest elected female would have been
over.

She's Not Done

This study of Nancy Pelosi now ends before her speakership is completed.
Any insights we have been able to glean about her and her speakership
are necessarily provisional. No speakership can be fully assessed until it is
over, and hers has more to come. Instead of putting a period to her story, it

remains for us here to frame its interpretation. We believe that Pelosi has demonstrated what a Speaker of the House needs to do in the era of the New American Politics and some of the pitfalls into which Speakers may fall. The Speaker's responsibility is majority management in all of its aspects: candidate recruitment, campaigning, fund-raising, and protection of incumbents. The Speaker must be a policy leader and not simply an institutional manager. This entails immersion in the details of major policies.

At the same time, the Speaker has institutional obligations. These extend to reliance on regular order, working in cooperation with the committees, and offering procedural fairness to the minority. A Speaker must be a strong leader, and can when necessary be a partisan battler. But the Speaker must also acknowledge an institutional obligation to comity and the conditions of deliberative government. The Speaker is the public face of the House and of her congressional party. The image she projects is the face of the institution and party she leads. In crisis situations, the Speaker has an obligation to rise above partisanship in the public interest. The skill of a Speaker is most clearly expressed in striking the appropriate balance between partisan and institutional obligations. In the era of the New American Politics, that balance is hard to achieve. Gingrich did not try. Hastert said that he wanted to be fair but in the end grounded his leadership on a majoritarian principle. Pelosi speaks with reverence for the House of Representatives and her obligation to its institutional values, but she is also a strong partisan whose partisan instincts sometimes lead her into trouble. Her attack on the House Republicans after the initial defeat of the TARP legislation in September 2008 is a case in point; her attack on the CIA in May 2009 is another.

In the end, Pelosi's speakership will likely be remembered for three things. Most obvious is her historical significance as the first woman speaker; that can never be taken away from her. The second is the way she has sought to manage the office. Future Speakers will, we think, look to her pragmatic recruitment of candidates, her fund-raising prowess, her integration of policy and message, the general harmony of her leadership team, her effective liaison with a group of talented committee chairs, her strategic approach to legislation, her pragmatic coalition building, and her cultivation of her image and say to themselves "That is what I need to do." They will also observe her sometimes awkward presentational style and hope to improve upon it. Her successors will differ in their personal qualities and political circumstances, and may pursue different legislative strategies than has she; but she has, as the first female Speaker well might, offered a recipe for success.

Equally or more important, Pelosi will be remembered for the legislative accomplishments of her tenure. The House of Representatives under her speakership has tackled an expansive agenda—reforming health care, redirecting energy and environmental policy, restructuring the financial services industry and regulations, and addressing student loans, food safety, technological innovation, highway and transit funding, among other issues. As we complete our study, it remains to be seen how much of the Democratic agenda will be enacted into law. Some see this agenda of issues as overly ambitious; others criticize the Democrats for being too willing to compromise on substance in order to pass the bills. Ironically, both critiques may prove true. Pelosi may both overreach politically and underperform substantively.

She is a Speaker who wants to be remembered for the way her policy leadership has produced a better world for children and families. In chapter 6, we wrote of the particular type of ambition that is emblematic of Pelosi: task ambition. As she herself has often stated, her policy goals are nothing short of saving the planet and improving the lives of future generations of children. Whatever the final disposition of the big issues of health-care reform and renewable energy, she will continue to fight the good fight on behalf of the policy goals that have defined her public service. And many important goals lie ahead.

As she approaches these and other issues, Pelosi will proceed as doggedly as she has so far—as she often puts it, "one step at a time." We have argued in this book that her skill set has matched the times in which she has been called on to serve. Many challenges and potential pitfalls lie ahead. She has become a polarizing figure, and there can be little doubt that Republicans will continue to attack her as the public face of "big government" and "San Francisco liberalism." If, or perhaps when, public opinion turns against the Democrats, these attacks may gain purchase. Rhetorical stumbles on her part may provide fodder for her enemies' attacks. The Democrats, by pursuing an active agenda, may put their majority at risk. If they lose control of the House on her watch, Pelosi's reputation will suffer. Still, it seems apparent that Nancy Pelosi has the opportunity to establish a record of legislative accomplishment of historic dimensions. In addition to the list of important items previously mentioned, the Democratic agenda includes a heady list of other reforms of the entitlement system, immigration policy, education, military affairs, the financial system, and, looming over all of it, the federal deficit. We cannot know now how she and her party will fare as they seek to address these enormously complex challenges. We can say that Speaker Pelosi has developed the tools and demonstrated the skills required of an effective Speaker in the era of the New American Politics.

NOTES

CHAPTER 1

1. Breaking new ground, Boehner presented the gavel to Pelosi with a kiss on the cheek. This was not, however, a harbinger of a harmonious relationship between the majority and minority parties.
2. See Lyndsey Layton, "Pelosi Aims to Recast Self, Party," *Washington Post*, December 22, 2006.
3. George Lakoff, *Morality Politics* (Chicago: University of Chicago Press, 2002).
4. On polarization and its effects on party leadership in the House see David W. Rohde, *Parties and Leaders in the Postreform House* (Chicago: University of Chicago Press, 1991); Barbara Sinclair, *Party Wars* (Norman: University of Oklahoma Press, 2006); Sean Theriault, *Party Polarization in Congress* (New York: Cambridge University Press, 2008).
5. Steve Gillon, *The Pact: Bill Clinton, Newt Gingrich, and the Rivalry That Defined a Generation* (New York: Oxford University Press, 2008).
6. Carol M. Mueller, ed. *The Politics of the Gender Gap: The Social Construction of Political Influence*. (Newbury Park, Calif.: Sage, 1988), and Richard A. Seltzer, Jody Newman, and Melissa Voorhees Leighton, *Sex as a Political Variable: Women as Candidates and Voters in U.S. Elections* (Boulder, Colo.: Lynne Rienner Publisher, 1997).
7. Hillary Clinton, *Living History* (New York: Simon and Schuster, 2003), 109.
8. Pew Research Center, "Audience Segments in a Changing News Environment," August 17, 2008, http://people-press.org/reports/pdf/444.pdf (accessed November 10, 2008).
9. See Jacob S. Hacker and Paul Pierson, *Off Center: The Republican Revolution and the Erosion of American Democracy* (New Haven: Yale University Press, 2005).
10. See Anthony Downs, *An Economic Theory of Democracy* (New York: Addison Wesley, 1997).
11. Morris Fiorina, *Culture War? The Myth of a Polarized America* (New York: Pearson Longman, 2005).
12. Michael Barone, "The 49% Nation," *National Journal*, June 8, 2001; David Brooks, "One Nation, Slightly Divided," *Atlantic Monthly*, December 2001.

13. Rick Perlstein, *Nixonland: The Rise of a President and the Fracturing of America* (New York: Scribner, 2008).

14. Tim Graham, "NBC Anchor Puffed Pelosi, but in '94 Brokaw Whacked 'Amoral' Gingrich," *NewsBusters*, November 14, 2006, http://newsbusters.org/node/9089 (accessed January 3, 2009); Michael Barone, "No Permanent Majorities in America," *Real Clear Politics*, January 3, 2009, www.realclearpolitics.com/articles/2009/01/no_permanent_majorities_in_ame.html (accessed January 3, 2009). Barone says: "The Republican Party throughout our history has been a party whose core constituency has been those who are considered, by themselves and by others, to be typical Americans."

15. We pick 1986 responses because of their proximity in time to Pelosi's first electoral effort. At that time, 21% of men also agreed with the statement. In 1998, 15% of men agreed that women should take care of the home rather than be concerned about running the country.

16. Spiro Agnew, "An Effete Corps of Impudent Snobs," speech delivered in Houston, May 22, 1972, www.geocities.com/pacific_future/speech_agnew220570.html (accessed October 1, 2008).

17. Center for Responsive Politics, OpenSecrets.org. "EMILY's List: Fundraising/ Spending by Cycle: 2008," based on Federal Election Commission reports. See http://www.opensecrets.org/pacs/lookup2.php?strID=C00193433&cycle=2008 (accessed September 27, 2009).

18. Partisan gerrymandering is, of course, a bipartisan phenomenon. Its master in the precomputer era was California Democrat Phil Burton, to whose congressional seat Pelosi was elected in 1987. See John H. Fund, "Beware the Gerrymander, My Son: Creative Redistricting," *National Review*, April 7, 1989, http://findarticles.com/p/articles/mi_m1282/is_/ai_7483113 (accessed January 4, 2009). For a good account of the development of redistricting technology see Kimbell W. Brace, "Technology and Redistricting," paper presented at Brookings Institute Conference on Redistricting, Washington, D.C, April 16, 2004 www.brookings.edu/gs/crc_Brace.pdf (accessed January 3, 2009).

19. The Democrats called their data base "Demzilla." It held over 170 million names. The Republican counterpart is called "Voter Vault." See Lev Grossman et al., "What Your Party Knows about You," *Time*, October 14, 2004, www.time.com/time/magazine/article/0,9171,995394,00.html (accessed January 22, 2009).

20. Cass R. Sunstein, *Republic.com 2.0* (Princeton: Princeton University Press, 2007).

21. Markos Moulitsas Huniga, *Taking on the System* (New York: Celebra Press, 2008).

22. Matt Bai, *The Argument: Billionaires, Bloggers, and the Battle to Remake Democratic Politics* (New York: Penguin Press, 2007).

23. Thomas E. Mann and Norman J. Ornstein, *The Permanent Campaign: Its Future* (Washington, D.C.: AEI Press, 2000).

24. These figures were calculated from data in U.S. Census Bureau, *The Statistical Abstract 2009*, Washington D.C., and prior year volumes, www.census.gov/compendia/statab/cats/population.html.

25. CAWP Women's Vote Watch, "Women's Votes Could Determine Election Outcome: Women Are a Clear Majority of Voters," October 10, 2008, www.cawp.rutgers.edu/press_room/news/documents/PressRelease_11–05–08_womensvote.pdf (accessed December 2008).

26. Anna L. Harvey, *Votes without Leverage* (New York: Cambridge University Press, 1998).

27. Ibid., chap. 6.

28. Betty Friedan, *The Feminine Mystique* (New York: Dell, 1964).

29. Kira Sanbonmatsu, *Democrats/Republicans and the Politics of Women's Place* (Ann Arbor: University of Michigan Press, 2002).

30. Barbara Burrell, *A Woman's Place Is in the House: Campaigning for Congress in the Feminist Era* (Ann Arbor: University of Michigan Press, 1996), 130.

31. Nonetheless, women still trail men among big dollar bundlers. See Fredereka Schouten, "In Presidential Fund-raising Ranks, a Gender Gap Is Closing," *USA Today*, July 31, 2008, www.usatoday.com/news/politics/election2008/2008–07–30-gender_n.htm (accessed January 22, 2009).

32. Glenna Matthews, *Just a Housewife: The Rise and Fall of Domesticity in America* (New York: Oxford University Press, 1987). Matthews argues that consumerism, technology, sexism, and modern feminism combined to reverse a century and a half of celebration of domesticity and its ability to connect and find avenues for expression in politics and public life in spite of women's lack of the vote and full citizenship.

33. From Jane Addams, *Women and Public Housekeeping* (New York: National Woman Suffrage, 1910), reprinted in John Pettigrew, *Public Women, Public Words* (New York: Madison House, 2002), 2:116.

34. The autobiographies of political women are replete with stories of balancing acts and analogies to housework. Among the most colorful is Pat Schroeder, *24 Years of Housework and the Place Is Still a Mess* (Kansas City, Mo.: Andrews McMeel, 1999). See also Barbara Mikulski et al., *Nine and Counting: The Women of the Senate* (New York: HarperCollins, 2000).

35. John Naisbitt, *Megatrends* (New York: Grand Central, 1988). Naisbitt coined the expression "high-tech and high-touch" and pointed out the fallacy of automating every business transaction without human interaction at some point.

36. As former Harvard president Larry Summers discovered, the assumption of women's weaker mathematical aptitude can no longer be taken for granted.

37. *Nielsen OnLine,* "Connection-seeking 'Power Moms' Twice as Likely to Give Online Advice," October 17, 2008, http://www.marketingcharts.com/interactive/connection-seeking-power-moms-twice-as-likely-to-give-online-advice-6426/ (accessed January 22, 2009).

38. Deborah Fallows, "How Women and Men Use the Internet," *Pew Internet and American Life Project,* December 28, 2005, www.pewinternet.org/pdfs/PIP_Women_and_Men_online.pdf (accessed January 22, 2009).

39. Auren Hoffman, "The Social Media Gender Gap," *Business Week,* May 19, 2008, www.businessweek.com/technology/content/may2008/tc20080516_580743.htm (accessed January 22, 2009).

40. CAWP Women's Vote Watch, "Women's Votes Could Determine Election Outcome: Women Are a Clear Majority of Voters," October 10, 2008, www.cawp.rutgers.edu/press_room/news/documents/PressRelease_11–05–08_womensvote.pdf (accessed December 31, 2008).

41. Ronald M. Peters, Jr., *The American Speakership: The Office in Historical Perspective,* 2nd ed. (Baltimore: Johns Hopkins University Press, 1997).

42. The literature on legislative leadership is large and growing. Interested readers can begin inquiry by consulting these studies: Joseph Cooper and David Brady, "Institutional Context and Leadership Style: The House from Cannon to Rayburn," *American Political Science Review* 75 (1981): 411–25; Gary Cox and Matthew McCubbins, *Legislative Leviathan* (New York: Cambridge University Press, 2007); Matthew Green, "Presidents and Personal Goals: The Speaker of the House as Non-majoritarian Leader," *Congress and the Presidency* 34, 2 (autumn 2007): 1–22; Rhode, *Parties and Leaders in the Postreform House,* 1991); Barbara Sinclair, *Legislators, Leaders, and Lawmaking: The U.S. House of Representatives in the Postreform Era* (Baltimore: Johns Hopkins University Press, 1998); Randall Strahan, *Leading Representatives* (Baltimore: Johns Hopkins University Press, 2007).

43. Peters, *American Speakership,* chap. 5. See also Julian E. Zelizer, *On Capitol Hill* (New York: Cambridge University Press, 2006), chaps. 8–9.

44. These are so-called special rules that govern the floor consideration of all legislation. All major legislation must be referred to the House Rules Committee by the committee of substantive jurisdiction. The Rules Committee then develops the special rule that determines the amount of floor time, its allocation between the majority and minority, and the amendments that will be made in order. Currently, there are four categories of special rules: open, modified, structured, and closed. An explanation of these rules and a list of special rules for the 110th and some preceding congresses may be found on the Rules Committee website, www.rules.house.gov/.

45. The House does most of its business in the Committee of the Whole, whose quorum is 100 members. Once bills are perfected in the Committee of the Whole, it rises (i.e. ends its session) and the House itself goes into session, whose quorum is half of the members plus one. This arrangement allows the House to do its business more efficiently. Teller votes were conducted by members lining up in yea or nay lines and counted as they walked past the official tellers (counters). Votes were not recorded by name. Teller votes only occurred in the Committee of the Whole. Final passage votes were recorded roll call votes taken by the House. With the advent of electronic voting in 1973, teller votes fell into disuse and were removed from the House rules.

46. A dramatic illustration of this tit-for-tat complaining may be found in comparing Richard B. Cheney, "An UnRuly House: A Republican View," *Public Opinion* (January–February 1989): 41–44, to David Price, "House Democrats under Republican Rule:

Reflections on the Limits of Partisanship," *Forum* (Miller Center, University of Virginia, (spring–summer 2004): 21–28.

47. Bills considered under Suspension of the Rules must receive a two-thirds majority to pass. No amendments are allowed, and debate is limited to 20 minutes. The purpose of suspensions is to facilitate floor consideration of noncontroversial (likely to gain a two-thirds majority) or minor (authorizing or appropriating less than $100 million) bills.

48. For a discussion and explanation of MTR, see "Motions to Recommit" in chapter 3.

49. Exceptions were the subcommittee chairs of the Appropriations Committee, the so-called cardinals, whose selection was subject to ratification by the full caucus.

50. Barbara Sinclair, *Majority Party Leadership in the U.S. House of Representatives* (Baltimore: Johns Hopkins University Press, 1983).

51. In the 1980s, conservative Democrats organized into the Conservative Democratic Forum and were nicknamed the Boll Weevils. In the 1990s, they recast themselves as the Blue Dogs and organized a formal caucus under that name.

52. Dennis Hastert, "Reflections on the Role of the Speaker in the Modern Day House of Representatives," in *The Cannon Centenary Conference: The Changing Nature of the Speakership* (Washington, D.C.: U.S. Government Printing Office, 2004), 60–64.

53. For Reed's well-known remark see Rules Committee website, *House Floor Procedures*, www.rules.house.gov/archives/jcoc2f.htm.

54. See Juliet Eilperin, *Fight Club Politics* (Lanham, Md.: Rowman and Littlefield, 2006); Thomas E. Mann and Norman J. Ornstein, *The Broken Branch* (New York: Oxford University Press, 2006); Barbara Sinclair, *Party Wars*.

55. The success of liberal Ned Lamont's primary victory over Connecticut senator Joe Lieberman is perhaps one of the more striking examples. Lieberman lost in the 2008 Democratic primary but ran as an Independent in the general election and defeated Lamont with the help of independent and moderate voters.

56. Mann and Ornstein, *Broken Branch*.

57. Speaker Hastert emerges as in some respects the outlier in this group, an "accidental" Speaker who, like Pelosi, entered the House at a relatively late age. He was elected Speaker in just his seventh term, having held no prior elected party leadership office. Unsurprisingly, therefore, he was relatively low on the seniority list when he became Speaker. The last person prior to Hastert to have been elected Speaker after seven or fewer terms was Charles Crisp of Georgia, who was first elected to the House for the 48th Congress in 1883 and was elected Speaker in the 52nd Congress in 1891. Hastert is alone among the recent Speakers in table 1.1 in never having sought or campaigned for the office. Nonetheless, he became the longest serving Republican Speaker.

58. The ideological polarization scores presented in table 1.1 are based on the difference between the Democratic and Republican mean "DW NOMINATE" scores for the first Congress in which each Speaker served as Speaker. The DW NOMINATE score, an acronym standing for dynamic, weighted, nominal three-step estimation, is

a measure of a member's place on an ideological continuum ranging from most liberal to most conservative. A mean score for a Congress of zero would indicate that no
ideological separation between the two parties existed; as the mean score approaches
one, the parties approach complete ideological divergence. Data and explanation of
this measure, which was developed by Keith T. Poole and Howard Rosenthal—may
be found at the VoteView web site at http://voteview.com/.

59. General Social Survey, National Opinion Research Center, University of Chicago,
Chicago, IL, www.norc.org/GSS+Website/.

60. Carl B. Albert, *Little Giant* (Norman: University of Oklahoma Press, 1990), 116;
Thomas O'Neill, Jr., *Man of the House* (New York: Random House, 1987), 272.

61. Cindy Simon Rosenthal, *When Women Lead* (New York: Oxford University Press,
1996); Patricia Lunneborg, *Women Changing Work* (Westport, Conn.: Greenwood
Press, 1990), 47; Marilyn Loden, *Feminine Leadership* (New York: Times Books,
1985), 120–31.

62. See for example, Judy B. Rosener, "Ways Women Lead," *Harvard Business Review*
68 (November–December 1990): 14–28; Mary M. Hale and Rita Mae Kelly, eds.,
Gender, Bureaucracy and Democracy (Westport, CT: Greenwood Press, 1989); David
C. McClelland, *Power: The Inner Experience* (New York: Irvington, 1979).

63. Carol Gilligan, *A Different Voice* (Cambridge, Mass.: Harvard University Press,
1993).

64. There is a robust literature on gender differences in the policy arena. Among the
key works are Debra L. Dodson and Susan J. Carroll, *Reshaping the Agenda: Women
in State Legislatures* (New Brunswick, N.J.: Rutgers University Center for American
Women and Politics, 1991). On advocating for policies that affect social well-being
and families, see Cindy Simon Rosenthal, ed., *Women Transforming Congress*
(Norman: University of Oklahoma Press, 2001), especially chapters by Christina
Wolbrecht, Michele Swers, and Noelle Norton. On speaking for underrepresented
groups, see Katherine Cramer Walsh, "Enlarging Representation," in Rosenthal,
Women Transforming Congress, 370–96; Debra Dodson, *The Impact of Women in
Congress* (New York: Oxford University Press, 2006). On introducing more femi-
nist and social welfare legislation, see Michelle Swers, *The Difference Women Make*
(Chicago: University of Chicago Press, 2002); Sue Thomas, *How Women Legislate*
(New York: Oxford University Press, 1994); Michelle A. Saint-Germain, "Does Their
Difference Make a Difference? The Impact of Women on Public Policy in the Arizona
Legislature," *Social Science Quarterly* 70, 4 (December 1989): 956–68. On investing
scarce legislative time in women's issues, see Karen L. Tamerius, "Sex, Gender, and
Leadership in the Representation of Women," in Georgia Duerst-Lahti and Rita Mae
Kelly, eds., *Gender Power, Leadership and Governance* (East Lansing: University of
Michigan Press, 1996), 93–114; Beth Reingold, "Concepts of Representation among
Female and Male State Legislators," *Legislative Studies Quarterly* 17, 4 (1992): 509–
37. On emphasizing constituency service, see Sue Thomas, "The Effects of Race and
Gender on Constituency Service," *Western Political Quarterly* 45 (March 1992):

169–80. On facilitating rather than dominating in committee communications, see Lyn Kathlene, "Power and Influence in State Legislative Policymaking: The Interaction of Gender and Position in Committee Hearing Debates," *American Political Science Review* 88, 3 (September 1994): 560–76.

65. James MacGregor Burns, *Leadership* (New York: Harper, 1982), 344.

66. Vera Katz, "The Leader and the Public," *Journal of State Government* 60, 5 (November–December 1987): 262–64.

67. Rosenthal, *When Women Lead.*

68. The epigraph from Rayburn is quoted by Joseph Alsop and Robert Kintner, "Never Leave Them Angry," *Saturday Evening Post*, January 18, 1941, 22.

69. The quotation from Anthony in the epigraph is from "Inspiring Quotes by Women," *Feminist.com*, www.feminist.com/resources/quotes/ (accessed January 22, 2009).

CHAPTER 2

1. The epigraph to this chapter is from Nancy Pelosi's statement upon her investiture as Speaker, reprinted in *Know Your Power: A Message to America's Daughters* (New York: Doubleday, 2008), 8.

2. In addition to the various articles we cite hereafter, our narrative draws on three recent books: Vincent Bzdek, *Woman of the House* (New York: Palgrave McMillan, 2008); Pelosi, *Know Your Power: A Message to America's Daughters* (New York: Random House, 2008); Marc Sandalow, *Madam Speaker* (New York: Modern Times, 2008).

3. For example: "Multinational corporations do control. They control the politicians. They control the media. They control the pattern of consumption, entertainment, thinking. They're destroying the planet and laying the foundation for violent outbursts and racial division." BrainyQuote.com www.brainyquote.com/quotes/ quotes/j/jerrybrown187894.html (accessed January 21, 2009).

4. Sandalow, *Madam Speaker*, 167.

5. This characterization of Speaker O'Neill was offered by first-term New York Republican John LeBoutillier in 1981. O'Neill took a personal interest in LeBoutillier's career, which ended with his defeat in 1982. Donald T. Critchlow, "When Republicans Became Revolutionaries," in Julian E. Zelizer, ed., *The American Congress: The Building of Democracy* (New York: Houghton Mifflin, 2004), 715.

6. Sandalow, *Madam Speaker*, 76–81, provides a brief overview. See also Phil Gailey, "Political Memo: Strange Encounters of the Post-election Kind," *New York Times*, December 13, 1984; United Press International, "No Governors' Endorsement," *New York Times*, December 16, 1984. In 2009 Paul Kirk was named by Massachusetts Governor Deval Patrick to replace Kirk's old boss, the late Senator Edward Kennedy.

7. Howell Raines, "Vote Aids Kennedy Ally's Effort to Head Democratic Committee," *New York Times*, February 1, 1985.

8. Howell Raines, "Unionists Accused of Sexism in Race to Lead Democrats," *New York Times*, January 29, 1985; Katherine Roberts, Michael Wright, and Caroline Rand Herron, "The Democrats Settle on a New Chairman," *New York Times*, February 3, 1985. According to Sandalow's account (*Madam Speaker*, 80), neither Mannatt nor Kirk thought gender was a decisive factor in the election.

9. Robert Lindsey, "Contest for House Growing Complex," *New York Times*, February 12, 1987. See also John Jacobs, *Rage for Justice* (Berkeley: University of California Press, 1995).

10. "San Francisco Mayor Shuns Race for House," *New York Times*, February 13, 1987.

11. Robert Lindsey, "Homosexuals' Political Power Tested in West," *New York Times*, April 5, 1987.

12. We explore this idea further in chapter 6.

13. Robert Lindsey, "House Race in West Goes to Runoff," *New York Times*, April 9, 1987; Associated Press, "Democrat Elected in San Francisco," *New York Times*, June 3, 1987.

14. Carl Albert had been an oil attorney. Tip O'Neill was an insurance agent and the first Democratic speaker of the Massachusetts General Court. Jim Wright had served as mayor of Weatherford, Texas, and one term in the Texas state legislature. Tom Foley was an attorney in private practice. Among Republicans, Gingrich had been a college professor, and Hastert a high school civics teacher and wrestling coach before serving in the Illinois state senate.

15. See Bzdek, *Woman of the House*; Pelosi, *Know Your Power*; Sandalow, *Madam Speaker*. See also John Jacobs, "Not Just a Party Girl," *San Francisco Chronicle*, July 12, 1992.

16. Carolyn Lochhead, "House OK's $2.5 Billion to Fight Aids," *San Francisco Chronicle*, October 8, 1993; Sheryl Gay Stolberg, "Clinton Decides Not to Fund Needle Program," *New York Times*, April 21, 1998; Louis Freedberg, "Pelosi Amendment Restores AIDS Funds," *San Francisco Chronicle*, March 3, 1995.

17. Sandalow, *Madam Speaker*, 133–38, describes Pelosi's work on the Presidio legislation. Speaker Pelosi herself offers the Presidio bill as an example of innovative leadership, a topic to which we return in chapter 7. See Pelosi, *Know Your Power*, 109–11. See also Carolyn Lochhead, "Presidio Bill Approved at Last Minute, *San Francisco Chronicle*, October 4, 1996.

18. Sandalow, *Madam Speaker*, 139–55.

19. Ibid., 153. Pelosi has found no inconsistency in decrying the influence of money in politics while building her career in substantial part on her fund-raising ability. For an account of business influence on this issue, see Keith Bradsher, "Pressure From Companies," *New York Times*, May 13, 1993.

20. See John Kruger and Mark Lewis, "Bill's Long March: When Money Talked, Clinton Retreated to George Bush's Policy," *Washington Post*, November 7, 1993; Kenneth J. Cooper, "House Backs HIV Immigration Ban," *Washington Post*, March 12, 1993; Barbara Crossette, "U.N. Talks on Women under Fire," *New York Times*, March 17, 1995; Nancy Pelosi, "On to Beijing," *Washington Post*, August 2, 1995; "Hillary Clinton and China Policy," editorial, *San Francisco Chronicle*, August 14, 1995.

21. Phillip Matier and Andrew Ross, "Pelosi's Candid Take on the Real Bill Clinton," *San Francisco Chronicle*, December 21, 1998.

22. Mark Sandalow, "Discarding Dogma, Leftist Democrats Swing to Clinton," *San Francisco Chronicle*, August 26, 1996.

23. Quotations in this paragraph are from Marc Sandalow, "Nancy Pelosi: Holding Out for Dreams," *San Francisco Chronicle*, June 9, 1996.

24. Steven Skowronek, *Politics Presidents Make* (Cambridge, Mass.: Harvard University Press, 1997).

25. Several members have claimed responsibility for initiating these dinners, including Russo, Downey, and Congressman Pete Stark of California.

26. Judy Sarasohn, "Pelosi's Dinner Club," *Washington Post*, November 14, 2002, A31.

27. Sandalow, *Madam Speaker*, 128.

28. *New York Times* columnist A. M. Rosenthal, especially enamored of Pelosi's vigorous advocacy of human rights in China, featured her in several columns. This further illustrates the extent to which Pelosi was building a national reputation as well as influence in the House. See for example: A. M. Rosenthal, "Here We Go Again," *New York Times*, April 9, 1993; A. M. Rosenthal, "Guide for Cleansers," *New York Times*, April 27, 1993; A. M. Rosenthal, "Grovel and Pander," *New York Times*, November 9, 1993.

29. While the circumstances at the Bank, Post Office, and Restaurant differed in point of detail, all three scandals involved members taking advantage of their status to obtain economic advantage.

30. For background on the Gingrich ethics probe see www.washingtonpost.com/wp-srv/politics/govt/leadership/ethics.htm.

31. Marc Sandalow, "Opposition to Gingrich Takes Shape," *San Francisco Chronicle*, January 7, 1997; Adam Clymer, "Parties Exchange Sharp Volleys on Handling of Gingrich Matter," *New York Times*, January 11, 1997; Adam Clymer, "The Gingrich Case: The Overview," *New York Times*, January 18, 1997; Marc Sandalow, "Pelosi Says GOP 'Sandbagged' Gingrich Ethics Investigation," *San Francisco Chronicle*, January 23, 1997. The Internal Revenue Service later ruled in Gingrich's favor, arguing that the content of the course and a related book were educational in character. See "IRS Clears Foundation that Aided Gingrich Course," *Washington Post*, February 4, 1999, p. A05.

32. Carl Albert was appointed whip in his fourth term and never authored a major bill. Tip O'Neill served on the Rules Committee, an exclusive appointment at the time, and never authored a major bill. Jim Wright rose to become influential on the Public Works Committee. Among these Democratic speakers, Tom Foley had the most impressive prior experience. A member of the Phil Burton circle, Foley benefited from the revolt against the chairs in 1974 to become chairman of the Agricultural Committee in 1974, his fifth term. He was elected chair of the Democratic Caucus in 1979. Two years later, he was appointed Democratic whip. Gingrich, the first Republican Speaker since 1954, had been a vocal minority backbencher with no

substantial bill to his credit. Hastert was a quiet minority backbencher and then an appointed chief deputy whip under Tom DeLay. Neither Gingrich nor Hastert had authored major legislation.

33. Pelosi, *Know Your Power*, 100.

34. Sandalow, *Madam Speaker*, 180, places this dinner in the summer of 1998. Juliet Eilperin, "The Making of Madam Whip," *Washington Post*, January 6, 2002, locates the series of dinners in July and August 1999. In another article, however, Eilperin describes Pelosi's "three year quest" to become whip: Juliet Eilperin, "Pelosi Finds Her Place in the House: Selection Ends Three-Year Quest," *Washington Post*, November 13, 2001. Bzdek, *Woman of the House*, 129, places the first dinner on July 13, 1999, but indicates (130) that the survey of members occurred in 1998. Our interviews indicate that initial discussion of the whip race began in the summer of 1998.

35. Jackie Koszczuk, "When Nancy Met Steny," *CQ Weekly*, November 20, 2006, 3095.

36. Sandalow, *Madam Speaker*, 180. See also Marc Sandalow, "Rep. Pelosi Aims to Become Top Woman in the House," *San Francisco Chronicle*, October 13, 1999.

37. Michael Barone, ed., *The Almanac of American Politics, 2002* (Washington, D.C.: National Journal, 2003), www.nationaljournal.com/pubs/almanac/2002/states/mo/mo03.htm (accessed January 23, 2009).

38. Eric Pianin, "House Democrats Say Defeat Has Chastened Them," *Washington Post*, December 27, 1999.

39. Ibid. It was, of course, Pelosi who had made the fight over China's trade status her signature issue, and it was Pelosi who sought to win her way into the House leadership in part on an argument that a woman should have a place in the top leadership.

40. Juliet Eilperin, "House Whip Race Seen as Indicator of Democrats' Future," *Washington Post*, October 8, 2001.

41. Eric Schmitt, "In Congress, Conflict of Comity and Gridlock," *New York Times*, February 18, 2000.

42. Carolyne Zinkle, "GOP Holds Lead in House Despite Losses in California," *San Francisco Chronicle*, November 9, 2000.

43. Sandalow, *Madam Speaker*, 205. See also: Brian Faler, "Pelosi Irks House Veteran by Donating to His Opponent," *Washington Post*, February 10, 2002.

44. Sandalow, *Madam Speaker*, 171–202. See also Adam Clymer, "Women in the News: A New Vote Counter—Nancy Patricia Pelosi," *New York Times*, October 11, 2001; Eilperin, "Pelosi Finds Her Place."

45. "Juliet Eilperin, "Democrats Pick Pelosi as House Whip." *Washington Post*, October 11, 2001.

46. Marc Sandalow, "Pelosi Breaks House Glass Ceiling," *San Francisco Chronicle*, October 11, 2001.

47. Eilperin, "Democrats Pick Pelosi."

48. Eilperin, "Pelosi Finds Her Place."

49. Carla Marinucci, "Fund Raising Crucial to Pelosi Win," *San Francisco Chronicle*, October 11, 2001.

50. There were two prior instances in which backbench members had won leadership elections due in substantial part to their fund-raising efforts: Tony Coehlo, elected Democratic Whip in 1986, and Tom DeLay, elected Republican whip in 1994. Interestingly, Gingrich won his whip race against Ed Madigan in 1989 not by virtue of his fund-raising prowess but by making an ideological and strategic appeal.

51. Gephardt did indeed retire from the House in 2003 to seek the 2004 Democratic presidential nomination. Interestingly, Nancy Pelosi was among a handful of House Democrats who endorsed him, in contrast to the dozens who had endorsed his 1988 bid. This demonstrated both Pelosi's pragmatism and the extent to which Gephardt had lost support in the Democratic Caucus.

52. Edward Epstein, "Pelosi Breaks with Gephardt on Authorizing War," *San Francisco Chronicle*, October 4, 2002; Allison Mitchell and Carl Hulse, "Threats and Responses: The Vote; Congress Authorizes Bush to Use Force against Iraq," *New York Times*, October 11, 2002.

53. David von Drehle and Hannah Rosin, "The Two Nancy Pelosis," *Washington Post*, November 14, 2002.

54. Marc Sandalow, "Pelosi's House Ascending: National Tour Boosts Her Leadership Role," *San Francisco Chronicle*, November 3, 2002.

55. "The Courage to Be Different," editorial, *San Francisco Chronicle*, November 8, 2002.

56. Harold Ford, "Why I Should Be Minority Leader," *Washington Post*, November 13, 2002. Some informants suggest that Ford's real objective was to present a more moderate image in anticipation of a Senate run in Tennessee. Pelosi was afterward dismissive of him.

57. Von Drehle and Rosin, "Two Nancy Pelosis." See also Marc Sandalow, "Pelosi Mocked as S.F.'s 'Latte Liberal,' " *San Francisco Chronicle*, November 13, 2002; Edward Epstein, "Conservatives Call S.F. Democrat's Rise Money in the Bank," *San Francisco Chronicle*, November 10, 2002.

58. Jim VandeHei, "Democrats on Hill Split on Agenda," *Washington Post*, March 4, 2003.

59. David Firestone, "Woman in the News: Getting Close to the Top and Smiling All the Way," *New York Times*, November 10, 2002.

60. Research indicates that there has been a systematic tendency by successful Democratic leadership aspirants to engage in polarizing rhetoric with respect to the opposition. Republican aspirants, by contrast, focus on demonstrating to the rank and file their consistent location at the ideological core of the party. Pelosi seems to us to have straddled both strategies. See Brian D. Posler and Carl M. Rhodes, "Preleadership Signaling in the U.S. House," *Legislative Studies Quarterly* 22, 3 (August 1997): 351–68.

61. Von Drehle and Rosin, "Two Nancy Pelosis."

62. "Pulling a Party Together," Editorial, *New York Times*, November 9, 2002.

63. "Courage to Be Different."

64. Zachary Coile, " 'I Can Take the Hit,' Pelosi Tells Critics Skewering Her," *San Francisco Chronicle*, November 18, 2002.

65. John Wildermuth and Carla Marinucci, "California Democrats Leaning Left," *Washington Post*, March 17, 2003.

66. "Have Democrats Found Their Voice?" editorial, *San Francisco Chronicle*, January 7, 2003.

67. David Firestone, "Bush Tax Plan Gives Pelosi an Opening," *New York Times*, January 26, 2003.

68. David Firestone, "Democrats Pulling Together United Front against G.O.P.," *New York Times*, March 3, 2003.

69. VandeHei, "Democrats on Hill Split on Agenda."

70. Adam Nagourney, "Threats and Responses: Democrats; Divided Democrats Concerned about 2004," *New York Times*, March 19, 2003.

71. Sheryl Gay Stolberg, "A Nation at War: The House Minority Leader; With Democrats Divided on War, Pelosi Faces Leadership Test," *New York Times*, April 1, 2003.

72. Nagourney, "Threats and Responses."

73. Dan Balz, "War Highlights Rift among Democrats," *Washington Post*, April 6, 2003.

74. William Safire, "On Language: Netroots," *The New York Times*, November 19, 2006. http://www.nytimes.com/2006/11/19/magazine/19wwln_safire.html?ex=132159 2400&en=a21ab052f4bda85e&ei=5090&partner=rssuserland&emc=rss (accessed September 17, 2009), and David Von Drehle, "Among Democrats, The Energy Seems to Be on the Left," *Washington Post*, July 10, 2003.

75. Robert Pear and Robin Toner, "Counting Votes and Attacks in the Final Push for Medicare Bill," *New York Times*, November 20, 2003.

76. House rules specify that the period for recording electronic votes on final passage is 15 minutes. Speaker Hastert held this vote open for three hours. When the Democrats took control in the 110th Congress, they emphasized that they would adhere to the 15-minute rule, which for the most part they did. In convening the 111th Congress, they recognized that on occasion it might be necessary to hold votes open for a longer period of time. Nonetheless, the Democrats did not hold votes open indefinitely.

77. David Firestone, "Congressional Memo: 11th-hour Bills Irk Lawmakers Left in Dark," *New York Times*, November 22, 2003, 1. Tom DeLay was later reprimanded by the House Ethics Committee after he threatened to withhold support from a Republican member's son who was seeking to succeed his father in office.

78. As Pelosi became more secure in her power, she demonstrated a willingness to at least threaten sanctions. In 2005, she threatened the committee assignments of two ranking members, Edolphus Towns of New York and Collin Peterson of Minnesota, for perceived lack of support of the leadership. In 2007 she threatened the committee assignments of members who had supported Steny Hoyer in his race against John Murtha. See Erin Billings, "Pelosi Threatens Towns' Slot," *Roll Call*, December 14, 2005.

79. Juliet Eilperin, "Democrats Laud Pelosi's Style; House Minority Leader Commended for Focus on Party Unity," *Washington Post*, November 30, 2003; Edward Epstein, "Pelosi Makes Democrats Toe the Line," *San Francisco Chronicle*, November 30, 2003. For Pelosi's view of loyalty, see Stolberg, "Nation at War."

80. Edward Epstein, "Democrats Attack Bush on All Fronts," *San Francisco Chronicle*, January 21, 2004.

81. Marc Sandalow, "Pelosi Won't Back Off Bush Condemnation," *San Francisco Chronicle*, May 21, 2004.

82. Charles Babington, "All Quiet on the House Side: Democrats Say GOP Is Evading Debate," *Washington Post*, May 11, 2004.

83. Harold Myerson, "Sounds of Democrats Not Fighting," *Washington Post*, June 2, 2004. On Democratic Party unity, see Mark Simon, "Local Posse Backs Pelosi in Quest for a Democratic House," *San Francisco Chronicle*, January 25, 2004.

84. Edward Epstein, "Pelosi Prediction: 'I Am Going to Be Speaker' in '05," *San Francisco Chronicle*, July 16, 2004.

85. Charles Babington, "Democrats Reassess Prospects to Win House," *Washington Post*, September 19, 2004.

86. Edward Epstein, "Pelosi, Colleagues, Challenge Bush on War," *San Francisco Chronicle*, September 18, 2004.

87. Charles Babington, "Democrats Vow to Hold Bush Accountable," *Washington Post*, November 10, 2004.

88. The Speaker's characterization of Emanuel as "reptilian" is taken from a confidential interview. Its substantive reference is to Emanuel's willingness to assess prospects cold-bloodedly, rejecting some potential candidates and denying funding to nominees he thought could not win.

89. Adam Nagourney and Anne E. Kornblut, "Dean Emerging as Likely Chief for Democrats," *New York Times*, February 2, 2005. Although Pelosi had opposed Frost for DNC chair, she would later demonstrate her capacity to care and heal. When Frost's wife passed away in September 2006, Pelosi took a half day away from the most important campaign of her career to attend the memorial service.

90. Sheryl Gay Stolberg, "For Democrats, Social Security Becomes a Defining Test," *New York Times*, January 30, 2005.

91. Sheryl Gay Stolberg and Robin Toner, "Republicans Are Chastened about Social Security Plan," *New York Times*, February 27, 2005.

92. James Traub, "Party Like It's 1994," *New York Times*, March 12, 2006. David Espo, "Pelosi Says She Would Drain GOP 'Swamp,'" *Washington Post*, October 6, 2006. Rick Klein, "Democrats Set an Agenda They Can Agree On," *Boston Globe*, August 4, 2006.

93. Adam Nagourney and Sheryl Gay Stolberg, "Some Democrats Are Sensing Missed Opportunities," *New York Times*, February 8, 2006.

94. Marc Sandalow, "Election Aftermath: How Pelosi Propelled Democrats to Power," *San Francisco Chronicle*, November 10, 2006.

95. For reference to the "homosexual" ad, see Adam Nossiter, "G.O.P. Collapse in Indiana Emblematic of Larger Loss," *New York Times*, November 12, 2006. See also: Kate Zernicke, "Seats in Danger, Democrats Proclaim Their Conservatism," *New York Times*, October 24, 2006; Sheila Dewan and Anne E. Kornblut, "In Key House Races, Democrats Run to the Right," *New York Times*, October 30, 2006; Jennifer Steinhaur, "With the House in the Balance, Pelosi Serves as Focal Point for Both Parties," *New York Times*, October 30, 2006; "G.O.P. Ads Star Democratic House Leader," *New York Times*, November 2, 2006; Adam Nossiter, "G.O.P. Collapse in Indiana Emblematic of Larger Loss," *New York Times*, November 12, 2006.

Chapter 3

1. Jennifer Yachnin, "Pelosi, Emanuel Cut Deal," *Roll Call*, November 13, 2006.
2. Dick Gephardt had taken a similar step toward diversity in appointing Rosa DeLauro assistant leader after she lost her battle against Martin Frost for conference chair in 2000.
3. The best account of the Wright-Burton fight is in John Jacobs, *Rage for Justice* (Berkeley: University of California Press, 1995), chap. 14.
4. Alan K. Ota, "Experience Counts in the House," *CQ Weekly*, November 13–17, 2006, 3128–3121.
5. Jonathan Weisman and Lyndsey Layton, "Murtha Stumbles on Iraq War Funding Curbs," *Washington Post*, February 25, 2007.
6. Jonathan Weisman, "In Backing Murtha, Pelosi Draws Fire," *Washington Post*, November 14, 2006. In fact, this was not the first time Pelosi had injected herself into a subordinate leadership contest. In 2002, Congresswoman Jan Schakowsky sought the position of vice chair of the Democratic Caucus. This position has often been held by a woman member, and it was natural for Pelosi to support Schakowsky, a strong supporter of hers. Schakowsky was opposed by Congressman Joe Crowley of New York, a more moderate member and a Hoyer supporter. When it appeared that Crowley had the votes to win, Pelosi lured John Larson of Connecticut into the race, and Schakowsky threw her support to him. Larson, a Pelosi supporter, continued as vice chair in the 110th Congress. Pelosi's commitment to Larson was strong. Chaka Fattah of Pennsylvania, though in the minority, was next in line by seniority to become ranking member of the House Administration Committee. Pelosi informed him that he would have to relinquish his coveted position on the Appropriations Committee in order to claim Administration. She then sought to appoint Larson to the Administration slot even though Larson was also a member of Ways and Means, the other most coveted committee. When Pelosi was challenged over this obvious preferment, she relented and gave Fattah the assignment. See Jill Barshay, "Woman of the House Brings a Sense of Power," *CQ Weekly*, November 13, 2006, 2970.
7. Ota, "Experience Counts in the House."

8. Ibid.

9. The most persuasive defense of Pelosi's advocacy on behalf of Murtha argues that even in defeat, she sent a strong message about the value she places on loyalty. In this view, her aim was didactic. It is also suggested that her late entry into the fracas was timed to ensure that it would not affect the outcome. Some of our informants believed that the decision to support Murtha was really driven by Pelosi lieutenants such as Congressman George Miller of California. Whatever weight might be attached to these interpretations, in the end, one conclusion is evident, as one participant put it to us: "Well, we lost." For the most comprehensive account of this episode see Matthew N. Green, "The 2006 Race for Democratic Majority Leader: Money, Policy, and Personal Loyalty," *PS* 41, 1 (January 2008): 63–68.

10. The fratricide in the Republican Conference during these 12 years makes the conflicts among the Democrats look like a tea party. DeLay managed Ed Madigan's unsuccessful whip campaign against Gingrich and then defeated Gingrich ally Bob Walker for whip in 1995. By the summer of 1997, DeLay and Republican majority leader Dick Armey were complicit in a coup to remove Gingrich from power. A year later, Appropriations Committee chair Bob Livingston challenged Gingrich for speaker, forcing Gingrich's resignation from the House. After Livingston withdrew his bid, DeLay engineered the election of his chief deputy whip, Hastert, election as Speaker. Then DeLay backed J. C. Watts in his successful effort to oust Republican Conference chair John Boehner. DeLay then immediately turned against Watts, seeking to control the Republican communications operation centered in the Conference. Hastert spent much of his time as Speaker defending himself against DeLay's assertion that Hastert was merely a "chairman of the board" while DeLay was the "chief executive officer." See Paul Kane and John Bresnahan, "New Leaders' Rivalries Carry Eerie Parallels to 1994," *Roll Call*, November 20, 2006.

11. In 1903, Republican speaker Cannon permitted Democratic leader John Sharp Williams of Mississippi to make the Democratic committee assignments. Prior to that time, the Speaker had made all committee assignments. In 1919, Republican James Mann of Illinois successfully moved to create a new Republican Committee on Committees on which each state would have one member and each member could cast a number of votes equal to that state's Republican House delegation. See Ronald M. Peters, Jr., *The American Speakership: The Office in Historical Perspective,* 2nd ed. (Baltimore: Johns Hopkins University Press, 1997), 98–103. This system remained in place until the Republicans came into power in 1995. Gingrich made himself a member of the Committee on Committees and gave himself an extra number of votes (see 294). Gingrich thus had controlling influence over committee assignments, but he did not make all nominations himself. A description of the Republican and Democratic committee assignment processes may be found at the Rules Committee website, www.rules.house.gov/lpp/Organization.pdf.

12. Johanna Neuman and Michael Finnegan, "Pelosi-Harman Friction Strains Democrats' Unity," *Los Angeles Times*, November 21, 2006.

13. In April 2009, it was revealed that by the time Pelosi was called on to select the member to chair the Intelligence Committee in 2006, she had been made aware that the FBI had wiretapped Harman's telephone in connection with a counterespionage investigation into the activities of two pro-Israeli lobbyists. It was alleged that Harman "had been overheard on a government wiretap agreeing to seek lenient treatment from the Bush administration for the two lobbyists in exchange for her support for her bid to be chairman of the House Intelligence Committee." Neil A. Lewis and Eric Lichtblau, "Lawmaker Denies Effort for Lobbyists," *New York Times*, April 22, 2009. While Pelosi denied that her knowledge of the investigation had influenced her decision not to appoint Harman, it seems likely that any attempt by the Israel lobby to pressure the Speaker would have only reinforced her predisposition to deny the chair position to Harman. It was also alleged that Attorney General Alberto Gonzales had intervened with the FBI on Harman's behalf because she had been "a valuable administration ally in urging the *New York Times* not to publish an article about the National Security Agency's program of wiretapping without warrants." Mark Mazzetti and Neil A. Lewis, "Gonzales Said to Have Intervened on Wiretap," *New York Times*, April 24, 2009. If in fact Harman had undertaken to squash the *Times* story, it would surely have been sufficient motive for Pelosi to have denied her the Intelligence Committee position. Harman denied all of the allegations. See Edward Epstein, "Pelosi Said She Knew Harman Was Wiretapped," http://breakingjist.com/ pelosi-said-she-knew-harman-was-wiretapped-cqpoliticscom/ *CQ Politics*, April 22, 2009; Neil A. Lewis and Eric Lichtblau, "Lawmaker Denies Effort for Lobbyists," *New York Times*, April 22, 2009; Tory Newmyer, "Harman Goes on the Attack," *Roll Call*, April 22, 2009; Mike Soraghan and Susan Crabtree, "Harman Fires Back on Audiotape," *Hill*, April 21, 2009.

14. Josephine Hearn, "Pelosi Riles Old Guard Chairmen," *Politico*, January 22, 2007, http:// dyn.politico.com/printstory.cfm?uuid=4CC295F1–3048–5C12–000803C7AB5EA6FD. Term limits for chairs were dropped for the 111th Congress. See below chapter 5, "The Committees," p. 160. We will have more to say about how her system of committee appointments dovetailed with fund-raising strategies in chapter 4's discussion of internal fundraising.

15. Rebecca Kimitch, "Democrats Opt to Spread the Power," *CQ Weekly*, April 16, 2007, 1080–83.

16. Ibid., 1081.

17. Michael Titelbaum, "Matsui Edges Out Christensen for Energy and Commerce Seat," *CQ Weekly*, June 9, 2008, 1553.

18. Pelosi decided to renew the charter of the select committee for the 111th Congress, indicating that she still saw the need for it even though Henry Waxman deposed John Dingell as chair of Energy and Commerce.

19. "2007 Vote Ratings," *National Journal*, www.nationaljournal.com/voteratings/house/ lib.htm (accessed January 23, 2009). For another measure of partisan polarization, see table 1.1.

20. *National Journal*, February 28, 2009, 31.

21. Shawn Zeller, "Parties Dig in Deep on a Fractured Hill," *CQ Weekly*, December 15, 2008, 3338.

22. It is interesting to compare the Blue Dogs, New Dems, and Progressives in this respect. At the beginning of the 110th Congress, there were 40 New Dems and 42 Blue Dogs (with 13 members overlapping) and 71 Progressives. The three most desirable and powerful House committees are Ways and Means, Appropriations, and Energy and Commerce. Among the 40 New Dem members, only one was appointed to one of these three committees. Among the 42 Blue Dogs, 14 (33%) served on these committees, including several who served as chairs or subcommittee chairs. The rural character of the Blue Dogs is confirmed by the fact that 20 of the 25 House Democrats on the Agriculture Committee were Blue Dogs. Among the Progressives, 24 of 71 (34%) served on one of the three committees.

23. The House can, of course, waive PAYGO requirements in adopting the special rule governing particular legislation, as it did in 2008 in dealing with the Alternative Minimum Tax and the economic stimulus package. Because of this, Blue Dogs have pushed for a statutory PAYGO requirement that would supersede the House rules. Speaker Pelosi and President Obama expressed support for this concept in 2009, but liberal Democrats were skeptical. See Mike Soraghan, "Left Distrusts Centrist Push on Pay-go Rule," *Hill*, June 22, 2009.

24. Richard E. Cohen, "Class Struggles," *National Journal*, September 22, 2007, 28–32.

25. On the revolt of the Hispanic Caucus, see Jennifer Yachnin, "CHC Revolts over Leadership Snubs," *Roll Call*, November 12, 2007.

26. Ryan Grim, "Pelosi Turns Democratic Caucus into 'Meet Market,' " *Politico*, October 10, 2007, http://www.politico.com/news/stories/1007/6274.html.

27. Jonathan Weisman, "Edging Away from Inner Circle, Pelosi Asserts Authority," *Washington Post*, July 9, 2007.

28. Barbara Sinclair, *Legislators, Leaders, and Lawmaking* (Baltimore: Johns Hopkins University Press, 1998).

29. Fyea Fiore, "Pelosi: Speaker, Listener, Conciliator, and Battler," *Los Angeles Times*, April 14, 2007.

30. See Jonathan Allen, "San Francisco Liberal Charts a Moderate Course," *CQ Today*, March 6, 2007; Richard Scammon, "Nancy Pelosi's Pragmatism Draws Heat," *Kiplinger Business Research Center*, June 15, 2007.

31. Jonathan E. Kaplan, "Rep. Pelosi Reminds the Left That She Is on Its Side," *Hill*, June 28, 2007.

32. Wes Allison, "Pelosi Keeps Democrats in Tow," *St. Petersburg Times*, June 2, 2007.

33. The Republicans typically used restrictive rules and often held votes open until the leadership could twist enough arms to reach a majority, most notably on final passage of the Medicare Part D prescription drug bill, on which the vote was held open for over three hours. When the House and Senate have passed different versions of a bill, each chamber appoints a number of conferees to a conference (sometimes

called a conference committee) to work out common language. As we discuss in "House-Senate Conferences" later in this chapter, the Republicans had often conducted negotiations with Senate Republicans, excluding Democratic conferees from the process. On Pelosi's Minority Bill of Rights see Charles Babington, "Pelosi Seeks House Minority 'Bill of Rights,'" *Washington Post*, June 24, 2004.

34. We discuss the Six for '06 legislation in more detail later.

35. The Speaker does not always travel on government airplanes. She also travels on private aircraft and commercially within the House rules.

36. U.S. House of Representatives, Committee on Rules, Rules Committee website, www.rules.house.gov/archives/recommit_mot.htm (accessed April 6, 2009).

37. As we discuss further in chapter 5, in organizing the 111th Congress the Democrats removed the option of "promptly" MTRs.

38. Jared Allen, "Armed with More Dems, Pelosi Poised to Get Tougher," *Hill*, November 5, 2008.

39. We return to this conception of bipartisanship in "Partisanship, Bipartisanship, and Postpartisanship" in chapter 7.

40. This discussion draws on Bart Jansen, "Capitol Hill's Conferences: Can They Be Revived?" *CQ Weekly*, January 5, 2009, 18–19.

41. The fast-track authority was authorized in the Fair Trade Act of 1974. The president has to formally submit proposed trade agreements for ratification, and then the Congress has to act within 60 days. Pelosi had the House vote to suspend the timetable, thus giving her control over CFA. For a background study see Todd Tucker and Lori Wallach, "The Rise and Fall of Fast Track Authority," *Public Citizen Global Trade Watch*, 2008, Public Citizen Web Site, www.citizen.org/documents/riseandfall.pdf (accessed December 3, 2008).

42. Carl Hulse, "Democrats Stall Trade Pact with Colombia," *New York Times*, April 10, 2008; Steven T. Dennis, "Pelosi Pockets Colombia Chip," *Roll Call*, April 14, 2008; Associated Press, "Bush Asks Congress to Reconsider Colombia," *Politico*, April 20, 2008, http://www.politico.com/news/stories/0408/9728.html.

43. This anecdote was reported to us by a person attending the meeting.

44. For a related discussion of Pelosi's approach to policy-making see Barbara Sinclair, "Orchestrators of Unorthodox Policy-making: Pelosi and McConnell in the 110th Congress," *Forum* 6, 3 (2008), www.bepress.com/forum/vol6/iss3/art5/ (accessed January 23, 2008).

45. Alan K. Ota, "Pelosi's Challenge: Enforce Party Discipline While Seeking Accord with GOP in House," *CQ Today*, May 9, 2006. See also David Nather et al., "Manifesto for the First 100 Hours," *CQ Weekly*, November 20, 2006, 3104–16; "Manifesto for the 'First 100 Hours,'" CQ Weekly—In Focus, *CQ Weekly*, November 20, 2006, 3104.

46. Thomas Edsall, "Happy Hours," *New York Times*, January 18, 2007. See also Fox News, "Democrats' 'First 100 Hours' Winds Down with Plenty of Time to Spare," January 19, 2007.

47. For an example of this trade-off, see Peters, *American Speakership*, 162–72.

48. The logic of this exclusion is that fruit and vegetables are perishables, not "durable" commodities.

49. David Rogers, "Pelosi Cultivates Her Own Style," *Wall Street Journal*, July 24, 2007.

50. The text of H.Res. 574 is available at the Rules Committee website, www.rules.house .gov/.

51. U.S. House of Representatives Roll Call Votes 110th Congress—1st Session (2007), http://clerk.house.gov/evs/2007/ROLL_700.asp. House passage of the farm bill was only the first step in a long saga. The bill was held up in the Senate until the end of 2007. In the meantime, authorization for the farm programs expired, and Congress was forced to pass short-term extensions. In 2008, the House and Senate finally sent a bill to President Bush, who vetoed it. Congress overrode that veto, but a technical error in the Clerk of the House of Representatives office led to the omission of an entire section of the bill he vetoed. Congress was forced to fix the bill and pass a second override vote, much to Pelosi's annoyance. See *Farm Policy Facts.Org*, "Déjà vu All Over Again," www.farmpolicyfacts.org/ne_Deja_Vu_All_Over_Again.cfm (accessed January 23, 2009); "Congress Overrides Farm Bill Again," *MSNBC.Com*, www.msnbc.msn.com/id/25244839/ (accessed January 23, 2009). During floor consideration, the farm bill produced another flap, when the chair gaveled closed a vote on a Republican motion to recommit while members were still in the process of changing their votes. Republicans claimed that this prevented the motion from carrying. The Speaker agreed to appoint a panel to examine the incident, but nothing came of it. See Jennifer Yachnin and Steven T. Dennis, "Panel to Probe Floor Uproar," *Roll Call*, August 6, 2007.

52. See Carol Davenport, "Dingell Stands Down on Energy Bill," *CQ Today*, June 18, 2007; Carol Davenport, "Pelosi, Dingell May Announce Deal on Energy Bill," *CQ Green Sheets*, June 18, 2007. Carol Davenport, "Battle of House Titans Reignited," *CQ Weekly*, June 18, 2007, 1828.

53. Jennifer Yachnin, "House Approves Energy Bill, Continues Long March to Adjournment," *Roll Call*, August 4, 2007.

54. Jennifer Yachnin, "It's 'Ping-pong' for Energy Bill," *Roll Call*, October 11, 2007.

55. For a summary of congressional action on P.L. 110–140 (H.R. 6) see Fred Sissine, "Energy Independence and Security Act of 2007," in *CRS Report for Congress*, Congressional Research Service, December 21, 2007. See also Fred Sissine, Lynn J. Cunningham, and Mark Gurevitz, "Energy Efficiency and Renewable Energy Legislation in the 110th Congress (updated May 15, 2008)," in *CRS Report For Congress*, http://www.fas.org/sgp/crs/misc/RL33831.pdf, Congressional Research Service, May 15, 2008.

56. For background on this discussion see Rebecca Adams, "The Big Three on the Defensive," *CQ Weekly*, June 18, 2007, 1824–31; Jeff Tollefson, "Senate Passes Compromise Bill," *CQ Weekly*, June 25, 2007, 1920–24; Rebecca Kimitch and Jeff Tollefson, "Wrangling over Energy Package Continues at House Markup," *CQ Weekly*, July 9, 2007, 2043; Richard Rubin and Jeff Tollefson, "Energy Package Generates

Conflict," *CQ Weekly,* August 13, 2007, 2466–67; Dina Cappiello, "Deal Near on Stiffer Mileage Standards," *CQ Weekly,* December 3, 2007, 3603; Dina Cappiello, "House Bill Is a Senate Challenge," *CQ Weekly,* December 10, 2007, 3654–55; Dina Cappiello, "Slimmer Energy Bill Nears Finish Line," *CQ Weekly,* December 17, 2007, 3722–23.

57. A CNN/Opinion Research Corporation poll issued November 12, 2006, showed public support for the war at 33%. Between November 2006 and August 2008, support for the war in the CNN poll fluctuated between a high of 35% in August 2008 and a low of 30%. Thus, unpopularity of the Iraq War was among the most consistent features of the political landscape of the 110th Congress.

58. The Republicans wanted to offer two amendments, one to implement the recommendations of the Iraq Study Group, the other to ensure continued funding for the U.S. military. Initially, Steny Hoyer and Rahm Emanuel indicated that the Republicans would be offered a substitute amendment. The leadership then shifted its position to impose a closed rule. See Jennifer Yachnin and Susan Davis, "GOP Boxed Out on Iraq," *Roll Call,* February 13, 2007.

59. For H.Con.Res. 63, go to http://thomas.loc.gov/. For the Pelosi and Boehner quotations, see Jonathan Weisman, "House Takes Up Resolution on Iraq," *Washington Post,* February 13, 2007.

60. Jonathan Weisman and Lyndsey Layton, "Murtha Stumbles on Iraq Funding Curbs," *Washington Post,* February 25, 2007. See also Josephine Hearn, "Dems: Murtha Upstaging Pelosi," *Politico,* March 1, 2007, http://www.politico.com/news/stories/0207/2941.html.

61. John M. Donnelly, "House Disapproves War Strategy," *CQ Weekly,* February 19, 2007, 542.

62. See Susan Davis and Emily Pierce, "Supplemental Sows Discord," *Roll Call,* March 5, 2007; Emily Pierce, "Consensus Slow to Build on Iraq Supplemental," *Roll Call,* March 6, 2007; Josephine Hearn, "Blue Dog Democrats Divided over Approach to War in Iraq," *Politico,* March 8, 2007, http://www.politico.com/news/stories/0307/3040 .html.

63. Jennifer Yachnin and Emily Pierce, "Pelosi Pushes for Clean Iraq Bill," *Roll Call,* March 15, 2007.

64. David Espo, "Democrats Want Iraq Pullout by Fall 2008," Associated Press via *Washingtonpost.com,* March 8, 2007, available at RedOrbit.com, http://www. redorbit.com/news/general/863354/democrats_want_iraq_pullout_by_fall_2008/ index.html. See also Jennifer Yachnin, "Democrats Roll Out Supplemental: Redeployment Timeline Included," *Roll Call,* March 8, 2007.

65. "The Pelosi Plan for Iraq," editorial, *Washington Post,* March 13, 2007.

66. Jeff Zeleny and Robin Toner, "Democrats Shore Up Support for Iraq Votes," *New York Times,* March 23, 2007. Josephine Hearn, "Anti-war Democrats Near Defeat on Spending Bill," *Politico,* March 21, 2007. Jennifer Yachnin, "House Narrowly Passes Iraq Supplemental," *Roll Call,* March 23, 2007.

67. Yachin, "House Narrowly Passes," op. cit.

68. David Rogers, "War-funds Bill Reveals Limits of Majority," *Wall Street Journal*, May 25, 2007.

69. See Thomas Ferraro, "Newly Empowered Democrats Draw Wrath of Voters," *Reuters*, June 18, 2007; Martha Angle, "Defying Bush, House Passes New Deadline for Withdrawal from Iraq," *CQ Weekly*, July 12, 2007; Jennifer Yachnin, "House Not Letting Go of Iraq Debate," *Roll Call*, July 23, 2007.

70. John M. Donnelly, "Hard-line Anti-war Votes Fail," *CQ Weekly*, September 24, 2007, 2760–62. John Bresnahan and Martin Kady II, "Dem Leaders Pressured to Alter War Strategy," *Politico*, December 21, 2007, http://www.politico.com/news/stories/1207/7498.html. Jonathan Weisman, "Weary, Wary, Lawmakers See Compromise as Way Forward," *Washington Post*, October 30, 2007.

71. H.R. 5140, the Recovery Rebates and Economic Stimulus for the American People Act of 2008, passed the House under suspension 385 to 35 (Republicans 169 to 25, Democrats 216 to 10) on January 29, 2008. Initial House passage was attained after late-night negotiations between Paulson, Pelosi, and Republican Boehner. In the Senate, the bill failed to attain cloture. The Senate added an amendment to provide that disabled veterans and senior citizens would receive rebate checks regardless of their tax status. This amended version was then approved. The Senate-amended bill received final House passage on February 8, 2008, by a vote of 380 to 34 (Republicans 165 to 28, Democrats 215 to 6). Bush signed the bill on February 13, 2008.

72. This complicated legislative history is summarized on the Library of Congress legislative web site Thomas.gov at http://thomas.loc.gov/cgibin/bdquery/z?d110:HR03221:@@@R.

73. See Jessica Holzer and Mike Soraghan, "High Gear on Housing," *Hill*, July 14, 2008; U.S. House Committee on Financial Services web site "House Passes Comprehensive Housing Rescue and Foreclosure Prevention Legislation," July 23, 2008, www.house.gov/apps/list/press/financialsvcs_dem/press0723082.shtml (accessed January 21, 2009).

74. David M. Herszenhorn, "Congressional Leaders Stunned by Warnings," *Washington Post*, September 20, 2008.

75. Reid Wilson, "Politics Plays a Role in Failed Bailout," *Real Clear Politics*, September 30, 2008, http://www.realclearpolitics.com/articles/2008/09/politics_plays_role_in_failed.html.

76. Ibid.

77. Dana Milbank, "A House Divided along Twisted Lines," *Washington Post*, September 30, 2008.

78. Glenn Thrush and Ryan Grim, "Leadership Beat by Bailout Shocker," *Politico*, September 30, 2008, http://www.politico.com/news/stories/0908/14108.html.

79. "Pelosi Floor Statement on Bipartisan Financial Rescue Legislation," press release from Speaker Pelosi's office, September 29, 2008. Pelosi had yielded the chair to Speaker pro tempore Ellen Tauscher of California during the debate, thus her reference to "Madam Speaker."

80. Klaus Marre, "Shadegg Says Blaming Pelosi Speech Is 'Stupid Claim,'" *Hill*, September 30, 2008. Jackie Kucinich, "GOP Backs Away from Pelosi Blame," *Hill*, September 30, 2008.

81. John Bresnahan, "House GOP Dazed after Bailout Failure," *Politico*, October 1, 2008, http://www.politico.com/news/stories/0908/14156.

82. Steven T. Dennis, "Anarchy Reigns over GOP," *Roll Call*, October 1, 2008.

83. Former GOP majority leader Tom DeLay was among the more vocal critics. He told MSNBC's Chris Matthews: "Well, I've got to tell you, this Congress under Pelosi's leadership has got to be the most incompetent Congress of my career." Of course, DeLay would have insisted that any such bill be written on Republican terms and passed with Republican votes. In this case, it is unlikely that he would have been able to do so, so the House would have failed altogether. After the 2008 election, DeLay changed course, saying that Pelosi would become the most powerful Speaker in a generation. See "'Hardball with Chris Matthews' for Tuesday September 30, 2008," *MSNBC.com*, September 30, 2008, www.msnbc.msn.com/id/26978984/ (accessed January 21, 2009); "DeLay: Pelosi will Rule Obama," *Hill: Blog Briefing Room*, November 4, 2008, http://briefingroom.thehill.com/tag/tom-delay/ (accessed January 21, 2009).

84. Mike Soraghan and Jared Allen, "Picking Up the Pieces," *Hill*, September 30, 2008.

85. Dan Balz, "A Political Meltdown," *Washington Post*, September 30, 2008; Jackie Calmes, "In Bailout Vote, a Leadership Breakdown," *New York Times*, September 30, 2008.

86. David Rogers, "Paulson Powerless: Pelosi Punts," *Politico*, November 18, 2008, http://www.politico.com/news/stories/1108/15711.html.

87. David M. Herszenhorn and David E. Sanger, "House Passes Auto Rescue Plan," *New York Times*, December 11, 2008.

88. Pelosi was also banking on the Democrats' ability to restore the green funding to Detroit under an Obama administration.

89. Don Wolfensberger, "Just Call the 110th 'The Little Congress That Couldn't,'" *Roll Call*, October 28, 2008.

90. The quotation from Bolling in the epigraph is from Richard Bolling, *Power in the House* (New York: Dutton, 1968), 266.

CHAPTER 4

1. Thomas E. Mann and Norman J. Ornstein, *The Permanent Campaign: Its Future* (Washington, D.C.: AEI Press, 2000).

2. The epigraph from Unruh is quoted in Hoover Institute, "Coming to Terms: A Money-in-politics Glossary," www.campaignfinancesite.org/structure/terms/m.html (accessed January 24, 2009). The epigraph from Yogi Berra is quoted in an article by W. David Patton, director of the Center for Public Policy and Administration, University of Utah, *Policy Perspectives*, "Yogi Berra on Improving Organizational

Performance," Vol.3 Issue 6, June 27, 2007, http://www.imakenews.com/cppa/e_article 000845413.cfm?x=b11,0,w, accessed January 24, 2009. Nancy Pelosi's statement reflects her thoughts when she was advised not to say anything during her swearing in as a new congressional member in 1987; Nancy Pelosi, *Know Your Power: A Message to America's Daughters* (New York: Doubleday, 2008), 87–88.

3. Douglas Harris, "The Rise of the Public Speakership," *Political Science Quarterly* 113 (1998): 193–212. The term "public speakership" was first used by Barbara Sinclair, but other scholars have acknowledged the role Speakers now play well beyond the halls of Congress. Where the old understanding of the Speaker's role emphasized the skills needed for insider negotiations and coalition building, the contemporary era requires a focus on public outreach and communications. Barbara Sinclair, *Legislators, Leaders, and Lawmaking: The U.S. House of Representatives in the Postreform Era* (Baltimore: Johns Hopkins University Press, 1995).

4. John Bresnahan, "Pelosi Concentrates Power in Office," *Politico*, June 3, 2008, http://www.politico.com/news/stories/0608/10781.html. John Bresnahan, "What Does Rahm Want?," *Politico*, July 16, 2008, http://www.politico.com/news/stories/0708/11782.html.

5. Naftali Bendavid, *The Thumpin'* (New York: Random House, 2007), 10.

6. John Bresnahan, "Pelosi's Power Reigns Supreme," *Politico*, November 12, 2008, http://www.politico.com/news/stories/1108/15536.html.

7. After the 2008 election, the Democrats held a margin of 78 seats over the Republicans, but the resignations of Kirsten Gillibrand and Rahm Emanuel reduced that margin to 76. Both districts were retained by the Democrats in special elections in 2009.

8. Robert Caro, *The Years of Lyndon B. Johnson: The Path to Power* (New York: Knopf, 1982).

9. For a history of the House congressional campaign committees see Robin Kolodny, *Pursuing Majorities* (Norman: University of Oklahoma Press, 1998).

10. A summary of current campaign contribution limits is available at the Federal Election Commission website, www.fec.gov/pages/brochures/contriblimits.shtml.

11. Seth Gitell, "The Democratic Party Suicide Bill," *Atlantic Online*, July–August 2003, http://www.theatlantic.com/doc/200307/gitell.

12. We thank Randall Strahan for drawing our attention to this point.

13. Alan K. Ota, "Lawmaker Says Pelosi Should Hit the Road—and Campaign," *CQ TODAY ONLINE NEWS*, June 3, 2009, http://www.cqpolitics.com/wmspage.cfm?docID=news-000003133967. Pelosi's staff reported to us that she had in fact visited 30 states in the 2008 election cycle. All but two were "blue" states. We take this to indicate that she is deeply engaged on behalf of members, but with real constraints imposed by her liberal image, unwelcome in conservative parts of the country.

14. John Harwood and Gerald F. Seib, *Pennsylvania Avenue: Profiles in Backroom Power* (New York: Random House, 2008), 79–81.

15. Lauren W. Whittington, "House Leaders Badger Members to Pay Dues," *Roll Call*, October 23, 2008, http://www.rollcall.com/issues/54_50/politics/29495-1.html

and Jared Allen, "House Chairmen Respond to Speaker Pelosi's Call for Cash," *Hill*, October 21, 2008, http://thehill.com/homenews/news-archive.

16. Damon M. Cann, "Modeling Committee Chair Selection in the U.S. House of Representatives," *Political Analysis* 16, 3 (summer 2008): 274–89; John E. Owens, "The Return of Party Leadership in the U.S. House of Representatives: Central Leadership—Committee Relations in the 104th Congress," *British Journal of Political Science* 27, 2 (April 1997): 247–72.

17. Joseph J. Schatz, "Lewis Wins Favor of GOP Leaders—and a Coveted Appropriations Chair." By contrast, when Henry Waxman (D-CA) challenged John Dingell (D-MI) for the chairship of the Energy and Commerce Committee in 2009, fund-raising was in play only insofar as Waxman had contributed money to more members than had Dingell. Waxman was chosen by members; Lewis was chosen by the leadership.

18. An interesting counterpoint to the Lewis example for the Republicans is Pelosi's nomination of Collin Peterson of Minnesota as chair of the Agriculture Committee. Peterson had not made any contributions to the DCCC for 10 years. He had often voted with the Republicans, even on the Medicare prescription drug bill, on which Pelosi, then minority leader, had sought a unified Democratic opposition. After his election as Agriculture chair, Peterson began to catch up on his party dues; but his prior record had not prevented his nomination. See Steven T. Dennis and Tory Newmyer, "Old Alliance Faces New Test," *Roll Call*, June 23, 2009.

19. Bendavid, *Thumpin'*, 22.

20. Party unity scores are taken from the website Voteview, http://voteview.com/ (accessed January 24, 2009).

21. John Bresnahan, "Brian Wolff: Staffer and Pelosi make perfect pair," *Politico*, June 3, 2008, http://www.politico.com/politicopros/brianwolff.html.

22. Richard E. Cohen, "Rolling..." *National Journal*, May 24, 2008, http://www.nationaljournal.com/njmagazine/cs_20080524_4869.php; Carl Hulse, "House Democrat Seeks a 2006 Repeat, His Own Way," *New York Times*, October 24, 2008.

23. Democratic Congressional Campaign Committee, Red-to-Blue press releases dated February 28, 2006, and August 1, 2008, and documents at www.dccc.org/page/content/redtoblue, http://dccc.org/newsroom/entry/Red_to_Blue, http://dccc.org/newsroom/entry/dccc_announces_fourth_round_of_red_to_blue/, and www.dccc.org/page/content/redtoblue (accessed December 31, 2008).

24. Juliet Eilperin, "The Making of Madam Whip," *Washington Post Magazine*, January 6, 2002, W27.

25. Opensecrets.org. The Center for Responsive Politics, "Democratic Congressional Campaign Committee 2000–2008," accessed at: www.opensecrets.org/politicians/summary.php?cid=N00007360&cycle=2008.

26. This difference is statistically significant ($p < 0.01$) even though the amounts in the larger scheme of campaign fund-raising are relatively minor.

27. Harris, "Rise of the Public Speakership"; Sinclair, *Legislators, Leaders, and Lawmaking*.

28. David H. Rohde, "The Gingrich Speakership in Context: Majority Leadership in the Late Twentieth Century," *Extensions* (Autumn 2000): 4–7; L. Marvin Overby, "Public Opinion Regarding Congressional Leaders: Lessons from the 1996 Election," *Journal of Legislative Studies* 12 (March 2006): 54–75.

29. Dan Nimmo, "Political Image Makers and the Mass Media," *Annals of the American Academy of Political and Social Science* 427 (1976): 33–44; and Costas Panagopoulos and Jim Thurber, "Do Imagemakers Need a Makeover? Public Attitudes towards Political Consultants," paper presented at the annual meeting of the American Association for Public Opinion Research, Phoenix, Arizona, May 11, 2004.

30. Lyndsey Layton, *Washington Post*, "Pelosi Aims to Recast Self, Party: New House Speaker Plans a 4-Day Fete," http://www.washingtonpost.com/wp-dyn/content/article/2006/12/21/AR2006122101865.html, October 15, 2009. This "rebranding" of Pelosi and the Democratic Party is described by Vincent Bzdek, *Woman of the House* (New York: Palgrave Macmillan, 2008), chap. 10.

31. *Meet the Press,* May 7, 2006. For critical commentary on Pelosi's performance, see Mark Leibovich, "Talk of Pelosi as Speaker Delights Both Parties," *New York Times,* May 30, 2006; Lois Romano, "The Woman Who Would Be Speaker," *Washington Post*, October 21, 2006.

32. But sometimes they have. Carl Albert was twice a national debating champion. He honed his skills by memorizing famous speeches and reciting them to his family. Henry Clay was a legendary speech maker. As a young man, he practiced speaking to the trees. Thomas Brackett Reed was one of the most famous epigrammatists in American history. Jim Wright was so glib that his opponents turned his style against him, labeling him a southern snake-oil salesman.

33. "Luntz Claimed Military Plane for Pelosi Is "Not a Security Issue," *Media Matters for America,* February 09, 2007, http://mediamatters.org/research/200702090019 (accessed June 9, 2009).

34. Michelle Malkin, "Queen Nancy: Fly as I Say, Not as I Fly," http://michellemalkin.com/2009/03/11/nancy-pelosi-the-jennifer-lopez-of-congressional-travelers/ (accessed June 10, 2009).

35. House of Representatives Republican Conference, "The Pelosi Premium: Out of Touch," April 25, 2008, accessed at http://www.youtube.com/watch?v=LlD1Pg_mbAY. In the interview, Pelosi described the price of gas as increasing three-fold from when President Bush first took office—"from a dollar something when he took office, now it's $2.56 on average, but it's higher in California." King then interrupted her to say, "No it's $3.50, they're saying," to which she responded "Down six cents [from $3.56], well it's higher in California, sad to say."

36. Glenn Thrush, *Politico*, "GOP Tweets clip of Hitler praising Pelosi," October 13, 2009, http://www.politico.com/blogs/glennthrush/1009/GOP_Tweets_clip_of_Hitler_praising_Pelosi.html, and Jordan Fabian, *The Hill's Blog Briefing Room*, "NJDC: Conservative Nazi rhetoric has reached 'epidemic proportions,' " October 13, 2009,

http://thehill.com/blogs/blog-briefing-room/news/62843-njdc-conservative-nazi-rhetoric-has-reached-epidemic-proportions.

37. E. J. Dionne, Jr., "Veteran Leadership: How the Eric Shinseki Appointment Could Help Heal the Wounds of Two Wars," *New Republic*, December 9, 2008.

38. Harwood and Seib, *Pennsylvania Avenue*, 163–66.

39. Project for Excellence in Journalism, "The Changing Newsroom: Gains and Losses in Today's Papers," (Washington D.C.: *Pew Research Center*, July 21, 2008).

40. All the blogs listed here have been included among the top 12 blogs in terms of authority by the blog-tracking website Technorati.com, www.Technorati.com (accessed January 24, 2009).

41. John F. Scruggs, "The 'Echo Chamber' Approach to Advocacy," interoffice correspondence, Philip Morris Companies Inc., December 18, 1998. See SourceWatch, "Echo Chamber," www.sourcewatch.org/index.php?title=Echo_chamber (accessed January 27, 2009).

42. Kathleen Hall Jamieson and Joseph N. Cappella, *Echo Chamber: Rush Limbaugh and the Conservative Media Establishment* (New York: Oxford University Press, 2008).

43. Daniel W. Drezner and Henry Farrell, "The Power and Politics of Blogs," paper presented at the annual meeting of the American Political Science Association, Chicago, September 2–5, 2004.

44. Markos Moulitsas Zuniga, *Taking on the System: Rules for Radical Change in a Digital Era* (New York: Penguin Books, 2008).

45. Daniel Libit, "The Commentocracy Rises Online," *Politico,* July 24, 2008, http://www.politico.com/news/stories/0708/11890.html.

46. Lada A. Adamic and Natalie Glance, "The Political Blogosphere and the 2004 U.S. Election: Divided They Blog," paper presented at the Third International Workshop on Link Discovery, Chicago, Illinois, March 4, 2005, www.blogpulse.com/papers/2005/AdamicGlanceBlogWWW.pdf (accessed January 24, 2009).

47. David D. Perlmutter, *Blogwars* (New York: Oxford University Press, 2008).

48. Karen Kedrowksi and Rachel E. Gower, "Gender and the Public Speakership: News Media Coverage of Speaker Nancy Pelosi," paper presented at the annual meeting of the Southern Political Science Association, New Orleans, January 7–10, 2009.

49. Lisa Tucker McElroy, *Nancy Pelosi* (Minneapolis: Lerner, 2008); Elaine Povich, *Nancy Pelosi* (Westport, Conn.: Greenwood Press, 2008); Dwayne Epstein, *Nancy Pelosi* (Farmington Hills, Mich.: Lucent Books, 2009); Sandra H. Shichtman, *Political Profiles: Nancy Pelosi* (Greensboro, N.C.: Morgan Reynolds, 2008); Amie Jane Leavitt, *Nancy Pelosi* (Hockessin, Del.: Mitchell Lane, 2008). An earlier biography for young readers was Hal Marcovitz, *Nancy Pelosi* (Philadelphia: Chelsea House, 2004).

50. Karina Newton, "The Exploding World of Political Web Video," Youtube, May 9, 2007, www.youtube.com/watch?v=JoNYaoLvim4&feature=user.

51. Tracking of blog posts was done through the monitoring tools of Technorati.com for a six-month period culminating with the financial crisis of late September 2008. During the same period, postings mentioning the three presidential candidates McCain,

Clinton, and Obama were of a magnitude four to five times greater than those mentioning Pelosi but also included coverage of the two parties' nominating conventions.

52. CQ Staff, "Pelosi to Revisit Old Tradition, Regular News Conferences by House Speaker," *CQ Weekly*, September 21, 2007.

53. George Lakoff, *Don't Think of an Elephant!* (New York: Chelsea Green, 2004).

54. Matt Bai, "The Framing Wars," *New York Times*, July 17, 2005.

55. Nayda Terkildsen, Frauke I. Schnell, and Cristina Ling, "Interest Groups, the Media, and Policy Debate Formation: An Analysis of Message Structure, Rhetoric, and Source Cues," *Political Communication* 15 (1998): 45–61; Douglas Arnold, *The Logic of Congressional Action* (New Haven: Yale University Press, 1990); Frank Baumgartner and Bryan Jones, *Agendas and Instability in American Politics* (Chicago: University of Chicago Press, 1993); Myra Marx Ferree, William A. Gamson, Jurgen Gerhards, and Dieter Rucht, *Shaping Abortion Discourse* (Cambridge: Cambridge University Press, 2002); Kim Fridkin Kahn, "The Distorted Mirror: Press Coverage of Women Candidates for Statewide Office," *Journal of Politics* 56, 1 (1994): 154–73; William A. Gamson, David Croteau, William Hoynes, and Theodore Sasson, "Media Images and the Social Construction of Reality," *Annual Review of Sociology* 18 (1992): 373–93; Pippa Norris, ed., *Politics and the Press: The News Media and Their Influences* (Boulder, Colo.: Lynne Rienner, 1997).

56. E. E. Schattschneider, *The Semi Sovereign People* (New York: Holt, Rinehart and Winston, 1960).

57. Murray Edelman, *The Symbolic Uses of Politics* (Urbana: University of Illinois Press, 1964); William A. Gamson, *Talking Politics* (New York: Cambridge University Press, 1992).

58. See Frank Luntz, *Words That Work* (New York: Hyperion, 2008).

59. Richard Weaver, *Ideas Have Consequences* (Chicago: University of Chicago Press, 1962).

60. Marc Sandalow, *Madam Speaker* (New York: Modern Times, 2008), 252.

61. Jack Trout with Steve Rivkin, *The Power of Simplicity* (New York: McGraw-Hill, 1999); See also Al Ries and Jack Trout, *Marketing Warfare* (New York: McGraw-Hill, 1986); Jack Trout, *Differentiate or Die: Survival in Our Era of Killer Competition* (New York: Wiley, 2001).

62. Rahm Emanuel and Bruce Reed, "Breaking Out of the Frame Game," *Blueprint Magazine* (DLC), October 18, 2006, www.dlc.org/ndol_ci.cfm?contentid=254080&kaid=127&subid=171 (accessed January 24, 2009).

63. Marc Cooper, "Thinking of Jackasses," *The Atlantic*, April 2005, http://www.theatlantic.com/doc/200504/cooper.

64. Matt Bai, *The Argument* (New York: Penguin Books, 2007).

65. Bai, "Framing Wars."

66. Speaker's Office, "A New Direction for America," October 4, 2008, www.speaker.gov/newsroom/reports?id=0074 (accessed January 24, 2009).

67. We devised the coding scheme and then coded the documents for analysis, with the help of two graduate student coders. The Speaker's office releases a variety of public information, including fact sheets, news media highlights ("In the News"), and press releases featuring the Speaker and others. Our subject matter codes generally employed the scheme devised by Frank Baumgartner and Bryan Jones for the Policy Agendas Project, with minor modifications. For example, particular codes were created to capture the frequency with which the Speaker's communications outreach dealt with the Iraq War, climate protection, and SCHIP, specifically. The original codebook for the Policy Agendas Project is available at www.policyagendas.org/codebooks/topicindex.html (accessed January 24, 2009).

68. The facilitative-conciliatory and competitive-confrontational dimensions have gender implications that we explore in more depth in chapter 6. We have been guided in our coding for these characteristics by prior research, for example, Jane Blankenship and Deborah Robson, "A 'Feminine Style' in Women's Political Discourse: An Exploratory Essay," *Communication Quarterly* 43 (1995): 353–66; Lyn Kathlene, "Power and Influence in State Legislative Policy-making—The Interaction of Gender and Position in Committee Hearing Debates," *American Political Science Review* 88, 3 (1994): 560–76; Charlotte Krolokke and Anne Scott Sorensen, *Gender Communication Theories and Analyses: From Silence to Performance* (London: Sage, 2006); Julie Dolan and Jonathan S. Kropf, "Credit Claiming from the U.S. House: Gendered Communication Styles?" *International Journal of Press/Politics* 9, 41(2004): 41–59; and Colleen J. Shogan, "Speaking Out: An Analysis of Democratic and Republican Woman-invoked Rhetoric in the 105th Congress," *Women and Politics* 23, 1 (2002): 129–46.

69. One anomaly of the coding system we used was that discussion of college benefits and health-care benefits for military families and veterans was coded under military affairs in the Policy Agenda Projects coding scheme. Thus, the New Direction Congress goals of college access and affordability showed as having few mentions. Another anomaly of our data is the absence of discussion on Social Security and retirement issues. These were prominent issues of the Democrats leading up to the 2006 election but were absent from the 110th Congress agenda.

70. Media releases had a lower threshold for coding as partisan due to their shorter length, single topics, and clearer intents. By contrast, most speeches were longer, often covering multiple topics, and combining purposes other than partisan point-scoring. The determination that a speech was partisan required a global assessment of the content and its intended purpose. Releases decline when the houses is in recess.

71. News from Speaker Nancy Pelosi, "Pelosi: House Votes to Crack Down on Price Gouging," May 23, 2007, www.speaker.gov/newsroom/pressreleases?id=0187.

72. See GasBuddy.com, www.gasbuddy.com/gb_retail_price_chart.aspx (accessed January 25, 2009).

73. CNN, "'Two Oil Men' to Blame for high Gas Prices, Pelosi Says," *CNN.com*, July 17, 2008, www.cnn.com/2008/POLITICS/07/17/congress.oil/index.html (accessed January 24, 2009).

74. Alexander Mooney, "Pelosi: Bush a 'Total Failure,'" *CNN.com*, July 18, 2008, www .cnn.com/2008/POLITICS/07/17/pelosi.interview/index.html (accessed November 11, 2008).

75. "Top Ten Questions for the House GOP on Energy," report from the Speaker's Office, August 6, 2008, www.speaker.gov/newsroom/reports?id=0064.

76. Martin Kady II and Patrick O'Connor, "Pelosi: At-risk Dems Back Drilling," *Politico*, August 5, 2008, http://www.politico.com/news/stories/0808/12304.html; Patrick O'Connor and Daniel W. Reilly, "Pump Primed for Fall Fight on Energy," *Politico*, August 19, 2008, http://www.politico.com/news/stories/0808/12630.html.

77. David Rogers, "Pelosi: 'I'm Trying to Save the Planet,'" *Politico*, July 29, 2008, www .politico.com/news/stories/0708/12122.html (January 24, 2009).

78. Lydia Saad, "Battle for Congress Suddenly Looks Competitive," *Gallup.Com*, September 12, 2008, www.gallup.com/poll/110263/Battle-Congress-Suddenly-Looks-Competitive.aspx (accessed December 18, 2008).

79. David Libit, "'Pelosi Premium' Runs out of Gas," *Politico*, December 10, 2008, www .politico.com/news/stories/1208/16397.html (accessed January 24, 2009).

80. "Pelosi 49% Favorable, Other Congressional Leaders Panned by Voters," *Rasmussen Reports*, February 5, 2007, www.rasmussenreports.com/public_content/politics/people2/pelosi_49_favorable_other_congressional_leaders_panned_by_voters (accessed January 24, 2009).

81. John Hibbing and Christopher W. Larimer, "The American Public's View of Congress," *Forum* 6, 3 (2008), www.bepress.com/forum/vol6/iss3/art6/ (accessed January 2, 2009).

82. Quoted in John Jacobs, "No Longer a Party Girl," *San Francisco Chronicle*, Image sec., July 12, 1992.

83. Marc Sandalow, "Pelosi Won't Back Off Bush Condemnation: 'Her Words Are Putting American Lives at Risk,' Says Her House Counterpart," *San Francisco Chronicle*, May 21, 2004.

84. Ibid.

85. Pelosi, *Know Your Power*, 49.

86. Marc Sandalow, "Pelosi Says GOP 'Sandbagged' Ethics Investigation," *San Francisco Chronicle*, January 23, 1997; Marc Sandalow, "Starr Went Too Far, Pelosi Says," *San Francisco Chronicle*, January 24, 1998.

87. Speaker Pelosi. "Transcript of Today's Speaker Pelosi Press Conference—May 15, 2008." Received by email:<SpeakerPelosi@mail.house.gov>.

88. *The Sean Hannity Show*, ABC Radio Networks, August 29, 2006.

89. John W. Lillpop, "Nancy Pelosi, President of the U.S.," *Conservative Voice* (blog), October 13, 2006, www.theconservativevoice.com (accessed January 24, 2009).

90. John W. Lillpop, "Can America Survive a Pelosi Plundering?" *Conservative Voice*, October 9, 2006, www.theconservativevoice.com (accessed January 24, 2009).

91. Lesley Stahl, "Pelosi: Two Heartbeats Away," *60 Minutes*, October 22, 2006, www.cbsnews.com/stories/2006/10/20/60minutes/main2111089.shtml (accessed January 22, 2009).

92. Ibid.
93. Pelosi, press conference, May 15, 2008.
94. Mike Soraghan, "The Subtle Art of Nancy Pelosi's Signals," *Hill*, June 6, 2008, http://74.125.95.132/search?q=cache:qrGbxJK04iIJ:thehill.com/leading-the-news/the-subtle-art-of-nancy-pelosis-signals-2008–06–17.html+Mike+Soraghan,+%E2%80%9CThe+Subtle+Art+of+Nancy+Pelosi%E2%80%99s+Signals,%E2%80%9D&cd=1&hl=en&ct=clnk&gl=us.
95. Pelosi, press conference, May 15, 2008.

Chapter 5

1. The departures of Rahm Emanuel and Kirsten Gillibrand created two vacancies that were later filled by Democrats in special elections. In November 2009 the Democrats picked up another seat in a special election in upstate New York's 23rd congressional district, bringing the number of Democrats to 258 on the eve of the health care vote discussed below. In the Senate, the party switch of Pennsylvania's Arlen Specter moved the Democrats to 59 seats while the outcome was awaited of the disputed Minnesota contest between Democrat Al Franken and Republican Norm Coleman. A Franken win ultimately brought the Democrats to the 60-vote threshold needed to break Republican filibusters.
2. John Bresnahan, "Pelosi's Power Reigns Supreme," *Politico*, November 12, 2008, http://www.politico.com/news/stories/1108/15536.html; Glenn Thrush, "With the 111th, the Age of Pelosi Dawns," *Politico*, January 8, 2009, http://www.politico.com/news/stories/0109/17105.html. See also Jared Allen, "Armed with More Democrats, Pelosi Poised to Get Tougher," *Hill*, November 5, 2008.
3. Mike Soraghan, "Anxiety among Democrats as Pelosi Tightens Grip," *Hill*, December 12, 2008.
4. Greg Giroux, "A New Democratic Demographic," *CQ Weekly*, April 20, 2009, 908–13.
5. Tory Newmyer and Keith Koffler, "Emanuel Move Shakes Up Democrats," *Roll Call*, November 6, 2008.
6. See Steven T. Dennis, "House Leadership Races Immediately Underway," *Roll Call*, November 5, 2008; Jared Allen, "Dems Back Off Leadership Challenges," *Hill*, November 10, 2008; Steven T. Dennis and Tory Newmyer, "House Leaders' Races Lack Zest," *Roll Call*, November 17, 2008; Victoria McGrane and Ryan Grim, "Crowley, Wasserman Schultz in Leadership Battle," *Politico*, December 3, 2008, http://www.politico.com/news/stories/1208/16178.html; Patrick O'Connor and Ryan Grim, "Why Becerra Rebuffed Obama," *Politico*, December 17, 2008, http://www.politico.com/news/stories/1208/16676.html; Steven T. Dennis, "Becerra's Snub of Trade Job Ices Others' Ambitions," *Roll Call*, December 17, 2008.

7. See Victoria McGrane and Ryan Grim, "Crowley, Wasserman Schultz in Leadership Battle," *Politico*, December 3, 2008, http://www.politico.com/news/stories/1208/16178. html#; John Bresnahan, "Pelosi Recruits Van Hollen for New Role," *Politico*, December 9, 2008, http://www.politico.com/news/stories/1208/16342.html.

8. Mike Soraghan, "Reps. Dingell, Waxman, Trade Salvos in Battle," *Hill*, November 11, 2008; John M. Broder and Carl Hulse, "Behind House Struggle, Long and Tangled Roots," *New York Times*, November 23, 2008; Mike Soraghan and Jared Allen, "Waxman Gains Edge from Steering Committee," *Hill*, November 19, 2008; Alexander Bolton, "Panel Fight Reaches up to Leaders," *Hill*, November 17, 2008.

9. Tory Newmyer, "Race for Gavel Hits Final Turn," *Roll Call*, November 19, 2008; Ryan Grim, "Dingell Pushes to Keep Chairmanship," *Politico*, November 15, 2008, http://www.politico.com/news/stories/1108/15638.html; Patrick O'Connor and Ryan Grim, "Dingell vs. Waxman Has Party Squirming," *Politico*, November 20, 2008, http://www.politico.com/news/stories/1108/15810.html.

10. Andrew Taylor, "Waxman Topples Dingell for Key Panel Chair," *Yahoo News*, November 20, 2008; John M. Broder, "Longtime Head of House Energy Panel Is Ousted," *New York Times*, November 21, 2008; Mike Soraghan, "Dingell Wins Support of Key Black Members," *Hill*, November 13, 2008.

11. Alexander Bolton, "Chair Fight Sparks Fear on Seniority," *Hill*, November 18, 2008.

12. Tory Newmyer, "Waxman's Coup Worries Moderates," *Roll Call*, November 10, 2008; Jonathan Allen, "Dingell's Defeat Part of a Pattern of Growing California Clout," *CQ Today Online News*, November 20, 2008.

13. Richard E. Cohen and Brian Friel, "Chairmen Rising," *National Journal*, January 24, 2009, 22–32; Glenn Thrush, "Congressional Bulls Guard Their Turf," *Politico*, April 3, 2009, http://www.politico.com/news/stories/0409/20841.html.

14. *Congressional Record*, Vol. 153, June 28, 2007, H7408.

15. Ibid., August 2, 2007, H9649.

16. Ibid., March 1, 2007, H2117; July 12, 2007, H7701.

17. Tory Newmyer and Jackie Kucinich, "New Rules Ignite Partisan Battles," *Roll Call*, January 6, 2009; Molly K. Hooper, "Pelosi's Power Move Leaves House Republicans Fuming," *Hill*, January 5, 2009. These categories apply only to MTRs "with instructions." A simple MTR, which kills the bill, remains available under the House rules.

18. Glenn Thrush, "Pelosi Draws Her Lines with Obama," *Politico*, January 20, 2009, http://www.politico.com/news/stories/0109/17650.html.

19. John Bresnahan, "Pelosi Butts Heads with Obama," *Politico*, February 27, 2009, http://www.politico.com/news/stories/0209/19389.html.

20. John Bresnahan, "Pelosi Lays Down the Law with Rahm," *Politico*, December 16, 2008, http://www.politico.com/news/stories/1208/16622.html.

21. Keith Koffler, "Schiliro Expected to Lead Obama's Legislative Affairs Team," *Roll Call*, November 5, 2009.

22. Jay Newton-Small, "Obama vs. Pelosi: Can the President Work with the Democrats?," *Time*, February 4, 2009.

23. Holly Bailey, "Obama's Pelosi Problem," *Newsweek*, March 9, 2009.

24. Speaker Hastert pushed the Bush agenda even when the right wing of his caucus opposed it, for example on immigration, Medicare prescription drugs, and federal deficit spending.

25. Froma Harrop, "Centrist Democrats: Dogged If They Do, Dogged If They Don't," *Real Clear Politics*, April 3, 2009, http://www.realclearpolitics.com/articles/2009/04/centrist_dems_dogged_if_they_d.html; Glenn Thrush and Patrick O'Connor, "The Blue Dogs Bark," *Politico*, February 5, 2009, http://www.politico.com/news/stories/0209/18434.html; Tory Newmyer, "Pelosi's Restless Team Seeks Voice," *Roll Call*, February 5, 2009; Jared Allen, "Freshman Dems Not Afraid to Defy Pelosi on Legislation," *Hill*, March 2, 2009.

26. "Remarks of Senator Barack Obama, Reno, NV," October 25, 2008, www.barackobama.com/2008/10/25/remarks_of_senator_barack_obam_147.php (accessed January 25, 2009).

27. See Reinhold Niebuhr, *Moral Man and Immoral Society* (Louisville, Ky.: Westminster John Knox Press, 1960), 34: "Wherever men hold unequal power in society, they will strive to maintain it. They will use whatever means are most convenient to that end and will seek to justify them by the most plausible arguments they are able to devise."

28. Richard Reeves, "A New Era of Bipartisanship?" *Real Clear Politics*, November 29, 2008, http://www.realclearpolitics.com/articles/2008/11/a_new_era_of_bipartisanship.html.

29. Jeff Zelny, "Initial Steps by Obama Suggest a Bipartisan Flair," *New York Times*, November 24, 2008.

30. Don Wolfensberger, "Can President Obama Change the Way That Washington Works?" *Roll Call*, December 1, 2008.

31. Stuart Rothenberg, "Can Anyone Bring America Together in an Era of Division?" *Real Clear Politics*, December 2, 2008, http://www.realclearpolitics.com/articles/2008/12/can_anyone_bring_america_toget.html.

32. John Harwood, " 'Partisan' Seeks a Prefix: Bi- or Post-," *New York Times*, December 7, 2008.

33. For one prominent example of deliberative democracy in political theory see Amy Gutmann and Dennis Thompson, *Democracy and Disagreement* (Cambridge, Mass.: Harvard University Press, 1996).

34. The epigraph is from Speaker Pelosi, "Transcript of Today's Speaker Pelosi Press Conference–November 5, 2008." Received by email:<SpeakerPelosi@mail.house.gov.>

35. *News Hour*, January 8, 2009.

36. Jared Allen, "Both Sides Wonder What Pelosi Means by 'Center,' " *Hill*, January 6, 2009.

37. Ibid.
38. Thomas Frank, "Bipartisanship Is a Silly Beltway Obsession," *Wall Street Journal*, February 18, 2009; Julian E. Zelizer, "Bipartisanship Is Not Always Good," *Politico*, February 11, 2009, http://www.politico.com/news/stories/0209/18671.html; James Morone, "One Side to Every Story," *New York Times*, February 17, 2009; Dan Balz, "Partisans Argue of Partisanship," *Washington Post*, April 12, 2009.
39. "American Recovery and Reinvestment Act: Bipartisan, Open and Transparent Legislative Process," Office of Speaker Nancy Pelosi Fact Sheet, January 27, 2009. Received by email:<SpeakerPelosi@mail.house.gov.>.
40. Nancy Pelosi, interview by Charlie Rose, *Charlie Rose Show*, PBS, March 13, 2009.
41. Ibid.
42. E. J. Dionne, Jr., "The Real Nancy Pelosi," *Washington Post*, April 9, 2009.
43. Glenn Thrush and John Bresnahan, "'I Am the Speaker of the House,'" *Politico*, February 2, 2009, http://www.politico.com/news/stories/0209/18279.
44. Tim Dickinson, "Pelosi Hits Back," *Rollingstone.com*, February 18, 2009.
45. Thrush and Bresnahan, "'I Am the Speaker of the House.'" See also Marie Cocco, "Chipper on the Hill," *Real Clear Politics*, March 5, 2009, http://www.realclearpolitics.com/articles/2009/03/chipper_on_the_hill.html.
46. Glenn Grunwald, "Obama to Release OLC Torture Memos; Promises No Prosecutions for CIA Officials," *Salon.com, April 16, 2009. http://www.salon.com/opinion/greenwald/radio/2009/04/16/aclu/.
47. Scott Shane and Mark Mazzetti, "In Adopting Harsh Tactics, No Inquiry into Their Past Use," *New York Times*, April 22, 2009.
48. Speaker Nancy Pelosi, "Transcript of Today's Speaker Pelosi Press Conference April 23, 2009." Received by email:<SpeakerPelosi@mail.house.gov>.
49. Porter J. Goss, "Security before Politics," *Washington Post*, April 25, 2009.
50. Glenn Thrush and John Bresnahan, "Pelosi Defense: Couldn't Object in '03," *Politico*, May 11, 2009, http://www.politico.com/news/stories/0509/22401.html.
51. Manu Raju, "GOP's Torture Strategy: Pelosi," *Politico*, May 9, 2009, http://www.politico.com/news/stories/0509/22348.html; Emily Pierce, "Boehner Turns Up Political Heat on Pelosi," *Roll Call*, May 17, 2009.
52. Scott Horton, "What Did Pelosi Know?" *Daily Beast*, May 11, 2009.
53. Jared Allen and Mike Soraghan, "Hoyer Wants Pelosi Facts Out," *Hill*, May 12, 2009.
54. Central Intelligence Agency, "Member Briefings on Enhanced Interrogation Techniques (EITs), May 8, 2009, http://online.wsj.com/public/resources/documents/briefings.pdf."
55. Mike Soraghan and Jared Allen, "Pelosi Claims CIA Lied to Her about Waterboarding," *Hill*, May 14, 2009.
56. Carl Hulse, "Pelosi Says She Knew of Waterboarding by 2003," *New York Times*, May 15, 2009.
57. Speaker Pelosi, "Transcript of Today's Speaker Pelosi Press Conference—May 14, 2009." Received by email: <SpeakerPelosi@mail.house.gov>.

58. Ibid.

59. Sam Youngman, "CIA Director Says Pelosi Received the Truth," *Hill*, May 15, 2009. Speaker Nancy Pelosi, "Pelosi Statement on Panetta Message to CIA Employees," Press Release, May 15, 2009.

60. Tory Newmyer and Steven T. Dennis, "Pelosi Knocked off Her Game," *Roll Call*, May 20, 2009; Martin Kady II, "Off Her Game," *Politico*, May 12, 2009; Alexander Bolton, "Democrats Pack July Agenda," *Hill*, May 13, 2009.

61. In the novel *Goldfinger*, Galore is a lesbian gang leader who, in the novel's last pages, is rescued from her wayward past and becomes an "obedient child" under the "ruthless" kisses of James Bond. Was the RNC thus offering a lesson in family values?

62. Andie Collier, "RNC's Below-the-belt Shot at Pelosi," *Politico*, May 23, 2009, http://www.politico.com/news/stories/0509/22882.html.

63. There was another important aspect to the timeline. Zubaydah was waterboarded 83 times in the month of August 2002. What were the interrogators trying to get from him? Some have speculated that the Bush administration was determined to establish a link between Al Qaeda and Saddam Hussein.

64. Glenn Thrush, "How Pelosi Botched CIA Script," *Politico*, May 20, 2009, http://www.politico.com/news/stories/0509/22795.html.

65. Mike Soraghan, "Liberals Back Speaker in Briefing Controversy on Interrogation Tactics," *Hill*, May 13, 2009; Emily Pierce, "Colleagues Blast Pelosi Critics," *Roll Call*, May 13, 2009; Robert Schrum, "The Case for Nancy Pelosi," *Week*, May 19, 2009, www.theweek.com; Julian E. Zelizer, "The Pelosi Factor," *Politico*, May 13, 2009, http://www.politico.com/news/stories/0509/22425.html.

66. In July, 2009 seven House Democrats issued a letter claiming that CIA Director Leon Panetta had acknowledged in a report to the House Intelligence Committee that the CIA had in fact misled the Congress on several occasions dating back to 2001, thus offering some vindication for Pelosi's statements. In October, 2009, House Intelligence Committee Democrats Jan Schakowsky of Illinois and Anna Eshoo of California, both close Pelosi allies, announced the findings of an investigation that indicated the CIA may have misled Congress five times since 2001. See: Siobhan Gorman, "Democrats Say Panetta Admits CIA Misled Them," *Wall Street Journal Online*, July 10, 2009, http://online.wsj.com/article/SB124709503805414883.html.66; Jared Allen, "Dems: CIA May Have Misled Congress Five Times Since 2001," *Hill*, October 27, 2009.

67. Matt Bai, "Taking the Hill," *New York Times Magazine*, June 7, 2009, http://www.nytimes.com/2009/06/07/magazine/07congress-t.html.

68. Richard Cohen, "Pelosi's Shift," *National Journal*, June 6, 2009, 31–34.

69. Whereas the president submits his budget proposals to Congress each year, the congressional Budget Resolution is an intramural document that guides authorizers and appropriators in developing actual tax and spending legislation; it does not require the president's signature.

70. Davie Clark, "Budget Moves on Hard Party Lines," *CQ Weekly*, May 4, 2009, 1036.

71. U.S. House of Representatives, Committee on Rules, "The Budget Reconciliation Process," n.d., www.rules.house.gov/archives/bud_rec_proc.htm (accessed May 26, 2009); Robert Keith, Congressional Research Service, "Budget Reconciliation Procedures: The Senate's "Byrd Rule,"= Report RL30862," March 20, 2008; and Center on Budget and Policy Priorities, "Policy Basics: Introduction to the Federal Budget Process," December 17, 2008, http://www.cbpp.org/files/3-7-03bud.pdf.

72. The policy deficit is the difference between the amount of money needed to honor the government's statutory obligations and the amount of revenue it reasonably expects to have available, both under current law. It is variously estimated at between $50 and $90 trillion over the next 75 years. Entitlement programs such as Social Security, Medicare, and Medicaid are the largest elements of the policy deficit.

73. Lynda Waddington, "National Health-care Conversation Being Shaped in Iowa," http://www.essentialestrogen.com/2007/08/national-health-care-conversation-being-shaped-in-iowa.html, *Iowa Independent*, August 24, 2007; "Corporate American Pushes Health Care Reform," *Medical News Today*, May 7, 2007; Bob Mook, "Health Care Alliance Is Launched," *Business Journal*, October 2, 2007.

74. "Conservative Groups Fault Health Care Agenda," *Wall Street Journal*, Digital Edition, May 27, 2009, http://online.wsj.com/article/sb124339409809957455.html; Dave Davies, "Obama Backers Now Set Organizing Sights on Health-care Reform," Philly.Com, January 22, 2009, archived at http://www.philly.com.

75. Steven T. Dennis, "Markey Making His Mark," *Roll Call*, April 1, 2009.

76. Jared Allen, "Van Hollen: Climate Bill Could Wait," *Hill*, April 27, 2009; Steven T. Dennis and Tory Newmyer, "Democrats Clash on Climate Change," *Roll Call*, May 4, 2009; Mike Soraghan, Dem Centrists Press Pelosi to Shelve Climate Bill," *Hill*, May 6, 2009.

77. Avery Palmer, "Waxman Reaches Deal on Emissions," *CQ Today*, May 12, 2009.

78. Ian Talley and Stephen Power, "House Panel Clears Plan to Cut Greenhouse Gases," *Wall Street Journal*, May 22, 2009. See also Jared Allen, "Cap-and-trade Showdown," *Hill*, May 20, 2009; Steven T. Dennis, "A Big Thaw for Climate Change," *Roll Call*, May 14, 2009; Avery Palmer, "Democrats Line Up behind Energy Bill," *CQ Today*, May 18, 2009.

79. Massachusetts et al. v. Environmental Protection Agency et al., 05-1120, 415 F. 3rd 50, April 2, 2007.

80. Jared Allen, "Pelosi Takes Reins on Climate Change," *Hill*, June 2, 2009; Vicki Needham, "Chairmen Plot Moves on Climate Bill," *Roll Call*, June 8, 2009; Jennifer Bendery, "Peterson: Democrats at Impass over Climate Change," *Roll Call*, June 10, 2009; Jared Allen, "Dem Mutiny on Climate Bill Grows, Says Peterson," *Hill*, June 10, 2009.

81. Jared Allen and Molly K. Hooper, "Climate Change Vote: Pelosi's Green Gamble," *Hill*, June 24, 2009. On the structure/policy trade-off see Terry Moe, "The Politics of Bureaucratic Structure," in John E. Chubb and Paul E. Peterson, *Can the Government Govern?* (Washington, D.C.: Brookings Institution, 1989), 267-314. For an explana-

tion of carbon offsets see: Jonathan L. Ramseur, *CRS Reports* "Voluntary Carbon Offsets: Overview and Assessment," Congressional Research Service, November 7, 2007, http://assets.opencrs.com/rpts/RL34241_20071107.pdf.

82. Patrick O'Connor and Glen Thrush, "Chaos and Arm-twisting Gave Pelosi Win," *Politico*, June 30, 2009, http://www.politico.com/news/stories/0609/24364.html. See also: Ronald Brownstein, "House Dems Hang Together on Climate Bill," *National Journal*, July 4, 2009; Richard E. Cohen and Brian Friei, "The Big Lift," *National Journal*, July 4, 2009, pp. 24–31; Carol Davenport and Avery Palmer, "A Landmark Climate Bill Passes," *CQ Weekly*, June 29, 2009, pp. 1516–1517.

83. John M. Broder, "House Passes Bill to Address Threat of Climate Change," *New York Times*, June 26, 2009. Press accounts indicated that Pelosi was surprised by the defection of four Democrats who had been expected to vote in favor—four more entries for her mental ledger.

84. Jared Allen and Mike Soraghan, "Climate Bill Pelosi's Biggest Triumph Yet," *Roll Call*, June 26, 2009; Lisa Lerer and Patrick O'Connor, "House Passes Climate Change Bill," *Politico*, June 26, 2009, http://www.politico.com/news/stories/0609/24232.html.

85. Steven T. Dennis, "Blue Dogs Jump on Health Care," *Roll Call*, May 13, 2009; Jeffrey Young and Jared Allen, "Blue Dogs Bare Teeth on Health Care," *Hill*, May 12, 2009; Robert Pear, "45 Centrist Democrats Protest Secrecy of Health Care Talks," *New York Times*, May 12, 2009.

86. Susan T. Dennis and David M. Drucker, "Democratic Health Care Deals Far from Sealed," *Roll Call*, July 30, 2009; Mike Soraghan, "Liberals Strike Healthcare Deal with Blue Dogs," *Hill*, July 31, 2009; David Shalleck-Klein, "House Panel Approves Healthcare Reform Bill, *Hill*, July 31, 2009.

87. See Ceci Connolly, "Kennedy Readies Health-care Bill," *Washington Post*, June 6, 2009; John Harwood, "Bipartisan Health Care Bill Is Possible, Leaders Say," *New York Times*, June 8, 2009; Alexander Bolton, "Baucus to Chop $600 Billion from Healthcare Bill," *Hill*, June 17, 2009.

88. See Jeffrey Young, "Dems Reel on Healthcare," *Hill*, June 16, 2009; David M. Drucker, "Health Care Bipartisanship Fades," *Roll Call*, June 17, 2009; CBO Director Douglas Elmendorf to Senator Edward M. Kennedy, July 2, 2009, http://www.cbo.gov/ftpdocs/104xx/doc10431/07–02-HELPltr.pdf.

89. Sheryl Gay Stolberg, "Obama to Forge a Greater Role on Health Care," *New York Times*, June 7, 2009; Sheryl Gay Stolberg and Robert Pear, "Obama Takes His Health Care Case to the Public," *New York Times*, June 12, 2009; Michael A. Fletcher and Shailagh Murray, "Obama Stumps for Health-care Reform," *Washington Post*, June 12, 2009; Alexander Bolton, "Pelosi Rejects Proposal to Skirt Government Healthcare," *Hill*, June 11, 2009; Patrick O'Connor and Chris Frates, "Dems Double Down on Health Care," *Politico*, June 10, 2009, http://www.politico.com/news/stories/0609/23560.

90. Jared Allen and Jeffrey Young, "Dems Launch Augusts Healthcare Defense," *Hill*, July 30, 2009; Alex Isenstadt, "As Recess Begins, the Heat Is On," *Politico*, August

3, 2009, http://www.politico.com/news/stories/0809/25719.html; Kate Ackley and Anna Palmer, "Recess Ads to Flow Freely," *Roll Call*, August 4, 2009.

91. John Kraushaar and Lisa Leher, "Health Care Town Hall Anger Rages On," *Politico*, August 14, 2009, http://www.politico.com/news/stories/0809/26049.html.

92. All of the survey results reported in this paragraph are available at http://www.gallup.com/tag/Congress.aspx.

93. Alex Isenstadt and Martin Kady II, "House Dems Plot Health Care Comeback," *Politico*, August 21, 2009, http://dyn.politico.com/printstory.cfm?uuid=7308622C-18FE-70B2-A8249CF156137AF8; Carl Hulse, "Conservative Democrats Expect a Health Deal," *The New York Times*, September 2, 2009; Tory Newmyer and Steven T. Dennis, "Key Liberals Willing to Bargain," *Roll Call*, September 8, 2009; Tory Newmeyer and Steven T. Dennis, "Democrats Still Seek Unity," *Roll Call*, September 8, 2009; Sheryl Gay Stolberg, "Despite Fears, Health Care Overhaul Is Moving Ahead," *The New York Times*, September 9, 2009.

94. Pew Research Center for the People and the Press, "Mixed Views of Economic Policies and Health Care Reform Persist," October 8, 2009, http://people-press.org/report/551/.

95. Jared Allen and Mike Soraghan, "Pelosi Chooses Healthcare Bill With Public Option Favored by Centrists," *Hill*, October 28, 2009.

96. Stephen T. Dennis and Jennifer Bendery, "House OK's Stupak Anti-Abortion Amendment," *Roll Call*, November 7, 2009.

97. Lori Montgomery and Shailagh Murray, "House Democrats Pass Health Care Bill," *Washington Post*, November 8, 2009.

98. "David Rogers, "'I'm Not Big on Showing Weakness," *Politico*, October 30, 2009, http://www.politico.com/news/stories/1009/28919.html.

99. Patrick O'Connor and John Bresnehan, "Tears, Tempers Fly in Pelosi Campaign," *Politico*, November 8, 2009, http://www.politico.com/news/stories/1109/29305.html.

100. Quotes in this paragraph are from: Jonathan Allen, "Speaker Pelosi Wins the Day," *Politico*, November 8, 2009, http://www.politico.com/news/stories/1109/29281_Page2.html.

101. Speaker Nancy Pelosi, "Pelosi Remarks at Press Conference Following Passage of the Affordable Health Care for America Act," Speaker.house.gov/.

102. The options available to the Senate were these. First, it might refuse to act on health care reform. Second, it might pass a Senate-originated bill and go to conference with the House. Third, it might take the House bill and amend it. Fourth, it might take a non-related House bill and replace its contents with the Senate version of health care. These options carried different strategic implications. Assuming that the Senate would pass something, it might prefer to ping-pong the House bill rather than suffer a potentially divisive conference. The fourth option, of packaging the Senate legislation in a House-passed bill would put the House in the position of either voting on the Senate bill or amending it, beginning the ping-pong process. The pressure to

simply vote on the Senate version of health care, presumed at the time of this writing to be more centrist than the House-passed bill, would be enormous. This possibility illustrates a centrist critique of Pelosi's leadership that we develop in chapter 7, "Too Liberal?" By pushing through on a narrow margin a bill too liberal to pass in the Senate, Pelosi puts the Senate in the driver's seat. We assess this claim in chapter 7.

103. O'Conner and Frates, "Dems Double Down," op. cit. n. 89.

CHAPTER 6

1. The three chapter epigraphs are from, respectively, Nancy Pelosi, *Know Your Power: A Message to America's Daughters* (New York: Random House, 2008), 75; quotation of Pelosi in Richard Cohen, "The Race for No. 2," *National Journal*, September 2001, 2923; quotation of Pelosi in Mike Allen and Alexander Burns, "Pelosi Says Polls Shortchange Obama," *Politico*, August 26, 2008, www.politico.com/news/stories/0808/12839_Page2.html (accessed January 25, 2009).

2. Jennifer L. Lawless and Richard L. Fox, *It Takes a Candidate: Why Women Don't Run for Office* (Cambridge: Cambridge University Press, 2005); Linda Witt, Karen M. Paget, and Glenna Matthews, *Running as a Woman: Gender and Power in American Politics* (New York: Free Press, 1994).

3. Mark Kann, *The Gendering of American Politics: Founding Mothers, Founding Fathers, and Political Patriarchy* (Westport, Conn.: Praeger, 1999).

4. Jeane Kirkpatrick, *Political Woman* (New York: Basic Books, 1974); Witt et al., *Running as a Woman*.

5. Timothy Bledsoe and Mary Herring, "Victims of Circumstances: Women in Pursuit of Political Office," *American Political Science Review* 84, 1 (1990): 213–23; Lawless and Fox, *It Takes a Candidate*, chap. 2.

6. Lawless and Fox, *It Takes a Candidate*; Cynthia Enloe, *The Curious Feminist* (Berkeley: University of California Press, 2004), 4–5; Jo Freeman, *A Room at a Time: How Women Entered Party Politics* (Lanham, Md.: Rowman and Littlefield, 2000); Georgia Duerst-Lahti, "Knowing Congress as a Gendered Institution: Manliness and the Implications of Women in Congress," in Cindy Simon Rosenthal, ed., *Women Transforming Congress* (Norman: University of Oklahoma Press, 2002).

7. Lawless and Fox, *It Takes a Candidate*, 149, credit data provided by Harvard University professor David King. See also David E. Campbell and Christina Wolbrecht, "See Jane Run: Women Politicians as Role Models for Adolescents," *Journal of Politics* 68 (May 2006): 233–47.

8. Joseph Schlesinger, *Ambition and Politics* (Chicago: Rand McNally, 1966), 10.

9. Rebekah Herrick and Michael K. Moore, "Political Ambition's Effect on Legislative Behavior: Schlesinger's Typology Reconsidered and Revised," *Journal of Politics* 55, 3 (1993): 765–76.

10. Lawless and Fox, *It Takes a Candidate*, 81.

11. Cindy Simon Rosenthal, "Climbing Higher: Opportunities and Obstacles within the Party System," in Beth Reingold, ed., *Legislative Women: Getting Elected, Getting Ahead* (Boulder, Colo.: Lynne Rienner, 2008).

12. The shift in focus from gender differences among individuals to gender as a feature of organizations and institutions is evident in the work of Joan Acker, "Gendered Institutions: From Sex Roles to Gendered Institutions," *Contemporary Society* 21, 4 (1992): 565–69; Sally Kenney, "New Research on Gendered Political Institutions," *Political Research Quarterly* 49, 2 (June 1996): 445–66; Georgia Duerst-Lahti and Rita Mae Kelly, eds., *Gender Power, Leadership, and Governance* (Ann Arbor: University of Michigan Press, 1995); Duerst-Lahti, "Knowing Congress as a Gendered Institution."

13. Irwin Gertzog, *Women and Power on Capitol Hill: Reconstructing the Congressional Women's Caucus* (Boulder, Colo.: Lynne Rienner, 2004), 42–43.

14. Alice H. Eagly and Linda L. Carli, *Through the Labyrinth: The Truth about How Women Become Leaders* (Boston: Harvard Business School Press, 2007).

15. Kathleen Hall Jamieson, *Beyond the Double Bind: Women and Leadership* (Oxford: Oxford University Press, 1995).

16. Ofer Feldman and Christ'l De Landtsheer, eds., "Epilogue: Where Do We Stand?" *Politically Speaking: A Worldwide Examination of Language Used in the Public Sphere* (Westport, Conn.: Praeger, 1998), 195.

17. Regina Lawrence and Melody Rose, "Playing the Gender Card? Media, Strategy, and Hillary Clinton's Campaign for the Presidency," paper presented at the annual meeting of the American Political Science Association, Boston, August 28–31, 2008.

18. Pelosi credits Congresswoman Lindy Boggs for the advice "Never fight a fight as if it's your last one"; *Know Your Power*, 148.

19. Schlesinger, *Ambition and Politics*, 8.

20. Virginia Sapiro, "Private Costs of Public Commitments or Public Costs of Private Commitments? Family Roles versus Political Ambition," *American Journal of Political Science* 26, 2 (1982): 245–79.

21. Bledsoe and Herring, "Victims of Circumstances."

22. Kira Sanbonmatsu, *Where Women Run* (Ann Arbor: University of Michigan Press, 2006).

23. Lawless and Fox, *It Takes a Candidate*, 81.

24. Nancy Woloch, *Women and the American Experience* (New York: McGraw-Hill, 1984), 78.

25. Irwin Gertzog, "Women's Changing Pathways to the U.S. House of Representatives: Widows, Elites, and Strategic Politicians," in Rosenthal, *Women Transforming Congress*, pp. 95–118.

26. Witt et al., *Running as a Woman*, 33.

27. This number does not include U.S. Senator Olympia Snowe, who succeeded her late husband in the Maine state legislature and then went onto a congressional career.

28. Gertzog, "Women's Changing Pathways," 102.

29. Ibid.
30. Hope Chamberlin, *A Minority of Members: Women in the U.S. Congress* (New York: Praeger, 1973), 76–81.
31. Witt et al., *Running as a Woman*, 33.
32. Ibid., 106.
33. Gertzog, "Women's Changing Pathways," 102–10.
34. This extensive literature on strategic politicians includes the initial work of Gary Jacobsen, "Strategic Politicians and the Dynamics of House Elections," *American Political Science Review* 83 (January 1989): 773–93; David R. Mayhew, *Congress and the Electoral Connection* (New Haven: Yale University Press, 1974). Other contributors to this literature include, among others, Schlesinger, *Ambition and Politics*; Jonathan S. Krasno and Donald Phillip Green, "Preempting Quality Challengers," *Journal of Politics* 50, 4 (November 1988): 920–36; Jon R. Bond, Cary Covington, and Richard Fleisher, "Explaining Challenger Quality in Congressional Elections," *Journal of Politics* 47, 2 (June 1985): 510–29; L. Sandy Maisel and Walter J. Stone, "Determinants of Candidate Emergence in U.S. House Elections: An Explanatory Study," *Legislative Studies Quarterly* 22, 1 (February 1979): 79–96; and Gary F. Moncrief, "Recruitment and Retention in U.S. Legislatures," *Legislative Studies Quarterly* 24, 2 (1999): 173–208.
35. Gertzog, "Women's Changing Pathways," 107.
36. In addition to the sources identified in note 38, several scholars have made special note of the role of gender in ambition, for example, Linda L. Fowler and Robert D. McClure, *Political Ambition: Who Decides to Run for Congress* (New Haven: Yale University Press, 1990); Robert Biersack and Paul S. Hernnson, "Political Parties and the Year of the Woman," in Elizabeth Adell Cook, Sue Thomas, and Clyde Wilcox, eds., *The Year of the Woman: Myths and Realities* (Boulder, Colo.: Westview Press, 1994), p. 161–180; John M. Carey, Richard G. Niemi, and Lynda W. Powell, "Are Women State Legislators Different?" in Sue Thomas and Clyde Wilcox, eds., *Women and Elective Office: Past, Present, and Future* (New York: Oxford University Press, 1998), 87–102.
37. Lawless and Fox, *It Takes a Candidate*, 28–32.
38. Ibid.; Gary Moncrief, Peverill Squire, and Malcolm E. Jewell, *Who Runs for the Legislature?* (Upper Saddle River, N.J.: Prentice Hall, 2001).
39. Marcia Lee, "Why Few Women Hold Public Office," in Marianne Githens and Jewell Prestage, eds., *Portrait of Marginality* (New York: Longman Inc., 1977), 131.
40. Lawless and Fox, *It Takes a Candidate*, 148–49.
41. Speaker Nancy Pelosi, "Just for Kids," video, www.speaker.gov/kids/ (accessed January 25, 2009).
42. Pelosi, *Know Your Power*, 55–56; John Jacobs, *A Rage for Justice: The Passion and Politics of Phillip Burton* (Berkeley: University of California Press, 1995), 446.
43. Pelosi, *Know Your Power*, 70.
44. Nancy Pelosi, "Remarks at a Democratic Women's Forum," Federal News Service, January 3, 2007, www.lexisnexis.com/us/lnacademic/results/docview/docview.

do?docLinkInd=true&risb=21_T5605430779&format=GNBFI&sort=RELEVANC
E&startDocNo=1&resultsUrlKey=29_T5605430782&cisb=22_T5605430781&tree
Max=true&treeWidth=0&csi=8104&docNo=1.

45. While the definition of "quality candidate" has evolved over time, officeholding remains a key characteristic. The definition of quality candidates as those having held prior office was first coined by Gary Jacobson and Samuel Kernell; see Gary Jacobson and Samuel Kernell, *Strategy and Choice in Congressional Elections* (New Haven: Yale University Press, 1981). Jonathon S. Krasno, and Donald Philip Green advocated a more sophisticated measure of candidate quality, including a variety of factors to assess the quality of those not holding office, e.g. professional status, political party activity, holding certain nonelective posts. See Gary Jacobson and Samuel Kernell, "Preempting Quality Challengers in House Elections," *Journal of Politics* 50 (1988): 920–36. Others have argued for an understanding of candidate quality that certainly includes factors Nancy Pelosi brought to the table in her first election. For example, L. Sandy Maisel, Walter J. Stone, and Cherie Maestas found that prior officeholding has an indirect effect on predicting electoral success and that strategic resources such as national party support and fund-raising potential are also important. See Maisel, Stone, and Maestas, "Reassessing the Definition of Quality Candidates," paper presented to the annual meeting of the Midwest Political Science Association, Chicago, April 15–17, 1999.

46. As we saw in chapter 2, Pelosi did not capture all of Burton's supporters. She had less support among gays and organized labor than Burton typically received.

47. Mark Z. Barabak, "Triumph of the 'Airhead,'" *Los Angeles Times Magazine*, January 26, 2003, 12.

48. Victoria Schuck, "Women in Political Science: Some Preliminary Observations," *PS: Political Science and Politics* 2, 4 (1969): 642–53.

49. Elaine Povich, *Nancy Pelosi: A Biography* (Westport, Conn.: Greenwood Press, 2008), 11.

50. Schuck, "Women in Political Science," 642.

51. Research on coeducational settings includes E. Arms and K. Herr, "Accountability and Single Sex Schooling: A Collision of Reform Agendas," *American Educational Research Journal* 41, 3 (2004): 527–55; D. G. Smith, "Women's Colleges and Coed Colleges: Is There a Difference for Women?," *Journal of Higher Education* 61, 2 (1990): 181–97. For insight into Catholic school educational advantages, see D. Neal, "The Effects of Catholic Secondary Schooling on Educational Achievement," *Journal of Labor Economics* 15, 1 (1997): 98–123.

52. Ruth Mandel, *In the Running: The New American Woman Candidate* (Boston: Beacon Press, 1981), 90.

53. Witt et al., *Running as a Woman*, 138.

54. Ibid., chap. 4.

55. Lawless and Fox, *It Takes a Candidate*, 148.

56. Jamieson, *Beyond the Double Bind*.

57. Pelosi, *Know Your Power,* 42–43.

58. Howell Raines, "Unionists Accused of Sexism in a Race to Lead Democrats," *New York Times,* January 28, 1985.

59. Witt et al., *Running as a Woman,* chap. 1.

60. Ibid., 82.

61. Richard F. Fenno, Jr., *Congressmen in Committees* (Boston: Little, Brown, 1973).

62. Kenney, "New Research on Gendered Political Institutions"; Duerst-Lahti and Kelly, *Gender Power, Leadership, and Governance.*

63. The notion of a glass ceiling was first coined in the mid-1980s by Fortune 500 business consultant Alice Sargent to denote an invisible barrier above which women's careers rarely ascended. "Sticky floor" refers to the predominance of female-dominated professions and jobs at the lowest pay levels. Rosabeth Moss Kanter, *Men and Women of the Corporation* (New York: Basic Books, 1977), notes that dead-end jobs might appear to have opportunities for promotion and advancement, but rarely to the top of the corporate ladder; for example, women who opt for community relations or personnel specializations cannot compete with men who travel career paths in finance or operations. The "mommy track" describes the more recent phenomenon of women (and the rare men) who voluntarily opt for less demanding work schedules in order to accommodate family obligations.

64. Michele L. Swers, *The Difference Women Make: The Policy Impact of Women in Congress* (Chicago: University of Chicago Press, 2002). African-American males have clearly benefited from their longer service, now chairing the House Ways and Means, Oversight, and Judiciary Committees.

65. In 2008, the number of women chairing full committees dropped to two when Representative Stephanie Tubbs Jones (D-OH) died. She had chaired the Committee on Ethics. Representative Louise Slaughter (D-NY), who was first elected to the House in 1986, chairs the Rules Committee, and Representative Nydia Velasquez (D-NY), who was elected to the House in 1992, chairs the Committee on Small Business.

66. Rebekah Herrick, "Seniority and Lost Power of Female House Members," paper presented at the Annual Meeting of the Midwest Political Science Association, Chicago, 2000.

67. While seniority earned former Representative Nancy Johnson (R-CT) clout as Ways and Means Health Subcommittee chair, her moderate politics limited her influence in the caucus. Representative Marge Roukema (R-NJ) fell short in her bid to become the first woman to chair a major House committee at the start of the 107th Congress, even though GOP term limits created the opportunity for her to secure a committee chair on the basis of her seniority. Representative Roukema, a moderate who is fiercely independent, lost out to Representative Michael Oxley (R-OH) in seeking appointment as chair of the Financial Services Committee.

68. Kanter, *Men and Women of the Corporation.*

69. Janice D. Yoder, "Rethinking Tokenism: Looking beyond Numbers," *Gender and Society* 5, 2 (June 1991): 178–92. Lyn Kathlene, "Power and Influence in State Legislative Policy-Making: The Interaction of Gender and Position in Committee Hearing Debates," *American Political Science Review* 88, 3 (1994): 560–76.

70. Rosenthal, "Climbing Higher."

71. Barbara Sinclair, *Party Wars* (Norman: University of Oklahoma Press, 2006).

72. Swers, *Difference Women Make*, 23.

73. Barbara Palmer and Dennis Simon, *Breaking the Political Glass Ceiling: Women and Congressional Elections* (New York: Routledge Press, 2006).

74. David B. Truman, *The Congressional Party: A Case Study* (New York: Wiley, 1959).

75. Douglas B. Harris and Garrison Nelson, "Middlemen No More: Emergent Patterns in Congressional Leadership Selection," *PS* 10, 1 (2008): 43–46.

76. Pat Schroeder, *24 Years of Housework…and the Place Is Still a Mess* (Kansas City: Andrews McMeel Publishing 1998). Barbara Boxer (with Nicole Boxer), *Strangers in the Senate* (Bethesda, Md.: National Press Books, 1994). Rosenthal, *Women Transforming Congress*; Karen Foerstel, *Biographical Dictionary of Congressional Women* (Westport, Conn.: Greenwood Press, 1999).

77. Barbara Mikulski, Kay Bailey Hutchison, Dianne Feinstein, Barbara Boxer, Patty Murray, Olympia Snowe, Susan Collins, Mary Landrieu, Blanche L. Lincoln, and Catherine Whitney, *Nine and Counting: The Women of the Senate* (New York: HarperCollins, 2000), 43.

78. Foerstel, *Biographical Dictionary of Congressional Women*, 245.

79. Foerstel, *Biographical Dictionary of Congressional Women*, 8.

80. Jessica Valenti, "Girl Politicians have Cooties," *Huffington Post*, November 12, 2006, www.huffingtonpost.com/jessica-valenti/girl-politicians-have-coo_b_33947.html (accessed January 25, 2009).

81. Jamieson, *Beyond the Double Bind*.

82. Interview with Meredith Vierra on the *Today Show*, www.msnbc.msn.com/id/21134540/vp/25884372#25884372 (accessed January 25, 2009).

83. John Jacobs, "Not Just a Party Girl," Image sec., *San Francisco Chronicle*, July 12, 1992.

84. Of course her opponent, Steny Hoyer, was also a member of the Appropriations Committee, enabling him to forge alliances as well.

85. Eleanor Clift, "Capitol Letter: Pelosi Power," *Newsweek*, 5 October 2001.

86. Harris and Nelson, "Middlemen No More".

87. Clift, "Pelosi Power."

88. Richard Cohen, "Race for No. 2."

89. Spencer S. Hsu, "Once More, Hoyer Aims for the Top," *Washington Post*, October 7, 2001.

90. Ibid.

91. Marc Sandalow, "Rep. Pelosi Aims to Become Top Woman in the House," *San Francisco Chronicle*, October 13, 1999.

92. Rosenthal, "Climbing Higher."

93. Carl Hulse, "House Democrats Seeking Leader to End Losing Trend," *New York Times*, November 8, 2002.

94. We explore these dimensions of Pelosi's persona further in Cindy Simon Rosenthal and Ronald M. Peters, Jr., "Who Is Nancy Pelosi?," *PS* 41, 1 (January 2008): 57–62.

95. Debra Dodson, *The Impact of Women in Congress* (Oxford: Oxford University Press, 2006), chap. 5.

96. Ibid., 116.

97. "Gender Stereotypes and Discussions of Armani Suits Dominate Media's Coverage of Speaker-elect Pelosi," *Media Matters for America*, November 20, 2006, http://mediamatters.org/ (accessed January 25, 2009).

98. "Yet Again, Media Figures Respond to a Pelosi Controversy with Attacks on Her Looks," *Media Matters for America*. May 18, 2009, http://mediamatters.org/research/200905180006 (accessed June 10, 2009.)

99. "Schultz Highlights Attacks on Nancy Pelosi's Looks," *MSNBC*, May 18, 2009, *Media Matters for America*, http://mediamatters.org/mmtv/200905180034 (accessed June 10, 2009.)

100. National Republican Congressional Committee, "Pelosi Knows Better, Slams McChrystal," October 6, 2009, accessed at http://nrcc.org/news/read.aspx.?id=863; Michael O'Brien, "Democrats decry Republican Party as sexist, out of touch and 'extreme,'" *Hill*, October 7, 2009, accessed at http://thehill.com/homenews/house/62157-democrats-decry-gop-as-sexist-out-of-touch-and-extreme-; and Glenn Thrush, "Dem: House GOP is "80 percent male, 100 percent white," *Hill*, October 6, 2009, accessed at http://www.politico.com/blogs/glennthrush/1009/GOP_urges_general_to_put_Pelosi_in_her_place.html.

101. "Savage Makes Degrading Comments about House Speaker, Other Prominent Dem Women," *Media Matters for America*, December 14, 2007, http://mediamatters.org/ (accessed January 25, 2009).

102. DeLauro was herself the beneficiary of a seniority skip to become chair of the Appropriations Subcommittee on Agriculture, Rural Development, Food and Drug Administration, and Related Agencies. She bypassed Congresswoman Marcy Kaptur, one-time Pelosi leadership rival, suggesting that more than gender was at play. Kaptur, however, was compensated with a seat on the Appropriations Subcommittee on Defense, becoming the first woman to have a seat on that panel.

103. By the end of the 110th Congress, the number of women chairing full committees had dropped to two with the deaths of Stephanie Tubbs Jones and Juanita Millender-McDonald.

104. We utilize the same categorization of subcommittees as women's issue subcommittees as developed by Michele Swers, *The Difference Women Make* (Chicago: University of Chicago Press, 2002).

105. Jane Blankenship and Deborah Robson, "A 'Feminine Style' in Women's Political Discourse: An Exploratory Essay," *Communication Quarterly* 43 (1995): 353–66, as quoted in Molly A. Mayhead and Brenda Devore Marshall, *Women's Political*

Discourse: A Twenty-first-century Perspective (Lanham, Md.: Rowman and Littlefield, 2005), 16.

106. Jamieson, *Beyond the Double-Bind;* see also Kathlene, "Power and Influence in State Legislative Policy-Making."

107. Witt et al., *Running as a Woman;* Jamieson, *Beyond the Double Bind.*

108. See, for example, Charlotte Krolokke and Anne Scott Sorensen, *Gender Communication Theories and Analyses: From Silence to Performance* (London: Sage, 2006); Julie Dolan and Jonathan S. Kropf, "Credit Claiming from the U.S. House: Gendered Communication Styles?" *International Journal of Press/Politics* 9, 41 (2004): 41–59; Blankenship and Robson, "'Feminine Style' in Women's Political Discourse"; Colleen J. Shogan, "Speaking Out: An Analysis of Democratic and Republican Woman-invoked Rhetoric in the 105th Congress," *Women and Politics* 23, 1 (2002): 129–46.

109. Kathleen A. Dolan, *Voting for Women: How the Public Evaluates Women Candidates* (Boulder, Colo.: Westview Press, 2004); Richard Seltzer, Jody Newman, and Melissa Leighton, *Sex as Political Variable* (Boulder, Colo.: Lynne Rienner, 1997); and Barbara C. Burrell, *A Woman's Place Is in the House* (Ann Arbor: University of Michigan Press, 1996).

110. Witt et al., *Running as a Woman,* 214.

111. Susan Carroll, "Representing Women: Congresswomen's Perceptions of Their Representational Roles," in Rosenthal, *Women Transforming Congress,* 50–68.

112. Quoted in Witt et al., *Running as a Woman,* 271.

113. Susan Molinari, "Keynote Address," *Extensions* (spring 2000), 11.

114. Karen Kedrowski, "Gender and the Public Speakership: News Media Coverage of Speaker Nancy Pelosi," paper presented at the annual meeting of the Southern Political Science Association, New Orleans, January 7–10, 2009.

115. Liz Cox Barrett, "A Girl's Got the Gavel! But What's She Wearing?" *Columbia Journalism Review,* January 24, 2007, http://www.cjr.org/behind_the_news/a_girls_got_the_gavel_but_what.php.

116. Lizette Alvarez, "Speaking Chic to Power," *New York Times,* January 18, 2007.

117. Ibid.

118. Robin Givhan, "Muted Tones of Quiet Authority: A Look Suited to the Speaker," *Washington Post,* November 10, 2006.

119. "Luntz on Pelosi: 'You Get One Shot at a Facelift. If It Doesn't Work the First Time, Let It Go,'" *Media Matters for America,* November 1, 2006, http://mediamatters.org/ (accessed January 25, 2009).

120. "Gender Stereotypes and Discussions of Armani Suits Dominate Media's Coverage of Speaker-elect Pelosi," *Media Matters for America,* November 20, 2006, http:// mediamatters.org/ (accessed January 25, 2009).

121. Vincent Bzdek, *Woman of the House* (New York: Palgrave MacMillan, 2008), 230.

122. Linda Campbell, "What Will Pelosi Do?" *Fort Worth Star-Telegram,* January 5, 2007.

123. Ethan Wallison, "The Nancy I Knew," *Real Clear Politics*, September 29, 2006, http://www.realclearpolitics.com/articles/2006/11/the_nancy_i_knew.html.

124. Povich, *Nancy Pelosi*, 142.

125. Nancy Pelosi, "Speech upon Being Elected Speaker of the House for the 110th Congress," January 4, 2007, www.speaker.gov/newsroom/speeches?id=0006.

126. Nancy Pelosi, "Pelosi: Our Nation Needs Action and We Need Action Now," January 26, 2009, www.speaker.gov/newsroom/speeches?id=0155.

127. The coding scheme comprised three dimensions: a style dimension that involved judgments about direct or indirect rhetoric and speech structure; a content dimension that required judgments about confrontational and competitive statements or conciliatory or facilitative comments; and a relationship dimension that involved judgments about references to others in a collaborative or autonomous approach. Coders were trained until a satisfactory degree of intercoder reliability was obtained. Only two coders were involved in the project: a graduate student and one of the coauthors.

128. Ronald M. Peters Jr. and Cindy Simon Rosenthal, "Assessing Nancy Pelosi," *The Forum.* 2008, volume 6, issue 3, accessed at: http://www.bepress.com/forum. For further discussion of congressional leadership theory see below, chapter 7, "Congressional Leadership in Theory."

CHAPTER 7

1. Seth A. Rosenthal; Todd L. Pittinsky; Sadie Moore; Jennifer J. Ratcliff; Laura A. Maruskin; Claire R. Gravelin, 2008-12-17, "National Leadership Index 2008", Harvard Kennedy School Center for Public Leadership, hdl:1902.1/12296, http://content.ksg.harvard.edu/leadership/index.php?option=com_content&task=view&id=413&Itemid=98.

2. Shawn Zeller, "Parties Dig in Deep on a Fractured Hill," *CQ Weekly*, December 15, 2008, 3338.

3. Barbara Sinclair, *Legislators, Leaders, and Lawmaking* (Baltimore: Johns Hopkins Press, 1998).

4. James MacGregor Burns, *Leadership* (New York: Harper, 1982).

5. Gary W. Cox and Matthew D. McCubbins, *Legislative Leviathan* (New York: Cambridge University Press, 2007).

6. Joseph Cooper and David W. Brady, "Institutional Context and Leadership Style: The House from Cannon to Rayburn," *American Political Science Review* 75 (1981): 411–25.

7. Matthew N. Green, "Presidents and Personal Goals: The Speaker of the House as Non-majoritarian Leader," *Congress and the Presidency* 34, 2 (autumn 2007): 1–22; Randall Strahan, *Leading Representatives* (Baltimore: Johns Hopkins University Press, 2007).

8. Cindy Simon Rosenthal, *When Women Lead* (New York: Oxford University Press, 1998).

9. Daniel Palazzolo, "Evaluating Majority Party Leaders in Congress," *Forum* 6, 3 (2008), www.bepress.com/forum/vol6/iss3/art1/.

10. Sarah A. Binder, Thomas E. Mann, Norman J. Ornstein, and Molly Reynolds, "Assessing the 110th Congress, Anticipating the 111th," *Mending the Broken Branch* 3 (January 2009): 8, www.brookings.edu/~/media/Files/rc/papers/2009/0108_broken_branch_binder_mann/0108_broken_branch_binder_mann.pdf (accessed January 23, 2009).

11. Barbara Sinclair, *Unorthodox Lawmaking* (Washington, D.C.: CQ Press, 2007).

12. Dennis Hastert, Remarks at Cannon Centennial Conference, Washington, D.C., November 3, 2003.

13. Jared Allen, "Panel Chairmen Fighting Mad over Snubs by Pelosi," *Hill*, January 15, 2009.

14. As reported by Pollingreport.com, www.pollingreport.com/P.htm (accessed November 7, 2008).

15. *Real Clear Politics* reported the following congressional job approval ratings in November 2008: Gallup 19%; Associated Press GfK 21%; Fox News 18%; CBS-New York Times 15%; George Washington University-Battleground 19%. The average was 18.4%. www.realclearpolitics.com/polls/archive/?poll_id=18 (accessed December 5, 2008).

16. Dianna Heitz, "Congressional Approval Ratings Rise," *Politico*, March 12, 2009, http://www.politico.com/news/stories/0309/19935.html reporting on the Gallup Poll conducted March 5–8, 2009. Glenn Thrush, "Congressional Approval Skyrockets," *Politico*, February 17, 2009, http://www.politico.com/blogs/glenn-thrush/0209/Congressional_Dem_approval_more_than_doubles. Pelosi's various approval ratings can be accessed at PollingReport.com. That of House Democrats was accessed at RealClearPolitics.com.

17. Lydia Saad, "Both Parties in Congress Near Record-Low Approval," *Gallup Poll*, September 17, 2009, http://www.gallup.com/poll/123011/Parties-Congress-Near-Record-Low-Approval.aspx?.

18. *Realclearpolitics*, "Generic Congressional Vote," accessed October 15, 2009 at http://www.realclearpolitics.com/epolls/other/generic_congressional_vote-901.html. A generic ballot poll asks respondents if, voting today, they would choose a generic Democratic or Republican to represent them in the House of Representatives. *Realclearpolitics* averages the responses to the generic ballot question. An average of survey results is, of course, non-scientific, but if each of the surveys included in the average are scientifically conducted the average result may be taken as approximating public attitudes on the question asked if the surveys are taken within a narrow space of time, here the first week in October, 2009.

19. *NBC-Wall Street Journal* survey reported by *Pollingreport.com*, "Speaker Nancy Pelosi," accessed October 15, 2009 at http://www.pollingreport.com/p.htm#Pelosi. The figures we report combine responses of "very positive" and "somewhat positive"

as approval, and responses of "very negative" and "somewhat negative" as disapproval. See also, reporting on *NBC-Wall Street Journal* poll by David Rogers, "Nancy Pelosi's lesson: 'You can't always get what you want', *Politico*, October 30, 2009, accessed at http://www.politico.com/news/stories/1009/28919_Page2.html.

20. Naftali Bendavid, "Pelosi Key to GOP 2010 Playbook," *The Wall Street Journal*, October 12, 2009.

21. Attacking Pelosi is one way Republican House leaders nurture support in the Republican Conference. See Jackie Kucinich, "Pelosi Slip Fuels Boehner Surge," *Roll Call*, June 18, 2009.

22. Sarah Wildman, "Power Walker," *Washington Post Magazine*, May 3, 2009, http://www.washingtonpost.com/wp-srv/artsandliving/magazine/features/2009/fitness/pelosi.html, accessed October 24, 2009.

23. Newt Gingrich, interview with Ronald M. Peters, Jr., Atlanta, GA, July 4, 1996.

24. As one illustration, the initial leadership campaigns of Speakers Wright, Foley, and Gingrich lasted only a few weeks. Hastert's occupied a few hours one afternoon. Pelosi's campaign for Democratic whip lasted three years.

25. This point is taken from Ronald M. Peters, Jr., and Cindy Simon Rosenthal, "Assessing Nancy Pelosi," *Forum* 6, 3 (2008), www.bepress.com/forum/vol6/iss3/art5/ (accessed January 23, 2009).

26. Dennis Hastert, interview with Ronald M. Peters, Jr., Washington, D.C., March 21, 2001.

27. Office of Speaker Nancy Pelosi Fact Sheet, October 9, 2008, Speaker.House.gov.

28. Charles O. Jones, *The Presidency in a Separated System* (Washington, D.C.: Brookings Institution, 1994), 19–23.

29. The quotation in the epigraph is from Fareed Zakaria, "How to Get Back to Growth," *Newsweek*, June 7, 2008.

30. Malcolm Gladwell, *Outliers: The Story of Success* (New York: Little, Brown, Company, 2009).

BIBLIOGRAPHY

Acker, Joan. "Gendered Institutions: From Sex Roles to Gendered Institutions." *Contemporary Society* 21, 4 (1992): 565–69.

Addams, Jane. *Women and Public Housekeeping*. New York: National Woman Suffrage, 1910), reprinted in John Pettigrew, *Public Women, Public Words*. Vol. 2. New York: Madison House, 2002.

Albert, Carl B. *Little Giant*. Norman: University of Oklahoma Press, 1990.

Arms, E., and K. Herr. "Accountability and Single Sex Schooling: A Collision of Reform Agendas." *American Educational Research Journal* 41, 3 (2004): 527–55.

Arnold, Douglas. *The Logic of Congressional Action*. New Haven: Yale University Press, 1990.

Bai, Matt. *The Argument: Billionaires, Bloggers, and the Battle to Remake Democratic Politics*. New York: Penguin Press, 2007.

Barone, Michael, ed. *The Almanac of American Politics, 2002*. Washington, D.C.: National Journal, 2003.

Baumgartner, Frank, and Bryan Jones. *Agendas and Instability in American Politics*. Chicago: University of Chicago Press, 1993.

Bendavid, Naftali. *The Thumpin'*. New York: Random House, 2007.

Biersack, Robert, and Paul S. Herrnson. "Political Parties and the Year of the Woman." In Elizabeth Adell Cook, Sue Thomas, and Clyde Wilcox, eds., *The Year of the Woman: Myths and Realities*. Boulder, Colo.: Westview Press, 1994, 161–80.

Blankenship, Jane, and Deborah Robson. "A 'Feminine Style' in Women's Political Discourse: An Exploratory Essay." *Communication Quarterly* 43 (1995): 353–66.

Bledsoe, Timothy, and Mary Herring. "Victims of Circumstances: Women in Pursuit of Political Office." *American Political Science Review* 84, 1 (1990): 213–23.

Bolling, Richard. *Power in the House*. New York: Dutton, 1968.

Bond, Jon R., Cary Covington, and Richard Fleisher. "Explaining Challenger Quality in Congressional Elections." *Journal of Politics* 47, 2 (June 1985): 510–29.

Burns, James MacGregor. *Leadership*. New York: Harper, 1982.

Burrell, Barbara. *A Woman's Place Is in the House: Campaigning for Congress in the Feminist Era*. Ann Arbor: University of Michigan Press, 1996.

Bzdek, Vincent. *Woman of the House*. New York: Palgrave MacMillan, 2008.

Campbell, David E., and Christina Wolbrecht. "See Jane Run: Women Politicians as Role Models for Adolescents." *Journal of Politics* 68 (May 2006): 233–47.

Cann, Damon M. "Modeling Committee Chair Selection in the U.S. House of Representatives." *Political Analysis* 16, 3 (summer 2008): 274–89.

Carey, John M., Richard G. Niemi, and Lynda W. Powell. "Are Women State Legislators Different?" In Sue Thomas and Clyde Wilcox, eds., *Women and Elective Office: Past, Present, and Future.* New York: Oxford University Press, 1998, 87–102.

Caro, Robert. *The Years of Lyndon B. Johnson: The Path to Power.* New York: Knopf, 1982.

Chamberlin, Hope. *A Minority of Members: Women in the U.S. Congress.* New York: Praeger, 1973.

Cheney, Richard B. "An UnRuly House: A Republican View." *Public Opinion* (January–February 1989): 41–44.

Clinton, Hillary. *Living History.* New York: Simon and Schuster, 2003.

Cohen, Richard. "The Race for No. 2." *National Journal* 33, 38 (September 2001): 2923.

Cooper, Joseph, and David W. Brady. "Institutional Context and Leadership Style: The House from Cannon to Rayburn." *American Political Science Review* 75 (1981): 411–25.

Costello, Barbara J. "Moving in the Right Direction: Developments in the Online Availability of Full-text Congressional Committee Hearing Transcripts." *Government Information Quarterly* 25, 1 (2008): 104–17.

Cox, Gary W., and Matthew D. McCubbins. *Legislative Leviathan.* New York: Cambridge University Press, 2007.

Critchlow, Donald T. "When Republicans Became Revolutionaries." In Julian E. Zelizer, ed., *The American Congress: The Building of Democracy.* New York: Houghton Mifflin, 2004, 703–28.

Dodson, Debra. *The Impact of Women in Congress.* New York: Oxford University Press, 2006.

Dodson, Debra L., and Susan J. Carroll. *Reshaping the Agenda: Women in State Legislatures.* New Brunswick, N.J.: Rutgers University Center for American Women and Politics, 1991.

Dolan, Julie, and Jonathan S. Kropf. "Credit Claiming from the U.S. House: Gendered Communication Styles?" *International Journal of Press/Politics* 9, 41(2004): 41–59.

Downs, Anthony. *An Economic Theory of Democracy.* New York: Addison Wesley, 1997.

Duerst-Lahti, Georgia, and Rita Mae Kelly, eds. *Gender Power, Leadership, and Governance.* Ann Arbor: University of Michigan Press, 1995.

Eagly, Alice H., and Linda L. Carli. *Through the Labyrinth: The Truth about How Women Become Leaders.* Boston: Harvard Business School Press, 2007.

Edelman, Murray. *The Symbolic Uses of Politics.* Urbana: University of Illinois Press, 1964.

Eilperin, Juliet. *Fight Club Politics.* Lanham, Md.: Rowman and Littlefield, 2006.

Enloe, Cynthia. *The Curious Feminist.* Berkeley: University of California Press, 2004.

Epstein, Dwayne. *Nancy Pelosi.* Farmington Hills, Mich.: Lucent Books, 2009.

Feldman, Ofer, and Christ'l De Landtsheer, eds. *Politically Speaking: A Worldwide Examination of Language Used in the Public Sphere.* Westport, Conn.: Praeger, 1998.

Fenno, Richard F., Jr. *Congressmen in Committees.* Boston: Little, Brown, 1973.

Ferree, Myra Marx, William A. Gamson, Jurgen Gerhards, and Dieter Rucht. *Shaping Abortion Discourse.* Cambridge: Cambridge University Press, 2002.

Fiorina, Morris. *Culture War? The Myth of a Polarized America.* New York: Pearson Longman, 2005.

Foerstel, Karen. *Biographical Dictionary of Congressional Women.* Westport, Conn.: Greenwood Press, 1999.

Fowler, Linda L., and Robert D. McClure. *Political Ambition: Who Decides to Run for Congress.* New Haven: Yale University Press, 1990.

Freeman, Jo. *A Room at a Time: How Women Entered Party Politics.* Lanham, Md.: Rowman and Littlefield, 2000.

Friedan, Betty. *The Feminine Mystique.* New York: Dell, 1964.

Gamson, William A. *Talking Politics.* New York: Cambridge University Press, 1992.

Gamson, William A., David Croteau, William Hoynes, and Theodore Sasson. "Media Images and the Social Construction of Reality." *Annual Review of Sociology* 18 (1992): 373–93.

Gertzog, Irwin. *Women and Power on Capitol Hill: Reconstructing the Congressional Women's Caucus.* Boulder, Colo.: Lynne Rienner, 2004.

Gilligan, Carol. *In a Different Voice: Psychological Theory and Women's Development.* Cambridge, Mass.: Harvard University Press, 1993.

Gillon, Steve. *The Pact: Bill Clinton, Newt Gingrich, and the Rivalry That Defined a Generation.* New York: Oxford University Press, 2008.

Gladwell, Malcolm. *Outliers: The Story of Success.* New York: Little, Brown, 2008.

Green, Matthew N. "Presidents and Personal Goals: the Speaker of the House as Non-majoritarian Leader." *Congress and the Presidency* 34, 2 (autumn 2007): 1–22.

———. "The 2006 Race for Democratic Majority Leader: Money, Policy, and Personal Loyalty." *PS* 41, 1 (January 2008): 63–68.

Gutmann, Amy, and Dennis Thompson. *Democracy and Disagreement.* Cambridge, Mass.: Harvard University Press, 1996.

Hacker, Jacob S., and Paul Pierson. *Off Center: The Republican Revolution and the Erosion of American Democracy.* New Haven: Yale University Press, 2005.

Hale, Mary M., and Rita Mae Kelly, eds. *Gender, Bureaucracy and Democracy.* Westport, Conn.: Greenwood Press, 1989.

Harris, Douglas. "The Rise of the Public Speakership." *Political Science Quarterly* 113 (1998): 193–212.

Harris, Douglas B., and Garrison Nelson. "Middlemen No More: Emergent patterns in Congressional Leadership Selection." *PS* 10, 1 (2008): 43–46.

Harvey, Anna L. *Votes without Leverage.* New York: Cambridge University Press, 1998.

Harwood, John, and Gerald F. Seib. *Pennsylvania Avenue: Profiles in Backroom Power.* New York: Random House, 2008.

Herrick, Rebekah, and Michael K. Moore. "Political Ambition's Effect on Legislative Behavior: Schlesinger's Typology Reconsidered and Revised." *Journal of Politics* 55, 3 (1993): 765–76.

Hibbing, John, and Christopher W. Larimer. "The American Public's View of Congress' "
    Forum 6, 3 (2008): Article 6, http://www.bepress.com/forum/vol6/iss3/art6/.

Hilley, John L. *The Challenge of Legislation*. Washington, D.C.: Brookings Institution,
    2008.

Huniga, Markos Moulitsas. *Taking on the System*. New York: Celebra Press, 2008.

Jacobs, John. *A Rage for Justice: The Passion and Politics of Phillip Burton*. Berkeley:
    University of California Press, 1995.

Jacobsen, Gary. "Strategic Politicians and the Dynamics of House Elections." *American
    Political Science Review* 83 (January 1989): 773–93.

Jacobson, Gary, and Samuel Kernell. "Preempting Quality Challengers in House Elections."
    Journal of Politics 50 (1988): 920–36.

———. *Strategy and Choice in Congressional Elections*. New Haven: Yale University Press,
    1981.

Jamieson, Kathleen Hall. *Beyond the Double Bind: Women in Political Leadership*.
    New York: Oxford University Press, 1995.

Jamieson, Kathleen Hall, and Joseph N. Cappella. *Echo Chamber: Rush Limbaugh and the
    Conservative Media Establishment*. New York: Oxford University Press, 2008.

Jones, Charles O. *The Presidency in a Separated System*. Washington, D.C.: Brookings
    Institution, 1994.

Kahn, Kim Fridkin. "The Distorted Mirror: Press Coverage of Women Candidates for
    Statewide Office." *Journal of Politics* 56, 1 (1994): 154–73.

Kaiser, Robert G. *So Damn Much Money: The Triumph of Lobbying and the Corrosion of
    American Government*. New York: Knopf, 2009.

Kann, Mark. *The Gendering of American Politic: Founding Mothers, Founding Fathers, and
    Political Patriarchy*. Westport, Conn.: Praeger, 1999.

Kanter, Rosabeth Moss. *Men and Women of the Corporation*. New York: Basic Books,
    1977.

Kathlene, Lyn. "Power and Influence in State Legislative Policymaking: The Interaction
    of Gender and Position in Committee Hearing Debates." *American Political Science
    Review* 88, 3 (September 1994): 560–76.

Katz, Vera. "The Leader and the Public." *Journal of State Government* 60, 5 (November–
    December 1987): 262–64.

Kenney, Sally. "New Research on Gendered Political Institutions." *Political Research
    Quarterly* 49, 2 (June 1996): 445–66.

Kirkpatrick, Jeane. *Political Woman*. New York: Basic Books, 1974.

Kolodny, Robin. *Pursuing Majorities*. Norman: University of Oklahoma Press, 1998.

Krasno, Jonathan S., and Donald Phillip Green. "Preempting Quality Challengers." *Journal
    of Politics* 50, 4 (November 1988): 920–36.

Krolokke, Charlotte, and Anne Scott Sorensen. *Gender Communication Theories and
    Analyses: From Silence to Performance*. London: Sage, 2006.

Lakoff, George. *Don't Think of an Elephant!* (New York: Chelsea Green, 2004).

———. *Morality Politics*. Chicago: University of Chicago Press, 2002.

Lawless, Jennifer L., and Richard L. Fox. *It Takes a Candidate: Why Women Don't Run for Office*. Cambridge: Cambridge University Press, 2005.

Leavitt, Amie Jane. *Nancy Pelosi*. Hockessin, Del.: Mitchell Lane, 2008.

Lee, Marcia. "Why Few Women Hold Public Office." In Marianne Githens and Jewell Prestage, eds., *Portrait of Marginality*. New York: Longman Inc., 1977, 118–38.

Loden, Marilyn. *Feminine Leadership*. New York: Times Books, 1985.

Lunneborg, Patricia. *Women Changing Work*. Westport, Conn.: Greenwood Press, 1990.

Maisel, L. Sandy, and Walter J. Stone. "Determinants of Candidate Emergence in U.S. House Elections: An Explanatory Study." *Legislative Studies Quarterly* 22, 1 (February 1979): 79–96.

Mandel, Ruth. *In the Running: The New American Woman Candidate*. Boston: Beacon Press, 1981.

Mann, Thomas E., and Norman J. Ornstein. *The Permanent Campaign: Its Future*. Washington, D.C.: AEI Press, 2000.

Marcovitz, Hal. *Nancy Pelosi*. Philadelphia: Chelsea House, 2004.

Matthews, Glenna. *Just a Housewife: The Rise and Fall of Domesticity in America*. New York: Oxford University Press, 1987.

Mayhead, Molly A., and Brenda Devore Marshall. *Women's Political Discourse: A Twenty-first-century Perspective*. Lanham, Md.: Rowman and Littlefield, 005.

Mayhew, David R. *Congress and the Electoral Connection*. New Haven: Yale University Press, 1974.

McClelland, David C. *Power: The Inner Experience*. New York: Irvington, 1979.

McElroy, Lisa Tucker. *Nancy Pelosi*. Minneapolis: Lerner, 2008.

Mikulski, Barbara, Kay Bailey Hutchison, Dianne Feinstein, Barbara Boxer, Patty Murray, Olympia Snowe, Susan Collins, Mary Landrieu, Blanche L. Lincoln, and Catherine Whitney, *Nine and Counting: The Women of the Senate*. New York: HarperCollins, 2000.

Moncrief, Gary F. "Recruitment and Retention in U.S. Legislatures." *Legislative Studies Quarterly* 24, 2 (1999): 173–208.

Moncrief, Gary, Peverill Squire, and Malcolm E. Jewell. *Who Runs for the Legislature?*. Upper Saddle River, N.J.: Prentice Hall, 2001.

Mueller, Carol M., ed. *The Politics of the Gender Gap: The Social Construction of Political Influence*. Newbury Park, Calif.: Sage, 1988.

Naisbitt, John. *Megatrends*. New York: Grand Central, 1988.

Neal, D. "The Effects of Catholic Secondary Schooling on Educational Achievement." *Journal of Labor Economics* 15, 1 (1997): 98–123.

Niebuhr, Reinhold. *Moral Man and Immoral Society*. Louisville, Ky.: Westminster John Knox Press, 1960.

Norris, Pippa, ed. *Politics and the Press: The News Media and Their Influences*. Boulder, Colo.: Lynne Rienner, 1997.

O'Neill, Thomas, Jr. *Man of the House*. New York: Random House, 1987.

Ornstein, Norman J. *The Broken Branch*. New York: Oxford University Press, 2006.

Overby, Marvin. "Public Opinion Regarding Congressional Leaders: Lessons from the 1996 Election." *Journal of Legislative Studies* 12 (March 2006): 54–75.

Owens, John E. "The Return of Party Leadership in the U.S. House of Representatives: Central Leadership—Committee Relations in the 104th Congress." *British Journal of Political Science* 27, 2 (April 1997): 247–272.

Palazzolo, Daniel. "Evaluating Majority Party Leaders in Congress." *Forum* 6, 3 (2008).

Palmer, Barbara, and Dennis Simon. *Breaking the Political Glass Ceiling: Women and Congressional Elections*. New York: Routledge Press, 2006.

Pelosi, Nancy. *Know Your Power: A Message to America's Daughters*. New York: Doubleday, 2008.

Perlmutter, David D. *Blogwars*. New York: Oxford University Press, 2008.

Perlstein, Rick. *Nixonland: The Rise of a President and the Fracturing of America*. New York: Scribner, 2008.

Peters, Ronald M., Jr. *The American Speakership: The Office in Historical Perspective*. 2nd ed. Baltimore: Johns Hopkins University Press, 1997.

Peters, Ronald M., Jr., and Cindy Simon Rosenthal. "Assessing Nancy Pelosi." *Forum* 6, 3 (2008): Article 5, http://bepress.com/forum/vol6/1553/art5/.

Posler, Brian D., and Carl M. Rhodes. "Pre-leadership Signaling in the U.S. House." *Legislative Studies Quarterly* 22, 3 (August 1997): 351–68.

Povich, Elaine. *Nancy Pelosi*. Westport, Conn.: Greenwood Press, 2008.

Price, David, "House Democrats Under Republican Rule: Reflections on the Limits of Partisanship," *The Forum*, Miller Center, University of Virginia (Spring/Summer, 2004): 21–28.

Reingold, Beth. "Concepts of Representation among Female and Male State Legislators." *Legislative Studies Quarterly* 17, 4 (1992): 509–37.

Ries, Al, and Jack Trout. *Marketing Warfare*. New York: McGraw-Hill, 1986.

Rohde, David W. *Parties and Leaders in the Postreform House*. Chicago: University of Chicago Press, 1991.

Rosener, Judy B. "Ways Women Lead." *Harvard Business Review* 68 (November–December 1990): 14–28.

Rosenthal, Cindy Simon. "Climbing Higher: Opportunities and Obstacles within the Party System." In Beth Reingold, ed., *Legislative Women: Getting Elected, Getting Ahead*. Boulder, Colo.: Lynne Rienner, 2008, 197–222.

——. *When Women Lead*. New York: Oxford University Press, 1996.

——, ed. *Women Transforming Congress*. Norman: University of Oklahoma Press, 2001.

Rosenthal, Cindy Simon, and Ronald M. Peters, Jr. "Who Is Nancy Pelosi?" *PS*, 41, 1 (January 2008): 57–62.

Saint-Germain, Michelle A. "Does Their Difference Make a Difference? The Impact of Women on Public Policy in the Arizona Legislature." *Social Science Quarterly* 70, 4 (December 1989): 956–68.

Sanbonmatsu, Kira. *Democrats/Republicans and the Politics of Women's Place*. Ann Arbor: University of Michigan Press, 2002.

———. *Where Women Run*. Ann Arbor: University of Michigan Press, 2006.

Sandalow, Marc. *Madam Speaker*. New York: Modern Times, 2008.

Sapiro, Virginia. "Private Costs of Public Commitments or Public Costs of Private Commitments? Family Roles versus Political Ambition." *American Journal of Political Science* 26, 2 (1982): 245–79.

Schattschneider, F. F. *The Semi-sovereign People*. New York: Holt, Rinehart and Winston, 1960.

Schlesinger, Joseph. *Ambition and Politics*. Chicago: Rand McNally, 1966.

Schroeder, Pat. *24 Years of Housework and the Place Is Still a Mess*. Kansas City, Mo.: Andrews McMeel, 1999.

Schuck, Victoria. "Women in Political Science: Some Preliminary Observations." *PS* 2, 4 (1969): 642–53.

Selzter, Richard A., Jody Newman, and Melissa Voorhees Leighton. *Sex as a Political Variable: Women as Candidates and Voters in U.S. Elections*. Boulder, Colo.: Lynne Rienner, 1997.

Shichtman, Sandra H. *Political Profiles: Nancy Pelosi*. Greensboro, N.C.: Morgan Reynolds, 2008.

Shogan, Colleen J. "Speaking Out: An Analysis of Democratic and Republican Woman-invoked Rhetoric in the 105th Congress." *Women and Politics* 23, 1 (2002): 129–46.

Sinclair, Barbara. *Legislators, Leaders, and Lawmaking: The U.S. House of Representatives in the Postreform Era*. Baltimore: Johns Hopkins University Press, 1998.

———. *Majority Party Leadership in the U.S. House of Representatives*. Baltimore: Johns Hopkins University Press, 1983.

———. "Orchestrators of Unorthodox Policy Making: Pelosi and—McConnell in the 110th Congress." *Forum* 6, 3 (2008).

———. *Party Wars*. Norman: University of Oklahoma Press, 2006.

———. *Unorthodox Lawmaking*. Washington, D.C.: CQ Press, 2007.

Skowronek, Steven. *Politics Presidents Make*. Cambridge, Mass.: Harvard University Press, 1997.

Smith, Daryl G. "Women's Colleges and Coed Colleges: Is There a Difference for Women?" *Journal of Higher Education* 61, 2 (1990): 181–97.

Strahan, Randall. *Leading Representatives*. Baltimore: Johns Hopkins University Press, 2007.

Sunstein, Cass R. *Republic.com 2.0*. Princeton: Princeton University Press, 2007.

Swers, Michelle. *The Difference Women Make: The Policy Impact of Women in Congress*. Chicago: University of Chicago Press, 2002.

Tamerius, Karen L. "Sex, Gender, and Leadership in the Representation of Women." In Georgia Duerst-Lahti and Rita Mae Kelly, eds. *Gender Power, Leadership and Governance*. East Lansing: University of Michigan Press, 1996, 93–112.

Terkildsen, Nayda, Frauke I. Schnell, and Cristina Ling, "Interest Groups, the Media, and Policy Debate Formation: An Analysis of Message Structure, Rhetoric, and Source Cues." *Political Communication* 15 (1998): 45–61.

Theriault, Sean. *Party Polarization in Congress.* New York: Cambridge University Press, 2008.

Thomas, Sue. "The Effects of Race and Gender on Constituency Service." *Western Political Quarterly* 45 (March 1992): 169–80.

——. *How Women Legislate.* New York: Oxford University Press, 1994.

Trout, Jack. *Differentiate or Die: Survival in Our Era of Killer Competition.* New York: Wiley, 2001.

Trout, Jack, and Steve Rivkin. *The Power of Simplicity.* New York: McGraw-Hill, 1999.

Truman, David B. *The Congressional Party: A Case Study.* New York: Wiley, 1959.

Weaver, Richard. *Ideas Have Consequences.* Chicago: University of Chicago Press, 1962.

Witt, Linda, Karen M. Paget, and Glenna Matthews. *Running as a Woman: Gender and Power in American Politics.* New York: Free Press, 1994.

Woloch, Nancy. *Women and the American Experience.* New York: McGraw-Hill, 1984.

Yoder, Janice D. "Rethinking Tokenism: Looking beyond Numbers." *Gender and Society* 5, 2 (June 1991): 178–92.

Zelizer, Julian E. *On Capitol Hill.* New York: Cambridge University Press, 2006.

Zuniga, Markos Moulitsas. *Taking on the System: Rules for Radical Change in a Digital Era.* New York: Penguin Books, 2008.

INDEX

Congressional Hispanic Caucus (CHC),
74, 75, 12, 127
congressional leadership theories, 26–27;
conditional party leadership theory,
230, 231; party cartel leadership
theory, 231, 231; principal-agent
leadership theory, 230, 231. *See also*
legislative leadership
Congressional Progressive Caucus, 74, 89,
138–40, 269n22
Conrad, Kent, 183
Conservative Opportunity Society, 5
Conservatives for Patient Rights, 178
Contract With America, 60, 77,
136–37, 238
Conyers, John, 164
Cooper, Marc, 137
copartisanship, 241–42
corporate average fuel economy
standards. *See* CAFE standards
Countrywide Mortgage, 103
Couric, Katie, 7
coverture, 198
Crider, Jennifer, 117
Crisp, Charles, 257n57
cross-partisanship, 241
Crowley, Joe, 158, 239, 266n6
Cullinane, John, 137
culture wars: role of in partisan politics,
9–10
Cunningham, Duke, 59
Cuomo, Mario, 32, 33

Daily Kos, 12–13, 138
D'Alesandro, Annunciata, 202, 203
D'Alesandro, Thomas, 4, 30, 46
Daly, Brendan, 54, 129, 131–32
Daschle, Tom, 110
Dean, Howard, 55, 58
deficits. *See* federal deficits
DeGette, Diana, 217
DeLauro, Rosa, 50, 121, 199, 209, 216–17
DeLay, Tom, 22, 49, 56, 59, 66, 129,
150, 239, 248, 262n32, 263n50,
267n10, 274n83
Democratic Caucus, 21; constituencies
represented by, 247; diversity
in, 71–72; Pelosi's relationship
with, 73–74, 75–76; and tensions

between moderates and liberals,
21, 74–75, 89–90, 96, 137–40,
176, 182, 185–87, 243–44; and the
2008 elections, 110. *See also* Blue
Dog Democrats; Congressional
Black Caucus; Congressional
Hispanic Caucus; Congressional
Progressive Caucus; New
Democrats
Democratic Congressional Campaign
Committee (DCCC), 17; and
candidate recruitment, 111,
116–18; Pelosi's fund-raising
for, 43, 111–12, 114–16, 118–22;
Pelosi's involvement in, 117–18,
152, 236; tariff structure of, 115–
16; transformation of, 111–15
Democratic Leadership Council (DLC),
32, 55
Democratic National Committee (DNC),
11–12; Dean chosen as head of, 58
Democratic National Convention (1984),
31–32
Democratic Party: characterizations of,
5, 10; divisions within, 8, 137–38,
245; reframing efforts of, 136,
137–38; organizational challenges
faced by, 11–12
Democratic Senatorial Campaign
Committee (DSCC), 17, 34
Department of Defense Reauthorization
bill, 97
Digg Dialogg, 133
Dingell, John, 47, 72–73, 90–93, 158–60,
187, 239
diversity: among House Democrats,
71–72, 75, 116, 156; in political
representation, 13–15
DividedWeFail.org, 178
Dodson, Debra, 215
Douglas, Helen Gahagan, 199, 206
Douglas, Melvyn, 199
Drudge, Matt, 125
Dunn, Jennifer, 209

Eagle Forum, 16
Eagly, Alice, 207
earmarks, 22
echo chamber, 130–31